THE ROUTLEDGE COMPANION TO ACTORS' SHAKESPEARE

The Routledge Companion to Actors' Shakespeare is a window onto how today's actors contribute to the continuing life and relevance of Shakespeare's plays.

The process of acting is notoriously hard to document, but this volume reaches behind famous performances to examine the actors' craft, their development and how they engage with play-texts. Each chapter relies upon privileged access to its subject to offer an unparalleled insight into contemporary practice.

Chapters consider the techniques, interpretive approaches and performance styles of the following actors:

Simon Russell Beale, Sinead Cusack, Judi Dench, Kate Duchêne, Colm Feore, Mariah Gale, John Harrell, Greg Hicks, Rory Kinnear, Kevin Kline, Adrian Lester, Ian McKellen, Marcello Magni, Patrice Naiambana, Vanessa Redgrave, Pyotr Semak, Antony Sher, Jonathan Slinger, Kate Valk, Harriet Walter.

This twin volume to *The Routledge Companion to Directors' Shakespeare* is an essential work for both actors and students of Shakespeare.

John Russell Brown is scholar, director, writer and teacher. He has been an Associate Director of the National Theatre, London, an Arden editor, author of a dozen books on Shakespeare and contemporary theatre by Palgrave and Routledge, and an energetic editor of many series on theatre history and practice.

Kevin Ewert is the Director of the Theatre Program at the University of Pittsburgh at Bradford, USA. He contributed to *The Routledge Companion to Directors' Shakespeare* and is one of the Series Editors for Palgrave's Shakespeare Handbooks.

THE ROUTLEDGE COMPANION TO ACTORS' SHAKESPEARE

Edited by
John Russell Brown

Associate Editor Kevin Ewert

Routledge
Taylor & Francis Group
LONDON AND NEW YORK

First published 2012
by Routledge
2 Park Square, Milton Park, Abingdon, Oxon OX14 4RN

Simultaneously published in the USA and Canada
by Routledge
711 Third Avenue, New York, NY 10017

Routledge is an imprint of the Taylor & Francis Group, an informa business

British Library Cataloguing in Publication Data
A catalogue record for this book is available from the British Library

Library of Congress Cataloging in Publication Data
The Routledge companion to actors' Shakespeare / edited by John Russell Brown; associate editor, Kevin Ewert.
p. cm.
Includes bibliographical references and index.
1. Shakespeare, William–1564–1616–Dramatic production. 2. Acting. I. Brown, John Russell. II. Ewert, Kevin, 1965–
PR3091.R68 2012
792.9'5–dc22
2010053567

ISBN: 978–0–415–48302–5 (hbk)
ISBN: 978–0–415–48301–8 (pbk)
ISBN: 978–0–203–81619–6 (ebk)

Typeset in Goudy by Taylor & Francis Books

MIX
Paper from responsible sources
FSC www.fsc.org FSC® C004839

Printed and bound in Great Britain by the MPG Books Group

CONTENTS

ACKNOWLEDGEMENTS

Several years have passed since I first thought of bringing together a collection of well-informed studies of actors who have thrived by performing Shakespeare and this idea gathered strength when talking about the project with numerous theatre and university colleagues. Having gained the approval and support of Talia Rogers at Routledge and, later, of Ben Piggott, I was able to develop editorial plans, decide on dates for completion of each stage, and start choosing actors for inclusion and authors to commission. By this time it had become clear that to avoid too long a gap between inception and completion, I needed an associate editor to help handle the submissions and most fortunately Kevin Ewert agreed to join me. He has contributed to my thinking and understanding, as well as more basic editorial tasks. He has lightened my way, for which I am most grateful.

My name features as editor of the book but without the unflagging help and wise advice of these three colleagues there would have been no book. My hearty thanks go to them and to each of the contributors with whom I had illuminating and practical discussions as the book slowly took shape. On more general questions about theatre and study, I have benefited from the generously expressed views of many others, chief among them in alphabetical order, Michael Freeman, Terry Hands, Pamela Howard, Peter James, Richard Nelson, Leon Rubin and Maria Shevtsova. My thanks are also due to the graduate seminar I have led at University College London for usefully and provocatively considering my questions and suggesting other conclusions.

INTRODUCTION

Actors can be said to possess Shakespeare's plays more deeply and thoroughly than any reader, scholar or theatre-goer, and to focus their attention on a text more minutely and intensely than a play director. To bring Shakespeare's plays to life on stage they have to memorize the words of the parts they play, speak them as if they belonged to the character they present and shape their performance to the unfolding of the whole play. Numerous books describe performances by leading actors and give some permanence to their achievements but reading about a performance is no substitute for experiencing it. Photographs reproduce what a camera can capture of the outward appearance of single moments but give little impression of the actor's mental involvement, and nothing of the progressive experience offered to an audience. Many photographs would be needed to study an actor's presentation of a single role.

Descriptions of an actor's use of a text at a number of key moments in a play are the best available means of learning from discoveries made in performance and so this book brings together twenty such accounts about twenty very different actors. Each one has unique abilities and a career that has shaped their understanding of the demands that Shakespeare's texts make on actors and the support that they offer. With the help of an index, a reader can explore a wide range of performances in the most frequently performed plays and compare the insights and achievements of leading actors.

Perhaps the greatest benefit of studying the plays as actors have known and used them is a growing awareness of the clues embedded in their texts to the physical beings and instinctive reactions of its characters as Shakespeare conceived them. This understanding is hard to define or to defend against rival readings of a part but studying how actors have brought a text to life on stage offers a unique and precious entrance to the lived experience that lay behind the writing of the plays, the fleeting but recurrent presence of which can be one of the most remarkable consequences of reading or performing the texts.

The choice of actors for inclusion sought a wide variety of talents and experience. With one exception they all perform in English so their response to the texts is not complicated by the use of translations. Pyotr Semak is included for the influence that he and fellow Russians have had on actors of the English Cheek by Jowl Company with whom they have worked closely. All the actors have met with success, judged not so much by journalistic reviews as by the new challenges that have followed each step in their careers over a number of years. Two exceptions to this are

Rory Kinnear and Mariah Gale who are included for strong runs of early successes. As this book goes to press all the actors continue to act in Shakespeare's plays. In recent years Ian McKellen and Judi Dench have rarely acted in theatres but, working in film and television, they continue to provide guides and touchstones for their successors. Because acting has to be seen to be believed only living actors are included and all the authors have seen numerous performances and had access to rehearsals, workshops, video recordings, personal correspondence or live interviews. Some actors are absent because an author was not available with sufficiently close or continuous experience of their performances, others because a choice was made between two actors with similar careers.

Full descriptions of performances are not possible because too many small details would be involved, some of them fleeting and almost imperceptible and many deriving from the progress and context of an entire production. For this reason the principal task of an author has been to show how an actor prepares, rehearses and sustains a performance in the context of a whole career. This may include the effect of early teaching or current training methods, the sequence of parts played or the companies and actors with whom the actor has worked, the theatres that staged the performances, the directors and designers involved or the audiences that came to watch. The task is huge since everything and everyone involved in a theatrical event affects a performance and, ultimately, everything that preceded it: authors have had to choose among innumerable details.

By concentrating on theatrical performances of Shakespeare's plays much of an actor's career will be excluded. Today acting in television and film contributes to the experience of almost all actors and so do productions of new plays and other 'classic' texts; for some, training or teaching responsibilities are a continuing part of their lives. Nevertheless, Shakespeare's plays remain a unique test of an actor's ability because they stretch the imagination and continually challenge understanding and technique. For readers, they provide examples that are likely to be familiar through both study and play-going.

The choice of authors was as difficult as that of actors because an ability to write about an actor's processes is more rare than the descriptive and analytical skills necessary to review performances. Many of the authors brought together in this book have worked as actors, directors or dramaturges and all have had first hand and repeated experience of their actor's performances and privileged access to rehearsals, workshops, discussions or interviews; many have known the actor personally for a number of years. For each chapter a biographical note on the author defines the perspective from which it was written; these show a spectrum of opportunities that a student might seek when studying theatre performances.

The form of the chapters varies with the sources on which each is based and the course of the actor's career. A concluding bibliographical note gives references that will help further study of the actor and suggest ways of studying other actors currently playing in English-speaking theatres. Comparatively few North American actors are included because their opportunities to perform in Shakespeare are less frequent than in Britain and their experience of the plays, in the absence of major reperatory theatres, shorter lived.

This *Routledge Companion to Actors' Shakespeare* is planned as a brother to the previously published *Companion to Directors' Shakespeare*. Both collect specially commissioned and researched studies of theatre practitioners but their differences are too great for the books to be twins. The directors' companion includes some pioneers whose careers are long finished whereas all the actors are active at the present time. This was a necessary difference because substantial evidence remains of a director's productions from years past, whereas every performance of an actor dies on the day it is created, leaving almost no trace behind. Nevertheless, the two books belong together, sometimes overlapping and often extending each other's view of the theatrical life that can be given to some of Shakespeare's most frequently staged plays. They also share an inevitable short-coming in that neither deals with the very youngest generation of actors and directors or those recent developments not yet tested by time. In compensation, established practices are studied over a long enough period to show their development and promise for the future; the creative energy that has brought these directors and actors to the present time is likely to find other outlets and new audiences.

1
Simon Russell Beale

Carol Chillington Rutter

> Actors are ambassadors from the playwright to his audience, but part of the message they bring is their own. A performance is a role seen through a temperament; an imaginary person realised through the perceptions and technical skills of a real one.
>
> John Peter, *Sunday Times*, 9 September 1990

> … actors are endlessly interviewed by outsiders who hope to pluck out their mystery, and who always fail …. Reviewers are seldom able to analyse what actors do. But they can describe it; this being the one undisputed service they can offer to the theatre.
>
> Irving Wardle, *Theatre Criticism*, 1992

1 Undisputed service

I enlist two of the finest theatre critics in the business to help me frame an account of one of the finest Shakespearean actors in the business, and I'll have in mind the terms of their critique as I proceed. But I begin with 'the one undisputed service' that I, a theatre viewer (and re-viewer), can offer, a performance memory, a spectator's 25-year-old memory (so a no doubt flawed memory): describing a place in the past where an actor – an 'ambassador' – delivered a message that was charged with something more than the playwright's dispatch, something all his own.

The theatrical conceit was conventional enough. A cry of players in doublet and hose led by an Edward Alleyn-esque strutter and bellower had arrived at a tavern where the cannikin clinkers didn't want any of that high falutin' 'O for a muse of fire' metropolitan stuff, but something with local colour. How about 'Bess Bridges', the 'girl worth gold'? The players groaned – but gave in. So the company book-holder – a swottish-looking, bungling sort of neurotic flop-haired youth, tubby, in big breeches and spectacles, flapping silently in the background – began passing out the players' parts. Not, you'd imagine, life-threatening work. Except that his every move made it just that. Crossing the stage, he might have been negotiating a minefield. His panic was palpable, and registered as both endearing and deeply silly. A stage manager – with stage fright! He retreated to invisibility, to prompt corner, to a stool set well back from the action where he huddled over his promptbook, a lump of apprehensiveness, making turning the pages look like handling gelignite.

Every time he noticed the audience, his goggle eyes bulged – risking head-on collision with his wire-rims. But worse was to come. Much worse: the awful moment in this actor-hungry adventure story when the players realised there simply weren't enough of them to fill all the parts. They froze. Where to find an extra? The penny dropped. They turned on their hapless bookholder – and frog-marched him into the play.

My memory is of the 25-year-old Simon Russell Beale playing Fawcett in Thomas Heywood's *The Fair Maid of the West* in 1986, his debut season with the Royal Shakespeare Company, when he also played Ed Kno'well in Jonson's *Every Man in His Humour* and – his first professional Shakespeare role – a gloriously idiotic, wonder-full Young Shepherd in Terry Hands's *The Winter's Tale* (by a wonderful symmetry, 23 years later, his latest Shakespeare role would be Leontes, of which more, anon). These first parts were epitomes, and promissory notes on a career playing Shakespeare that would take Beale from prompt corner to centre stage, from the RSC to the National, the Almeida, the Old Vic, playing Thersites, Navarre, Richard III, Ariel, Edgar, Iago, Hamlet, Macbeth, Cassius, Malvolio, Benedick, by way of Chekhov, Ibsen, Marlowe, Middleton, Farquhar, Pinter, Stoppard, Brecht: a list stretching from the gormless, dopey and ineffectual to the consummately Machiavellian, the traumatically broken, and the terrifyingly, yet gleefully, psycho-pathological to demonstrate the critic's observation that Beale is 'typecast to defy expectations' (*Independent*, 28 June 1993). But Fawcett, Ed and Young Shepherd gave audiences the first measure of this actor, drafted his performance signature: the ability to embody contradiction, to play both the cornered soul and the klutzy clown, to break spectators' hearts while he has them doubled over with laughter. If, as John Peter writes, performance is a role 'seen through a temperament', it's also seen through a body, and it's the body of this actor I'll look at first, observing how he uses the physical to address Shakespeare.

2 Body consciousness

Let's take the actor's body as his instrument, and analogise that to the orchestra (apt enough in Beale's case since he wasn't supposed to be an actor: a boy chorister who graduated to choral scholar at Cambridge, he originally went to the Guildhall School of Music and Drama to study singing). Pursuing the analogy, one actor's body is a flute, another's a cello, a bassoon, a trumpet, each excellent in its own terms, with a range, register, repertoire. And limit. The instrument must observe decorum, the 'Cyrano effect': like the man with the ludicrous snout who can't 'do' love, the grumpy bassoon can't 'do' madrigals. Or *can* it? Can a lover woo his lass any more beguilingly than with Frescobaldi's 'Canzona Prima' scored for basso?

The pleasure in performance of the limit defied is as great as the limit observed, and Beale is an actor who delivers that anarchic, even dangerous, defiant pleasure. Paul Taylor sees him as 'the very incarnation of paradox', a 'walking, built-in drama', a squat, unmade bed of a man, mountain-bellied (like Ben Jonson), a face out of Brueghel, someone whose 'flesh seems to have played a spiteful practical joke on the fastidious intellect that is trapped inside it': Caliban's body, perhaps, holding Ariel's mind hostage (*Independent*, 14 January 2005). David Leveaux dryly comments that

Beale's self image is 'not exactly a love affair', and Beale deprecates himself as tending 'to walk on to a stage sideways' (David Lister, *Independent*, 22 February 2008). But – Leveaux again – 'when he acts you have the sense that he is completely in his body'. 'Sensual', able 'to communicate thought and feeling on the same waveband', he's turned 'lack of self-esteem into an art form', a body evidently built for laughs into an engine to probe alienation, exclusion, the serious grotesque, the kind of self-loathing that flips from mischief to menace and that, his performance habitually discovers, has at its core a devastated sense of disappointed love.

Trying to fix this art form into words, you can feel reviewers outbidding each other for comparisons. Beale's skin-head, bunch-backed Richard in his full-length black leather trench coat (that had to be gathered around the collar to allow for the extravagant hump) was 'the unhappy result of a one-night stand between Pere Ubu and Gertrude Stein' (Paul Taylor, *Independent*, 13 August 1992), a 'depraved blend of Mr Punch and A. A. Milne's Piglet' (Benedict Nightingale, *Times*, 13 August 1992), a 'collision of Magwitch, Big Daddy and Mussolini' (Michael Coveney, *Observer*, 16 August 1992). His Thersites 'makes your average dosser look like a fitness fanatic'; 'he reminds you of an anthropomorphised storybook animal – Toad, say, dressed up as the washerwoman' (Paul Taylor, *Independent*, 30 April 1990). His Cassius might have been 'a Marxist don embittered by the undeserved promotion of a conservative colleague' (Benedict Nightingale, *Times*, 22 April 2005). His Ariel, in blue Mao jacket and kohl-rimmed eyes, the perfect colonial civil servant, moving with weird balletic gestures at half-speed, was a 'dauntingly glacial' subaltern who, freed, gave Prospero as 'a parting present' a 'gob' of spit 'full in his face' (Paul Taylor, *Independent*, 4 September 2000).

Uniquely, Thersites and Richard were parts he 'built from the outside in' (interviews with the author conducted in 2009; all otherwise unattributed quotations come from these interviews). Thersites looked like a walking spoil heap or midden, 'botched together by a sort of stream of consciousness': wrecked pinstriped trousers held up by old Etonian and MCC ties; flasher's mac blazoned with CND and GAY PRIDE badges; leather bonnet strapped under his chin, ear holes cut out, like a pilot's – or 17th-century alchemist's – cap, surgical gloves (borrowed from prep school days, the memory of 'a boy who used to have iodine on his feet, for eczema, who had to put them in plastic bags at night to sleep'), nicotine yellow with sweat, put on backwards, making the thumbs flap. He was a palimpsest of cross-cultural signifiers that registered this pro-war protester's body as constitutionally, insistently and ironically dissident: 'The CND badge made me laugh! Thersites is the *least* likely member of CND.' But given Thersites's intellectual disdain for the indolence and stupidity around him, he had to be read as an oxymoron. It was hard to tell, for instance, whether he wore those surgical gloves 'to cover some hideous disease or to protect himself from contamination by forced fraternizing with dolts whose suicidal idiocy might be infectious' (Rutter: 2001, 141). Here, says Beale, 'once we discovered the grotesque – and I have a *joy* in the physical – we had the part'. None of the physical was gratuitous or 'designer decorative'. The body – and this defines Beale's physical process – was the beginning of what the actor expressed, seeing Thersites as 'thwarted', 'a cynic', but 'like any cynic, actually the most romantic man in the play; someone who *profoundly* believes in Achilles's greatness, wants him so badly to be great, and is just so staggeringly disappointed! Thersites believes in FAME – Homeric FAME – and Achilles is being *just lazy*! If we'd come out to Troy and *done Homer* – if we'd done *The Iliad*! But we were doing "wars and lechery". What a *waste*!' Thersites's body became the walking comment on that waste.

Beale claims to be 'terrible with props'. Perhaps. But he uses them to capture character, to contain a history or inform a world. His Richard was heard long before he arrived, tap, tap, tapping his way down some distant corridor, then entering, standing under the dim light of a single naked bulb, leaning his monstrous bulk on his little, but bizarrely rather elegant, Charlie Chaplin walking stick – which he later, eye-balling the audience with his gob-stopper eyes like some somnolent toad, with a gesture so quick it couldn't be followed, plunged straight through the neat, tied-up-with-string-and-sealing-wax brown paper parcel in which Hastings's head had been delivered. His Malvolio, roused from bed in the caterwauling night kitchen scene, was a man discovered to sleep in a hairnet; his Cassius was 'the lone grammar school boy amongst a load of Etonians', and 'furious', socially – but then 'got seduced by nice cuff-links' (Rutter: 2006, 208); his Benedick arrived home from the wars (to a Beatrice who sat at breakfast absorbed in reading) carrying a single rose and a parcel of books tied with a ribbon.

Even more significant than the body work he does with props is the way Beale expresses character through gesture. Leontes wiped Mamillius's 'smutch'd ... nose'. Then he lingered, seeking paternity in the boy's face by measuring Mamillius's little nose against his own, a gesture (and doubt) he absent-mindedly remembered later, settling the child to sleep, singing a lullaby under his breath, when he gently tweaked the child's nose – and half-consciously remembered again, sixteen years later, meeting a girl called 'Perdita', when he reached out a hand instinctively as if – strange impulse! – to touch her nose. His Iago, dead-eyed as a gutted fish, endured Emilia's hungry kiss – then wiped it off his mouth. Rubbing Othello's mind raw with pornographic images ('Lie with her? Lie on her?') that finally felled him in a seizure, his Iago tugged his uniform straight, settled himself onto a wicker couch and calmly observed the spasming body, leaning forward, when its convulsions eased, without emotion to prod it with his boot. Then suddenly he himself doubled over and retched. Konstantin in *The Seagull* (the part Beale thinks of as his audition piece for *Hamlet*, as he thinks of Chekhov as sustaining his most important actorly cross-conversation with Shakespeare) stood almost paralysed over his desk, tidying papers, destroying writing, a two-minute silence re-playing a whole damaged life before exiting to suicide. His Hamlet was a son grieving for the loss of *two* loved parents, who, in the closet scene, reached out arms to the Ghost and to Gertrude. His Macbeth – counter-intuitively for a warrior who can 'unseam' an opponent from 'the nave to the chops' with a single up-swing of sword – spent the final act of the play screwed to his throne as his 'sticking place', 'waiting for the world to come to me'. Earlier, he'd stood apart, supervising the slaughter of Macduff's household. Killing Duncan had been, astonishingly, 'a gift', his 'gift to his wife', to 'heal the trauma' of the loss of their own dead child. At Macduff's, he needed to know what the death of a child looked like, and he observed 'the prolonged death throes of his thane's wife with detached fascination' as if watching 'a fluttering moth beating itself to death at a window'. Sitting still for the end, Beale had an image in mind of

'Stalin trapped in his paranoid little room'. He wanted to see Macduff coming, 'to explore what it's like for Macbeth finally to meet the father of the children he has had murdered'. But he had something else in mind. Consciously denying the physical, the body's exhibitionism, the extreme work timed in Shakespeare's performance text to explode in the final showdown with Macduff, he was making space for what Shakespeare's *playtext* was doing. 'The last bit of the play,' he comments, 'is linguistically and spiritually very interesting.' That move to language takes me where I want to go next.

3 Vocal register/actorly acoustics/textual play

Beale is an actor who's earned Ulysses's review of Cressida: 'There's language in her eye, her cheek, her lip – Nay, her foot speaks'. But the voluble body is articulated, too, in a voice that not only produces an extraordinary acoustic range but that works on Shakespeare the way a Stradivarius works on Bach in the hands of Pablo Cassals. His 'enunciation is matchless', writes Paul Taylor. 'He can pounce on a phrase with a plump, voluptuous relish, and comically switch to recoiling, fastidious distaste in a twinkling. No one can inflect a passage of verse with such haunting insight or such subtle variations of pace and dynamics' (*Independent*, 14 January 2005). To wit, his Richard, in the opening soliloquy, started deadpan, a man droning the shipping forecast, when, twelve lines in, he hit a vocal oil-slick: 'the lascivious pleasing of a *lute*'. The last word bloated in his mouth to an act of obscenity, the 't' snapping open a trapdoor plunging listeners down a vocal shaft into the black hole of Richard's hatred. His Benedick, cannon-balling into Leonato's garden pool to 'hide' from Don Pedro and Co., bobbed to the surface, wide-eyed, learning of Beatrice's suicidal 'dotage': 'Love *me*? WHY?' Then, the frog turned prince, all breathless grace: 'It must be requited.' Iago's monotone monosyllabic final utterance was a heart monitor going flat: 'What you know, you know.' 'Sssatisfy? ... *sssssatisfy*?', erupted from Leontes like projectile vomiting. 'Paddling palms', 'pinching fingers', 'practis'd smiles' sluiced around in his mouth like mucky sludge. 'GOOOD queen?' landed a staggering punch on Paulina's jaw.

This is a voice prepared to take risks. It's a voice pitched at D below Middle C in conversation ('Tongue-tied our queen?'; 'I had rather be a tick in a sheep ...') that can dive two octaves for hilarious (or horrible) effect ('But to be *Menelaus*!'; 'My wife is *slippery*'). It can squawk ('What, think you we are *Turks* or *infidels*?'), chuckle (low, like a dog woofling), soothe; bark ('Gentlewoman!'), giggle with teeth sucking delight, speak wonder ('if the sins of your youth are forgiven you, you're well to live!'), insinuate ('She did deceive her father marrying you'), tune ethereally up an octave to the exalted music of the spheres ('Full fathom five your father lies'), and return to a simplicity of utterance, all on one note, that makes a miracle of the ordinary: 'I do love nothing in the world so well as you – is not that strange?' Catching the quality of Beale's Thersites, Taylor wrote that 'Vocally, he produces what Sir Fopling Flutter, after a century on skid row, might sound like in a play by Berkoff' (*Independent*, 30 April 1990). Analysing his Iago, Jeremy Kingston observed that 'His voice makes use of the mocker's trick of evacuating breath on a word to point the follies of all pretension – and all honour too (*Times*, 18 September 1997).

This is a voice that, whatever tonally and technically it's doing, is delivering thought on stage, giving listeners direct access to a mind discovering itself in words. Beale's Cassius is a good example. In *Julius Caesar* 1.2 Beale offered a masterclass in speech as rhetorical persuasion as political thought, speech that simultaneously (*inter alia*) anatomised one deep thinker's needy interiority. This Cassius, the potato-faced, rumple-suited grammar school swot amongst the sleek Armani Etonians (and with twice their collective political savvy), knew he didn't have the right face to fit the political bill in a Rome designed by Norman Foster (you saw him stung by Caesar's jibes: 'Would he were fatter'). To get rid of Caesar, he'd have to fashion a face that did. So in 1.2.25–176, 307–321, he went to work on Brutus (played here by Anton Lesser as a petulant neurotic – and a walking political disaster). At first, Cassius played the deferential school fag, presuming nothing: 'Will you go see the order of the course?' Then, bolder, 'Brutus, I do observe you now of late ...', making a hesitant – but there it was, risky, *spoken* – claim: 'I have not from your eyes that ... / *love* [lifted vocally] as I was wont to have'. He accepted Brutus's brush-off ('Be not deceived'): he was used to such class humiliations masquerading as apology. He backed off: 'Then Brutus, I have much mistook your passion.' But he was manoeuvring, taking a breather before Iago-ing Brutus with one of those questions so obvious that you snap an answer – to discover only later that you've been suckered into a speculation that's drilled a worm hole into your brain that you'll scratch at for the rest of your life: 'Tell me, good Brutus, can you see your face?'

'No' was the (instant) right answer, but that produced what Beale's Cassius was bargaining for, and released him into allusive circumlocution on the theme of seeing by 'reflection', lifting audibly the words he wanted bored into Brutus's brain: 'mirrors', 'hidden worthiness', 'eye', 'shadow', 'best respect', 'eyes'. The parenthetical remark was casually dropped in (only hinting at sarcasm, only momentarily giving away emotion), 'Except for immortal Caesar'. There was nothing agitated about this speech. Nothing 'invested'. It was donnish; an exercise in practical criticism. But Brutus was alert to something more: 'Into what dangers would you lead me, Cassius...?' – a question that invited Cassius to continue.

So Cassius did, offering to stand as proxy mirror, 'your glass', to 'discover to yourself' the self 'which you yet know not of', the Brutus who, Cassius claimed, was Caesar's equal. You had to marvel at Cassius's smarts, picking up exactly the right metaphor, the flattering metaphor, which, expertly, he enabled in this discourse by draining it of flattery ('Were I a common laughter ...'). The verbal sleight of hand was dazzling – and astute. For if this coup was going to succeed it needed a poster boy. It needed Brutus because Brutus's face on conspiracy's side (as Casca would observe) 'like richest alchemy' would 'change [offence] to virtue and to worthiness'. With Cassius playing for those stakes, his cool was staggering: forcing nothing, waiting for Brutus (startled by the noises off, the cries of the people in the market place at line 75) to introduce into the conversation, protesting peevishly, his 'honour', a word Cassius scooped up off-handedly: 'Well, honour is the subject of my story'.

And 'speech craft' was its method. What you heard as Cassius proceeded was him shedding the role of diffident underling, emerging as the most sophisticated political lobbyist in Rome, constructing, verse paragraph by verse paragraph, a rhetorical world fit for Republicans. He mobilised anecdote, exemplum, memory; analogy, comparison, anaphora ('both'/'both'; 'god'/'god'; 'shake'/'shake'), the rhetorical question, the exclamation for effect, amplification, the stunning *non sequitur*; articulating this verbal performance with such clarity that its grammatical logic ('For', 'And', 'Why', 'But') persuaded you of the political case. The story of the wager, Caesar betting he could swim the Tiber in a storm, nearly drowning, Cassius fishing him out, recounted in a voice that 'girled' the floundering Julius crying 'Help me, Cassius', was a positional memory, certainly, but rhetorically, by Beale, it aimed at momentum, gathering pace, refusing interruption to bear down on the conclusion: 'and this man / *Is now become a god.*'

Each round of shouting from 'off', from the market place, raised the temperature on stage, prompts for Cassius to raise the ante. But the latest tipped him into personal uproar: 'Why, man, he doth bestride the narrow world / LIKE A COLOSSUS' – an explosion that shocked, that discovered the ugly molten interior of Cassius's social rage. And perhaps shocked him. He retreated. Into conceit: weighing names. Into apostrophe: 'Age, thou art shamed'. Into comparison: 'There was a Brutus once … in Rome'. And, *inter alia*, he recited, as academic and inarguable as an aphorism, the proposition that would wreck Brutus's life: 'The fault, dear Brutus, is not in our stars / But in ourselves, that we are underlings.'

What Antony would later do to the mob, telling stories, fantasising a Caesar who 'loved you', we heard Beale's Cassius doing first to Brutus. Love was Cassius's claim, too. He was 'a friend that loves you'. This persuasion scene, then, Beale made also a wooing game – fuelled not just by the political emergency (Cassius's need to instil public commitment in sulking Brutus) but by a personal crisis, Cassius's *neediness*, which expressed itself paradoxically in self-loathing, all its raw hurt exposed in two lines:

> I had as lief not be as live to be
> In awe of such a thing as I myself.

It sounded like republican critique, this two-liner as hypothesis, not least because of the way Beale raised the grain of the first line, inflecting 'lief'/'live', 'be'/'be'. But reaching its conclusion, it had settled into bleak self-disgust. He was saying 'Caesar is no god'; 'Caesar's just a man – like you, like me'; 'Caesar doesn't deserve our awe'. Caesar was the 'thing'. But the 'thing' then became 'I', 'myself' – and it was 'myself' that stuck like bile in Cassius's throat.

What was heard in this scene were not thought-out speeches, but public speaking producing thought in progress; peeling off layers of skin; exposing nerve endings; probing emotional interiority. As wooing, it worked. Brutus exited promising the next meeting: 'Come home to me.' Til then, replied Cassius, the republican idealist, 'Think of the world.' But then, alone, he turned. Gazed blank-faced. And cast an eye backward that wasn't just jaundiced but sickened. He'd won. But the winning – his neediness, needing to win – disgusted him. The flat voice that assessed what it now signalled as a 'performance' (by an inflection on 'yet') came from the actor's bowels:

thought in progress / public speaking

> Well Brutus, thou art noble: yet I see
> Thy honourable mettle may be wrought
> From that it is disposed. Therefore it is meet
> That noble minds keep ever with their likes

('likes' not, we heard, 'like' me)

> For who so firm that cannot be seduced?

(That last word, almost a sigh that broke into something between pity, apology, and contempt).

This kickback was astonishing. It forced listeners into instant reassessment. What (really) had we just heard? A political system imagined? A love letter delivered? Shabby manipulation? Spin? Or all of that? The cross-currents that swept through Beale's performance registered what was happening in Rome as history-in-the-making, certainly, but also as a lopsided love affair that would end in personal tragedy.

4. The play of mind/the actorly job of work

Whatever he plays, Beale shows characters thinking. Perhaps because they're absorbing, projecting the thinking the actor is doing. But his real achievement – as with Cassius – is to show them *feeling* thought, too. It's part of his actorly equipment to bring to Shakespeare intelligence of the heart *and* the head, and as he talks about the process of working on Shakespeare's roles – what he's doing in the final section of this piece, in interviews conducted with me in 2009 and in an unpublished lecture, 'Without Memory or Desire: On Acting Shakespeare' – he moves fluently between these two ways of knowing the playwright.

He does 'this work for the intellectual fascination', his job being 'to lead the audience through a detailed, thought-through argument or series of arguments', and to do that, 'before you do anything else', 'before you begin overlaying thought with emotional stuff that you think the character's about', 'you have to get the character's thought clear in your head – which sounds simpler than it is; it takes three quarters of the rehearsal time.' He gives an example:

> When Leontes [*The Winter's Tale*, 1.2.108] says 'Too hot, too hot!', that's quite a specific thought. It's not 'hot'; it's '*too* hot'. I know that sounds quite simple, but you've got to get that really firmly in your head, the difference between a Hermione whose behaviour he sees as 'hot' or 'too hot'. Because if you say '*too* hot' you're allowing 'hot', you're allowing a certain amount of leeway for these two friends to touch each other – but then you're saying, "That's over-stepped the mark", that's *specifically* 'too hot'. Once you've got those sorts of specifics firmly in your head, doors open all over the place. For me, in the case of Leontes, that this was actually a *reasonable* man, being reasonable, saying, "well, of course, this sort of behaviour is the sign of a graceful personality, a giving, generous woman, and I accept that. But what

> *that* is, is *too* hot." Then a whole series of emotional reactions open up that you don't expect – which was that for me Leontes was about the *rational* not the *irrational*.

Beale begins building a part – paradoxically – by stripping away: getting 'rid of what I know', getting 'rid of preconceptions' to 'see what's *there*' so that he can approach the part 'without memory or desire', a phrase he's adopted from the psychoanalyst Wilfred Bion, finding that it aptly tropes his actorly practice. So: 'get rid of "Thersites the clown"'; 'get rid of "Cassius the political manipulator", "Leontes the jealous tyrant", "the moody Dane".' To 'see what's *there*', Beale constantly observes: 'There's something in the writing ....' What he found 'in the writing' for Cassius was repeated threats of suicide: 'in every scene – until the scene when he does it.' 'That was a discovery that opened an emotional life I didn't expect.' What he found 'in the writing' for Iago was not the dazzling machiavel of critical commonplace but the 'dullest man in Shakespeare': 'with no charm (like Richard's); no wit (like Thersites's). A man whose vocabulary, his use of language, except when he's talking about sex, is imitative or workmanlike, dull and grey. Playing him was like walking around with a large lump of basalt in my stomach.' What he found 'in the writing' for Richard was a man who 'makes every exit to lunch or dinner – until Bosworth, when someone says, "Oh my god; he's not eating"'; for Thersites, not the impacted punning that makes Shakespeare's fools frequently tedious because inaccessible to modern audiences but someone 'genuinely funny'. 'He constantly gives you lines like "Agamemnon ... has not so much brain as ear wax" that make you *howl* with laughter!' But more than that: he found 'in the writing' 'this desperate cynicism' born of disappointment, whose source he located in a kind of bewildered innocence, a Thersites 'who doesn't understand sex', who's 'never been with a woman', who, 'when (in our production) he picked up Cressida's scarf that Troilus had discarded and sniffed it and smelled her perfume, experienced an alternative universe; it would take a lobotomy to get that smell out of his head'.

The academic in Beale (he took a First in English from Cambridge) relishes the part of the actor's job that is about study: 'a process that's between me and the text'; 'seeing those huge soliloquies and thinking, this is going to be enormous fun'; pedantically finding out 'the meaning of the words at their simplest level': 'do I know what "calumny" means? Am I sure what a "bodkin" is?' (I remember Fawcett poring over his book back in '86: a neat, and persistent trope.)

In the rehearsal room, 'all the big ones' – edition-wise – are on the table: the Oxford and Norton, Cambridge and Penguin. But Beale prefers to study Shakespeare in Arden editions:

> I don't like to be on the rehearsal floor with a book – so I don't need one I can carry around (like the Penguin); I can learn from a great, big whopping edition like the Arden before rehearsals start. And I'm starting to learn earlier and earlier. Partly it has to do with age. I learned the whole of Benedick before we started rehearsals.

But he 'learns neutrally' so that the part can 'be flexible in rehearsals'. (That Benedick line that he made 'Love *me*? WHY?', in the Arden edition is, 'Love me? Why, it must be requited'). The clichéd question actors get at the stage door (and mock), 'How do you learn *all those lines?*' is actually, says Beale, 'a very interesting question. And we only mock it because *we don't know the answer.*' For him, learning the part is 'a combination of muscle memory and making sense of the words'. But 'it's not a quick process; it's quite plodding, really'.

Technically, he starts working on a speech by 'doing that really boring thing of working out the stresses, where the line endings are, listening for antithesis, repetitions, the sounds of the words'. He demonstrates with Macbeth's soliloquy that opens 1.7, 'If it were done, when 'tis done, then 'twere well / It were done quickly'. It's a speech he admits having a 'peculiar relationship' to, because it's the first one he ever 'learned off by heart, independent of doing it in a play', so to do it 'without memory or desire', he needs to 'get rid' of the deep recall of 'being in my school dormitory'. Starting over, he begins tapping out the regular iambic metre: 'If ít / were dóne'. Then experimenting with changing the stresses, still tapping: 'Íf it were done'; 'If it were dóne'. 'Trying to get this sort of thing sorted out in my head takes a long time', because in a line like this one, locating the stress locates the line's meaning. His Macbeth finally settled a single light stress on 'it', 'If ít were done', which had the effect of inflecting, but then rushing the line past, the euphemism, the 'it' that means 'murder'. But this non-committal 'it', repeated (as if normalising, habituating 'it'?) in the following line ('It were done quickly'), spectacularly has its cover blown in the word that ends that second line, that names 'it', a word (Beale observes, remembering his Arden gloss) that Shakespeare invented in *Macbeth*, 'assassination'. The five syllables of 'assassination' stretches, swells the enormity of the 'it' Macbeth is contemplating, and hisses 'it' with a string of 'sssses'.

Learning line endings – in this speech, 'catch', 'blow', 'here', 'time', 'cases', 'teach', 'return': all of them, stressed – Beale locates the narrative, the story of the speech, what the speech is about as the iambic pentameter line arrives at its individual destination in a word, but he also internalises the structure *in order to forget it*. 'I don't remember where any of the line endings are in *Winter's Tale*' – the play he was going to be on stage playing that night. 'Except one. In the trial scene, when Leontes opens the "sessions", arraigning Hermione. And he says, "the party tried / The daughter of a king, our wife, and *one* / Of us too much beloved"'. That 'one' in Beale's performance hung suspended at the end of the line, producing a second's pause as though Leontes were trying to run through the catalogue of possibilities of what this 'one' might be.

Listening for sounds ('Could trammel up the consequence, and catch / With his *surcease success*') and repetitions ('we but *teach* / Bloody instructions, which, being *taught* return') is learning how the character's thinking, what's on his mind, the contours of his imagination. ('There's something in the writing.') Looking at Macbeth's pre-murder soliloquy, Beale casts forward, to observe that Macbeth is a man who's going to end 'his life imprisoned in the present'; a man who won't be able to 'look back to the past – where there's a dead child, a murdered king, a once-happy marriage that cannot be healed'; or to the future, where there's 'no heir' and a 'continuing reign significant only in its potential to create more misery'. He'll live 'in a state of almost total self-alienation ("To know my deed 'twere best not know myself")', trying to 'survive and preserve his sanity by cutting off all human contact'. 'A murderer. A "butcher".' And yet – here's the paradox – 'this naturally taciturn man, surprised by the intensity of his experience', will find 'a poetic voice': he'll be released into a 'dark, circling, introspective verse' that will 'explore his internal life and his growing unhappiness'. And the beginnings of that 'dark ... verse' can be found here, in this soliloquy – in the image of 'Pity', the 'babe' (line 21).

'I can't get over that image,' says Beale. '"Pity, like a naked new-born babe striding the blast"':

> I have dreams – there's some sort of pathology to this – it's a symptom of something – anyway, in dreams I see things growing – faces, organs, livers, *growing*, monstrous. And this image – it's nightmarish – of a *huge* baby, a fleshy-thighed, fat-armed, round, neutral-faced baby. I find it absolutely horrific. Children and babies in *Macbeth*: I think they do become nightmares, great big moon-faced monsters, and very accusatory, day-of-judgement type figures, pointing fingers.

If you're Simon Russell Beale, what you do with such images 'is that they become the focus of the speech': they show you 'where you're going with the speech'.

But then he reflects:

> The interesting thing about any of these analyses of speech is not the technical things – because we all know about antithesis, line endings; they *are* important; you have to acknowledge that they're there. Because if you don't observe the structure, it's almost impossible to *do* Shakespeare's speech physically – you can feel the language slipping away from you through your fingers. You have to go to the end of the line because if you don't, the line doesn't make sense; it's not about beauty or a question of aesthetics. If the audience can't hear the last word of the line, they can't get the thought. So the thought's wasted.

For an actor to have technical intelligence and control, then, 'is great'. But the 'really interesting thing is *beyond* the technical. It's what that image – Macbeth's image of the monster baby – is doing *to me*, Simon, and how I can somehow transform that into something the audience can grasp.' Therein lies an answer to the mystery Irving Wardle was pondering at the top of this essay, asking how actors (imagined as latter-day alchemists) 'transform their base metals into gold'. Body, voice and mind, in Beale's case, are the philosopher's stone. The 'magic' is to make them connect through Shakespeare's script (where 'every word spoken carries the freight of the speaker's attitude') by suturing thought to emotion (which, in any case, 'are separated only for the purposes of analysis in the artificial environment of the rehearsal room'), making the 'figure' – in both senses of 'figure' as body *and* poetic trope – 'come alive onstage' by 'the thought processes, the argument, being galvanised by some emotional energy'. Alchemy, indeed.

But as Beale stands slightly back from the characters he's played and remembers them, the insights he offers exactly demonstrate this bonding between 'thought processes' and 'emotional energy', and show, fascinatingly, that its interface is, time and again, a love relationship. Of the crook-backed demon king he says:

> The Richard I played was missing his dad – always talking about his dad, what his dad did. Because *he loved me*; treated me, the *cripple*, just like the other boys, with equal status, equal love. Then my mother: she loathed me. When she cursed me, it was a shock, but not unexpected; it's what I'd always known, that she hated me from birth.

Of Hamlet, grieving (a part Beale rehearsed in the months following his mother's death):

> So much of this play is about love that has been abused or destroyed – and the unpredictable muggings administered by grief. Grief is like being mugged. Things are going along fine and then suddenly it hits you.

Hamlet's soliloquies were 'the moments when he's mugged'. When they dry up, when Hamlet stops talking to the audience in Act 5, Beale found the prince beginning a 'slow retreat from and ultimate denial of direct, human contact' which, for the audience, 'is to begin a process of grief'. Beale calls Hamlet 'Iago's benign stepbrother':

> If Iago's actions come to constitute a last throw of the dice, a suicide mission, then Hamlet finds himself in a similar situation. Hearing the commission from his father's ghost, he must feel that his own death sentence has been pronounced. The rest of his short life is an extended suicide.

So it rather astonished him that he 'unexpectedly' found in Hamlet 'a "sweet prince"': 'Sweetness was where our work led me.' And if the audience grieves for him, Hamlet himself doesn't. Where 'Macbeth turns in on himself' Hamlet, says Beale, 'remains sane, clear-eyed, even serene'. That's 'Shakespeare's gift' to the audience, that our 'grief for Hamlet is transformed into a grief for ourselves'.

Of Iago:

> Love was acute in my Hamlet and Macbeth. Iago's a different case – which is why I found him fascinating. He's absolutely without love. He can't understand it. Has no mental vocabulary to construct love. That's the hell he lives in – deep in the grain of his soul, a rooted lovelessness, *that he needs someone else to experience*.

Of Benedick:

> What makes him remarkable is not his love for Beatrice but his *courage*. He's one of the bravest men I've played. In a world where men and women are essentially segregated, with the prejudices and insensitivities that breeds, Benedick takes an extraordinary decision to support a wronged woman against an army (quite literally an army) of men. That scene in the church – after the wedding's wrecked, 4.1, when Beatrice and Benedick are left behind – is the best love scene Shakespeare ever wrote. They have the space to squeeze out a few words – mostly simple monosyllables.

'What's wonderful here is the ordinary, the commonplace.' The transformative power of love in this play 'seems somehow within our grasp. The joy at the end is on a human scale.'

Simon Russell Beale knows why he's an actor who needs Shakespeare. 'It's what Tom Stoppard said to me, after the dress rehearsal of *Winter's Tale*: "He exercises all your muscles, Shakespeare, doesn't he?"' He's an actor who knows – and generously acknowledges – what part directors have played in his career: Terry Hands ('so great; so shrewd; he told me – me, just out of drama school, with "ideas" – "Young Shepherds go on to play Hamlet" – code for "Keep your head down (smart ass) and learn your craft!"'); Sam Mendes ('the most productive professional relationship of my life'; 'a soul mate'; 'his sentimental streak – he wanted Thersites to carry around a *wind-up victrola*! – balances my love for the grotesque – the Thersites who'd have a bog-standard kitchen radio playing Sinatra's "Lover Man"'); Deborah Warner (her particular 'genius' is to release an actor 'into his personal territory of crisis'; her 'gift to me' was 'to remember physically', 'to be less interested in what a character is saying than in the precise situation of his speaking': Cassius, in 'the night, the thunderstorm, the clothes plastered to the body', the sensation 'of the wet shirt, sticking to me').

But, bringing this piece back round to where it began, with the 'ambassador' and the 'message', he's also an actor who knows, playing Shakespeare, that he needs the audience. Because it's the audience – each 'individual audience member' – that 'determines what is seen and understood'. It's the audience that operates as 'a sort of theatrical uncertainty principle' upon the 'generative imprecision' of the actor's performance. ('I have no idea what the last scene of *The Winter's Tale* means. I can't make it conveniently comprehensible.') He's an actor, then, who, finally, wants 'the audience to do its work'. Fair enough. From this ambassador, we accept the commission.

Selected chronology

1986–87	RSC. Fawcett (*The Fair Maid of the West*); Ed Kno'well (*Every Man in His Humour*); Young Shepherd (*The Winter's Tale*).
1988–89	RSC. Clincher Senior (*The Constant Couple*); Lord Are (*Restoration*); Sir Fopling Flutter (*The Man of Mode*).
1990–91	RSC. Edward (*Edward II*); Navarre (*Love's Labour's Lost*); Konstantin (*The Seagull*); Thersites (*Troilus and Cressida*).
1992–93	RSC. Richard (*Richard III*).
1993–94	RSC. Ariel (*The Tempest*); Edgar (*King Lear*); Oswald (*Ghosts*).
1997–98	NT. Iago (*Othello*).
2000	NT. Hamlet (*Hamlet*).
2002	Donmar Warehouse. Malvolio (*Twelfth Night*); Vanya (*Uncle Vanya*).
2005	Almeida. Macbeth (*Macbeth*); Barbican Theatre. Cassius (*Julius Caesar*).
2007	NT. Benedick (*Much Ado About Nothing*).
2009	The Bridge Project. Leontes (*The Winter's Tale*); Lopakhin (*The Cherry Orchard*).

Bibliography

Beale, Simon Russell (1993) 'Thersites in *Troilus and Cressida*' in Russell Jackson and Robert Smallwood (eds), *Players of Shakespeare 3*. Cambridge: Cambridge University Press, 160–73.

——(2003) 'Hamlet' in Robert Smallwood (ed.), *Players of Shakespeare 5*. Cambridge: Cambridge University Press, 145–77.

——(2006) 'Macbeth' in Michael Dobson (ed.), *Performing Shakespeare's Tragedies Today: The Actor's Perspective*. Cambridge: Cambridge University Press, 106–18.

Rutter, Carol Chillington (2001) *Enter the Body: Women and Representation on Shakespeare's Stage*. London: Routledge, 104–41.

——(2006) 'Facing History, Facing Now: Deborah Warner's *Julius Caesar* at the Barbican Theatre', *Shakespeare Quarterly* 57:1, 71–85.

——(2008) 'Deborah Warner' in John Russell Brown (ed.), *The Routledge Companion to Director's Shakespeare*. London: Routledge, 474–92.

About the author

Carol Chillington Rutter is Professor of English and Comparative Literary Studies at the University of Warwick where she is Co-Director of the Institute for Advanced Teaching and Learning. A Shakespeare scholar and historian of the Elizabethan theatre who specialises in performance studies, her books include *Documents of the Rose Playhouse* (1984); *Clamorous Voices: Shakespeare's Women Today* (1988); *Enter the Body: Women and Representation on Shakespeare's Stage* (2001); *Henry VI in Performance* (co-authored, 2006); and *Shakespeare and Child's Play: Performing Lost Boys on Stage and Screen* (2007). She writes the annual review of 'Shakespeare Performances in England' for *Shakespeare Survey*. As Director of the CAPITAL Centre (Creativity and Performance in Teaching and Learning) at Warwick, 2006–10, she was responsible for leading innovation in pedagogy and practice – for example, with her module, 'Shakespeare without Chairs'. She was honoured with a Warwick Award for Teaching Excellence in 2007 and named a National Teaching Fellow in 2010. She's been a fascinated watcher of Simon Russell Beale since that moment when he arrived, shoved, centre stage in *The Fair Maid of the West*.

2
Sinead Cusack

Andrew James Hartley

Sinead Cusack had no formal training as an actress. She disavows an allegiance to any particular "school" or approach to acting, and says she has no consistent process. In spite of this, she has become a commanding figure in the modern theatre, having played to critical acclaim many of Shakespeare's most demanding roles for the Royal Shakespeare Company and other organizations including, most recently, the Bridge Project, for which she played Paulina in *The Winter's Tale* directed by Sam Mendes. The apparent paradox speaks to her success as an instinctive actor who has honed her craft through experience, and who is able to keep what she calls "the essential humanity" of the roles she plays uppermost.

Though she never went to drama school, Cusack came from a deeply theatrical family. Her grandparents were traveling players and her father, Cyril, had an extensive resume as an actor for the RSC, the Abbey Theatre, Dublin, and numerous other theatres as well as almost a hundred films including Zeffirelli's *The Taming of the Shrew*, *The Day of the Jackal*, *Harold and Maude*, and *My Left Foot*. As a girl, Sinead watched her father prepare, helped him learn his lines and saw up close the man's careful and conscious use of technique. She learned from him "osmotically," but never adopted his deliberation where craft was concerned, so that many of the tools she uses on stage—vocal projection, for instance—tend to be accessed reflexively. What she did get is a conviction that detail work is crucial in the construction of character, so that—as in her father's film work—the impression of personhood, of a fully rounded thinking and feeling presence is always specific and concrete, not generalized.

Her first forays into Shakespeare were unsuccessful, she says—citing her "disastrous" Juliet at the Shaw Theatre in 1972 and her Desdemona at the Ludlow Festival in 1974—largely because of her assumptions about what Shakespearean acting was. Shakespeare, she thought, was to be declaimed—shouted even—with the eyes front and a suitably elevated look on the face. There was to be no smiling or laughing, no spontaneous movement, no naturalism of any kind: no sense of character as a living, breathing person. Shakespeare was an idea manifested by poetic sound. In short, she was playing Shakespeare's reputation, his Cultural Significance, not his characters. She was still getting cast, partly because of a "quality" derived from her look, her youth, perhaps even her Irishness, and she had a facility with poetic language which was aided by the natural mellifluousness of her voice (she grew up speaking Gaelic), but—at least where Shakespeare was concerned—she wasn't treating the characters as human beings. This despite the fact that she had established herself as an actress with a gift for naturalism in modern drama, and it seems that her inability to see Shakespeare in the same terms came from a sense of intimidation augmented by her self-identification as an "Irish peasant."

The change came around 1980 and it originated in a couple of different factors. On the one hand she had simply (and in her own words) "become a better actress" by paying attention to the craft issues she had not formally studied: how to relax into a part, how to project, to persuade and so forth. The successful application of such things to Shakespeare, however, continued to prove elusive for her, until two crucial experiences provided the necessary epiphany. The first occurred while rehearsing Celia in Terry Hands' RSC *As You Like It*. Early in the process, she was shown the set model with its green color palette and the design for her dress which was also green. Timidly she approached Hands and pointed out that, being the same color as the walls, she would disappear into the set. "Sinead," Hands replied, "Celia *is* the set."

She resolved—with characteristic spunk—not to be, injecting the part with wit and dynamism designed—more than anything—to stay alive and visible. Not only did the performance get her noticed, it got her laughs, and this—to her, an extraordinary and astonishing feat quite at odds with that rarified notion of what Shakespeare was—altered her sense of the characters and went some way to breaking down the respect with which she had approached them. The incident also serves to pin point a key element of her process, the deliberate fusion of her own personality with that of the character, in this case a kind of performative defiance, a refusal to vanish, to become the dramatic equivalent of furniture, and that spark of Cusack herself gave life to Celia.

The second incident of the year which proved enlightening and transformative occurred while she was rehearsing Olivia opposite Felicity Kendal's Viola in John Gorrie's production of *Twelfth Night* filmed for the BBC. Confronted in part with the naturalized and smaller acting necessary for television, and working with actors used to the medium, she found the power and playfulness of Olivia's situation, its romantics and erotics, forced her to confront the character as a human being: a person, not an idea, albeit a person in a preposterous predicament, a woman responding to that predicament rather than a mouthpiece for authorial poetry. She was suddenly aware of her Olivia wanting things from Viola/Cesario. The situation suddenly struck her as something real, something edgy and charged with humor and sex in ways that had not registered before. These were ordinary people in remarkable circumstances: flawed, complex, familiar people, frail in every sense, driven by the same doubts and passions, the curiosities, terrors and thrills that she knew in herself. The unsmiling model of English nobility vanished, the face-front declamation disappeared, the wheeling out of lofty characters thinking lofty thoughts evaporated. She had found herself in the part by finding its heart and mind, a playable human presence glimpsed, then grasped, through the text. She would—in all subsequent roles—begin her process with a quest for that human presence.

Cusack's Irishness is important to her, but as that ironic reference to her "peasant" stock suggests, the intimidating nature of Shakespeare (even as she stands on the boards of the RST playing Portia) might verge on the oppressive, even the politically—and colonially—unsavory. Finding a specific human presence within Shakespeare's characters, however, provides a kind of ownership which overrides such negative concerns, giving her a sense of the familiar, of people she knows and can play. For her, Shakespeare transcends England and Englishness, tapping into broader emotional and political truths. Moreover, the richness of the writing allows her to find the details she can use to shore up her instinctive approach. In both ways, then, she turns what was once off-putting into a method of tackling Shakespeare in which she is an equal maker of the resultant character. The process gives her the special theatrical power of ease, of seeming—in exact contrast to those early attempts—at home with the characters she plays.

That "process," however, is not static and consistent. Each part, she says, is different, as is each director, each method of rehearsal. She adapts to what seems required and will work in whatever way her director wants—be it research-heavy (for Adrian Noble when playing Lady Macbeth), improvisationally inventive (as it was when she played Paulina for Sam Mendes) or using Max Stafford-Clark's "actioning" process, which she used for *Our Lady of Sligo* and which is premised on a degree of detail and control from the director that she initially baulked at. ("Actioning" involves the breaking up of the script into individual beats and assigning each beat a transitive verb. Cusack used it throughout the *Our Lady of Sligo* rehearsals, and her performance garnered the *Evening Standard* and *Critics Circle* awards for Best Actress. She has subsequently tried "actioning" by herself but could not make it work without Clark.) Her "process" as an actor is necessarily shaped and retooled for each production through an awareness of herself as a collaborative artist working with other actors, with a director and an entire staff of designers and technicians. Most importantly, it is determined by the demands and feel of the role itself: "It's always the character who dictates my process."

That said, there are certain features which seem fairly consistent for the way Cusack generates character and they begin with a deep and close analysis of the text itself. She reads and rereads the play numerous times, absorbing the whole of it, and combing it for everything she can find about the character she will be playing. She calls this process "mining"—a deep probing for details, for clues, for facts of back story, for given circumstances, for the tone and nuance which will inform her final realization of who the character is. She searches for the hard evidence of age, class, geographical origin, level of education, past experience—professional or domestic—for indicators as to who she would have been raised with, spent time with, what she might know, her beliefs (religious or otherwise), her passions, instincts, tastes, desires and so on. She also looks for things implied by phrasing or word choice, the images she uses and what they say about her, her brand of humor, how she deals with her inferiors, with power and powerful people and—particularly—with adversity. Though at this stage of the process (before rehearsal) such discoveries are being registered on almost a subconscious level, each of these details will become threads in the tapestry she will weave as she builds a more conscious sense of who the character is.

I refer to who the character *is*, rather than who she might *become* because for Cusack there will be one Paulina, one Beatrice, one Lady Macbeth, and that one character is there for the finding in the intersection between the details of the script and the actress herself. She doesn't expect other actors to find the same Cleopatra that she did—each actor bringing "their own values, their own DNA, their own baggage" to a role—but she sets out to discover who the character is for her. This is, in other words, not a range of possibilities from which she will choose, but a sense of the unique character which emerges from the details of the script as mediated by the actor's sense of self and personal history. What will appear on stage is the hybrid result of that symbiosis, one in which role informs actor and actor informs role, a character which is singular, true and specific. The personal nature of her performances (and a sense of being intimidated by other performers) makes her unwilling to see other actors performing the same role or research prior productions. She has to own the part, and to do so requires—to an extent—the gradual banishing of alternate possibilities, point by point, detail by detail, until a single figure emerges. This character will grow and develop in the course of rehearsals and performance, but its core is Cusack herself though deeply imbued with every detail and implication of the play script.

Alongside this mining of the script, Cusack also reads around the subject, researching in particular any relevant history and politics that will help her to get a grasp on the forces shaping the play and the character. For *Winter's Tale* she read Marxist criticism of the play. For Michael Attenborough's 2002 *Antony and Cleopatra* she pored over historical biography to try to separate the actual person of Cleopatra from the myth, particularly that of the Siren so demonized by the Romans. What she found—the physical plainness of the Egyptian queen and her political savvy—helped break down her fear of the role by giving her a sense of the person behind the icon. Because if there is one thing she has come to work against in her acting more than any other, it is generalization. To find specificity in a character requires actual connection—for her—to the character as a personality with a particular set of experiences, a full symbiotic transfer between actor and role. Fuelled by this demystified sense of who Cleopatra actually had been, she returned to the script and found new weight in her first line: "If it be love indeed, tell me how much." "This was not the voice of a love affair at its height," she says. "It was love in decline. It was the desperation of a woman convinced he [Antony] was going to leave her. It was the cry of the mistress." From that point she understood Cleopatra in ways she hadn't before, a way that cut through the legend and made her playable. It is also illustrative of her general approach. She does not need to like her character—and she feels that many of her greatest successes have come when she is playing monsters—but she does have to empathize with them. She has no interest in cleaning them up for the audience, in sentimentalizing or emphasizing extremes, always wanting instead to (in John Barton's phrase) "embrace the ambiguity" of the character, and to do that she must understand her.

Once some sense of the character has begun to emerge in her own private reading and before rehearsals have begun, Cusack likes to embrace a relevant physical discipline. For Kate in *Shrew*, she pumped iron for toughness and self-reliance; for Cleopatra, she did Pilates to build core strength and flexibility; and for Beatrice she learned ballet. The Beatrice she had found in reading was mercurial, elegant and quick-witted, and she wanted a graceful physicality that would mirror that, focus it. Again she recognizes that this is *her* sense of the character, one other actors or scholars might dispute, but it is not simply a choice. It's what—reading through the lens of her own personality, experience and selfhood—she found in the script. Again, the choice of discipline is instinctive, a gut-level decision of what "feels right" according to her sense of the character.

The decision to take on a physical discipline for several weeks before rehearsal requires considerable forethought, and if the character does not leap out at her reasonably quickly—as was the case for her Paulina—that may not be possible. It is certainly true that she often goes into rehearsal without a clear sense of the character she will play but she still mines the script to find those humanizing touches that will make the character feel real in her mind: a person, not an abstraction. Specifically it's often about finding "what damage was done to the character": something that might not fully explain who that person is in the play—and certainly not excuse it—but might provide access to who they are in private. For Cleopatra it was that sense of being the mistress. For Lady Macbeth (opposite Jonathan Pryce for the RSC in 1986) it was having lost a child. The mining of the script is then balanced with a mining of herself, her memories, anything that will allow the necessary symbiotic connection to happen. Sometimes this connection is literal, as she describes in her piece in Carol Rutter's *Clamorous Voices* [1994], in which she details drawing on her experience as a sleep walker for the specifics of her Lady Macbeth. Those specifics go beyond sleepwalking, however, and the chapter shows the detail with which she finds images and emotions for every word in order to keep the scene from becoming generalized—a particular problem, she says, with playing madness. At this stage she attempts to get extremely familiar with the text—the whole play, not just her own lines—but she does not yet learn her part.

Once in rehearsal, her process is very much dictated by the director and the nature of the company's work. This is not simply a pragmatic concession to the conditions of practical theatre-making, but an embrace of the collaborative process which is, in some sense, political. Whatever sense of character she brings in to the rehearsal process does not solidify until she is engaged with the other actors, relating to and interacting with the other people in the story. It is telling, for instance, that she does not learn her lines until the scene is roughly blocked, and that even the method of that learning is designed to emphasize her character as part of a scene, defined at least in part by her organic and active engagement with the other characters on stage. She covers her lines with a piece of cardboard and then reads aloud everyone else's lines—not just her cues—so that even her attempts to get her own lines right are done within the interactive context of the scene. She cannot grasp her character in a vacuum and needs the entirety of the play and its characters to comprehend the world of the production and her place in it. The decision not to learn her lines until a scene is blocked also serves to bind action and word together so that the words are made physical and utilizes a kind of muscle memory in which the body and its sense of space becomes a species of mnemonic. Moreover, it binds utterance and movement into a single impulse, fusing speech, gesture and action at the level of intent, immersing the actor in the role in ways producing naturalized character. The fusion of script and action reinforces that impulse towards the learning of physical disciplines where it "feels right." Cusack's Shakespeare does not exist merely at the mental or vocal level being crucially physical in ways generating a potent stage presence. Even in *Winter's Tale* in which her physical presence was limited by the nature of the part she was quickly defined by the way she moved, the long, stately processional entrance with which she crossed upstage, and the graceful, energized stillness with which she stood. Both emblematized her stature and strength of character.

Her attitude to the lines themselves, though alert to form, is content driven, and she makes no conscious attempt to address scansion and verse form. Generally, she says, her instinct about such things is good, and she will only count out syllables if she is having difficulty understanding the sense or intention behind a line. In any case, whether it's that latent Irish musicality to her voice, or years of experience, the lack of deliberation where scansion is concerned seems to have no effect on her effective handling of the verse, though she will occasionally deviate from the rhythm for particular emphasis. This is in keeping with her statement that she has "no tricks up [her] sleeve" and is "the least technical actor I know," which is to say the least *deliberately* or *consciously* technical, since she is more than competent in handling iambic pentameter. Similarly she does not worry about communicating with an audience while making eye contact with a fellow actor, even in intimate moments. Her stage craft has become instinctive rather than deliberate or intellectual, so it makes sense that—in contrast to other actors and directors—she says "I have no rules when it comes to Shakespeare ... I cherry pick."

The quest for revelation continues throughout the rehearsal process—according to the methodological dictates of the director—and she does not follow a set pattern in this phase of the production. She has no particular exercises or habits that she takes into the rehearsal room beyond close attention to the text, a constructive inquisitiveness which continues to draw on her own life experience, and a willingness to work with whatever approach the director has chosen to use. For her, rehearsal often comes down to answering key questions, particularly questions she cannot answer alone and needs input from the company in order to get a sense of the dynamics at work. Why, for instance, is Paulina absent from the first court scenes? And how is she able to stand up to Leontes without fully experiencing his tyrannical wrath? Both are crucial because the script seems to reveal so little about who Paulina is, and while Cusack saw value to maintaining some sense of the mystery surrounding the character, she needed to answer such things if she was to play her. In such matters she operates as elsewhere, mining the script and herself to make sense of what is there, building back story only from what is clearly evidenced by the play and certainly never in contradiction to it. But in rehearsal she adds the crucial component of the other actors and the director to help her work towards the kinds of answers that would help to root the character, particularly where the script is unhelpful. At this stage, she is testing her initial assumptions, her subconscious response to the character, and trying to figure out whether her impulse is right. If it seems like it is, it will harden, complicate and clarify, but answering these questions will give her the necessary foundation from which to build. In this case, she (with director Sam Mendes) concluded that Paulina had been away—perhaps because she had been abroad, perhaps because she lived not at court but in the country with her daughters—and she entered the prison scene with luggage: newly returned and astonished by the news which has reached her from court. The second question about the curious sense of license she seems to have is a good deal trickier and goes to the heart of who Paulina is.

Paulina's ability to tell truth to power without apparent fear of consequence smacked, to Cusack, of blood kinship: as if she had been in the king's life a long time, perhaps all of it, like a great aunt or a nanny (though not literally a wet nurse, a possibility she ruled out as unhistorical). Cusack and Simon Russell Beale characterized Paulina as resembling a formidable relative who would give every niece and nephew a dressing down but would reward them with marvelous gifts. Her attitude to both Rebecca Hall's Hermione and Simon Russell Beale's Leontes was cerebral but also fiercely maternal in both "the dolling out of punishment and the dolling out of love … She's very direct, and says what she feels without apparent fear of consequence. She's strong. She's feisty. She's also honest and loving." The notion of her maternal nature derives from Antigonus' reference to their three daughters, but the notion of its centrality to Paulina's sense of self comes from Cusack's own identity as a mother. Paulina as written never discusses it. (Paulina's marital relationship gets minimal treatment in the play and this provided more anxiety. Cusack perceived a certain pride in Antigonus' self-deprecating discussion of her strength, and saw real weight in her reference to mourning the loss of her "turtle" [dove] but saw no need to build a stronger sense of their relationship.) This is the symbiosis which is integral to her process, using the lines of her own life to connect the dots of what is scripted, and testing them in the presence of the director and cast till they solidify and become "right."

The result was a Paulina refreshingly marked with tenderness and compassion, even hope, and not simply a dictatorial harridan, a Paulina who could—alone of those in the court—lay hands upon the king and was merciless in her account of his wrongs, but who also did all for the best. She was still and stately on stage, very slightly aristocratic but always plausibly real and human, a thinking, feeling presence of depth, passion and complexity.

I should say before proceeding that for Cusack, there is no question that Hermione never dies, that while Shakespeare allows for the possibility of a mystical resurrection, the reality of the situation was, for her, absolutely and unequivocally realist. It was a plan—part punishment or test of Leontes, part protection of Hermione, and part an active participation in the oracle's cosmological scheme. This is, again, a choice made out of a deep personal sense of what the play was about, and having made it, it shaped the character significantly. The production did not finally make a clear choice to support Cusack's reading (and its cutting some of the lines about Hermione's wrinkles may suggest the opposite) but her sense of the situation gave her performance urgency and immediacy, as was particularly clear in the "cry woe" speech. The idea that she was waiting for the fulfillment of the oracle—as well as reinforcing her maternal presence—was further emphasized at the end of 5.1 when, as everyone else left the stage, she alone recognized Perdita.

Among other things, this conviction that Paulina is preserving a live Hermione gives a particular urgency to the moments between the announcements of the death of Mamilius and his mother: a scant thirty lines, considerably less if Paulina's plan is already afoot in her "Look down and see what death is doing." (Cusack chose to read the scene this way which meant that the decision to pursue the plan takes rough shape in only four lines.) In this sliver of stage time Paulina has to conceive the scheme to hide Hermione away from further tyranny at least in the short term, though she can take longer over the decision not to reveal the living queen until the oracle is fulfilled with Perdita's return and Leontes has redeemed himself. This sense of the character's improvisational quality was central to Cusack's conception of the part and it was palpable on stage: she clearly thought through each moment as it was happening, beginning with the decision to take the baby to Leontes in the prison scene. From that point, each action was clearly a response to the immediate conditions of the moment and each one came from impulses that seemed to be taking shape before the audience's eyes.

So she picked her way through various strategies of persuasion in the course of 2.3, *risking* laying the baby down within Leontes' reach, or reacting to her husband with a dire and heartfelt warning ("forever unvenerable be thy hands if thou tak'st up the princess ...," her only direct exchange with her husband), and the plotting of the "statue scene" was part of this improvisation. Indeed, it continued through that scene, since it was clear that she was monitoring Leontes carefully throughout before *deciding* that the statue would indeed be permitted to come down. She approached the scene as a "minefield" in which Leontes could, by his actions, delay the "revival" of the "statue," an idea which grew out of her general impulse that a Shakespearean character, far from sitting back complacently as if everything she says and does has been planned out (scripted, even), is always thinking, acting on impulse, on the line, alert and engaged in what Patsy Rodenburg calls "the state of readiness." Cusack rarely takes a pause unless (as before the "cry woe" speech, in the shift between "O, cut my lace, lest my heart, cracking it / Break too" and "What studied torments, tyrant, hast for me?") it seems called for by a significant change in direction or mood, and her rule of thumb is that you can do "almost everything on the line."

In this context, the "Cry woe" speech (3.2. 174-203) becomes a deception, but it contains so much truth that it need not play as such at all, and Cusack's delivery, however finally (and with hindsight) untrue as far as Hermione's true fate is concerned, was done in earnest. The truth of the speech came, she says, in how clearly it manifested the character elsewhere in the play—and it was in this capacity that it became a point of revelation. The idea of thinking on the line is common to some teachers of verse speaking and it partly explains her tendency to rely on the language rather than silence. She sometimes has to force herself, she says, to "take her moment," and is generally more comfortable speaking—a character trait she identifies as a form of shyness.

Given its length and centrality, it is perhaps not surprising that the key moment in Cusack's journey towards creating Paulina came while they were rehearsing the "Cry woe" speech. Sam Mendes is a very collegial director and uses a circle in which everyone has to perform the role various different ways in the early, exploratory stages of rehearsal. Cusack confesses to finding this terrifying and embarrassing but also empowering, breaking down her resistance and helping her become comfortable enough to try anything regardless of who was watching. The process freed her up for making new, deeper discoveries once she got the book out of her hands—which is, for her, when her sense of the character tends to deepen most. In this context, the "cry woe" speech, when it was rehearsed for the first time off book, brought many of her more general impulses about Paulina to the fore and laid out who she was. The speech begins, "What studied torments, tyrant, hast for me?" a remarkably direct—even reckless—standing up to the supreme earthly authority. For Cusack it came from the woman's passion, her love, disappointment, anger and even humor—the bitterly ironic list of Leontes's former wrongs culminating in the death of his wife. But she observed that the list also suggests a coolness and composure, a deliberation however improvisatory. Suddenly the character fell into place, confirming her less conscious assumptions and leanings. Armed with this new holistic sense of Paulina's power, integrity and depth of feeling, she was able to work back through the play with a new sense of clarity which, in turn, gave her a solid foundation from which to build the specifics of each moment. That sense of bleak humor, for instance, surfaced in Paulina's first scene in which she persuades the jailor to release the baby with a wry reference to the delivery as a liberation from the prison of the womb.

Once her conception of the character has taken hold she is loath to let it go, and the process from then on—a process which extends into previews and performance—is one of finding new colors, new "threads in her tapestry" to enrich the character rather than reshape or significantly shift it. One such moment came to her after the *Winter's Tale* production had opened in New York, moved first to Madrid, and then to London's Old Vic and was almost ready to close. In that litany of Leontes' tragic errors in the "cry woe" speech, she says "O, think what they have done / And then run mad indeed, stark mad!" Initially she was giving special emphasis to the first "mad" but suddenly realized the weight of "then": you may have thought you were mad before this, but after you hear what I'm about to say *then* you'll run mad... It was a completely different inflection and one perfectly in keeping with the character. These small adjustments and discoveries characterize her work throughout the later stages of rehearsal and performance, and she sees them as clarifying distillations rather than as redirections. Once she feels she understands the character, can get inside her, she is able to add these new threads in the tapestry not so much by invention as by a kind of empathetic discovery. The evolution is constant, always informed by the specifics of both the script and her own personal life.

That said, there are times when these discoveries push her away from where she—or the director—initially thought the character was going, and she confesses to a certain toughness on behalf of the character as she conceives her. In 1982 she appeared in Barry Kyle's RSC *Shrew*, and her Kate developed such a profound sense of defiance and anti-authoritarian self-sufficiency that—five weeks into rehearsal—she found the prospect of playing her in Bob Crowleys' gorgeously silken, luxuriant and jewel-studded costumes utterly confounding. Eventually she approached the director who referred her to the designer himself and she approached Crowley and laid out why she, as Kate, couldn't wear the costumes into which the wardrobe department had put all their time. Her Kate would not wear anything so lavish and decorative, particularly if—as was evident—it had been supplied by her father or, for that matter, her husband. It was three days till dress rehearsal. Crowley, though sympathetic, was at a loss. There was no contingency plan as far as costumes were concerned and Kate's sumptuous wardrobe had already absorbed all allocated resources. Cusack suggested that they desecrate them: cut them up, and that she shave her head and wear the formerly resplendent dresses with Wellington boots and a cheroot. There was a long pause then Crowley "to his eternal credit said, 'will you make the first cut or will I?'" For Paulina the resistance was not so drastic—the private ditching of a corset—but followed a similar faith in the integrity of the character as she had found her, in this case a need to find a slightly more rounded, maternal form that was comfortable in a different kind of authority and appearance than that of the other court women: again the decision was finally and simply about what "felt right" for her Paulina.

Because of the way she establishes and then pursues a clear sense of character—albeit discovering extra nuance along the way—her performance itself is more about relaxing into the role and relying on those issues of craft which are sufficiently ingrained to function without deliberate intent. That relaxation is also her primary strategy for dealing with stage fright—manifested as a slight nausea and a physical tension particularly in her shoulders. If she is tense when she goes on stage, she is less "in" the character and more likely to stumble on a line, and the same is true for those distractions which inevitably invade the performative moment—whether it's a lingering issue in the actor's mind which may have nothing to do with the play or the invasion of audience coughs or cell phones. In such moments her strategy—unsurprisingly—is to "just get on with it" and attempt to relax back into the moment.

Sometimes, of course, a director will point out something needing adjusting—either late in rehearsal or during the actual run. In such cases she will, she says, "fight her corner" if she disagrees, but has the flexibility to reshape where necessary—particularly if she realizes that something is slightly off. In *Winter's Tale*, for instance, her sense of the closeness between Paulina and Leontes—a closeness intensified into a kind of mutual dependence during the long sixteen-year gap between Hermione's "death" and Perdita's return—produced a feeling at the top of act five that they were like an old married couple. In one moment they sat together on a bench, their lives clearly intertwined. Mendes thought it was now too much and separated them a little, so as not to detract from the centrality of Hermione to Leontes. Cusack takes such direction affably, recognizing that this "sent the wrong message," because she never loses sight of her part in a larger organism, despite her commitment to character. In accord with her remark that she loves to be directed she counts herself "almost ridiculously open to suggestions from all and sundry," ideas that she sifts, tries out and keeps or discards according to what seems to work for the character she has built.

When asked, for instance, about her sense of Paulina's last minute marriage to Camillo she responds almost as an audience member: "I think it's a hoot!" she says. "I love it! A moment of sheer joy and comedy." She felt no need to seed some form of relationship earlier in the play—something which is extraordinarily difficult to do given the characters' minimal interaction—and has no interest in trying to create a wholly psychological through line for that particular moment. Rather she sees it as a kind of theatrical closure, something to be accepted without a great deal of soul searching or the extra textual invention of a long correspondence (as some actors have done) between Camillo and Paulina over the last sixteen years. There are times when character—however crucial—must give place to theatrical effect.

She has no regrets about the characters she plays, no agonizing over whether she should have played them differently. Sometimes—as with Cleopatra—she would like to revisit them because she thinks there's still more to mine, but her thoughts on Paulina are indicative of both her usual stance on past roles and the means with which she achieved them: "I think I'm happy with what I gave her and she gave me." This mutual or symbiotic exchange is the root of her ownership of roles.

Acknowledgements

In preparation for this piece I augmented the usual archive work with multiple viewings of the Bridge Project's *Winter's Tale*, in which Cusack played Paulina, and conducted lengthy interviews with the actress herself. I am deeply indebted to Sinead for her assistance. Her candor, curiosity and generosity made her a delight to work with.

Bibliography

Carol Rutter (1994) *Clamorous Voices: Shakespeare's Women Today*. Trafalgar Square Publishing.
Patsy Rodenburg (2004) *Speaking Shakespeare*. Palgrave/Macmillan.
Interviews by author with Sinead Cusack, August 10 and November 23, 2009.

Selected chronology

1972	*Romeo and Juliet*, The Shaw Theatre (as Juliet)
1974	*Othello*, The Ludlow Festival (as Desdemona)
1978–9	*Measure for Measure*, RSC, (dir. Kyle), (as Isabella)
1980	*Twelfth Night*, BBC (dir. Gorrie), (as Olivia)
1980–1	*As You Like It*, RSC (dir. Hands), (as Celia)
1980–1	*Richard III*, RSC (dir. Hands), (as Lady Anne)
1981	*Merchant of Venice* (dir. Barton), (as Portia)
1982–3	*The Taming of the Shrew*, RSC (dir. Kyle), (as Kate)
1982–5	*Much Ado About Nothing*, RSC, then Gershwin Theatre, New York, (dir. Hands), (as Beatrice); Tony nominated
1986–7	*Macbeth*, RSC (dir. Noble), (as Lady Macbeth)
1998	*Our Lady of Sligo*, National Theatre, (as Mai O'Hara)
2002	*Antony and Cleopatra*, RSC, (dir. Attenborough), (as Cleopatra)
2009	Bridge Project *Winter's Tale/Cherry Orchard*; began at the Brooklyn Academy of Music in February, transferring in March to the Singapore Repertory Theatre, Auckland New Zealand's EDGE Performing Arts Centre, Madrid's Teatro Español and Germany's Ruhrfestspiele Recklinghausen before settling at the Old Vic for a May through August run.

About the author

Andrew James Hartley is the Russell Robinson Professor of Shakespeare at the University of North Carolina in Charlotte. He is the author of *The Shakespearean Dramaturg* (Palgrave, 2005), and the editor of the performance journal *Shakespeare Bulletin*, published by Johns Hopkins University Press. His articles focus on the theory and practice of contemporary performance and he is completing the Manchester University Press 'Shakespeare in Performance' book on *Julius Caesar*. He is also a popular novelist.

3
Judi Dench
Stanley Wells

Judi Dench stands along with three other great Dames – Ellen Terry, Edith Evans and Peggy Ashcroft – in the line of women performers of Shakespeare over the past century. As an older contemporary of Dame Judi, I have been able to see many of her performances, some of them several times, and have reviewed some for the press. I have taken part in discussions with her before groups of students and members of the general public, and I have had the privilege of being able to talk to her informally about her work. She is modest, self-deprecating and private, not given to theorizing about her professional activities, or indeed to talking much about herself. Her intelligence is great but it is intuitive rather than analytical. She has written little about her approach to her art. There are some published interviews, and she is named as the author of a delightful if anecdotal essay, 'A Career in Shakespeare', published in 1996 (it was I believe transcribed and edited from an interview by Professor Russell Jackson). And though popular biographies and a celebratory volume – *Darling Judi*, edited by John Miller, 2004 – which includes illuminating essays by practitioners with whom she has worked, such as Peter Hall, Gregory Doran, Richard Eyre and Trevor Nunn have been published, I know of only one extended study of her as a Shakespeare actress, the excellent final chapter of Russ McDonald's book *Look to the Lady: Sarah Siddons, Ellen Terry, and Judi Dench on the Shakespearean Stage* (2005). There are also, besides the usual reviews in newspapers and periodicals, longer studies of individual productions in which she has appeared including a chapter on John Barton's *Twelfth Night* in my *Royal Shakespeare: Studies of Four Major Productions at Stratford-upon-Avon* (1977) and Tirzah Lowen's *Peter Hall Directs 'Antony and Cleopatra'* (1990), which gives a detailed, day-by-day account of the production in rehearsal.

Judi Dench developed an interest in the theatre as a child. She had ambitions as a ballet dancer, and saw school performances of Shakespeare given by her elder brother Jeffery, who also became a professional actor. As a schoolgirl she played her first Titania, as well as Ariel in *The Tempest* and the Queen in *Richard II*, and she took part in the York Mystery Plays, for which her mother was wardrobe mistress. At first, however, she wanted to be a stage designer, and enrolled at an art school in her home town of York with this in mind. Still uncertain about a career, she followed her brother as a student at the Central School of Speech and Drama in London where, after a shaky start, she graduated with a first class degree and won a gold medal as outstanding student of her year. Already she had worked with Cicely Berry as voice trainer, as she was to continue to do especially in her years with the Royal Shakespeare Company. Her debut performances as Ophelia at the Old Vic in 1957 were harshly criticized in the press: Richard Findlater called it a debacle. But she was learning fast. In an interview some twenty years later she said

> When I was first at the Old Vic in 1957 I played Ophelia. It was during the Asian flu epidemic which I caught, and I walked on to the stage and played the nunnery scene with tears streaming down my face. When I came off, John Neville, who was playing Hamlet, came up and really shook me and said 'Never do that again! The audience comes to see Shakespeare's *Hamlet* and you're privileged to be playing Ophelia. Don't think they come to see you with the flu or in tears because one of your family has died, or because you've got a headache, or that you can't be bothered.' I thought at the time that that was a very harsh thing to do. I realize now that it was one of the most extraordinary and marvellous discipline lessons.
>
> (Wells, 1976, p. 82)

She was replaced by another, slightly older actor, Barbara Jefford, when the production went on tour in America. But she persevered, playing Maria in *Twelfth Night* and other roles at the Old Vic in London and on Broadway.

Her performance a little later as Juliet in Zeffirelli's Old Vic production of 1960 appears to have forced her to think hard about the balance in classical acting between psychological verisimilitude and the demands of poetic drama. The production's innovative nature, with an emphasis on adolescent passion and Italianate *verismo*, caused it initially to receive bad reviews, with several critics complaining about neglect of the play's poetry; about one-third of the text was cut. The *Times* critic wrote 'Miss Judi Dench and Mr John Stride are young players who act their parts competently but cannot yet make anything like constant touch with the poetry within them' (qu. Miller, 1998, p. 46). Dench herself has said that Zeffirelli 'had no respect for the verse at all, and cut it appallingly, hacking at it, for which he was rightly criticized. He left the text to the actors, and it didn't survive at all well' (McDonald, 2005, p. 116). But the production's fortunes changed when Kenneth Tynan wrote that Zeffirelli had worked 'a miracle ... a revelation, even perhaps a revolution ... so abundant and compelling was the life on stage that I could not wait to find out what happened next' (Miller, 1998, p. 47). Judi Dench appears to have taken criticism of the verse speaking to heart in a way that may well have had a formative influence. Interviewed by Gareth Lloyd Evans years later, she said, 'Although I was learning about the poetry I didn't understand about it as I understand now, after so many years ... Therefore, it took up all our energies, in this production, in order to play the passion and the emotions.' The passion, she felt, 'carried it through' but 'there were many many people who simply couldn't take that – because there was no poetry. I would love to play it again ... now because I do know about the poetry, and I think I could still retain the passion' (Lloyd Evans, 1974, p. 138).

In 1961 Judi was invited by Peter Hall to become a founder member of the Royal Shakespeare Company, scoring a great success as Titania in his 1962 production of

A *Midsummer Night's Dream*. (She was to reprise the role, also under Hall's direction and with no less success, in 2010, at the age of 75.) By now, perhaps because of Hall's influence, her verse speaking was especially commended.

More perhaps than any other major actress in the history of the British theatre, Judi Dench's career is notable for versatility. She has never been susceptible to type casting. Though some of her greatest successes have been in Shakespeare, she has also acted to acclaim in classic and modern plays covering a wide range of dramatic styles, as well as in musicals and television situation comedies. She has starred in comedies by Ben Jonson, Wycherley, Congreve, Chekhov and Wilde, in Jacobean tragedies by Thomas Middleton and John Webster, in serious dramas by Ibsen and Shaw, Brecht and O'Casey, Pinter, David Hare and Edward Bond, and in light comedies such as Noel Coward's *Hay Fever* and Keith Waterhouse's *Mr and Mrs Nobody*. On film her roles have ranged from Queen Elizabeth 1 (in *Shakespeare in Love*), through Queen Victoria (in *Mrs Brown*), to Iris Murdoch (in *Iris*). No doubt her breadth of experience in a wide range of drama has fed into her Shakespearian roles, extending her technique and stimulating her imagination.

Inevitably given the theatrical conditions of the time, her career has been largely shaped by external forces. She has not, like an actor manager, been able to determine in which plays she would appear, but rather has responded to the needs of companies for which she has worked, such as the Old Vic, the Oxford and Nottingham Playhouses, the Royal Shakespeare Company and the National Theatre. A regrettable result of the system is that she has not been given the opportunity to play on stage roles for which she seems well suited such as Rosalind, Cressida and the Nurse in *Romeo and Juliet*, and that her Volumnia was given only in a limited number of performances in Chichester. And only three of her major Shakespeare roles can be seen on commercially available film – Titania, Lady Macbeth and Adriana in Trevor Nunn's musical adaptation of *The Comedy of Errors*. She is however a memorable and moving Mistress Quickly in Kenneth Branagh's film of *Henry V*, and can be seen and heard briefly but piercingly as Hecuba in his *Hamlet*. Notable among audio recordings are her Nurse in Branagh's *Romeo and Juliet* and Goneril to John Gielgud's King Lear. She has of course been able to turn down roles that she did not wish to play, but in responding to invitations she has, it would appear, relied much on the guidance of trusted colleagues, such as Peter Hall, Trevor Nunn, John Barton and Richard Eyre, as well as her late husband, the actor Michael Williams.

Trusting in the judgement of others has often required an exercise of faith, but it has also helped to extend her range in ways that might not have happened without external guidance. She has been willing to take risks, to be cast against type, to defy personal limitations and to spring surprises, even on herself. She has, writes John Miller in relation to her acceptance of a role (which injury forced her to abandon) in the musical *Cats*, 'made it a cardinal policy to try to move from a success in one dramatic form to a new challenge as different as possible from the last' (Miller, 1998, p. 169). And Richard Eyre has written that 'Every part she takes on has to test her; it has to be something that she thinks she might not be able to do' (Miller, 2004, p. 40). In a 1974 interview she spoke of having played Lady Macbeth on tour in Africa while saying that she 'would never be asked' to play it in England. 'Nor Cleopatra. That's not my scene. I wouldn't know how to approach them, actually'

(Lloyd Evans, 1974, p. 141). In later years she was to triumph in both roles. Similarly with the transition from stage to film. In 1973, asked 'Have you acted in films?', she replied 'Yes. I don't like it very much' (Wells, 1976, p. 82). She was to conquer her aversion enough to star later in many films, being nominated for an Oscar six times (so far), and winning one for her Queen Elizabeth in *Shakespeare in Love* (1998). But she retains her preference for the challenges of theatre. Interviewed by a fellow actor, Oliver Ford-Davies, in 2007, she said 'In *Antony and Cleopatra* there was a line I knew should get a laugh, and I couldn't get it. We did the hundredth performance and that night the laugh came. That's why the theatre wins over film and television every single time: *you* get more out of it, and the audience teach you so much' (Ford-Davies, 2007, p. 218).

Any actor's career is determined in part by inherent and inescapable physical and intellectual attributes, though these may be extended and developed by training. Judi Dench is short – five feet two inches. There is nothing much she can do about that, as she knows. McDonald writes, 'Having accepted Peter Hall's invitation to do *Antony and Cleopatra* at the National Theatre in 1987, she began the first rehearsal by saying to him "Well, I hope you know what you're doing. You are setting out to direct Cleopatra with a menopausal dwarf"' (McDonald, 2005, p. 111). Over the years she has, especially when playing romantic heroines, had to fight a tendency to embonpoint. Her features are regular, her eyes large and expressive. In youth she had a delicate, luminous beauty which has mellowed over the years, her face illuminated by her penetrating intelligence and radiant, often mischievous smile. Though she is not gifted with the 'voice beautiful' of the Terry family, she has a wide vocal range of both pitch and volume, along with a huskiness that has been seen as a trademark and as both an asset and a handicap. It is frequently said that a notice appeared outside a theatre in which she was appearing reading 'Judi Dench does not have a cold, this is her natural speaking voice'; John Miller's book about her is called *Judi Dench: With a Crack in Her Voice*.

Throughout the interviews that she gives there runs an emphasis on the actor's need for training, and especially, in performing Shakespeare, for training in vocal delivery and in understanding the demands of the verse. She has paid tribute to her teachers in this – among them Cicely Berry, John Barton and Peter Hall. She rightly sees herself as the bearer of a tradition, and she can be quite fierce in talking about deficiencies in the voice training offered nowadays to young actors. In both prose and verse, her vocal delivery is of exemplary clarity and energy, reminiscent of that of her great predecessor Peggy Ashcroft. The voice is fully supported and projected. The vowels are pure, the consonants crisp. Every syllable is required to make its contribution. She can speak fast if the situation demands it. Her mental agility means that she can, as her fellow actor Michael Pennington writes, 'move from a thought to a related half-thought, complicate it with a burst of feeling and move on to a physical action that incorporates all three, like mercury, at the speed of light' (Miller, 2004, p. 60). For all the speed, however, there is never an impression of unintended haste. In verse, she is conscious of rhythm, but does not overstress it. She knows where the caesura, the break within the verse line, occurs, and she can use it, perhaps with a scarcely perceptible pause, a little silence, that suggests the working of the character's mind, the thought processes in which meaning and poetry coalesce. She has often stressed the importance in verse speaking of what musicians call *legato* – the carrying over of the tone from one note or syllable to another, producing an apparently seamless flow of sound. She can convey an impression of this through a technical and imaginative mastery that is a result of a highly developed artistry. Gregory Doran, who directed her as the Countess in *All's Well That Ends Well*, wrote that:

> to listen to her deliver the text was to hear a master class in Shakespeare's verse. She would feel the verse line, beating out the iambic rhythm on her hand if in doubt about where the stress lay. And in early stages she would not be able to remember the line if the pulse was wrong. She'd seek to release the easy natural effect of the line endings, never pausing, so much as lifting and considering the end of a line before completing the sense with the next. For example, when the Countess (in Act One, Scene Three) says to Helena as she dissembles her love for Bertram:
>
> My fear hath catch'd your fondness; now I see
> The mystery of your loneliness, and find
> Your salt tears' head. Now to all sense 'tis gross:
> You love my son...
>
> at the end of the first line, where others may have run on, Judi would lift the word 'see', allowing the next phrase ('the mystery of your loneliness') to be considered precisely, and compassionately expressed. And lifting the end of the second line allowed her to land on the next four monosyllables with tough maternal love, leading on to the revelation that she wants to flush out of Helena: 'You love my son.'
>
> (Miller, 2004, p. 175).

It is often said of her preparation for roles that she does not read in advance the plays in which she is to appear. According to Doran, when he asked her to play the Countess she said 'I don't know the play. Never seen it, read it, or been in it. You're going to have to tell me the story' (Miller, 2004, p. 171). But this is clearly not always true. Maybe she will sometimes agree to act in a new play of which she has not seen the script, but there are after all times when she has undertaken a role that she has already played before. And nothing should give the impression that she does not prepare seriously for her roles. Absence of preconceptions before rehearsals start may enable her to throw herself the more fully into the creative process once it begins. The work is often done in private, by allowing her subconscious mind to mull over and solve the problems of the rehearsal room. I have been aware sometimes that deep down a process of absorption of a role was taking place. She is a great assimilator. Late in 1986 I saw her and her husband, Michael Williams, in *Mr and Mrs Nobody*, Keith Waterhouse's dramatization of *The Diary of a Nobody*, by George and Weedon Grossmith. It was an enchanting performance of a delightful if slight comedy of manners. In her dressing room afterwards she told me that her next role was to be Cleopatra, and asked me about the meaning of a line in the play.

Already she was thinking about it, and I have no doubt that the role grew steadily in her imagination as she pursued her daily tasks well before rehearsals began. Seriousness of approach is not however incompatible with a sense of fun. She is a great joker, a giggler, a husky chuckler, and a hearty laugher, famous for the jokes she plays on her fellow actors in rehearsal and even on stage, and for corpsing. She tells of an incident in a performance of *The Merchant of Venice*:

> In the casket scene Michael Williams was standing in the centre of the stage as Bassanio, about to make his choice. There was the wind band at the back of the stage, Peter Geddes as Gobbo, Polly James waiting to sing 'Tell me where is fancy bred', and my brother Jeff and Bernard Lloyd as monks. I was supposed to say
>
> I speak too long, 'tis but to peize the time,
> To eke it, and to draw it out in length,
> To stay you from election.
>
> But I said 'erection'. The band just put down their instruments and walked off, as did the monks, leaving Polly James to sing on her own. I have never been in such a state, and the scene had only just started.
>
> (Dench, 1996, pp. 204–205)

This irrepressible sense of fun, the lack of self-importance that it betokens, the ability, even the desire, to laugh at herself, is among the qualities that make her a natural team player – and also, ever since she has been a star, the natural leader of any company in which she appears. And jokiness both in rehearsals and during a run may well keep everyone on their toes, militating against staleness.

The seriousness that Judi brings to technical matters of verse speaking is no less apparent in her characterization of roles. She looks for the humanizing touches, the person below the style. This was true even in Trevor Nunn's farcical musical based on *The Comedy of Errors*. The performance can be seen on video. A high spot is the wordless interpolated moment when Judi appears on a balcony, impatient for her husband Antipholus to come in to dinner, and sees his identical twin brother, of whose existence she is oblivious, in the courtyard below. Drawing herself up to her full (not very great) height in a wonderfully imperious manner, like a latter-day Sarah Siddons, she glares at the hapless twin, and with a gesture like that of an exasperated traffic policewoman directs him into the house for what can only be going to be an exceedingly uncomfortable confrontation. This is splendid, but Judi knows that farce needs to be grounded in reality, and her performance succeeds in the way in which she underlies the exaggerations required by the production style with touches of true feeling that draw sympathy for Adriana in her plight.

The production style of *The Comedy of Errors* constricted the play's emotional range, which though relatively slight makes it so clearly a precursor of Shakespeare's other play about twins in search of each other and so of themselves, *Twelfth Night*. Judi played Viola in John Barton's RSC production 202 times, from October 1969 in Stratford, and later in Australia, then London, Stratford again and finally, in 1972, in

Japan. She has written of her love for this play's 'melancholy. The degrees of love that everyone is in, sometimes with themselves, sometimes with someone else in disguise – and everyone with their idea of love.' 'Shakespeare,' she says, 'takes so many textures of that emotion, and gives it so many forms' (Dench, 1996, p. 202). John Barton spoke in similar terms: '[T]he text contains an enormous range of emotions and moods and most productions seem to select one – farce or bitterness or romance – and emphasize it throughout. I wanted to sound all the notes that are there' (Interview with Barton in *Plays and Players*, November 1969, p. 49). Many-texturedness is a prime quality of Judi's acting. In writing about this production a year or two after it closed, I tried to suggest something of this in her interpretation of Viola, and about the ways in which she conveyed it through movement, gesture, facial expression and vocal inflection:

> When she first appeared at court, Valentine, congratulating Cesario on the Duke's favours, disconcertingly slapped her on the bosom; moments later, when the Duke had entered, he pointed to a stool and pulled it close to him, indicating that Cesario should sit on it; she pulled it away before sitting down; he pulled it back to him. The actress's momentary flinchings, signs of nervousness that would be understandable in a boy newly promoted to favour at court, held an extra dimension of meaning for those who knew the boy was a girl; and so a bond of complicity was entered into with the audience. Left onstage at the end of the scene, she could reveal to us her sympathetic amusement at her own situation: 'Whoe'er I woo, myself would be his wife.' There was intelligent irony as well as wistfulness in the delivery of the line, showing us Viola's independent resilience as well as her affectionate nature. In her next scene with the Duke, we were given an initial reminder of the true situation as he pulled her stool towards him and held on to her to prevent her moving away, but the scene was played for its full emotional power. Judi Dench spoke her lines about 'Patience on a Monument' with a quietly beautiful intensity, and late in the scene there came a brilliant fusion of a comic apprehension of an irony with a sense of deep emotion. 'But died thy sister of her love, my boy?', asked Orsino. 'I am all the daughters of my father's house, / And all the brothers, too ...', replied Cesario; and a tiny pause followed by a catch in the voice took us movingly from the fictional situation of Viola speaking equivocally to conceal her own disguise, to the reality of the situation in which she genuinely believed that she had lost her brother.
>
> (Wells, 1977, p. 50)

A studio recording of part of the scene made by Judi many years later, in 1998 (*Shakespeare His Life and Work*, 2 CDs), permits an analysis of how she spoke it. The voice is fresh, every syllable clear, but there is no hint of oratory. She opens in an almost casual, story-telling mode:

> My [emphasis on both 'My' and 'fa-'] father had a daughter [emphasis on 'daugh-'] loved a man [distinct pause],
> As it might be, perhaps, were I a woman [upward inflection, a smile in the voice, expressive of the impossibility],

I [slight emphasis] should your lordship.
ORSINO And what's her history?
VIOLA [slight pause, lowering of the tone and volume] A blank, my lord. [Momentary pause] She never told [emphasis on 'told'] her love,
But let concealment, [barely perceptible pause at the caesura] like a worm i'th'bud, [slight pause]
Feed on her damask cheek. [Longer pause] She pined [the voice opens out on the vowel, pace reduces] in thought, [slight pause]
And with a green and yellow melancholy, [pause at the end only of this and the following line, upward inflection on the last syllable]
She sat like patience on a monument,
Smiling [emphasis on 'smi-'] at grief. [Pause] Was not this [slight pause] love [emphasized] indeed?
[Pace picks up] We men may say more, swear more, but indeed
Our shows are more than will; for still we [slightly emphasized] prove
Much in our vows, but little in our love. [Emphasis points the antithesis of 'vows' and 'love']
ORSINO But died thy sister of her love, my boy?
VIOLA I am all the daughters of my father's house, [pause at the end only of this line]
And all the brothers too; [pause; volume reduces, last words whispered as if to herself] and yet I know not.

This analysis, crude though it is, may help to demonstrate something of the technical basis of Judi's speaking, showing the use she can make of her awareness of the way the verse works, of how observance of line endings, of caesuras (when they exist), and of antithesis (on which John Barton, very rightly, never tires of insisting) can help the performer to release the full emotional and intellectual potential of the lines.

The thoughtfulness that Judi brings to the preparation of a role can result in interesting freshness of interpretation. When she came to play Beatrice in John Barton's 1976 *Much Ado About Nothing*, also for the RSC, she softened the character's asperities by picking up on the suggestions in the text that Beatrice and Benedick had had a love affair in the past. The key line comes in response to Don Pedro's words 'Come, lady, come, you have lost the heart of Signor Benedick.' 'Indeed, my lord', she replies, 'he lent it me a while, and I gave him use for it, a double heart for his single one. Marry, once before he won it of me, with false dice.' When I mentioned to Judi that the line was often omitted, she replied that she had agreed to take the role only on condition that it was retained. It was part and parcel of her portrayal of Beatrice as a woman of some maturity, of a wisdom born of not entirely happy experience. There was enormous fun in her performance – the slightly bawdy comedy of the scene (3.4) with her girl friends, in which she has a cold, was as funny as I have ever seen it – but the ground bass of seriousness had been sounded again at the end of the second deception scene, when she emerges from hiding after hearing herself criticized. 'What fire is in mine ears?' she says. 'Can this be true? / Stand I condemned for pride and scorn so much?' I have heard the speech spoken farcically, but Judi knew better than this. Written in the form of an abbreviated sonnet, it is a turning point in the action:

> What fire is in mine ears? Can this be true?
> Stand I condemned for pride and scorn so much?
> Contempt, farewell; and maiden pride, adieu.
> No glory lives behind the back of such.
> And, Benedick, love on. I will requite thee,
> Taming my wild heart to thy loving hand.
> If thou dost love, my kindness shall incite thee
> To bind our loves up in a holy band.
> For others say thou dost deserve, and I
> Believe it better than reportingly.
>
> (3.1.107–116)

Responding to the speech's lyrical style, Judi, with a tenderness that did not deny an element of self-mockery, nevertheless showed that this is a response to a learning experience, that Beatrice is a wiser woman at the end of the scene than she had been at its beginning.

Judi's mastery of verse speaking is recognized by other members of the profession. A colleague, Dearbhla Molloy, cast as Lady Macbeth, writes that 'I rang Judi and asked her if she'd teach me how to speak the verse, which she did. We didn't use *Macbeth* as the text, for obvious reasons, we used Cleopatra, which she was playing at the time. I wrote down the rules that she gave me:

1. Remember it's a play, not reality.
2. Obey the metre.
3. Start scenes.
4. Earn a pause.
5. Don't separate.
6. Drive through the speech.
7. Antithesis, pauses up at the end of lines.
8. Economy, simplicity, and negotiate with humour.
9. You don't have to carry the message, the play does it for you.
10. Trust the play, and your casting.

(Miller, 1998, p. 221–222)

Most of these maxims are clear – 'start scenes', I understand, is shorthand for 'if you speak first in a scene, give it a kick start'. Though the advice clearly reflects Dame Judi's long experience, it also echoes to some degree advice given to her by the director of the production, Peter Hall, who has indeed been a lifelong mentor. She has said: 'When we did *Antony and Cleopatra* Peter Hall gave me the two best notes I've ever had. First, remember you don't have to play the whole of the character in each scene. You may only have to play a very small aspect of the character, and then at the end the character should be whole. Second, remember not everybody speaks the truth about your character' (Ford-Davies, 2007, p. 217).

For all the emphasis that Judi herself, as well as those who write about her acting, has placed on her mastery of the speaking of both verse and prose, she is a mistress too of body language. I felt this in her performance of Perdita in Trevor Nunn's production of *The Winter's Tale* (in which she also played a gravely beautiful Hermione). Her dancing in the pastoral scene was imbued with a kind of innocent eroticism, a rapt enjoyment of the music and of the sensuous movement of her own limbs that fully justified Florizel's praise:

> When you do dance, I wish you
> A wave o'th'sea, that you might ever do
> Nothing but that, move still, still so,
> And own no other function.
>
> (4.4.140–143)

Body language seemed especially important too, not least because it assisted depth and originality of interpretation, when Judi moved to the National Theatre to play Gertrude in Richard Eyre's 1989 production of *Hamlet*. I saw the play on its first night, when Daniel Day-Lewis played Hamlet – after withdrawing from the production he was succeeded by Jeremy Northam, and then by the dying Ian Charleson. In response, perhaps, to the broad dimensions of the Olivier stage and auditorium the play was performed in a presentational manner, formal rather than intimate. Characters stood far apart, speaking often with little or no movement, facing out to the audience rather than addressing one another. This production style held the audience at arm's length, encouraging observant neutrality rather than involvement in the characters' emotions and in the excitement of the action. Only in the closet scene between Gertrude and Hamlet did body language come into full play. As Hamlet's passion mounted he bestraddled his mother; her evident tenderness for him sought physical expression, and their climactic kiss was a naked and mutual acknowledgement of desire that shocked her. She addressed 'What shall I do?' to herself, acknowledging the discovery within herself of depths she could not fathom. As Hamlet left she collapsed, and for the rest of the play was a broken woman. Judi's acting communicated emotional complexity with great economy of means, and set the play's heart beating as it had not done until that point.

Economy is indeed a keynote of her acting, nowhere better exemplified than in the final scene of *All's Well that Ends Well*. As its director writes, 'The Countess says nothing when Helena returns, as if from the dead, at the end of the play. Her new daughter-in-law turns to the Countess with the line, 'Oh, my dear mother, do I see you living?' There is no reply. There can't be. Judi's choice was for the Countess to stare at Helena, almost unable to move, and finally, slowly turned her outstretched hands palm up to signal silent welcome, acceptance, and profound relief. It was a moment to haunt you with its stillness, and she created it with such economy and truth, the effect was devastating' (Doran in Miller, 2004, p. 177).

In the event, the Shakespeare role that gave Judi the greatest scope for the full range of her talents is the one she thought she would never play, Cleopatra. In Hall's 1987 production she embraced its challenges and opportunities with joyous acceptance of all it has to offer, extending herself into every aspect of the role, from the sordid to the sublime, while never losing the sense of a unifying self that could encompass the character's 'infinite variety'. Tirzah Lowen's book is revealing about the relationship between actor, role, company and director during the rehearsal process. 'When not in a scene, Judi Dench sits quietly in a corner, blocking out distraction as she studies her lines.' She is 'Wholly still and focused.' Day by day she 'is absorbing the many facets of the character, and tapping her own qualities to give them substance: the energy, the quick intelligence and wit, the "gutsiness", the femininity, the playfulness, the authority, the pensiveness and vulnerability.' But preparation for the role is not an entirely solitary process. 'Both on and offstage, a warm relationship with Cleopatra's entourage has developed (and it is not surprising to learn, later, that it is with the Cleopatra who had the common touch and inspired great loyalty ... that Dench most identifies)' (Lowen, 1990, pp. 57–58).

There are links with the past. Peter Hall had spoken to Peggy Ashcroft, who had played the role with Michael Redgrave as Antony to great acclaim thirty-five years previously, and did not underestimate its difficulties: 'You know you'll never get there, but it's quite clear where you're going' (Lowen, 1990, p.23). And Judi herself spoke to her great predecessor, gaining insight into the emotions behind the words: 'in reply to Antony's taunt that she save herself by sending his grizzled head to Caesar, Cleopatra's "That head, my lord?" should contain all her love for him' (Lowen, 1990, p. 80). Clearly too she had great confidence in her director, learning from him while also maintaining her independence.

All this showed in her performance. From her first appearance this was clearly a woman of volatile passions, physically restless, richly sensual yet with a shrewd, instinctive intelligence that probed suspiciously, vulnerably, behind the appearances with which she was presented. She realized the comedy of the role with perfect timing and brilliant transitions. As she questioned the messenger about Octavia, her self-confidence grew until, as he said 'I do think she's thirty', the smile froze on her face and, gathering her skirts, she swirled abruptly around, ran towards the door, and almost left the stage. The poetry of the role, too, was fully realized, climactically when, her restlessness subdued, she spoke 'I dreamt there was an Emperor Antony ...' with rapt, hushed lyricism to a Dolabella who stood in the auditorium aisle with his back to us, so that she was addressing us as well as him. The audience's silence was palpable. We were united in a single emotional response. This was great acting achieved through a perfection of vocal technique along with the highest physical economy.

An actor is nothing without an audience. Judi Dench's long love affair with those who come to see her act is reflected in the admiration and affection in which she is held by countless admirers. The generosity of her art reflects and is enabled by the generosity of a great spirit. She is the best loved English actress since Ellen Terry, and her success on stage, like Ellen Terry's, is indivisible from the personality that enables it.

Chronology (concentrating on Shakespeare)

Born York, 1934

1957	debut with the Old Vic Company playing Ophelia, etc.
1960	Juliet in Franco Zeffirelli's production of *Romeo and Juliet* and other roles at the Old Vic

1961	joins Royal Shakespeare Company: 1962 Isabella in *Measure for Measure*, Titania in *A Midsummer Night's Dream* (filmed 1965, on DVD), etc.
1963	Nottingham Playhouse Company: Lady Macbeth in *Macbeth*, Viola in *Twelfth Night*, and on tour in West Africa
1965	Nottingham Playhouse Company: Isabella in *Measure for Measure*
1969–71	Royal Shakespeare Company; roles include Hermione and Perdita in *The Winter's Tale*, Viola in *Twelfth Night* (both 1969), Portia in *The Merchant of Venice* (1971)
1975–80	Royal Shakespeare Company: 1976, Beatrice in *Much Ado About Nothing*, Lady Macbeth in *Macbeth*, Adriana in *The Comedy of Errors* (this and *Macbeth* also Thames Television, available on DVD); Regan in *King Lear*; 1979, Imogen in *Cymbeline*
1987	National Theatre Company, Cleopatra in *Antony and Cleopatra*, 1988, created Dame of the British Empire
1988	Mistress Quickly in Branagh's film of *Henry V*; directed *Much Ado About Nothing* for the Renaissance Theatre Company
1989	National Theatre Company: Gertrude in *Hamlet*
1991	Chichester Festival Company: Volumnia in *Coriolanus*
2003	Countess in *All's Well That Ends Well*, 2006, Mistress Quickly in *The Merry Wives: the Musical*, both Royal Shakespeare Company
2005	created Companion of Honour
2009	Titania in *A Midsummer Night's Dream* Rose Theatre, Kingston-upon-Thames

Bibliography

Dench, Judi (1996) 'A Career in Shakespeare', in *Shakespeare: An Illustrated Stage History*, ed. J. Bate and R. Jackson. Oxford: Oxford University Press, pp. 197–210.

Dench, Judi, and John Miller (2005) *Scenes from my Life*. London: Weidenfeld and Nicolson.

Evans, Gareth Lloyd (1974) 'Judi Dench talks to Gareth Lloyd Evans', *Shakespeare Survey 27*. Cambridge: Cambridge University Press, pp. 137–142.

Ford-Davies, Oliver (2007) *Performing Shakespeare: Preparation, Rehearsal, Performance*. London: Nick Hern Books.

Lowen, Tirzah (1990) *Peter Hall Directs 'Antony and Cleopatra'*. London: Methuen, 1990.

McDonald, Russ (2005) Look to the Lady: Sarah Siddons, Ellen Terry, and Judi Dench on the Shakespearean Stage. Athens and London: Georgia University Press.

Miller, John (1998) *Judi Dench: With a Crack in Her Voice*. London: Weidenfeld and Nicolson.

Miller, John, ed. (2004) *Darling Judi: A Celebration of Judi Dench at 70*. London: Weidenfeld and Nicolson.

Wells, Stanley (1976) 'An Interview with Miss Judi Dench', *Cahiers Elisabéthains* 10, pp. 69–83.

——(1977) *Royal Shakespeare: Four Major Productions at the Royal Shakespeare Theatre*. Manchester: Manchester University Press.

About The Author

Stanley Wells, Chairman of the Shakespeare Birthplace Trust and Honorary Fellow of the Shakespeare Institute, is General Editor of the Oxford and Penguin editions of

Shakespeare. He is Honorary Governor Emeritus of the Royal Shakespeare Company, and was for many years Vice-Chairman of the Board. His books include *Shakespeare: For All Time* (Macmillan, 2002), *Shakespeare & Co.* (Penguin, 2006), and *Shakespeare, Sex, and Love* (2010). His writings on theatre include *Royal Shakespeare* (listed above), *Shakespeare on Stage: An Anthology of Criticism* (Oxford, 1997), review articles in *Shakespeare Survey*, and numerous reviews of individual productions in e.g. the TLS and elsewhere.

4
Kate Duchêne

James Loehlin

In the summer of 2010, Kate Duchêne—an actress with over two decades of theatrical credits from the West End, the Royal Shakespeare Company and the Royal National Theatre—played her first Shakespearean lead on a London stage. She appeared to broad acclaim in the role of Queen Katharine in Mark Rosenblatt's production of *Henry VIII* at Shakespeare's Globe. Her performance provides an instructive instance of what a gifted and experienced actor can bring from non-Shakespearean work to a challenging part in one of the most demanding Shakespearean venues. This essay will focus on Duchêne's performance as Katharine—both process and product—and will be informed by my interview with her at Shakespeare's Globe on 19 August 2010 (from which all quotations are taken).

Duchêne had done some previous Shakespeare, but mostly quite early in her career: Mariana in *Measure for Measure* while at Cambridge in 1981, the Princess of France in *Love's Labour's Lost* at Chichester in 1989, Queen Elizabeth in the tour of Sam Mendes' RSC *Richard III* in 1992–3, Jessica in David Thacker's RSC *Merchant* in 1993–4. Since 2000 much of her theatre work was with the avant-garde director Katie Mitchell, including a series of productions at the Royal National Theatre. These productions encompassed classical and modern texts together with intensely detailed acting and innovative stagecraft. Duchêne appeared in Mitchell's RNT productions of *Iphigenia at Aulis* (Euripides, 2004), *Waves* (based on Virginia Woolf, 2006–8), *Attempts on Her Life* (Martin Crimp, 2007), and *Women of Troy* (Euripides, 2007). Mitchell's meticulous rehearsal techniques were a significant influence on the process by which Duchêne built up the role of Katharine.

She had also done film and television work throughout her career, most prominently in the television series *The Worst Witch* in 1998–2000. As Constance Hardbroom, a severe deputy headmistress at a school for young witches, she developed a popular following; she opted out of a similar role in the *Harry Potter* series of films. Her air of intimidating authority served her again as Carey Mulligan's Latin teacher in the Oscar-nominated *An Education* (2009), and it was an important dimension of her characterization of Queen Katharine. She has excelled in roles that, like Katharine, Hecuba, or Queen Elizabeth, combine imperiousness and vulnerability. She was a heartbreaking Varya in Adrian Noble's 1995 RSC *The Cherry Orchard*, maintaining order in the crumbling household while enduring her own hidden griefs.

Kate Duchêne's physical presence contributes to this distinctive combination of power and pathos. She is above medium height, with pale skin, dark hair, and piercing dark eyes. Onstage she strikingly resembled the surviving portraits of Katharine of Aragon, with the same strong jaw, tight mouth, and heavy-lidded dark eyes, framed in deep rounded sockets. Her voice and bearing conveyed a regal dignity, while her drawn face and haunted eyes conveyed the suffering that was the keynote of her characterization, and which provided the emotional heart of Rosenblatt's production.

Why did Kate Duchêne choose to take on such a difficult Shakespearean role, after concentrating on new and experimental work for so long? 'I'll say something blasphemous,' she said near the end of the run of *Henry VIII*. 'I've never been particularly interested in playing any of the big Shakespearean women, because there's such a feeling in England that people aren't really here for the story.' She commented on the frequency with which the major plays are produced, and the critical interest in interpretive variation among a few key roles. 'Everybody knows Lady Macbeth, everybody knows Gertrude—they're here to see how somebody's going to do it, what this production's going to be like,' Duchêne said. 'I want people to be wondering what's going to happen next, and lost in the story, not thinking about technical things, in essence. So I've never been that desperate to do Shakespeare, and I know that's peculiar.'

Duchêne was attracted by the fact that *Henry VIII* is seldom played, so that while people may know the historical events depicted, the character of Katharine is relatively unfamiliar to most audiences. 'I've loved working on this play because people don't know the play,' she said. 'They know the history but they don't know the play. They don't know how they're going to feel about Katharine, how they're going to feel about Henry, how they're going to feel about Anne Boleyn.' At the time of Rosenblatt's Globe production, *Henry VIII* had not received a major London production in half a century, apart from RSC Stratford transfers in 1970, 1984, and 1998. Nonetheless, a popular interest in the Henrician court, fostered by books like Phillipa Gregory's *The Other Boleyn Girl* and Hilary Mantel's *Wolf Hall* as well as the Showtime television series *The Tudors*, meant that many audience members knew the background to Shakespeare's play and had at least some sense of what was at stake for the character of Katharine.

In preparing the role, Duchêne combined the process she typically uses for modern plays with a consciousness of the particular demands of Shakespeare and the Globe. 'In terms of preparation, I've tried to do the things that Katie [Mitchell] has given me as guidelines, which are essentially very Method,' she recounted. Among these was preparing a detailed chronological outline of the character's life history. This exercise is a key step in Mitchell's own creative process, detailed in her book *The Director's Craft* (2009), and one she encourages all of her actors to undertake. With a character like Queen Katharine, who had a well-documented historical existence, the actor has both more available material and more restrictions on creative license. 'Often I have to make things up … to extrapolate from the text what I know and what must have happened,' she recalled. Katharine of Aragon's biography, by contrast, provided a wealth of detail that was valuable for the actor. 'You know when all of her children died,' she observed, focusing on a set of data that proved crucial for her development of the character's emotional life and, in the end, for the shape of the production. By building up her character not only as a Queen, a Spaniard, and a devout Catholic, but as 'a woman who had survived five dead children,' Duchêne found a deeply personal connection to the role. She also foregrounded what became a vital thematic element in the production: childlessness and the loss of children. In several key scenes, Henry was accompanied by a Fool, played by Amanda Lawrence, who manipulated a puppet representing a young boy in regal garments. Sometimes the puppet seemed to represent simply the dream of a male heir for Henry; but sometimes, in the response of Henry (and later Katharine) to this figure, it seemed to be the actual son born to the couple, who died not long after his birth in 1511. 'He lived for fifty-two days, which is enough time to be a baby you'd grieve fully,' Duchêne said, emphasizing the importance accorded to this figure in the scheme of the production, both emotionally and historically. 'Had their son lived, this country would probably still have been Catholic.'

Her preparation also included the kind of improvisational work that is an important part of Katie Mitchell's long rehearsal periods. While the Globe schedule precluded extensive work of this sort, the director Mark Rosenblatt encouraged it, especially for developing the relationship of Katharine and Henry. 'He wanted to see Henry and Katharine as quite human in their domestic drama, and we did improvisations around a divorce lawyer rather than a trial scene and stuff like that.' This work enabled Duchêne and Dominic Rowan, who played Henry, to have a strong connection, even though they only appear on stage together in two scenes of the text. Rosenblatt often overlapped scenes so that Henry and Katharine appeared on stage simultaneously in moments where only one or the other is actually present in the text, further reinforcing the importance of their relationship.

Preparing Katharine, then, involved much of the same kinds of work Duchêne would have undertaken with any role, combined with particular technical demands. 'In a way, the emotional preparation was the same, but alongside it was a much more technical preparation, to do with the verse, and with marrying an accent to the verse.' She recalled, as a young actress, working with Judi Dench, and asking her about how to do Shakespeare: 'She said, "It's very easy darling, you just observe the punctuation—go up at the end of the lines and observe the punctuation."' Duchêne retained this basic rule of thumb in her work on Katharine, sophisticating it with verse training from the Globe's text coach, Giles Block. From Block she learned to respond to the forward movement and rhythm of the lines, as well as how to make use of irregularities such as trochaic inversions of the first foot, where the stress falls on the first rather than the second beat of a line. 'Using the rhythm, of course, can really unlock things,' she noted, though technical effects were subordinated to her overall performance. 'I now have forgotten all about that, but I hope that it's there somewhere in what I'm doing.' In performance she generally observed a fairly pronounced iambic rhythm in conjunction with Katharine's accent: the labored, measured diction of someone who knows English well but lacks the throwaway ease of a native speaker.

The strong Spanish accent was one of the first important creative decisions Duchêne made about the role. She adopted it before rehearsals began, drawing on her training in Modern Languages at Cambridge and her own experience teaching in

Spain while a student. 'I tried to do it straightaway at the read-through in order not to imprint the verse in my head in another way,' she said. 'It's not possible to do a completely authentic Spanish accent and be intelligible, because the Spanish don't pronounce the ends of their words, so in this space it wouldn't be possible,' she said, noting the vocal challenges posed by the Globe.

Working in the Globe space put a lot of pressure on the various dimensions of Duchêne's approach to the role—'I had to marry the accent, the verse, and the naturalism that Mark really wanted'—while at the same time sending her performance out to fifteen hundred people surrounding the stage on all sides. 'You have to give it a lot of welly, this theatre—you have to really push it out, I think.' She had been apprehensive about working at the Globe, and had never sought work there previously: 'I was scared of working outside. Because at University I did some shows outside, and I felt the energy just went all over the place.' In practice, however, although the vocal demands were considerable, she found that the structure of the Globe did give focus to the performance.

> I've found the Globe fascinating and really illuminating about Shakespeare … It doesn't feel as if the energy goes all over the place. All you see when you go out there is a bank of faces… It's amazing. You're completely surrounded by people, just faces, waiting for a story. … There's something visceral about acting in the open air, and seeing the sky, but you're still very contained within this circle of people.

Queen Katharine appears in only four scenes of Shakespeare and Fletcher's *Henry VIII*, but she dominates most of them. With 391 lines, she has only the third-largest part in the play, though her role is fairly comparable to those of Henry (461) and Wolsey (439). Her first appearance, in 1.2, is the one that Kate Duchêne found most difficult to handle, since the personal stakes for Katharine are not especially well defined. The Queen is shown advocating on behalf of the people against ruinous new taxes, and then defending the Duke of Buckingham against the charges that are being levied against him. The scene establishes Katharine as in an almost Marian role as intercessor and defender of the weak and persecuted; but it didn't give Duchêne the emotional purchase she felt in the later scenes. 'In an odd way the first scene in which Katharine appears I find the most challenging because it's the blankest for her,' she said.

What came through strongly in Duchêne's performance of the scene was her regal bearing—she made a strong entrance from the yard of the Globe onto the platform set up in front of the stage, stopping the scene in its tracks as she knelt before the King—and her devotion to Henry. She gave an unfeigned smile on seeing him, and always kept seeking his eye with a sincere and interested regard as the various political topics were discussed. She showed a concern with the way he was conducting his affairs that came across as almost maternal. The production highlighted the age difference between Henry and his queen (Katharine of Aragon was six years Henry's senior), with Dominic Rowan playing a very young King, especially in the early scenes. Katharine was almost deferential to him, but clearly a woman of principle who would stand up for her beliefs. The scene made a point of her opposition to

Cardinal Wolsey, on both the taxation and Buckingham questions. After arousing Henry's ire against the new taxes, Katharine turned aside to enjoy a private smile as the King shouted at Wolsey. In the Buckingham scene, the text gives Katharine only a few brief expressions of charity and concern. Duchêne amplified these through non-verbal actions: fingering her rosary and crossing herself, as well as glaring angrily at Wolsey and his agent, Buckingham's disloyal surveyor. In scene 1.2 Katharine has the fewest lines, and though she made a strong impression here, one can understand Duchêne's feeling that it didn't give her much to chew on from an acting perspective: 'The relationship with Henry is a bit blank, it's public—whereas once she's being dumped, and fighting for her life, and then dying, you know what territory you're on.'

Katharine's next scene in the text (2.4) is her trial, but Rosenblatt amplified her part by making her visible during the previous two scenes, 2.2 and 2.3, in which Henry wrestles with his conscience and Anne Boleyn learns that she has caught the favor of the King. These scenes made use of one of the key features of Angela Davies' design for the production: a division of the large Globe platform into a kind of inner stage, defined by the pillars, and red-carpeted 'corridors of power' around the edge. This device, inspired by the 'walk-and-talk' scenes of the White House TV drama *The West Wing*, both created a sense of dangerous intrigue and allowed Rosenblatt to create effective, almost split-screen episodes. Queen Katharine was visible, a duteous and industrious presence seated at her embroidery, as Henry revealed his determination to Wolsey. Looking straight at the sweetly smiling Katharine, who is not present in Shakespeare's scene, Henry gravely intoned,

> O my lord,
> Would it not grieve an able man to leave
> So sweet a bedfellow? But conscience, conscience,
> O, 'tis a tender place, and I must leave her.
>
> (2.2.139–43)

As the action passed into the next scene, Katharine had obviously learned of his determination; she collapsed to her knees, her women flocking around to comfort her. Meanwhile, in the carpeted corridor downstage, Anne and the Old Lady played their scene. The split-screen effect heightened the irony as Anne, as yet unaware of her new fortune, avowed that she would never want to be queen, while the kneeling Katharine, fully conscious of her fate, sobbed in grief. This non-textual simultaneous staging heightened the rise-and-fall pattern that is one of the play's most obvious structural devices.

Katharine had thus been onstage for several minutes when the courtroom finally assembled around her for the trial scene, 2.4. Accordingly, she was able to begin the scene at a high emotional pitch, with the audience acutely conscious of her situation and very much on her side. Duchêne undoubtedly brought out the Queen's grief and anger in the scene, but one of the surprising keynotes of her performance was its rhetorical command and precision. Her Katharine was very conscious of her audience, and altered her performance, moment to moment, as her focus shifted. She acidly glared at Wolsey in declaring him her 'enemy' (29), shook her finger angrily at the King in challenging him to 'prove' any misconduct on her part (37), and appealed directly to the galleries of the Globe in asserting that both her father and Henry's had declared their marriage lawful (42–51). But she showed vulnerability and desperation at other times, falling to her knees before the King in beseeching him to allow her the counsel of her Spanish advisors. While Wolsey was speaking, she went and stood next to the King as he sat in his throne, assuming what she believed to be her rightful place, and, with a fierce yet controlled gaze, daring Henry to drive her from it. Her defiant attitudes were rooted in research into the historical Katharine's violations of protocol, and represented a woman who was, as Duchêne put it, 'fighting for her life'. Her final exit was both proud and exhausted.

Her next scene, with the two Cardinals (3.1), again highlighted Katharine's bitterness and anger. At one point she chased the cardinals out of the room, making a circuit of the red-carpeted corridor before returning to the center of the stage where her ladies-in-waiting had been busily eavesdropping on the quarrel. The ladies were deployed effectively throughout the scene, and helped serve to highlight the conflict between Katharine and Anne. While the other ladies wore shades of grey, Anne stood out in blue, marking a visual contrast with both Katharine's regal purple and Wolsey's scarlet. The conflict came to a head at the end of the scene, when Katharine asks desperately 'What will become of me?' (146). The text here indicates the Queen's concern for her ladies, 'poor wenches', whose fortunes will fall with those of their mistress. Yet Duchêne's Katharine singled out Anne from among the rest, challenging her aggressively. (Anne's presence in the scene is unscripted and, given her elevation to Marchioness of Pembroke, perhaps unlikely, but it was used here to great dramatic effect.) As Anne sat, unable to meet the Queen's gaze, Katharine advanced on her and physically grabbed her face, forcing her to look on 'the most unhappy woman living' (147).

Duchêne's most original and emphatic performance choices were reserved for Katharine's final scene, 4.2, in which the dying Dowager forgives her enemy Wolsey and witnesses a vision of 'spirits of peace' (83). Both of these moments were given a very different tone than the text suggests. Her performance was grounded in the brutal physical reality of Katharine's medical condition. 'She's dying of cancer with no pain relief,' and from her first entrance this harsh fact dominated the scene. This choice was justified by the text—in the scene's first line Katharine announces she is 'sick to death!'—and Duchêne never let the audience forget it. She entered leaning on a stick, her hair unkempt and sweaty, and spoke all of her lines with grimacing effort, racked sometimes by spasms of agony. There were notes of bitter humor in the scene, as Katharine learned of the decline of Wolsey: 'Alas, poor man!' she snapped insincerely, getting a huge laugh from the audience for her well-earned *schadenfreude* (16). When Griffith spoke of Wolsey's 'repentance' (27), she uttered a short, snorting laugh, and her denunciation of him was ferocious, building to a shouted 'nothing!' (42). Her eventual forgiveness of Wolsey was overwhelmed by her pain, with none of the gentleness the words imply. Likewise, the 'vision' was far from the 'blessed troop' promising 'eternal happiness' suggested by the text (87–90). 'The vision scene happened very late, and I had no idea what the vision should be,' Duchêne said. 'Mark kept talking about, maybe it should be Spanish, maybe it should be a vision of her home, maybe it should be heaven.' In the end, it became something altogether grimmer. The puppet-ghost of Katharine's dead son appeared out of a chest, guided by the Fool and flanked by the ghosts of Buckingham and Wolsey. The '*garland*' they offered her was the crown, which they took away as soon as they had given it, so that the vision ended in hysterical frenzy rather than peace and resignation to death. Duchêne again found sharp humor in Katharine's vexation with the 'saucy fellow' who fails to show her adequate reverence, but for the most part the scene was one of grueling suffering. In her last speech, Katharine's lines came in short bursts of four to five syllables as she fought for breath.

'Many people have felt that what I'm doing in the vision scene is over the top, but I don't think it is,' Duchêne said, noting that a nurse had confirmed the accuracy of her representation of the medical effects of cancer. 'I don't quite know how to make it feel real without playing the condition, so that's what I'm doing.' In the last moments of the scene, however, the physical pain dropped away for a final, unscripted confrontation with the King. In another instance of Rosenblatt's non-textual simultaneous staging, Henry had appeared to observe her last speech; as the dying Katharine moved toward the exit door, declaring that she 'was a chaste wife to my grave', she suddenly stopped, straightened up, and walked back toward the middle of the stage, addressing her final lines directly and accusingly to the King. It was a powerful final moment in a performance that in many ways dominated the production. This Katharine, to the end, was no docile Dowager, but a fierce and unyielding Queen. 'She's an amazingly brave woman,' Duchêne said. 'I feel a lot of responsibility towards her, I feel very moved by her.' Duchêne's combination of historical research, emotional exploration, and technical mastery culminated in a performance that made a strong case for Katharine as a major Shakespearean heroine.

The London critics almost universally praised the production, though their compliments often backhanded the play. Few critics could resist opening their reviews with an ominous mention of the 1613 performance that burned the original Globe to the ground. Paul Taylor's leading paragraph in the *Independent* is representative:

> *Henry VIII* is notorious as the play which burned down the original Globe when its thatched roof was set on fire by the cannon shot saluting the entrance of the King in an early scene. To modern taste, that disaster has come to look like a shrewd critical verdict on the play. It's no surprise that the reconstructed Globe has only now got round to presenting the play in a vivid, robust, and winningly well-conceived production by Mark Rosenblatt.
> (27 May 2010)

Taylor found Duchêne's Katharine 'awesomely fiery and confrontational, a foreign-accented outsider who explosively squares up' to Wolsey. Other critics thought her 'regal', 'eloquent', 'touchingly dignified', 'defiant, wounded, magnificent' (John Peter, *Sunday Times*, 30 May 2010; Susannah Clapp, *Observer*, 30 May 2010; Sarah Hemming, *Financial Times*, 26 May 2010; Dominic Maxwell, *The Times*, 26 May 2010). Some felt, with Michael Billington, that she 'over[did] the discarded queen's vituperative anger' (*Guardian*, 26 May 2010). Dominic Maxwell, in *The Times*, found fault with the painful naturalism of her death scene, but conceded that 'She injects so much heart into the show that you can forgive her doing quite so much wailing when she's later ailing' (26 May 2010).

Such critical responses reflect both the intensity and originality of Duchêne's performance. Bringing her years of experience and experimentation in non-Shakespearean drama to Shakespeare's last great female role, Kate Duchêne gave the London stage a queen who was both regal and human, vulnerable and defiant. Developing a characterization grounded in text and history but infused with deeply personal passion, she created a Katharine who fully embodied the words she speaks in the trial scene:

> Sir,
> I am about to weep; but, thinking that
> We are a queen, or long have dream'd so, certain
> The daughter of a king, my drops of tears
> I'll turn to sparks of fire.
>
> (2.4.67–71)

Selected chronology

1981	MEASURE FOR MEASURE, Mariana, dir. Stephen Unwin, Cambridge Mummers
1989	LOVE'S LABOUR'S LOST, Princess of France, dir. Sam Mendes, Chichester Festival
1991	THE MISER, Elise, dir. Steven Pimlott, RNT
1992/3	RICHARD III, Queen Elizabeth, dir. Sam Mendes, RSC
1993/4	THE MERCHANT OF VENICE, Jessica, dir. David Thacker, RSC
1995/6	THE CHERRY ORCHARD, Varya, dir. Adrian Noble, RSC
2004	IPHIGENIA AT AULIS, Clytemnestra, dir. Katie Mitchell, RNT
2006	WAVES, dir. Katie Mitchell, RNT
2007	ATTEMPTS ON HER LIFE, dir. Katie Mitchell, RNT
2007	WOMEN OF TROY, Hecuba, dir. Katie Mitchell, Royal National Theatre
2010	HENRY VIII, Queen Katharine, dir. Mark Rosenblatt, Shakespeare's Globe

Bibliography

Duchêne, Kate. Interview with James Loehlin. Shakespeare's Globe Theatre, London, 19 August 2010.

Mitchell, Katie (2009) *The Director's Craft: A Handbook for the Theatre*. London: Routledge.

Shakespeare, William (1997) *The Complete Works of Shakespeare*, ed. David Bevington. Updated Fourth Edition. New York: Longman.

About the author

James Loehlin is Shakespeare at Winedale Regents Professor of English at the University of Texas at Austin. He is the author of the *Henry IV* volume in the

Palgrave *Shakespeare Handbooks* series, edited by John Russell Brown; editor of the Cambridge *Shakespeare in Production* edition of *Romeo and Juliet*; and author of the Manchester *Shakespeare in Performance* volume on *Henry V*. He has also written two books on Chekhov for Cambridge University Press. He has directed more than forty productions of Shakespeare.

5
Colm Feore

Kevin Ewert

The actor is the instrument for playing Shakespeare. That is a very intimate relationship; whatever else may be going on, ultimately the actor is the one who has to go on stage in front of everyone and speak, make sense of, and embody what Shakespeare wrote. But the actor's relationship with Shakespeare is only one of many different, interdependent relationships in the collaborative enterprise of making theatre out of Shakespeare's words. The actor's relationship with Shakespeare is interwoven with his or her relationships with other actors, the director, the space, the concept, multiple designers, multiple design elements, the company, the audience. These relationships resonate and play off one another, sometimes harmoniously, sometimes in a contrapuntal manner that results in a complex kind of harmony, and sometimes, in spite of everyone's best intentions, in a way that creates dissonance. Trying to understand the actor's Shakespeare necessitates some wrestling with and unraveling of the dual/dueling narratives of productions and performances.

Colm Feore is a star in Canada, for his many years and leading roles at Stratford, which most people know about, and for his screen work, which many more people have actually seen. He played the bon part in the highest-domestic-grossing Canadian film of all time, *Bon Cop/Bad Cop*, as well as the title role in a much-watched CBC mini-series – if Patrick Stewart is often better known as Jean-Luc Picard, Feore has to live with having been Pierre Elliot Trudeau. He's amassed a truly heroic number of entries on IMDB, including roles in major films – *Pearl Harbor*, *Changeling*, *Chicago* – and popular tv shows – *24*. He has never worried about moving back and forth from stage to screen. Working with good writing like Shakespeare's only helps him when he has to breathe life into writing that is not so good, and his only aspiration for big screen success is to be the best guy to hire to make the plot make sense. He is a brilliant film actor when the material allows – his performance in the compellingly experimental, anti-music-bio-pic *Thirty-Two Short Films About Glenn Gould* is a wonder both of impersonation and invention. As far as his other film work, anyone wishing to hold *The Chronicles of Riddick* against him should remember that Judi Dench is in it too.

Feore likes to keep busy. That was his approach to his time at Stratford, both in his earlier work when he'd play three, four, even five different roles in a season, and to his recent returns – added to the 2006 Coriolanus was Fagin in *Oliver!* and Moliere's *Don Juan*, in both English and in French. It explains his belief in "cross-pollination" of the roles he plays – Coriolanus, Fagin, Don Juan: all lonely men with high standards; Macbeth and Cyrano (his other 2009 role): both defiant, independent souls, just going in different directions. It describes what he's up to in the dressing room before performances, still doing all the exercises he learned at theatre school that would seem in any way to apply. It's the way he is at home, where he'll stop in front of his bookshelf and pull out *Hamlet* because something suddenly dawned on him that he didn't see when he played the role. And apparently it applies to trips to the grocery store:

> I'm always using [Shakespeare] to be ready for something else. I use the first 40 minutes of *Julius Caesar* as my scales if you will, playing all the parts, and I just sort of wander the streets doing that. Not only does it amuse me, but you get a sense of trying to improve the facility, in the firm belief you will achieve another level of understanding if you keep practicing.
>
> (Interview with the author August 15, 2009; all quotes are taken from this interview unless otherwise noted)

While he believes his theatre school training was an excellent foundation for his work in the classics, Feore maintains that whatever skills he has primarily come from playing these huge Shakespearean roles in repertory for lengthy runs over a great number of years. That accords with my critical recollections of his work: his 1984 Romeo showed an actor who looked right and was good if not great; his 1986 Leontes saw him really being stretched by the material and for the most part rising to the occasion; and by the time of his 1990 Cassius I knew I was watching a compelling actor the quality of whose performance I needn't worry about.

He played Cassius again, on Broadway in 2005 opposite Denzel Washington, and here it was strikingly easy to see the tree from the forest, this actor's work from the over-busy production and uneven ensemble around it. In the opening section of the play, where it can seem that Cassius rather than Brutus is the main character, Feore displayed a virtuosity with the text and a facility with the language that no one else came close to. This was partly vocal technique – speed, clarity, precision, variety of inflection – and partly verse-handling skills – making perfect sense of every word, phrase, image and intention that he spoke. For some of the other actors, the lack of facility with Shakespeare's text meant that everything – words, sense, intention, psychology, emotion – became a muddled kind of Shakesgibberish. Perhaps unsurprisingly, many reviews used Feore's performance as a stick with which to beat the rest of the cast.

Feore saw this as having absolutely nothing to do with "talent" but only with opportunity:

> [North American actors] don't get a lot of practice at [performing Shakespeare], and so the trouble is when you finally do get a show on people say, 'You know, they're not very good.' Well, why aren't they very good? Well, because they do two Shakespeares in a lifetime instead of 75...We had some great guys in *Caesar*, they were all terrific, but they were all the guys who stay in New York. If you stay in Manhattan...it's tough to get the experience you need to play [Shakespeare] at a level that is acceptable at $100 a ticket.

Feore commends actors like Kevin Kline and Liev Schreiber for keeping the profile up by regularly acting Shakespeare on stage, but starry productions with big budgets to go with the big names cannot create depth all through a company for classical playing. Actors who go to San Diego or Ashland or Stratford Ontario will have more opportunities with Shakespeare; however, the vagaries and pressures facing large festival companies that ply for tourist dollars with *Twelfth Night* and *Midsummer Night's Dream* and *Hamlet* popping up in the repertory every few years mean all that practice can't necessarily guarantee good productions or great performances either.

Feore has had lots of practice. At the same time, in my experience of his long career at the Stratford Festival, he has never been able to "save" entirely on his own a production suffering from an unhelpful concept, uninspired direction or an uneven acting company. The 2009 *Macbeth* in many ways encapsulates both his individual strengths as well as the recurring hazards of his working life in Shakespeare. He gave an intelligent, well-spoken, emotionally accessible, physically committed performance, in a production that was decent but conceptually muddy and often over-enamored of big production elements that seemed unhelpful for the story and out-of-place on the Festival Theatre's thrust stage.

Actors, directors, productions, performances

Feore is quick-witted and exuberant, but one question during our interview elicited a long pause. We had been talking about directorial concepts and unsubtle lighting and intrusive music and I asked him if he ever had the chance to be in a simple, stripped down production of one of Shakespeare's plays. He was silent a while, then started reaching for examples he knew didn't work. He thought of the NY *Caesar*, but that had Broadway pretensions with big sets and lots of people. He thought of his recent *Coriolanus*, but it was at Stratford with its tendency towards imposing production values on the play and the open space. He thinks of the *Macbeth* as pretty pared down because from an acting standpoint there was nothing particularly useful in the larger production design – in early rehearsals he told Yanna McIntosh, playing Lady Macbeth, that it didn't really matter what eventually came up around them, as their scenes together were simple, straight-up two-handers. But lots of things did come up around them. After several more tries, he finally said, "I guess the short answer is 'no'...Most of the productions I've done have been somebody's big idea." He wants to do Shakespeare on a big scale, as fully and completely as possible, but that puts him in a catch-22. His experience with the plays has led him to a much simpler trust in Shakespeare's words and his own skills in serving them up, but he only performs with large companies that put up large-scale productions for large audiences. So, he does his work within someone else's big idea and hopes for the best.

As befits someone who has no desire to be a director – and, perhaps more importantly, as befits someone who is married to a director – Feore doesn't mind being told what to do. Generally speaking, "actors want to be in the service of directors," and he says he is willing to "do anything that doesn't deny the evidence of the text." After two seasons in the regular company at Stratford, a period where he admits he had no idea what he was doing, he became part of Michael Langham's Young Company for 1983. Langham loves to move his actors about in tightly blocked, carefully choreographed patterns. This didn't bother Feore, as it gave him skills in finding his way through a Shakespeare play with eminently practical, useful results: "Some of these plays are so complicated that if you don't have something that says 'Here; now, here; focus there' then you're completely lost." He felt Langham left the actor with plenty of "internal" work to do:

> It was up to the actors to rise to the occasion and be able to sustain all that [choreography] and find their way logically, intelligently, emotionally, all the things that actors are supposed to be doing at home that they then come and infuse [into rehearsals]. If you just do what he asks you to, it's an automaton, it's moronic.

To Feore, Langham's tight choreography of his actors is not old-fashioned rigidity. It helps actors gain a foundational understanding of how the physical narrative of Shakespeare's plays unfolds, in terms of their responsibility for serving up complex material to the audience: "It's no good if they can't see you, it's no good if they can't hear you, and it's no good if they don't actually know who they're supposed to be looking at at any given moment." Langham's tight control can actually be freeing: "You have an enormous amount of confidence in the 'production'...and so I feel that it's easy to throw myself 'into the service of'."

The most extraordinary production I've seen Feore in was Stratford's 1986 *Cymbeline*. I met him on the set of a tv movie in Toronto – he was starring, I was an extra – shortly after that season ended, and praised his performance as Iachimo. He just looked at me and said "Ah, The Robin Phillips Show." Since then I'd wondered if he thought his good work was all the director's idea, that he was just going through the prescribed motions like one of Gordon Craig's fantasized puppet-actors. More than 20 years later Feore told me no, and suggested that it didn't matter. He is happy to admit Phillips is a genius, recognizes that his productions are always beautifully produced and layered with ideas, but most importantly he knows Phillips gives each of his good ideas a lot of thought. A highly conceptual approach works if, from the actor's standpoint, the ideas all check out:

> I'd say "yes, but my text says—" "Mmm, of course it does, of course, dear boy, it does, it's great, and it fits there, see?" and he'd be right. I'd think "that works, that works, that works, that works, that works" so I'm just joining the dots of what works.

Feore's Iach-in-the-box entrance into Imogen's bedroom in 2.2 was one of those moments worth the price of admission: in a green velvet top, jodhpurs and high leather boots, snaking though the room and around her bed, the stubble of his beard rasping slowly over the silk of her nightie amplified disturbingly, erotically for all to hear, his voice picked up by his body-mic so that he seemed to be whispering over one actress' and a couple thousand audience members' shoulders all at once.

It's also part of the actor's life sometimes to be in productions that don't have enough ideas, big, good, bad or otherwise. When Feore played Hamlet he made a vow – do it honestly or give up acting; he felt he succeeded personally, but from where I was sitting the production made no compelling argument for its existence. When he returned to the Festival over a decade after his last Shakespearean role there, he wanted a challenge, and chose Coriolanus precisely because it would be harder than Hamlet; unfortunately the production seemed mostly to strand him in empty heroic poses. I don't remember a single thing he did as Iago, even though his reviews were good, because at the performance I attended I was mesmerized, not in a good way, by an Othello in blackface, in 1987, on the Festival stage – the star black actor got sick, a lot, and his understudy was white. But perhaps there's no point here to kicking long-dead productions. Playing Iago and Coriolanus and Hamlet was useful practice over the long run for Feore, even if the productions were less instructive to this audience member at only a single viewing.

Macbeth, 2009

His reading list included Machiavelli, Voltaire, Isaiah Berlin, Kant, Christopher Hitchens and the Bible, and he started collecting and learning how to sharpen Japanese knives, but Feore felt his most important "research" for his first time in *Macbeth* was having already played everything else, especially Iago, Coriolanus and Hamlet:

> This is the most distilled and most edited of [Shakespeare's] plays. It's the one where he says, "You know my stuff, right, there's no need to do all those extra scenes in *Hamlet* or any of that stuff in *Othello*, we're just going to jump from, you know, out of your pajamas, you're king, okay, cut, move on."

Feore's requirements for a productive rehearsal period are relatively simple. It's good for actors to understand what they are saying. He likes for a director to know what he or she is doing. It's helpful if the cast, director, designers, "all of us are in service of the same thing, and we all agree we're telling the same story so we're all on the same page…in a collaborative effort to make things clear." After that, it's a mixture of being very familiar with the text and always remaining open to change. Feore likes to throw a lot of things in the air, run with a director's first idea, then offer other possibilities, but everything has to be checked and rechecked against what Shakespeare actually wrote. It's here that being all "on the same page" becomes an elusive ideal in collaborative storytelling:

> I have great difficulty if the conceptual superimposition on the text takes us in a direction the text doesn't support simply because it's impossible to act. I'm not that good an actor. I can't do [it] if it's just not making sense. So you go through the rehearsals trying to find out how much of this you can *make* make sense.

In *Macbeth* rehearsals, there were instances where Feore couldn't make the concepts make sense with the text. The first concerned the appearance of Duncan's body in 2.3. Feore was convinced that Shakespeare in the text actually draws attention to the body's absence by having Macbeth talk about the wounds in a ridiculously hyperbolic way that suggests a) the body remains offstage, b) that the audience is being invited to imagine something more horrible than could actually be shown, and c) that Macbeth is acting, desperately, badly, in front of his assembled audience. When the body came on in rehearsal, Feore's initial thought was to offer to just cut his lines. He then tried pulling out the knife he always carried and opening the wounds up for an over-dramatic display to go with the hyperbolic language: "Here lay Duncan, his silver skin..." The director thought he shouldn't do that; Feore thought the director shouldn't be doing this. The stand-off was the result of differing priorities: Feore was concerned about what bringing the body *on* did to his understanding of the lines he had to say, while the director was interested in what he could do when the time came to take the body *off* at the end of the scene, so that section of the play could end with the image of the dead king on a 14-foot aluminum table being carried away in a solemn funeral procession.

Towards the end of the production, Macbeth sat at a desk as his world began falling apart. Another smaller desk, upon which sat a small computer screen to echo huge projection screens hanging high above the stage, was brought on in rehearsals and placed a little way in front of him. When the messenger rushes in to give the news of the marching woods and gets accused of lying, he was going to indicate the screen – No, look! – where images of the moving wood were to be projected, as they would be on the larger screens. Feore pointed out that if Macbeth could see the moving wood on the little computer screen then they could just cut the messenger. He also asked, if he could see the wood advancing on this computer screen, why he would later use the conditional "If that which he avouches does appear, / There is no flying hence nor tarrying here" – there would be no "if" if what the messenger avouches was apparent right there on the screen. Feore knew he wouldn't win the battle over the addition of Duncan's body to set up a funeral procession, but he set out to get rid of the unnecessary iBook:

> I said, "Hmm, ah, no, I can't act my lines..." and so it was one of the saddest moments of rehearsals as [the director] very reluctantly dragged the computer and the little desk and the little chair off.

Of course, everybody thinks they are helping the process. The language is dense and imagistic, so a director wants to make those images manifest and physicalize the language with added stage action and visual display; lighting designers want to expand impressions and enhance atmospherics that descriptive language merely suggests; and composers want to underline or heighten the emotional content of the big speeches. But while all this is going on, the actor still has to act the words that started this torrent of production creativity.

When Feore played Marcus in Julie Taymor's film *Titus*, he was perfectly happy to lose many of his lines upon discovering the raped and mutilated Lavinia in 2.4; no need to spend all that time talking about crimson rivers of blood flowing from her mouth when there could just be a shot of blood flowing from her mouth. What Feore has difficulty with are staging or design choices that contradict or, worse, render superfluous whatever he is trying to act, either with his lines or in the life of the character he builds up between them.

> What happens when they play that moody music stuff? I say "Stop, don't play the music, because you're acting what I'm supposed to be acting, and if you do what I'm going to do I forget my lines"...Directors go "I have this fabulous image for this, it's going to be great," and you say "Okay, great, then I don't need to say these words." I would much rather go ahead and do one or the other. I don't need to do both. I have no particular prejudice one way or another...but I don't want anything to be redundant. I don't want the audience to be that far ahead of me.

Such a moment of acting/production overlap occurred in *Macbeth* around Duncan's naming of his successor, which was played as a press conference with a slew of photographers scurrying in. In the slight hesitation at the end of the line "We will establish our estate upon..." one of the photographers swung his camera in Macbeth's direction, then swung it the other way when Malcolm was named. The photographer evidently thought it was going to be Macbeth, so the audience was being shown how the succession could have gone. Watching all these photographers the first time I saw the production, I wondered if it was really worth having them run in and out for their ten seconds of stage time. Watching it again I got my answer. Since I knew I wasn't interested in the photographers, I didn't bother watching them rush on and get set up; instead, this time I saw what Feore was doing. He was standing there with a huge smile, clearly imagining the final element of the prophecy about to drop in his lap. He was practically lighting up the space with joyful anticipation – and when it didn't happen he stood there with a pained smile stuck on his face while the succession moved on without him. I missed all of this the first time around – material, I later found out, crucial to Feore's interpretation of his character – in the rushing about of that gaggle of photographers to make the same point Feore was acting.

Early on Feore's Macbeth seemed less like a hardened killer and more like a wide-eyed little boy, a bit freaked out but completely caught up in the wonder of what might befall him. After speaking with him, I found that this was crucial to his conception of the character and the play, right from the beginning of rehearsals.

> I was doing "Gosh it might be great to be king!" acting early on and it may have come across as "happy." [The director] was less interested in that, and I said you know, it's got to look like a good idea, because our moral compass for the play, Banquo, says "What's your problem? This sounds great! You've got this present grace, the promise of noble having with Cawdor, and then royal hope. This is terrific!"

Feore didn't want to begin in a terribly dark place – "It doesn't become a horror movie just because these witches say it's so!" – and he kept looking to Banquo, who he felt marks the middle of the road Macbeth veers off of. Following the prophecies, even Banquo is thinking there might be something in all this for him, and Feore also wondered how Banquo knows about instruments of darkness winning us to our own harm. He thought there must be something of that in Banquo's own experience – and he's the "good guy":

> I think Shakespeare's telling the audience that it's tempting, it's very tempting – now, if you go a bit too far you're that guy, but if you hew to the straight and narrow you're still tempted.

If Macbeth and Banquo don't start out that differently, it makes it easier for actor and audience to follow Macbeth's journey.

Once Banquo suggests the prophecy sounds good, Feore's intentions/interior monologue ran something like: *This is good – well, I might have to kill my friend – but things are falling into my lap, maybe I don't need to do anything, maybe Duncan will just drop dead, or maybe I'm going to be named successor, maybe Duncan's lines about "I have begun to plant thee..." mean it's going to happen, right here, right now, I feel like I'm inflating, it's happening, and...it doesn't. Prince of Cumberland? Now what?*

Even after the murder of Duncan, Feore kept trying to act where Macbeth had started rather than only where he was headed. In 3.1, he was cool, arrogant and deliberate with the murderers until just near the end when suddenly everything came out in a crazy rush. After arranging for Banquo, Feore said he wanted to signal Macbeth struggling "to come to grips with trying to find the right words that are suggestive and yet unambiguous about what he'd like to have done, which for him is morally repugnant" – that is, adding Fleance to the body count. The sudden rushing of the lines was meant to bulldoze it through, "even though Macbeth is responding against his better nature and trying to overwhelm his better nature by using the momentum that he himself has created" – the sudden burst of speed pushes them all over the edge. The pacing shift, and accompanying move into a higher, less-stable vocal register, had an emotional and psychological payoff: the sudden reluctance to kill Fleance reminded us and showed us something of the humanity that was slipping away, and threw into sharper relief his later ease about killing all the Macduffs.

Feore was convinced that the story of Macbeth doesn't *start* wrong; it *goes* horribly wrong, and even then it might still go right. Every time he went into the theatre before a performance he would tell everyone "I feel really good about today. I think I'm gonna win today! I'm going to be king a lot longer." He felt there should be nothing predetermined about any of it:

> I don't like the idea of him being just monstrously masculine and he comes charging on. Shakespeare sets all that up, we know he can do it, that's easy. What's not easy is to drag people back in time to a moment when they can accept wonder and be open to possibilities. Macbeth does nothing but talk about the possibilities. He does nothing but imagine what might happen if things were different. I think you have to seduce people into going along on that journey and one of the ways to do it is to say, "Hey, listen, why not?"

His was a Macbeth who smiled a lot early on: a very striking attribute – when you could see it.

When Feore described to me the charming, heartbreaking scene he and Tim Stickney as Banquo played during 2.1, with smiles and warmth and lots of reaching out to each other in the last gasp of a friendship of equals, it came as a revelation to me – because I hadn't seen it. What I saw in the theatre were two guys lurking at the front of the stage in the brooding dark. Feore was not altogether surprised:

> The director had ideas about isolating and darkness and just shafts of light and you come up against a conceptual notion that you're not going to be able to overcome all that readily, or that may be at cross-purposes with what you're doing.

At times the production was giving off signals that differed significantly from Feore's performance.

Macbeth's first line comes three scenes in: "So fair and foul a day I have not seen." Feore was convinced he wasn't talking about the weather: "He doesn't come on as a killer, he comes on saying this is the worst day of my life, I mean it's the best day of my life but really it's been horrible." He had no interest in just playing a ruthless killer, and believes that is not what Shakespeare wants either:

> We're supposed to identify with him...Why does Shakespeare have this very horrible guy as the hero if not to show us something about ourselves, and we can't see something about ourselves if we're so convinced we should come at him with garlic and crosses.

But the production began with a mute prologue, staging the bloody rebellion with explosions, gunfire, smoke, soldiers rushing about, and so with Macbeth making his first appearance a few scenes early to dispatch his enemies on stage for our viewing pleasure. Feore knew the added prologue was unnecessary at best, and at worst pointed the audience almost 180 degrees – "Oh, I get it. That's cool. He's Rambo." – from what he was trying to convey, yet some reviews talked about how the production started off promisingly enough. He knew that the essential thing about the character is his overactive imagination, how he sees nothing but possibilities, yet some critics complained Feore was in one of his maddeningly cerebral modes. At least that negative review matches Feore's understanding of Shakespeare's play: "it's a very cerebral, lean exercise in 'What if you killed the only friends you have?' What does that do to you?"

Some of the simplest visual choices worked extremely well in this production: Macbeth delivering most of his lines in 2.3 while looking at Lady Macbeth – she's inspired him to some wildly improvisational performance art in the two "extra" murders in the next room and, as Feore put it, he's looking to get her review; Macbeth and his wife sitting together but not together on a bed in 3.2, a huge distance looming between them; Macbeth spinning slowly around in his desk chair upstage at the beginning of 4.1 as the witches round and round their cauldron go downstage; Lady Macbeth, after the sleepwalking scene, wandering through another scene, uncommented upon by her husband, to further emphasize isolation and loss. That "geography" as Feore calls it, of characters staking their places in the open space for mute storytelling, works well on the thrust; it helps the story, and "then the text should be able to go just that one step higher." That kind of visual work, which is all spatial relations and character proxemics and therefore actor-centered, is different from the imagistic add-ons many productions feel they need to have and that lead to what Feore identifies as an essential conundrum of modern productions of Shakespeare, regardless of the space they are performed in:

> One of the dangers of having...explosions and guns and all that other nonsense with prologues – I say nonsense advisedly, I mean ideas – the danger finally is that once you've exploded all your bombs and cleared the smoke, it's just going to be two people talking, and that will be by comparison disappointing. An audience led to expect Michael Bay gets Cassavetes and goes "What the fuck, it's just two people talking." My point is that should be the zenith of our achievement...just Shakespeare deftly handled, which is in the right hands just people talking.

The actor's Shakespeare

Some stage productions try to make Shakespeare more like the movies by adding elaborate special effects, extended action sequences and richly scored soundscapes. But Feore considers Shakespeare cinematic from the actor's standpoint. The Festival Theatre's Guthrie/Moiseiwitsch neo-Elizabethan thrust stage is a three-dimensional space requiring three-dimensional acting. Used well, Feore believes it lets actors call the shots, based on their mastery of their body and their voice: this is the wide shot because you're stretching your body and reaching through the space to another actor or to the audience, then you can switch to a medium shot, then you can pull the audience in for a close up, then hold everything in an extreme close-up where the audience only needs to watch your mouth make the words "To be or not to be." With the audience wrapping around you, you must be aware of all those individual "cameras" trained on the action, and find ways to stay in motion so everyone gets the essential information and no one's frame gets obstructed for long. With the audience wrapping around you, all your intentions must be physically expressed three-dimensionally as well – "acting out of the back of your head" as Feore puts it. To Feore, this is "the enormous control you have as an actor on that stage." It's also the kind of control actors usually give up when they make movies. Actor-centered work is often overwhelmed when stage productions of Shakespeare add "cinematic" extras that actors have to learn to live with: "All this other stuff" – moody lighting and intrusive soundtracks – "makes me crazy. But I'm not the director. I know I can't direct. It's not my thing. I'm just an actor in service of."

When he walks on stage at Stratford, Feore knows he is playing for two audiences. One is experienced with Shakespeare; one booked for the musical in the afternoon and then stayed for whatever was playing that evening.

> How do you as an actor bring those two disparate groups together for the same experience, which will be to each of them individually a very different experience, but you can only ring *one* bell, you can just sound *that* note and send it out. The vast history of my experience with Shakespeare has led me

> to the confidence to trust that, if properly served up by the actor, just hitting that one note is correct, that's the way to do it. If the instrument is ringing appropriately the overtones and undertones of everything else you are sending out [will be there].

For the production to start adding on – "unless it is very, very carefully considered from every possible point of view" – means that those audience members who have a lot of experience with Shakespeare will sit back in their seats and disengage, and those who have a hard enough time following Shakespeare at all won't know why they're going on an elaborate detour. The simpler and clearer the delivery, the richer the theatrical experience. Feore sees his job as serving up how the play in its verse form makes sense, and after that he assumes Shakespeare knew what he was doing in terms of its effects on a wide variety of audiences.

Once lighting cues, sound cues, video cues, etc. are added, there are certain limitations put on the actor – somebody presses "play" and the whole apparatus starts running. But over a run Feore looks for things that remain within the actor's control that he can improve or reinvent.

> It's one of the only reasons not to do theatre: you have to keep paying attention…so we have to find a new way to inspire ourselves every day…So I started doing entrances coming on backwards, so [for example in 2.2] I could be surprised and shocked when [Lady Macbeth] said "My husband." Why did I come on backwards? Because I was still looking at those two guys whose door was closed…whatever that scene was that takes place offstage I decided to keep playing and bring that life on with me.

This didn't occur to him in rehearsals, because in the empty rehearsal hall he was more focused upon, and trying to give something to, the other actor. Once he got to play the space a while, he found new opportunities for improvisation. The course of a long run and the distance it provides from the pressures of opening night encourages revision and reinvention: "It's not until you get the chance to do it and do it and do it that these ideas occur."

After *Macbeth* had been running for several months, Feore started playing with the words "tomorrow" and "nothing" whenever they came up before the well-known bit; he would hit them with a little extra pressure to get them to ring out. He was interested in the thought of Shakespeare building something, and that by hitting those words he might make the most famous speech in the play begin to resonate earlier and in a more interesting manner.

> What is Shakespeare doing there? I don't know, but maybe he's doing something, and if the actor is aware of it it's just nothing more than the way Glenn Gould would say "Hit that note because contrapuntally in the Bach scheme of things that's important."

It's detective work, except he's not trying to prove anything or create a moment. He just believes that if he offers it up, utilizing all the skills his theatre school training and his experience in playing it have given him, then "something 'greater than' will happen."

Practicing

At the National Theatre School in Montreal, Feore received conservatory-style acting training – tuning the instrument to get it up to speed to play the notes. Pierre Lefevre, his mask teacher, in assessing Feore's class looked at him and said "That's a classical actor." This was not based on achievements: "It wasn't that I showed any particular talent or skill. At all. I think it was the combination of body type, voice, demeanor, big enough nose to be seen at 60 feet, big enough voice hopefully to be heard." When Feore was there the NTS was run by people who had worked at Stratford and wanted to produce actors who could then go to the Stratford Festival and the Shaw Festival and do the big plays – even his audition to get in was for Douglas Rain, a Stratford stalwart. When he left he went to the National Arts Centre in Ottawa to do a number of roles in a *Henry V* and not long after that went on to Stratford: "The trajectory I've had has been the natural evolution of 'Oh, you'd be better as a classical actor than as a clown on the street-corner' – though I recognize the connection between the two."

Perhaps the most important influence his training has had on his career is how it shaped his attitude. His teachers at the National Theatre School made it very clear that, as an actor, "you are simply not very interesting, and you not going to get more interesting. Hamlet is interesting. What you must do is find a way to have your skills serve Shakespeare's vision, or Moliere's or Chekhov's or Bertolucci's or Sidney Lumet's," and this created in him "a desire to hammer away at a lifetime of perfecting the craft in order to be 'in service of…'" (2007 Banff World Television Festival). Training gives you certain skills to put in your bag of tricks, and Feore believes there is nothing dishonorable about having a bag of tricks. There is nothing wrong, even, with "fake it till you make it" when you don't yet really know what you are doing, provided you are open to learning from practice in order to catch up:

> All this acting in theatre school and all the very skilled people I'd worked with had only got me to a certain point and even standing on the Festival stage for two solid years was the merest shred of an apprenticeship in the craft of acting, and so for me the uphillness of it all and the sense of how large and daunting a process it would be simply to become a decent actor was ingrained early on.
> (2007 Banff World Television Festival)

I asked Feore if there was anything Canadian about his relationship to Shakespeare, and he practically pounced. He feels the intelligent Canadian actor looks at the historical importance of the British system and the unavoidable proximity of the American way and wants the best of both worlds.

> Take the lessons of what England has to offer, and that is: technique is not an ugly word, it doesn't harm you to know what's actually happening. But wouldn't it be good if you really felt it, wouldn't it be alarming if you actually were bloodcurdlingly real whenever you stepped out, and that you tried to grab as much of that at-the-minute, improvisational, holy-shit-I-don't-know-what-the-next-word-is-I-don't-know-what-I'm-going-to-do, something of that

> American experience, and infuse our understanding of Shakespeare and of classical playing with it.

Feore was also influenced by negotiating between French and English. He grew up in English Canada while attending French-speaking schools. He was then in the English class at the NTS in French Montreal, where the English students loved the freedom of passionate emotional expression they saw in the French students, while the French appreciated the English students' restraint and stillness. Here too, Feore thought success would be found somewhere between these opposing worldviews. Since, historically, Stratford was welcoming of all influences, he thought the thing to do was to take the best ideas everyone had and use Stratford "as a laboratory cradled environment in which to develop."

When Feore played Mercutio at Stratford, he was messing around with line readings just after his ill-fated duel with Tybalt. He came up with something he thought was new and amusing for "I'm hurt" but "afterward, one of the senior company members came up to me and said 'Ah, the Richardson of '53, very good choice!' like you pick them off a wine list." If you give up the notion that you can ever be entirely original, Feore sees benefits to being in a leading classical company that has some continuity to it: "The history of acting Shakespeare is there present, vibrantly going on." It's there for an actor to use – whether by stealing what works, or by getting a heads-up to avoid the blind alleys someone else has already gone down. A repertory system generates two other things in a classical actor: humility towards those who have come before – "If you go in thinking that there's in any way a responsibility to be better than the last one, or clearer, or more intelligent, you're deluding yourself" – and generosity towards those just starting to figure it out for themselves.

Colm Feore is a big fan of Christopher Plummer. When we spoke, he had recently seen a documentary on Plummer and was fascinated by the amount of work Plummer and his contemporaries did in their early days – bi-weekly repertory, evening theatre performances, live television during the day, films, live radio. Feore was not in envy of his idol's talents or success, but of the amount of work he got to do. That is his model and ideal for acting Shakespeare:

> Your facility, finally, when you did your third *Antony and Cleopatra*, your second or third *Hamlet*, you go "I'm getting better at this, I'm working out the bugs." It's just putting it into the repertory so you can keep practicing and keep playing. Because you know that the resonances and impact and real mysteries are only going to be revealed by very careful peeling back and peeling back and peeling back. How do you get good at that? You just keep doing it. It's the only way.

Selected chronology

1980	Graduated from National Theatre School, Montreal
1981	Joined the acting company at the Stratford Shakespeare Festival
1983	Joined Michael Langham's Young Company; Claudio, *Much Ado About Nothing*

1984	Romeo
1985	Orsino
1986	Leontes; Iachimo; Antipholus, *The Boys From Syracuse*
1987	Iago
1988	Richard III; Petruchio; Athos, *Three Musketeers*
1990	Cassius
1991	Hamlet; Benedick
1992	Mercutio; Angelo; Berowne
1993	Oberon; title role in *Thirty Two Short Films About Glenn Gould* (film)
1994	Cyrano; Pirate King, *Pirates of Penzance*; left the Stratford acting company
1999	Claudius, *Hamlet*, Public Theatre, NYC; Marcus in Julie Taymor's film *Titus*
2002	Title role in *Trudeau* (television series)
2005	Cassius, *Julius Caesar*, Belasco Theatre, NYC
2006	Coriolanus; title role in *Don Juan*; Fagin in *Oliver!* all at Stratford Festival; Martin Ward, *Bon Cop/Bad Cop* (film)
2009	Macbeth and Cyrano at Stratford Festival

Bibliography

Banff World Television Festival 2007, interview conducted by Kevin Tierney [online] Accessed at: http://blip.tv/file/818088 June 2007.

Colm Feore, interview conducted by the author, August 15, 2009.

Cushman, Robert (2002) *Fifty Seasons at Stratford*. Toronto: McClelland and Stewart.

About the author

Kevin Ewert grew up half an hour from the Stratford Festival. He attended student matinees every year when he was in high school, had a job in the Festival's archives for two summers when he was an undergrad, and came back to review multiple seasons when he served as a theatre critic for a Toronto radio station. He is Associate Professor and Director of the Theatre Program at University of Pittsburgh at Bradford, where he teaches a variety of acting and theatre studies courses. He directed for many years with the Unseam'd Shakespeare Company in Pittsburgh, and now directs regularly with Manbites Dog Theatre in Durham. He contributed a chapter on Michael Langham to *The Routledge Companion to Directors' Shakespeare* and wrote the volume on *Henry V* for Palgrave's *Shakespeare Handbooks*.

6
Mariah Gale

Clare Smout

Introduction

Mariah Gale is the most junior of the actors in this volume, but already an established presence on the Shakespearean stage: since graduating in 2003, she has performed in over a dozen Renaissance plays. It is unusual now for actors to devote so much of their early career to Shakespeare and especially unusual for a woman to have such an opportunity. This chapter explores Gale's escalating engagement with Shakespeare and the development of her own distinctive voice and working process, focusing on the early stages of a professional life in a twenty-first-century context.

Slight and slim with long fine brown hair, Gale has an unconventionally attractive face with a strong jaw, and is capable of unusual intensity. She has yet to play any character as a passive victim or a traditionally innocent blonde maiden. Paradoxically, the very qualities which make her least suited for a string of ingénue roles are the qualities for which she was cast in them, by directors seeking an actor capable of redefining such parts.

Early performances as Hero at the Globe and Viola at Regent's Park were followed by roles at the RSC which progressed from Octavia and Portia (in *Julius Caesar*) to Miranda, the Princess of France, Ophelia, Celia and Juliet. In between she played Annabella, the tragic incestuous co-protagonist of Ford's *'Tis Pity She's a Whore* at Southwark Playhouse – a sidestep which will be discussed in more detail later.

Gale's approach to Shakespeare's heroines leaves behind not only the idealised purity of Victorian (male) criticism and its accompanying stage tradition but also the campaigning reinterpretations of late twentieth-century feminism. She seems determined not to sentimentalise or idealise her characters, but neither could they be patronised with the term 'feisty'. Her acting is raw and vulnerable; she is willing to take risks and to explore darker options. She constantly juxtaposes contradictions, refusing to make obvious choices or pre-empt outcomes. She is as comfortable barefoot as displaying aristocratic assurance, playing an awkward teenager or corseted royalty. Her work is distinguished by intelligence and clarity of thought as much as by emotional intensity, and her early roles showed an earnestness and seriousness: comic parts such as Audrey and Jacquenetta are notably absent from her CV. However, in recent years a lightness and controlled humour have extended her range significantly, while she has had gradually increasing opportunities to explore the sensuality for which her Annabella was so highly praised.

Gale describes herself as having 'fallen into Shakespeare' accidentally, yet this was clearly serendipitous: there is a clear match between the demands of his roles and Gale's values and strengths as an actor. She sets high value on his ambiguity, openness and ambivalence, while adding, 'Shakespeare articulates [the big] things we can't' (Personal conversation with the author; all otherwise unattributed quotations come from these conversations). His parts demand immense courage of the actor but are exhilarating at the same time, forcing one to be bold about choices. She sees the actor's job as 'exploring taboos and exploding boundaries...going to the ends of experience'. Shakespeare of all playwrights both enables and demands that. The more Shakespeare you do the more you develop as a person and an actor. She observes further, however, that part of the skill is stepping back and paring down: 'The words are so exquisite you don't really need to act as much as you think...be a channel for the voice – let him speak.' While this may sound clichéd at first, it becomes gradually clear that Gale's focus on the language is paramount.

Gale's working process has moved from reliance on Stanislavskian principles and Renaissance social conventions towards an increasing emphasis on language, minimalism and a relish of character inconsistencies. Meanwhile her status has risen: she has begun to be offered roles unsought rather than having to audition for them and her voice is more often listened to in the rehearsal room. The challenges have also become greater. The unanimous critical adulation that met her earlier performances has become more mixed, as she takes risks with iconic moments about which reviewers have fixed preconceptions. Her choices nevertheless remain ground-breaking.

Gale's approach is as distinctively twenty-first-century in its technical underpinning as in interpretation. She comes from a theatrical generation for whom the large auditorium is once again the norm, after three decades during which the move towards intimate staging even for large-cast classics seemed unstoppable. Yet the most significant of the modern Shakespeare venues (the Swan, Courtyard and Globe) differ markedly from their predecessors: the exposure of the thrust stage and the visible audience demands a very different approach to acting (and interacting) from that required by the respectful silence and glass-wall segregation of the proscenium arch tradition. The redesigned and rebuilt Royal Shakespeare Theatre perpetuates this new dynamic.

Gale is unusual in having worked the full range of relevant venue and audience configurations, though her Shakespeare career has unfolded almost entirely in large auditoria. She has a marked preference for the 'shared room' model and the wrap-around audience, relishing the constant two-way tension and instant feedback, the perpetual opportunity for direct address, and what is to her a 'naturalistic' playing style. She has a high tolerance of teenage and tourist audiences, finding their restlessness a challenge rather than an irritation. She is undeterred by auditorium size and strongly resists the common assumption that the Globe necessitates broad-brush acting and big effects, arguing that Mark Rylance was able to communicate to the whole auditorium by simply raising an eyebrow and that the Globe is 'acoustically amazing' in the subtlety it permits. In contrast, she found it unexpectedly difficult transferring *Hamlet* from the Courtyard to the West End. She felt herself suddenly cut off and disconnected from an audience whose engagement consisted of observing not interacting, safely distanced from the danger her madness had posed in Stratford.

Training and early years

Gale comes from a non-theatrical background. As a shy fourteen-year-old she discovered that acting paradoxically enabled her to find a voice by speaking through an alternative persona. This revelation occurred through improvising a middle-aged dinner-lady in one school production and playing the deaf Daft Lizzie in another, suggesting that Gale was comfortable embracing extremes and unconventionality from the outset. She describes the key attraction of acting as its power 'to make you realise you contain a broader spectrum of personae than you usually acknowledge' combined with the opportunity to explore the variety of hands life could deal you and the different ways of approaching such variety.

Several years with the local youth group and Theatre Studies A-level followed. Gale then went to Birmingham University to read Drama and Theatre Arts. This gave her a space to grow up and experiment, in contrast to the later very focused professional training of drama school. The part-practical, part-academic course offered her little direct exposure to Shakespeare's work. However, playing Mary Betterton, one of the earliest Shakespearean actresses, in April de Angelis's *Playhouse Creatures* provided her first real taste of Shakespeare's language and emotional potential and whetted her appetite for more.

The transition to drama school shows Gale becoming aware of her own strengths and beginning to establish her theatrical identity. Having failed to get into RADA using conventionally appropriate audition speeches, she opted for pieces she felt passionate about and could relate to. She gained a place on the three-year acting course at Guildhall School of Music and Drama using a 'bold and visceral' Dario Fo monologue written for a much older woman. She describes this application process as the single most terrifying experience of her career, demanding that she present her personality and ability for assessment unmediated by the usual considerations of suitability for a specific role. Her choice of comfort zone and of persona to commit to is an indicator of her self-perception at the time.

Gale categorises her Guildhall training as 'rigorous without being over-invasive', requiring students 'to start from scratch [with] pure movement and voice' and, in Head of Acting Wyn Jones's words, 'to combine the fire of insight with the ice of technique'. Tutors also emphasised that learning to act is a career-long process. Gale still imagines herself with 'miniature versions of them in [her] pocket giving advice' and clearly continues to observe and learn from fellow actors: she repeatedly makes appreciative references to colleagues' technical skills and specific insights she has gained from them.

Guildhall's approach to Shakespeare is demonstrated by their choice of a voice coach to teach the subject. Patsy Rodenburg's principles are set out in detail in her publications [see 1998 and 2005]. For Gale these are now ingrained: '[C]onnect to your breath – keep it free, low – be on your front foot, in your forward space, "on voice" – don't be closed or unforthcoming – follow the arc of the thought – don't let the end of the thought drop – make it accessible – find *your* voice, let it come from *you*.' More unexpectedly in this context, she adds, 'Don't patronise the character.'

At Guildhall, Gale played both Isabella (the point where she 'really fell in love with Shakespeare') and Rosalind. The very limited rehearsal period for the latter gave her only a 'tantalising taster' of the role but it was enough to gain her an agent (from a major agency), something only a small proportion of students achieve before leaving drama school. The two have developed a strong relationship based on mutual trust and respect for each other's professional judgement. Gale instances the production of *'Tis Pity She's a Whore* at the tiny Southwark Playhouse – a return to 'fringe' work (virtually unpaid and usually low profile) which many agents would have advised against at that stage in her career. She was eager to play the incestuously passionate Annabella made pregnant by her brother and then murdered by him in Ford's 'Tarantino *Romeo and Juliet*' and knew that the production would enable her to develop creatively. Her agent supported her decision.

Up to that point, Gale's roles had included Hero in *Much Ado* at the Globe and a season at Regent's Park. She had also worked at Chichester and for Oxford Stage Company. The official blog she kept as part of the Globe's Adopt-an-Actor scheme is still available online. In this diary of her first Shakespearean role she speaks in detail about her rehearsal process, about coming to terms with the demands and exhilaration of the space, and about her transition from drama school to the professional environment. Fainting in an over-tightened corset alerted her to some of the implications for Elizabethan women of period clothing and she drew heavily on research into social history. She automatically and explicitly applied a Stanislavskian approach to her character.

The Globe production opened her eyes to the potential unleashed by making active rather than passive choices, an insight which has guided her ever since. In the wedding scene she refused to fall back on her accompanying women in the crisis, instead standing up for herself independently, using her repeated 'my Lord' (4.1.62, 67) to claim Claudio as husband even as he disowned her, and offering loving support during what she confidently saw as his madness. Instead of stereotyping Hero as intimidated or self-censoring Gale solved the problem of lengthy silences, faced so often by Shakespearean actresses, in the same way actors regularly approach lengthy speeches – by refusing the assumption they will continue.

Her stint at Regent's Park in *Cymbeline* and *Twelfth Night* was a less productive experience, despite the positive reviews: she found the space itself challenging and feels now that she was not yet ready to play Viola. After the elaborate support systems of the Globe this must have been a difficult and exposing leap. The return to fringe in *'Tis Pity* was exactly what Gale needed. The production enabled her to step aside from the commercial context and build on her first two years in the professional world with a brief return to experimentation and training. After playing large open-air theatres she welcomed the intimacy of the venue, the close direct contact with the entire audience and the added immediacy it gave to asides. In the context of both the Globe and RSC Gale has spoken appreciatively of the advantages of a company with varying levels of personal and professional experience; in *'Tis Pity* she enjoyed the different benefits of a group of equals, young actors all at a similar career stage.

The role itself enabled her to explore sexual and emotional extremes she had not previously encountered: a different kind of Renaissance voice, a tragic dimension, the deliberate breaking of one of society's strongest taboos. Both play and part resonated with everything Gale believes theatre should be about. Most significantly of all, however, director Ed Dick introduced her to the acting system developed by Declan Donnellan and articulated in *The Actor and the Target*. This approach rejects the traditional focus on a character's back-story, desires, motivation, tactics and unifying super-objective. Instead it encourages the actor to privilege externals, delivering a constantly modulating response to what is *seen*, the 'target' of attention, often another (unknowable and fluctuating) character. Additionally, it emphasises a constant awareness of contradictory dualities – what is the best possible outcome, what is the worst possible outcome, this character might love me, this character might hate me – pushing the actor to explore the counter-intuitive as well as the obvious. It requires the actor remain reactive and 'in the moment' rather than planning for the future.

Gale repeatedly references Donnellan's principles in conversation, and their effect can be seen running throughout her work: in her unpredictability, and her ability to find humour in unexpected places, to combine vulnerability with poise, and to generate detail and variety, development and contradiction, in even the shortest of speeches. *'Tis Pity* was a major artistic turning point. Gale still credits Ed Dick as the most important influence on her working process.

Her agent's confidence in Gale's judgement also paid off in career terms. Her performance catapulted her to critical notice, and won her the prestigious Ian Charleson Award as well as Most Promising Newcomer awards from Time Out and Critics' Circle. It opened doors to a new level of possibilities, including her first RSC season.

RSC, 2006–7: Rome and the Arctic

Gale's first RSC season started with two small roles in the Roman plays and concluded with her gauche home-schooled Miranda in Rupert Goold's controversial *Tempest*. In all three cases her interpretations broke markedly with accepted tradition.

Playing a passionate and troubled Portia in Sean Holmes's *Julius Caesar* Gale deliberately avoided the stereotype of the 'noble wife' (2.1.302). She focused on the underlying insecurities and desperate sense of exclusion which led to the character's suicide rather than on her self-claimed Stoicism. Her performance in this tiny debut role was singled out for praise across the broadsheets.

Her unexpectedly forceful Octavia in Greg Doran's *Antony and Cleopatra* evolved from a rehearsal suggestion by Patrick Stewart (Antony) that it would raise the stakes if they treated their marriage as potentially successful. This coincided with Gale's preference for active choices and her new openness to contradictory possibilities. Her interpretation consequently challenged the established reading privileging Antony's comparison of Octavia to a 'swan's-down feather, / That stands upon the swell at full of tide, / And neither way inclines' (3.2.48–50). This 'widow' of 'thirty' (3.3.27–28), 'admired Octavia' (2.2.125), was no meek virgin but an elegant, dignified and above all independent-minded Roman matron ready to take her place as both

Antony's political consort and his sexual partner. Nor was she emotionally dependent on her brother. Her only audible farewell was the clear instruction, 'Look well to my husband's house' (3.2.45). Like her historical counterpart, this Octavia was very much the elder sister.

Gale's Octavia subsequently stood up to first husband then brother, proactive in her determined attempts to reconcile them. 'Wars 'twixt you twain would be / As if the world should cleave, and that slain men / Should solder up the rift' (3.4.30–33) became not a lament but a warning of the enormity of what Antony was considering. She was equally firm with Caesar. Only when it became undeniably clear that Antony had abandoned her did Gale briefly put a hand to her face and look away, recovering mid-sentence however and turning back with defiant stresses on 'two friends' to emphasise her enduring allegiance to both sides (3.6.77). These choices transformed the character to an individual with her own tragic journey: the first collateral damage of the ensuing war.

Goold's ice-bound *Tempest* demanded a substantial imaginative gear-shift for actors and audience. Gale's forthright Miranda was no beach-beauty but a self-reliant Scandinavian adolescent well wrapped-up in a full-skirted knee-length red coat, thick leggings and stout boots; a single heavy plait hung down her back. Her endearingly child-like, morally conscientious and vigorously compassionate performance was based on research into home-educated children with no experience of socialising with others.

This production demonstrates more sharply than usual the difficulties of isolating an individual contribution. Just as Gale's performance was influenced by directorial concept, so Miranda was shaped by interaction with her father. Gale explicitly replicated towards Caliban the treatment Miranda received from Stewart's Prospero: summoning him for dinner, kneeling to make eye contact, recounting her earlier attempts to educate him, delivering moral judgement. Yet, however strong a director's vision, it is the actors who have to realise it. It is frequently claimed that 90% of a director's success lies in casting, finding actors who can contribute what the director is looking for, but to attribute Gale's interpretation here solely to Goold or to Stewart is to underestimate the collaborative nature of the process.

After the West End transfers that concluded the season, Gale moved briefly away from Shakespeare, feeling a need to 'get perspective and explore other territories, other mediums'. This work included a feature film, some TV drama, and a couple of modern stage plays. However within a year she was back at the RSC, this time by invitation, to join Greg Doran's unusually starry autumn ensemble.

RSC, 2008–9: Playing the Courtyard: Ophelia and the Princess of France

Gale's roles here included the Princess of France in *Love's Labour's Lost* and Ophelia to David Tennant's Hamlet. The season was staged entirely in the RSC's temporary home, the Courtyard, the large thrust venue which was the prototype for their redesigned main theatre. This cross between the Swan and Globe was challenging: its apparent wrap-around intimacy and very visible stalls audience were set in a cavernous auditorium with a high balcony and much distant seating; its acoustics were notoriously tricky. The space required actors to play the diagonals, find natural opportunities to look over a shoulder, change stance or upper-body angle, and vary the elevation of the gaze, so that no area of the audience was excluded. However, the range of venue types Gale had already played stood her in good stead. The Courtyard quickly became her favourite performance space, though she observes that playing any large auditorium remains a matter of ongoing trial and error, and uncertainty of what is being 'read'.

Love's Labour's Lost boasted the most lavish, jewel-encrusted Elizabethan costumes seen in Stratford for years, and a set complete with flowered Fragonard swing. Gale claims to have found it difficult to achieve the sparkling playing style the production demanded while simultaneously immersed in the suffering of Ophelia. However, this apparent drawback to the repertoire system seems to have generated a breakthrough in her range, liberating a playfulness and comic touch not evident before; this has persisted into her later work.

Gale's Princess had an upper-class hauteur and was visibly conscious of her responsibilities, with echoes of Miranda's earnestness; she was justifiably offended by Navarre's ill-timed vow and her lack of welcome. The almost wistful tone of her early comment 'God bless my ladies, are they all in love?' (2.1.77) betrayed she had never felt the emotion herself. As a result, when she used her silent half-line at 2.1.106 to face the King for the first time, having deliberately kept her back to him for 16 lines of duologue, their inevitable instant attraction was both comic and moving, the more powerful for having been delayed, expected by the audience but not the characters.

The Princess of France provided Gale with her first opportunity to play a Shakespearean heroine in control of events and dominating those around her. Nevertheless, the character has no soliloquies and functions as the 'head lady' (4.1.43) of a foursome, usually on a crowded stage with multiple semi-simultaneous transactions, in a play with a heavily choreographed structure. The role offers little leeway for significant individual development during the run. In contrast, Gale's apparently powerless Ophelia took centre stage, refusing to be controlled, determined to confront both king and queen, enforce a public acknowledgement of Polonius's death, enact a public ceremony of mourning, and go out 'not with a whimper [but] in a blaze of glory'.

Ophelia's mad scenes present a challenge to the modern actor attuned to naturalism rather than theatrical 'turns', as they demand a reprise of her repertoire of songs and madness only 80 lines after her exit. Gale played these two sequences very differently. In the first she was still trembling on the edge of sanity, mad enough to have lost her inhibitions and social conditioning, sane enough to have some idea what she was doing and why. She used the freedom and unpredictability madness offers as the only weapons available to her. The parallels with Hamlet's tactics as well as his situation were subtly evident. This was a potentially dangerous Ophelia, a threatening complement to Laertes's armed uprising.

She entered barefoot and running, alternating throughout the scene between lucidity, mania and parodies of madness: singing discordantly, skipping erratically in wild circles round Gertrude, pinning her to the spot, jumping up and down as she screamed out her repeated demand for attention, 'Nay, pray you, mark' (4.5.28, 34).

This was an ugly and violent performance, which took control of the whole stage. When Claudius appeared, Gale challenged him with an obviously feigned fit and suddenly attempted to undress him; prevented from this she stripped off her own dress and slip instead. Flipping back into apparent sanity, she mockingly echoed the king's posture and intonation, then, sincere and grief-stricken, returned to her father's death with 'I cannot choose but weep to think they should lay him i'th' cold ground' (4.5.68–69). When Gertrude shushed her and tried to wrap her own shawl round her, Gale rejected both garment and concern with a scream, before turning with a cold, clear, sane threat to Claudius on 'My brother shall know of it' (4.5.69).

By Ophelia's re-entrance, however, perhaps five minutes later, her wits had totally gone. The tone was very different, changed 'to favour and to prettiness' (4.5.187) underpinned by a raw grief and vulnerability. She entered slowly, still in her underwear but scratched and muddy, carrying a formless collection of three-foot weeds. A quiet self-absorption replaced the hyperactivity, and the singing was heart-piercingly beautiful rather than aggressively raucous. She claimed the centrespot and remained there, rather than whirling round the periphery.

The performance revealed Gale's readiness to open herself to the emotional extremes that Renaissance Drama demands of its tragic protagonists, in her first opportunity to do so since Annabella three years earlier. She was immediately invited to stay on and join the RSC's next long-term ensemble, playing roles that would start with Celia and culminate in Juliet. This segue into a further two-year commitment was difficult to accept but finally impossible to refuse, despite Gale's reservations about the personal and professional costs of being out of London for so long at this point in her career and as she turned 30. It was a gruelling schedule, with rehearsals overlapping the London transfer, understudy responsibilities (Rosalind), a highly physicalised schools Shakespeare tour (*Errors*), the televisation of *Hamlet*, and further roles in a Russian premiere, a Malory adaptation, and newly commissioned work all demanding energy and attention. It was a rewarding and varied programme, with medium-term job security and all the resources of the RSC onstage and off but offering little time to look back and reflect.

RSC, 2009–11: Playing Juliet

Playing Juliet gave Gale a new form of input into the creative process. Renewing her working relationship with Goold meant she started from a position of familiarity with the director. She was now also a protagonist. She and her Romeo, Sam Troughton, were consulted over costume. Their preference for contemporary over period clothing fitted well with Goold's vision. The pair started in modern dress, while the rest of the ensemble wore Elizabethan costume with a few deliberate anachronisms. The final act saw this situation reversed: Gale was laced into Renaissance corsetry for her enforced marriage to Paris, the physical constraints of the unwanted wedding dress part of the trap she was caught in; Troughton used a friar's habit to re-enter Verona unnoticed. The decision facilitated a nuanced, very modern reading for the main characters, opening up body language and interpretational choices which would have seemed inappropriate accompanying traditional costuming.

Accordingly, Juliet was initially seen wearing Converse trainers and a dark charcoal knee-length cotton dress (later she would wear skinny jeans and a baggy T-shirt, later still Romeo's hoodie). Her long brown hair was loose and she carried a rope in her hand, a toy which glowed brightly at one end when spun. She stood silent and apart while mother and nurse discussed her future, her obedience cautious, reserved. It suddenly became obvious how few lines Juliet has in this introductory scene. Only the varying speed and angle of the glow-rope and the extent to which she put her whole body into whirling it gave any indication of her feelings; it both revealed subtext and kept others at a distance. Gale eschewed the traditional intimate, tactile relationship with the Nurse, being older, self-contained, and in no need of babying. Whereas many Juliets start as a child and end as a woman, this Juliet was a teenager throughout, complex and conflicted, maturing along a briefer but more deeply etched spectrum. She lacked Margot Fonteyn's cherished doll, and the wide-eyed innocence of Zeffirelli's Olivia Hussey; she would have looked deeply out of place in Claire Danes's angel wings. Susannah Clapp described her as 'a frank hoyden' (*Observer*, 21 March 2010) and Michael Coveney praised her 'adolescent sulkiness' (*Independent*, 24 March 2010). Gale herself comments that Juliet is 'good at lying', repeatedly keeping her own counsel, concealing her emotions and her life not just from her parents but from her nurse at the start as well as at the end.

At the ball, Juliet remained in her original cotton dress, with bare legs, arms and neck, and hair still flowing, the only one not masked or elaborately costumed. Her exhilaration gave her a natural beauty that shone from within rather than from packaging and presentation. In her first encounter with Romeo, Juliet was clearly in control, still on a high from the dancing. The first kiss she accepted and the second she responded to, before pushing him away laughing, breaking the encounter even before the nurse interrupted.

As she waited to learn Romeo's identity, 'If he be marrièd, / My grave is like to be my marriage bed' (1.5.133–34) was a joke rather than a foreshadowing. Shared with the audience, it was part of a continuing direct relationship. The discovery was the more painful for its unexpectedness: Gale's repeated disbelieving stress drew out the irony of her situation, 'My *only* love sprung from my *only* hate' (1.5.137, actor's emphasis). Her explanation to the nurse, 'A rhyme I learnt even now / Of one I danced withal' (1.5.141–42), was not just a deceptive put-off but also a bitter truth.

Goold repeatedly placed Gale in positions of extreme vulnerability and isolation for an actor. In the balcony scene she was positioned alone and fully lit on the upper platform without even a rail as a physical or psychological prop, and with minimal room to manoeuvre as the scene developed. In contrast, Romeo initially played much of the scene far downstage, semi-lit, even at times in the audience, while later filling the entire stage with his jubilation.

This sequence was remarkable for the variety Gale brought to it; the influence of Donnellan's methodology on her work was clear. Sitting, legs dangling, she wrestled intellectually with the problem of Romeo's name: she was diverted by excitement at the solution of denying her own, displayed adolescent bravado with the innuendo of 'any other part / Belonging to man', and built to a hallooed offer to the empty night 'Take all myself' (2.1.75–91). At Romeo's response she fled instantly, but returned to modulate between threats, recognition, warnings and curiosity (2.1.94–121). As her confidence grew, her long speech was progressively amused, child-like, concerned, slow and sincere, rejoicing (2.1.127–48). Her second attempt to stop Romeo swearing was fast and passionate, the third matter of fact, developing into a would-be final speech which started by being sensible, searching for words to express her disquiet, before closing with four lines of self-consciously poetic farewell (2.1.154–66). Her subsequent speeches alternated between laughter (2.1.170) and an unexpected sadness at the depth of her love (2.1.175–78). When Romeo scaled the balcony at the end she joined him in the beginnings of a passionate embrace.

Gale applied a similar approach to the iconic 'Gallop apace' soliloquy (3.2.1–31), controversially delivered not with the usual desperate urgency but as a sequence of ritualistic invocations, broken up with explanatory asides to the audience and a conscious, deliberate use of its imagery.

The verbal and emotional variety Gale deployed was paralleled by her use of physical contradictions. In 2.5, Juliet entered running, hastening to her marriage, only to trip and fall headlong (neatly embodying Friar Laurence's metaphorical warning 'They stumble that run fast', 2.2.94). The audience's gasp, converted to relieved laughter, was silenced in turn by the stillness and intensity between Juliet and Romeo and maintained by the pair as he retrieved her flowers and knelt to present them. As in the meeting of Navarre and the Princess in *Love's Labour's Lost* the use of contrast both intensified the emotions and crystallised a specific key instant. In 4.1 Gale disconcerted the audience again, refusing to provide a predictable experience but rather opening up uncomfortable possibilities. Encountering Paris at the Friar's cell, she was openly rude to him, yet when he kissed her on the lips, her body, newly wakened to sexuality, instinctively responded: she briefly put her arms round his neck before dropping them in horror.

Encouraged by Goold 'not to ring the tragedy bell' at the start, both Gale and Troughton explored the humour and exuberance in the characters, the rush of joy, the exhilaration of risk. These were the most triumphantly ecstatic lovers Stratford had seen for a long while. Gale views the play as a celebration of impulse and passion: 'You don't earn going into the dark if you haven't explored the highs'. Yet it also required delicacy. In line with the design image of fire, Gale sees the couple as 'the fallout, the ash', adding 'all Romeo and Juliet's scenes are so fleeting, if you grip them too hard, it destroys them'.

Yet the eventual tragedy was given full weight. Faced with the enforced bigamous marriage to Paris, Gale screamed at the Friar, 'Be not so long to speak. I long to die!' (4.1.66). Her threats of suicide were genuine, graphically reinforced by the knife which she held resolutely to her throat for over 20 lines and surrendered only in exchange for the potion. The split-second mistiming of the final catastrophe was reinforced by Juliet's unnoticed indications of returning life as Romeo prepared to drink the poison. On awakening, Gale looked directly at Romeo's corpse as she enquired for him, her brain still too fuddled to take in immediately what she was seeing. She showed one last flicker of wry amusement at the emptiness of the drinking vessel, before the implications of her horrified discovery 'Thy lips are *warm*' (5.3.167, actor's emphasis) generated desolate weeping. Her actual death was violent, painful and (in initial performances) gory, swiftly executed when interruption seemed imminent.

Current working process

Gale singles out Greg Doran and Rupert Goold as directors with whom she particularly enjoys working, who 'speak [her] language' in the rehearsal room. Her praise of Goold for 'bold choices that are apparently off the wall but illuminate idiosyncrasies in the text that are usually smoothed out or squashed' says as much about her own style and values as his. She still sees herself as 'a conduit for the director's vision as well as the writer's', yet she relishes the freedom offered by directors who trust their actors to explore and follow their own instincts, who are adaptable rather than overly prescriptive, and who allow dialogue in rehearsal and flexibility in blocking. She is canny enough, however, to appreciate that 'the best of these directors' are nevertheless imperceptibly influencing the outcome.

Her rehearsal process is eclectic, varying according to the demands of the specific play, director and role. For Juliet she researched modern honour killings; for Ophelia she ran through the Stratford meadows gathering weeds. She repeatedly praises Shakespeare for his emotional 'insights', the points of connection with her own experiences or with 'our story as women'. She still uses a drama school technique of giving her characters a secret, however trivial, that never gets shared.

Despite these psychological hooks, Gale has become increasingly wary of naturalistic character-based approaches, relying now almost wholly on the verse. Since joining the RSC, her early training by Rodenburg has been reinforced by the work of John Barton [see 1984] and Cicely Berry [see 1987]. Her conversation keeps returning to the primacy of the language: 'The role is in the verse and the text – enjoy the musical score – the uber visceral words – use the monosyllables – look for the internal rhymes – stress the first and last words of the line – start with the music – let the text speak.' She rigorously observes shared lines, half-lines, the emotional force of 'O'. She frequently finds the Folio capitalisation helpful and is very conscious of varying forms of address. She sees this engagement with the text as an ongoing exploration, 'a life-long journey' that she has barely begun.

She now explicitly rejects Stanislavski, using Juliet's line 'No, madam, we have culled such necessaries' (4.3.7) to demonstrate: the cold consonants open up insights into the relationship and subtext which she could never have achieved by considering her 'motivation'. Of fluctuations and inconsistencies she says 'This is who I am: now I'm someone completely different. I love that about Shakespeare'. She refers back to Donnellan's methodology, which complements her text-based approach. Her priorities have become 'to learn how to unlock open-mindedness and relaxation…engage with the here and now – find each thought and find it fresh – find the character in the moment'.

One side-effect of this concentration on language is her unusual vocal clarity, stemming partly from technical expertise, partly from an intellectual and emotional connection with her dialogue through pushing meaning not volume. This is aided by Gale's exploitation of direct address, her delivery of imagery and classical references as comparisons deliberately chosen by the character rather than subconsciously expressed poetry, and her constantly varying energy which hooks the audience into attention rather than allowing them to be lulled by the iambic rhythm.

During performance runs, Gale's daily regime always includes the optional vocal warm-up led by RSC voice coach Alison Bomber. She sees this as an essential way to prepare for the show, connecting the imagination, voice and brain, exploring the extremes of her range, opening up where she can go in performance, bringing her into the world of the play and making contact with the other actors. For *Romeo and Juliet* she also attended the full company physical warm-up, a deliberately playful and varied ritual, enabling the cast to put aside the pressure of rehearsal day and private lives and come together as a group. Individual preparation for her specific role then follows.

*

As this volume reaches the shops, Mariah Gale will be in New York with the RSC, playing Juliet and Celia, making her international debut. What lies ahead for her is uncertain. She is ready for a change, needs 'to explore some uncharted waters'. However, she sees her engagement with Shakespeare as an unending development process and an 'addiction' that feeds her creativity. She comments simply, 'He is the best.' It seems unlikely to be long before she is back on the Shakespearean stage.

Selected chronology

2003	Ensemble, *The Lost Child* (dir. Andy Brereton) Minerva Theatre, Chichester Emily, *Stealing Sweets and Punching People* by Phil Porter (dir. Crispin Bonham-Carter) Latchmere Theatre, London
2004	Hero, *Much Ado About Nothing* (dir. Tamara Harvey) Shakespeare's Globe, London
2005	Annabella, *'Tis Pity She's A Whore* by John Ford (dir. Edward Dick) Southwark Playhouse, London (Critics' Circle Award for Most Promising Newcomer; Time Out Live Award for Most Promising Newcomer; First Prize, Ian Charleson Award) Viola, *Twelfth Night* (dir. Timothy Sheader) Open Air Theatre, Regent's Park, London Klara, *Musik* by Frank Wedekind (dir. Deborah Bruce) Oxford Stage Company, Arcola Theatre, London
2006	Miranda, *The Tempest* (dir. by Rupert Goold) RSC, Royal Shakespeare Theatre, Stratford, plus Novello Theatre, London Portia, *Julius Caesar* (dir. Sean Holmes) RSC Octavia, *Antony and Cleopatra* (dir. Greg Doran) RSC, Royal Shakespeare Theatre, Stratford, plus Novello Theatre, London
2007	Taylor/Ella, *Vernon God Little* by D.C.B. Pierre / Tanya Ronder (dir. Rufus Norris) Young Vic Theatre, London
2008	Ophelia, *Hamlet* (dir. Greg Doran) RSC, plus Novello Theatre, London (Special Commendation, Ian Charleson Award), televised 2009, BBC Princess of France, *Love's Labour's Lost* (dir. Greg Doran) RSC First Fairy, *Midsummer Night's Dream* (dir. Greg Doran) RSC, plus Novello Theatre, London Rose, *The Sea* by Edward Bond (dir. Jonathan Kent) Theatre Royal, Haymarket, London
2009	Celia, *As You Like It* (dir. Michael Boyd) RSC

	Courtesan, *The Comedy of Errors* (dir. Paul Hunter) RSC and Told by an Idiot, Young People's Tour
	Masha, *The Grain Store* by Natal'ia Vorozhbit (dir. Michael Boyd) RSC
2010	Juliet, *Romeo and Juliet* (dir. Rupert Goold) RSC
	Elaine of Astolat / Ensemble, *Morte D'Arthur* by Mike Poulton (dir. Greg Doran) RSC

Bibliography

Mariah Gale and I met to discuss her work on four occasions during this period (December 2008, March 2010, May 2010, August 2010).

Reviews and interviews

Bosanquet, Theo, http://www.whatsonstage.com/interviews/theatre/london/E8831273509906/Brief+Encounter+With+...+Mariah+Gale.html [Accessed 14 September 2010]

Dobson, Michael, 'Shakespeare Performances in England, 2006', *Shakespeare Survey* 60 (2007), 284–319

Gale, Mariah, *Adopt-an-Actor Globe Blog* http://www.globelink.org/resourcecentre/muchadoaboutnothing/hero/ [Accessed 14 September 2010]

Rutter, Carol Chillington, 'Shakespeare Performances in England (and Wales), 2008', *Shakespeare Survey* 62 (2009), 349–85

Smout, Clare, 'Review of *Love's Labour's Lost*, directed by Greg Doran for the RSC at the Courtyard Theatre, Stratford, and directed by Peter Hall at the Rose Theatre, Kingston', *Cahiers Élisabéthains*, 75 (2009), 68–74, 76

Theatre Record, Vols XXVI (2006), Issues 8, 10, 16–17; XXVII (2008), Issues 16–17, 21; XXX (2010), Issue 6

Walker, Greg, 'Review of *The Tempest*, directed by Rupert Goold for the RSC at the Royal Shakespeare Theatre, Stratford', *Cahiers Élisabéthains*, special issue (2007), 48–49

What's On Stage http://www.whatsonstage.com/index.php?pg=209&name=Mariah%20Gale [Accessed 14 September 2010]

Woods, Penelope, 'Review of *Hamlet*, directed by Greg Doran for the RSC at the Courtyard Theatre, Stratford', *Cahiers Élisabéthains*, 74 (2009), 58–59, 62

Other references

Barton, John (1984) *Playing Shakespeare*. London: Methuen, reissued 2009.

Berry, Cicely (1987) *The Actor and the Text*. London: Virgin, reissued 2000.

Donnellan, Declan (2002) *The Actor and the Target*. London: Nick Hern Books.

Rodenburg, Patsy (1998) *The Actor Speaks: Voice and the Performer*. London: Methuen.

——(2005) *Speaking Shakespeare*. London: Methuen.

Shakespeare, William (2005) *William Shakespeare: The Complete Works*. Gen. Eds. Wells and Taylor, 2nd edition. Oxford: Clarendon Press.

About the author

Clare Smout completed a B.A. at Oxford University and an M.A. at the Shakespeare Institute in Stratford. She is currently a doctoral student at Magdalen College,

Oxford, researching brother/sister relationships in Renaissance drama. Recent publications include: 'Actor, Poet, Playwright, Sharer...Rival? Shakespeare and Heywood, 1603–4', *Early Theatre*, 13 (2010); 'Staging the N-Town Plays: Theatre and Liturgy', with Elisabeth Dutton, *ROMARD*, 49 (2010); and 'Royal Shakespeare Company Performance History' sections for *The Winter's Tale* (2009), *The Merry Wives of Windsor* (2011) and *Timon of Athens* (2011), edited by Jonathan Bate (RSC/Macmillan). Smout writes regular theatre reviews for the journals *Shakespeare* and *Cahiers Élisabéthains*, and has also provided performance history research for RSC Education and Arden Online. She lectures for the University of Birmingham and has taught for the Universities of Oxford and Cambridge and at many leading drama schools.

Previously Smout spent 20 years in professional theatre. She worked as PA to John Barton, Assistant Director to Alan Ayckbourn, and Associate Director to Howard Barker. Her own directing has included *Measure for Measure*, *Much Ado about Nothing*, *The Winter's Tale*, *Merry Wives* and Dryden's *Marriage A-La-Mode*, combined with regular dramaturgical work and a career-long commitment to developing new writing from contemporary playwrights. She has seen all of Mariah Gale's Shakespeare performances at least once, apart from those at Regent's Park.

7
John Harrell

Jeremy Lopez

> ...during our final performance of *Richard II* on Sunday I had an epiphany. It was too late for this production, but next time I have anything to do with that play, as a director I hope, I will make sure that Richard drops the warder [in 1.3] accidentally. Imagine it. Richard's whole gig is that as king he literally (and only literally) never puts a foot wrong. He watches that scene, idly toying with his warder just as he toys with Bullingbrook and Mowbray. Then at the big moment he bobbles the prop and it crashes to the floor. The other characters look at the thing in shock and the audience has no clue whether it's an actor's mistake or not. Then the Lord Marshall yells, "Stay! The king hath thrown his warder down!" What is Richard to do? He leaves the stage, abandoning Mowbray and Bullingbrook to stare awkwardly at each other, then he comes back and banishes them. This staging might help mitigate the abrupt feeling of the banishment, and it impishly posits that all the ensuing strife between the Lancasters and the rest of the Plantagenets hinges on a fumbled stick.

It's the kind of interpretation that infuriates Shakespeare scholars. There is no historical warrant for a staging in which Richard II drops his warder accidentally, and as far as I know, no production has staged the play this way. Although the actor's rationale makes a kind of thematic sense, one cannot help but feel that such a staging would trivialize the scene, and perhaps the entire play. Such a staging would draw a laugh at a tense, climactic moment. It would raise a distracting question in the minds of spectators unfamiliar with Shakespeare or with medieval history: is that the way it *really* happened? The energy created by the audience's uncertainty about the intentionality of the mistake would, after the Lord Marshall's clarifying line, be neutralized by the audience's expectation that similar moments of slapstick or burlesque would occur throughout the production. Shakespeare's tragic meditation upon the entrenched conventions of monarchic power would, in this way, become a modern theatre company's satire on the entrenched conventions of Shakespeare's text in performance. Shakespeare's King Richard would disappear behind the person of the self-consciously witty actor.

Of course, entirely valid objections such as these run into some difficulty when we consider the fact that both theatrical interpretation and literary criticism of the past century or more have been largely in agreement that Shakespeare's King Richard *is* a self-consciously witty actor.

John Harrell, who has been performing with the American Shakespeare Center (ASC) at their Blackfriars-replica playhouse in Staunton, Virginia since 2002, is both a self-conscious and a witty actor, but it is unlikely that many who have seen him act would call him self-consciously witty. Your eye is immediately drawn to him because of how perfectly straight he always seems to be standing on the stage, even when he's not, and his line-readings are so chiseled and deliberate that you hang on every word, waiting to see how the phrase or sentence is going to turn out. But the dominant quality in his striking stage-presence is modesty. He is unassuming, in that he does not seem to assume that you will, or ought to, look at him. He is interesting to look at, and to listen to, because the things he does and says seem to be interesting to him.

Why is John Harrell, a very good actor at a small regional American repertory theatre, important? It might, of course, be fair to ask why *any* Shakespearean actor is important, but the cultural visibility, high-end box-office drawing power, and, not insignificantly, the Britishness of most of the actors featured in this volume, from Simon Russell Beale to Harriet Walter, means we don't have to. Tickets at the ASC are relatively inexpensive, and neither the actors nor the theatre can be said to have a high cultural visibility (indeed, many of the actors seek greater visibility, when not working at the ASC, in theatre, television, and film work in New York and Los Angeles); the core group of performers is just small and unstable enough that the quality of acting varies noticeably from production to production and season to season; and, because of the theatre's geographical isolation, the audiences are relatively small, are drawn from the immediately surrounding area (approximately 80% of the theatre's audience lives within 200 miles of the theatre, and 50% lives within 50 miles), and have a large student contingent (sales to student groups make up about 30% of ASC sales in any given month). Harrell's position is undoubtedly identical to the position of any number of surprisingly good actors who anchor small regional theatre companies throughout North America. Ian McKellen, Antony Sher, and Judi Dench arguably have had and continue to have a demonstrable impact upon the way "Shakespeare," as a constellation of theatrical artifacts and cultural ideas, signifies in contemporary British and North American popular and academic culture. John Harrell, on the other hand, like the vast majority of classical actors in the contemporary world, might simply be laboring in obscurity.

What distinguishes the ASC from other small regional American theatre companies is, of course, its remarkable theatre space—a best-guess historical replica of the Blackfriars theatre in London in which the King's Men began performing plays in the early seventeenth century. Deliberately unassuming on the outside (Steve Hendrix of the *Washington Post* wrote in 2001 that the theatre's exterior "has an upscale alpine look, like a fire station in Telluride"), the theatre is spectacularly beautiful on the inside—a bare plank stage surrounded on three sides by subtly ornate galleries constructed from Virginia white oak, and backed by a *frons scenae* painted with a black marble faux-finish. There is, in my experience, no other theatre like it—not even the Globe, the effect of whose similarly gorgeous interior always seems (to me) somewhat diminished by the incongruity of its garish, theme-park-style exterior in the midst of the hyper-modern South Bank landscape. When you walk into the Blackfriars, you feel transported—not really into "another time," which is the obvious intention of a theatre like the Globe, but rather and more simply into another place; this place is distinct from the world outside of it, but the portal through which you leave one to get into the other allows for a seamless transition. You don't quite notice that it's happening, but you suddenly notice that it *has* happened. There is a productive analogy to be made between the kind of theatrical experience this space provides and the kind of theatrical experience John Harrell's acting provides: in each case your engagement with something apparently familiar or quite ordinary gives way imperceptibly to an engagement with sharply delineated alterity. And the two kinds of engagement remain perceptibly, dialectically intertwined.

The complex relationship between Harrell and the Blackfriars theatre, in both its contiguities and its tensions, is what makes Harrell an important actor. Besides its regular season of Shakespeare plays, and besides its "Actors' Renaissance Season," where less familiar early modern dramas (such as *A King and No King*, or *The Blind Beggar of Alexandria* or, in 2011, *Look About You*) are produced without directors and according to an approximation of the early modern rehearsal process, the American Shakespeare Center hosts a biennial academic conference dedicated to the works of Shakespeare and his contemporaries in performance. Because of this conference, the NEH (National Endowment for the Humanities)-funded summer scholarly institutes (four since 1995) hosted at the theatre, and the constant traffic of academic spectators these events help to create year-round; because of the M. Litt and MFA graduate programs in Shakespeare performance studies at nearby Mary Baldwin College; and also because of its increasingly close collaboration with the educational arm of Shakespeare's Globe Theatre in London—because of all these things, it is not nearly as presumptuous as it might initially seem that a 300-seat theatre in a small town on the far western edge of Virginia calls itself the American Shakespeare *Center*. There is nowhere else in North America—or, arguably, even in the United Kingdom—where there are so many productions of the works of Shakespeare and his contemporaries going on and, at the same time, so much intimate, productive contact between scholars who study early modern drama and a company of actors performing that drama. John Harrell is at the center of that center—and also, in terms of the roles he plays, his attitude toward the theatre's "original practices" mandate, and even his relationship to professional acting *per se*, on the periphery of that center.

Harrell is not a member of the Actors' Equity Association and indeed has no "formal" training as an actor. His rigorous study of play-texts and his remarkable theatrical instincts give him the confidence to assess both the scholarly underpinnings of an "original practices" playhouse and the mystified ideals of late-modern naturalistic acting with a mischievous expediency.

> My obsessive preparation of verse is probably a waste of time from any sensible historical perspective. The text is unstable, we have no idea of what a line reading sounded like 400 years ago, etc. But an actor's attention to patterns of detail helps to render his performance visible. In a way, I think, it doesn't matter what lunacy a performer indulges in his preparation or process, as long as it forces him to do something deliberate. Certainly I have ideas of what a scene or an exchange of lines "means," but I have no control over whether an audience member perceives this meaning. This is the artist's side of aesthetic positivism. If someone in the audience thinks that

> he is witnessing my bared soul, or somehow reading my mind by "reading" my face and body, well, maybe he'll buy a season ticket. (2010)

Like many of the most established actors in the resident troupe, Harrell lives in Staunton, probably a twelve-minute walk from the theatre. His wife, Jenny McNee, is a costume designer for the theatre. He has played more roles (76) in more productions (69) than any other actor at the ASC. He teaches classes on acting in the Mary Baldwin College MFA program. His is probably the most familiar face in Staunton and at the Blackfriars theatre, and this familiarity combined with his extraordinarily clear way of speaking verse, and an unpredictable, idiosyncratic physicality means that he is the focus of an audience's attention from the moment he walks onto the stage—even if it's simply to make the obligatory pre-show remarks about cell phones and exits.

At the same time, Harrell only infrequently receives top billing at the Blackfriars. The self-consciously witty and theatrical Richard II, whom Harrell played in 2008, was actually somewhat of a departure for the actor. Since 2002, he has played an enviable number of Shakespearean roles, but very rarely the leading man. A representative (but far from complete) list would include: Feste, Quince, Justice Shallow, Old Gobbo, Polonius, Parolles, Friar Laurence, Silvius, Ariel, Gravedigger, Paris, Holofernes, Malvolio, Bottom, Ford, Lear's Fool, Saturninus, and Roderigo. To a greater and lesser degree, what these characters all have in common, and what distinguishes them from Richard II, is that they tend to require an actor to draw focus to himself from the periphery. Moreover, their best and most characteristic theatrical effects tend to be not only comic, but *unintentionally* comic; the characters are unaware of how comic, and often how theatrical, they are. These are roles where the actor-as-character can seem almost beside himself, surprised and yet powerless to stop, and ultimately grateful for, the bizarre or obtuse things the character-as-character will say and do. The pleasure of watching Harrell in roles like these comes from watching him demonstrate or suggest, with clarity and precision, that the characters are acting *him*.

*

Richard II is often performed as beside himself, watching himself act and demonstrating that he is being acted, and Harrell played him this way as well. The difference between Richard II and characters like Polonius or Holofernes is that Richard knows where his theatrical effects should or will come. In this way Richard II is like one of the only other lead Shakespearean roles Harrell has played at the Blackfriars, Richard III. The ASC's production of *Richard III* (in 2002, when the company was still known as Shenandoah Shakespeare) was Harrell's first in the Blackfriars playhouse, and happens to be the first production I saw there as well. I remember very little specific about this production, now at the remove of nearly eight years, though one of my most specific memories is of Harrell's body. Early in the play (I don't recall exactly when), at the beginning of a scene, a naked foot pushed through the curtain of the upstage-center entrance. The foot was attached to Harrell, who followed it shortly, being pushed onto the stage on a kind of wheelchair or cart. Around his neck he wore a hideous fur stole, and the end of his blasted right arm was covered with a misshapen leather ball. Along with this vivid memory, I can recall the cumulative effect of the production's stylizations: the production design—and this production *was* designed, a somewhat controversial fact about which I will have to say more later—was inspired by the visual and gestural rhetorics of silent film, vaudeville, and Edward Gorey cartoons. It conveyed a jagged or oblique, yet extremely precise, approach to what the director and cast assumed (justly) were the extremely familiar language and characters of Shakespeare's play. A contemporary review of *Richard III* by Joel Jones of the *Charlottesville Weekly*, praising Harrell's performance, might help to express what the production was like:

> ...Harrell's acting technique is strange and wonderful. Most actors look inward, digging into themselves for truth to project. You can often see them onstage trying literally to be deep. Harrell is so obstinately shallow he bursts out of the other side of shallow, creating his character's emotions live. (2002)

Also useful, perhaps, are some of director Thadd McQuade's notes to the cast just before opening night, which have been preserved in the American Shakespeare Center's archive:

> You already have all the material you need to score every moment of the play....Don't use everything in one scene....Use reductions, expansions, repetition, alteration of time and orientation to make one piece of source material serve many ends....Take a piece of vocabulary developed with the hand or arm, and put it in your legs or feet, or head. Only repeat something exactly when you wish to create an historical or metaphorical link between two moments...(2002)

McQuade's idea of an innovative, precise but eerily dislocated physicality is one reason that this production was, of all the productions I have seen at the Blackfriars, the most harmonious with the theatrical space and with Harrell's acting technique and style.

By the time McQuade directed Harrell in *Richard III* at the Blackfriars, the two had been working together in the theatre for some years, first in the traveling-company antecedent to the American Shakespeare Center, the Shenandoah Shakespeare Express (SSE; founded by Ralph Alan Cohen and Jim Warren in 1988—Harrell joined in 1991 and McQuade in 1994), and then in a Charlottesville, Virginia-based physical-theatre ensemble called Foolery (founded by Harrell, McQuade, and others in 1997.) These two extremely different theatre companies provided the majority of Harrell's theatrical experience and training, and their almost diametrically opposed styles and approaches to text and performance continue to define both the unique energy and the internal conflicts of Harrell's acting, its relationship to the American Shakespeare Center's theatre-space and theatrical mission, and the relationship of the American Shakespeare Company to its audiences.

The SSE was founded on the principle that Shakespeare's language must be the central element of any production of any of his plays, and that if you take care of the language—if you deliver the lines clearly and rapidly—everything else will take care of itself. The SSE was renowned for their essentially costumeless productions (monochromatic base garments, high-top sneakers, and the use of single accessories—often simply a hat or a colored sash—to distinguish characters), their under-two-hours performance time, their extensive doubling of roles, and their commitment to universal lighting. The correspondence between SSE's stated mission—to make Shakespeare communicate directly and freshly to modern audiences in a modern idiom—and its execution of that mission was so perfect as to make even academics and journalists agree about their productions. Reviewing SSE's 1992 *Comedy of Errors* for the *Washington Post*, Pamela Sommers praised the company's "playing to and with the spectators—the houselights never dim, and the actors think nothing of roaming the aisles or perching in strangers' laps"; this informal, interactive style "immediately established a sense of give-and-take" (1992). Writing in *Shakespeare Quarterly* that same year, about SSE productions in 1991, Stephen Booth noted that "the company performs in 'universal' light;...there is thus one less barrier than is usual on the modern stage between action and audience....Stripped of the time-consuming ruffles and riffs with which later traditions have stuffed out Shakespearean production...[SSE productions] have the sort of confidence, clarity, and gusto one hears in *a cappella* singing and sees in Leonardo's notebook sketches" (1992, 479).

Foolery, on the other hand, was founded upon the principles of European "total theatre." As its still-active website, www.foolery.org, explains, the troupe (which disbanded in 2004) "explored the possibilities of physical storytelling, combining traditional techniques of clown with modern research concerning the relationship between playmakers and playgoers." Paul Menzer, who worked with Foolery as a dramaturg and in other capacities, notes that they were "inspired by groups like Serbia's Dah Theatre," and worked "to make the body *visible* onstage, through restraint, tensions, angularities, held motions, etc." It was largely his work with Foolery, Menzer says, that gave Harrell "the physical vocabulary to complement the vocal abilities" (2010) that were his primary asset when he began his acting career with the SSE. In a 2008 interview on a Virginia arts and culture website (monkeyclaus.org), Foolery founding member Martha Mendenhall (now Director of Education of the North Carolina Shakespeare Festival), said that the company was in fact founded partly as a reaction to the SSE.

> We had worked as performers with given text and we had all worked with...Shenandoah Shakespeare—the founding members of Foolery. But Thadd McQuade, who was the artistic director of Foolery, and I both had an incredible love for silent comedy, for Chaplin and Keaton...and a kind of Vaudevillian sort of approach to performance that you don't see a lot in modern plays that are very text based. So we were trying to find a way to get away from text....We were, and I still am, interested in working physically and seeing...from an acting perspective, not dance, what story can you tell?

Foolery's inaugural show, performed by Harrell, McQuade, Mendenhall, and Kara McLane, was a silent, clown-show adaptation of *Cyrano de Bergerac*. It was performed in Virginia and also at the Edinburgh Festival Fringe, where it was nominated for the

Total Theatre Award for Most Innovative Production, and where it won the BBC Radio Award for Most Innovative Production. Later productions included adaptations of Shakespeare's *Winter's Tale*, and a non-text adaptation of *Twelfth Night* called *Cesario*.

These rival traditions, all language and no language—or, perhaps, all verbal language and all physical language—intersect at the core of John Harrell's identity and efficacy as an actor. In preparing his roles, Harrell does a great deal of metrical work, which he sees as adding "a whole other layer of memorization" to the work of learning lines.

> At first, verse is easier to learn because you can hear yourself screwing up lines, but once you start taking into account the questions about final beats of lines and opening trochees and all that stuff, it gets heavy. And I really examine these things because I've been listening to actors for a long time and I'm convinced that it matters. A verse play should sound like verse, or at least it shouldn't *not* sound like verse. I take a crankish pride in knowing that all of my line readings scan, or that if they do not I have a reason for it that I can discuss.

This intensive verse-work pays off. In my experience, Harrell is one of the very few actors—John Gielgud is another—whose verse-speaking spectators are eager to talk about almost before they talk about anything else. Fred Franko finds that Harrell's "speaking of verse is almost palpable. It's riveting without being showy. It directs his body, or, better said, his body becomes indistinguishable from his speech." (2009). For James Loehlin, "Harrell is very sensitive to changes in inflection and pronunciation suggested by metrical demands, and the acting opportunities these provide" (2009).

The other thing people are eager to talk about when they talk about Harrell is the way he uses his body. Describing Harrell's reading of Quince's "you speak your parts all at once, cues and all," Matthew Kozusko says that,

> he did one of those signature Harrell things, going a little pigeon-toed as he turned his chair incrementally counter-clockwise with his left foot and looked down at his director's papers with the also-signature-Harrell countenance of bemused or affable derision. The intonation of the delivery, sort of fey, with an edge on it, matched. (2009)

Jeremy Fiebig remembers that in the 2006 ASC *Tempest*, Harrell "performed the entire run of the show walking only on his toes or the balls of his feet, or the sides of his feet, or his heels. Never the whole thing" (2009). I recall Harrell's first appearance as Chapman's Blind Beggar of Alexandria: in dumbshow and to the accompaniment of music, his eyes covered with a large bandage or blindfold, the Beggar emerged from the central-upstage entrance carrying a large and obviously very heavy boulder. Sinking low to the ground under its weight, he plopped one foot comically forward, then the other, progressing to center of the stage. This prop would serve throughout the production to identify the location of the Beggar's cave. At the end of the scene, the Beggar having dispatched his various clients, the music started up again and Harrell exited in dumbshow, picking up the light-as-a-feather boulder (it was just *papier-mâché*, after all) and letting it bounce once in his hands as he made a rapid turn upstage—all of this in a single movement.

What one tends to hear or remember less about Harrell's performances are what we might think of as his characterizations. This has to do both with the kinds of roles he is given to play and his technique as an actor: he tends to be given "character parts," parts that depend upon vivid and rapidly achieved effects at discrete moments, and his natural inclination is to play the very discreteness of these moments—to eschew what we might think of as the "character arc." These are characters on the margins of the plays they inhabit, characters who would have us think as much of them as they do of themselves; fortunately for these characters, in spite of their peripheral roles, a good actor's gravity pulls them back toward the center of the mind's eye. As Lars Engle puts it, Harrell has the "capacity to project a character's narcissistic self-investment that draws all eyes to him, whether he is imposing his will in a comparatively self-effacing way as Octavius or being a learned Latinist idiot as Holofernes" (2009). Engle's terms correspond to my sharp but nevertheless quite general recollected impressions of Harrell's character work: his relentlessly stupid Lussurioso (in *The Revenger's Tragedy*, 2009), who took refuge behind a simpering, sneering smile; his unexpectedly moving Vermandero (*The Changeling*, 2009), who was completely oblivious to the psycho-sexual tortures afoot behind the doors of his castle's chambers; his vacant and trivial Lucifer, who moved like a bug (*Dr. Faustus*, 2010).

I like to think it is not only a trick of memory, but also significant that the plays of Shakespeare's contemporaries most readily spring to mind as I try to come up with a way of expressing the character of Harrell's characterizations. Less familiar to audiences and actors alike, produced (at the Blackfriars) under deliberately straitened circumstances with a minimum of rehearsal and without a director, these plays more urgently demand that actors give the spectators definite personalities to take from the theatre in their memories. In the case of Shakespeare, spectators bring their memories—of actors, characters, productions—*to* the theatre; much of the work of characterization, especially of characters like Polonius, Malvolio, or Peter Quince has been done by the audience, mentally and in advance. Harrell seems to be aware of this, and what he seeks to put into the spectator's memory is the distinctive, minute physical gesture, the surprising, oblique verbal intonation—something that just cracks the hard surface of theatrical convention and theatre history.

What you leave the theatre with, then, is a memory of John Harrell, and of highly precise physical and verbal work that is very difficult to reconstruct in words—which is why the popularity and admiration Harrell enjoys among both general and scholarly audiences is in exactly inverse proportion to the mentions he gets in journalistic and academic considerations of the ASC's work. For the spectator who hopes to find a *realization* of Shakespeare's text in a given theatrical production, Harrell's form of acting is probably somewhat frustrating—and we might glance back, at this point, to the discussion of *Richard II* with which this essay began. This is, of course, why Harrell is generally not cast in leading roles: as dedicated as the

American Shakespeare Center is to—and as effectual as it has been in—changing the way Shakespeare is performed in professional repertory theatres, it is inevitably and perhaps of necessity bound to the imperatives and conventions of post-modern realistic theatre, which is in turn bound to the imperatives and conventions of Hollywood screen-acting and story-telling. Harrell's acting is so arresting because it almost always successfully cuts against the grain of the mode and style of a theatre that is itself trying (*not* always successfully) to cut against the grain of the modes and styles of contemporary popular commercial entertainment. Harrell is one of the main reasons that people come to the Blackfriars theatre, and the main reason for this is that people want to see what he is going to do—with a line, a character, a scene—and, on some even more important level, I think, they want to try to figure out *what he is doing*. For, there is often a gap between what Harrell does and what the apparatus of the theatre (both in a broad cultural sense, and in a narrow physical sense particular to the Blackfriars) wants him to do, or suggests he should do. In playing that gap Harrell does what all the best actors, in any medium, manage to find a way to do: he creates desire.

*

Watching audiences watch Harrell, one might get an idea of what Henry Peacham was talking about when he recalled the effect of Tarlton's head merely being seen as it peeped out between the tiring-house door and tapestry. Academic and non-academic spectators alike are filled with expectation when they see Harrell walk onto the stage. This expectation feeds and is fed by what Brett Gamboa [2010] describes as the actor's "exuberant confidence" on the stage, the sense he conveys both of total ownership of the space and of his willingness to (or the possibility that he might) simply leave it at any moment and withdraw into the secret and delightful world that nurtures his particular talent.

If we follow out my analogy to Tarlton, we might say that Harrell also gives us an idea of how early modern repertory playing might as often as not have been something that modern scholars—who optimistically cherish the sometimes-mutually-exclusive virtues of subtlety and broad popular appeal—would not care for if they had the opportunity to experience it first-hand. Harrell's exuberant confidence, Gamboa goes on to say, allows him to be

> fully committed to anything, and the audience at the playhouse—at times too much of a "home crowd"—has perhaps allowed him to feel as though he can do little wrong. In turn, he allows himself to leak through his characters, or to enjoy alongside his audience, the intrusions of reality and topical reference into the fiction.

Holly Pickett provides a recollection of Harrell as Volpone which illustrates with a specific instance the complicated vacillation between two kinds of enjoyment which concerns Gamboa:

> The scene that surprised me the most was the attempted rape scene between Celia and Volpone. I had just been discussing with my class the previous day how disturbing the scene was and how it threatened to break the

> comedy of the play irreparably. The next day, when I took my class to see the play at the Blackfriars, I had to eat my words. The scene was hysterical. John Harrell was running around in his underwear...which managed to be funny in and of itself. Then, he had some kind of remote control in his hands which he could press to turn on sultry "Let's Get It On" type music. Finally, the attempted rape itself was so stylized, it recalled a kind of vaudeville skit or early cartoon, with Celia's legs, clad in lacy long pantaloons inside exaggerated hoop skirts, straight in the air in a kind of tug of war with Harrell as Volpone. Her legs would "snap" shut every time Harrell would try to pry them apart. (2009)

As with Harrell's idea about Richard's dropped warder, it is easy to imagine how some spectators in Pickett's position—spectators, that is, who know the play well and teach it to undergraduates—might assess this rendition of *Volpone* less generously. The imaginative and physically stylized staging does seem to convey something true about the play: that is, in the series of scenes involving Celia, Volpone *is* a ridiculous slave to his lust; Celia *is* a hyperbolical, almost cartoonish figure of chastity; the contest between them *is* one in which each adopts a highly conventionalized moral and rhetorical posture. Nevertheless, this staging also arguably gets something, and perhaps a great deal, wrong about the play, at least as it has been understood by critics and as it might be taught to students. One way of expressing what the staging gets wrong would be to say that it seems to develop a hyperbolical visual language based on Victorian prudishness and twenty-first-century pathetic masculinity out of a hyperbolical poetic language based on seventeenth-century satirical misogyny and classical images of bestial masculinity. The misalignment between these two (or perhaps four) languages is a characteristic example of how performances at the Blackfriars end up effecting a divide between two kinds of spectator: the academic spectator feels, to some extent justly, that the non-academic spectator is laughing at the wrong thing, and is doing so precisely because of the theatre's (often Harrell's) proficiency in achieving an intentional theatrical effect that is more self-referential than aware of the play-text that frames it.

And yet this line of critique itself almost surely gets something wrong about theatrical experience in assuming that it ever is, was, or could be anything other than self-referential. The reconstructed Blackfriars theatre itself does, of course, imply that the most valuable theatrical experience gestures to something beyond, and antecedent, to itself. Arguably, the original Blackfriars theatre, partly modeled on Court or great-hall playing spaces, implied this as well: one index of the effectiveness of the implication might be the persistence to this day of the idea that Blackfriars audiences were somehow more sophisticated than audiences at the outdoor theatres. But there is a direct line of descent between Fitzdotterel's satirical description of Blackfriars-audience behavior in *The Devil is an Ass* and modern scholarly complaints that universal lighting serves mainly to reveal that the highly responsive spectators don't quite understand what it is they're supposed to be responding to, and are often responding merely in order to make a spectacle of themselves. The persistence of the complaint might certainly suggest that audiences never really understand what the theatre is about; but it also might suggest that the complainers are looking at the problem the wrong way around. That is, it might be the case that the vital energy of theatrical experience always arises out of and is constituted by *misunderstanding*, or a misalignment of competing understandings—of the text by the actors, of the audience by the playwright, of the play by the audience, and so on.

The moment in *Volpone* described by Pickett involves a history of conflicted intention and interpretation which most spectators in the audience could not have the means to understand. The stylization of the attempted rape in the manner of a "vaudeville skit or early cartoon" derives not only from the actors' present desire to communicate the play's thematic concerns freshly and vividly to a modern audience, but also from Harrell's idiosyncratic aesthetic sensibility, and from his work in Foolery and in productions like Thadd McQuade's *Richard III*. The aesthetic sensibility so harmonious with the physical-theatre company Foolery is on one hand the resource upon which Harrell draws to enable a form of acting which seems to yield "discoveries" about early modern play texts. On the other hand, it is a sensibility that has caused considerable vexation at the Blackfriars: McQuade's production of *Richard III* was notoriously difficult and internally controversial because of the way its filmic/vaudevillian design concept seemed to misunderstand the mandates of an "original practices" theatre *and* because of the way its stylized acting resulted in alienating, non-naturalistic characterizations that seemed to misunderstand the mandates of a regional American repertory theatre trying to reach out to the broadest possible audience. Those two mandates are themselves not at all harmonious, and one manifestation of the ongoing conflict between them can be seen in the way the ASC handles more difficult (because less familiar), less box-office-worthy play-texts like *Volpone*: it produces them with *less* rehearsal time and *without* a director, thus encouraging the use of *more* discrete, stylized theatrical effects that are developed out of individual actors' idiosyncratic aesthetic sensibilities and theatrical histories. As a result, the plays of Shakespeare's contemporaries, those plays which one might expect to be most locked in to the historical conditions to which the theatre-space itself insistently alludes, end up seeming most to jar with that space's particularity as a reconstructed historical artifact.

This might not actually be something to worry about; or, to worry about it might be a productive misunderstanding of the character of theatrical experience which can help us to understand early modern theatricality in a new way. Perhaps early modern theatrical experience was, for its original audiences, just as bafflingly stylized, just as obviously constituted out of conflicting conventions of speech and embodiment, as are post-modern reconstructions of it. Both seem to require of audiences a great deal of attention to and puzzling over *what an actor is doing*, right now, in the moment. And that is why John Harrell is such an interesting actor, and why the way audiences respond to and think about Harrell is so useful for understanding the interpretive and phenomenological pleasures and problems created by productions of early modern drama in the twenty-first century.

Prefacing his description of Harrell's Quince which I quoted earlier in this essay, Matthew Kozusko explains that his initial experience of Harrell in the role was one of frustration: Harrell seemed to be "missing all the obvious jokes. It was the first play I'd seen [at the Blackfriars], and I just figured he'd been miscast" (2009). But as Harrell went on to reveal that it was *Quince* who was missing all the obvious jokes, Kozusko was struck by the force of the actor.

> Readings like that, which at first seem to misunderstand something about the role, work because a coherence emerges as the part unfolds, and though at any given instant the reading seems somehow off, you end up totally absorbed and persuaded. (2009)

Character, actor, and audience try to make sense of the role together. "I've never had much trouble with the grammatical or syntactical parts of Shakespeare's English," Harrell says, "and when I do hit a snag I genuinely enjoy trying to puzzle out a sentence's structure."

Ralph Alan Cohen recalls directing a 1996 production of *As You Like It* in which, for time's sake, he decided to cut three of Jaques's lines:

> He that a fool doth very wisely hit
> Doth very foolishly, although he smart,
> Not to seem senseless of the bob.

Harrell objected to the cut, but Cohen said that he had not been able to hear the sense of the lines in rehearsal. As Cohen tells the story,

> John said, "I promise you, Ralph, I'll make it clear or you can cut it." And of course he *did*, by managing to keep "doth very foolishly…not to seem senseless" as a single thought by actually *stressing* the turn on "although he smart" in the middle of that thought. John's approach always seems to me to be to embrace the difficulty as a way of solving it. So rather than rush "although he smart" to keep it from disturbing the main thought, he slowed down and emphasized the interruption as a way of achieving that goal of *not* interrupting. (2010)

Not surprisingly, Harrell has a particular fondness for the moment in *Richard II* where, having explained quite precisely why he cannot compare his prison to the world, Richard decides, in the second half of a line, that he'll give it a try anyway: "yet I'll hammer it out."

In the end, then, Harrell both creates and satisfies the desire to see how acting happens, and what it means for the actor as it happens. He cultivates a transparency that suggests you're in the presence of the real thing, even when (or precisely because) the thing turns out to be different from what you expected it to be. But, as with all great actors, at the heart of this transparency—or, perhaps, visible as a shadow on its periphery—is something held back, unfathomable. This is the mystery of technique: not only the ability but also the desire to subordinate the self to craft. My most vivid recent memory of Harrell on stage is his delivery of the song Lear's Fool sings when Kent is in the stocks. Sitting on stage, holding against his left shoulder a death's-head bauble (his constant companion throughout the show), he half-sang, half-intoned the lines, his voice fragile yet forceful; and as he spoke, he slowly turned the bauble around and around so that the skull seemed to survey the entire audience. The significance of this staging is quite clear, perhaps even conventional, as both an interpretation and a realization of *Lear*. What makes it linger in the mind is the position of the actor's body: he sat with his back to the audience.

Acknowledgements

I am very grateful to the following people, without whose time and generosity I could not have written this essay: John Harrell, Paul Menzer, Ralph Alan Cohen, Sarah Enloe (Director of Education at the American Shakespeare Center), Julia Bolotina (my research assistant at the University of Toronto), and the numerous colleagues cited in this essay who responded to my email request for responses to and thoughts on Harrell's acting.

Selected chronology

1996	*As You Like It*, Shenandoah Shakespeare Express (touring) – Jaques
1997	*Cyrano*, Foolery (Charlottesville, VA and Edinburgh) – Christian
1999	*The Winter's Tale*, Foolery (Charlottesville, VA) – Autolycus
1999–2000	*Cesario*, Foolery (Charlottesville, VA)
2002	*Richard III*, Shenandoah Shakespeare (Blackfriars Playhouse) – Richard III
2004	*A Midsummer Night's Dream*, Shenandoah Shakespeare (Blackfriars Playhouse) – Quince
2005	*A King and No King*, American Shakespeare Center (Blackfriars Playhouse) – Bessus
2005	*All's Well that Ends Well*, American Shakespeare Center (Blackfriars Playhouse) – Parolles
2007	*Love's Labours Lost*, American Shakespeare Center (Blackfriars Playhouse) – Holofernes
2008	*Richard II*, American Shakespeare Center (Blackfriars Playhouse) – Richard II
2008	*Volpone*, American Shakespeare Center (Blackfriars Playhouse) – Volpone
2009	*The Revenger's Tragedy*, American Shakespeare Center (Blackfriars Playhouse) – Lussurioso
2009	*The Changeling*, American Shakespeare Center (Blackfriars Playhouse) – Vermandero
2009	*The Blind Beggar of Alexandria*, American Shakespeare Center (Blackfriars Playhouse) – Cleanthes

Bibliography

Booth, Stephen. "The Shenandoah Shakespeare Express." *Shakespeare Quarterly* 43.2 (1992) 476–83.
Cohen, Ralph Alan. Personal correspondence with the author. May 5, 2010.
Engle, Lars. Personal correspondence with the author. October 30, 2009.
Fiebig, Jeremy. Personal correspondence with the author. November 6, 2009.
http://foolery.org/. Accessed May 7, 2010.
Franko, G. Fred. Personal correspondence with the author. October 30, 2009.
Gamboa, Brett. Personal correspondence with the author. February 8, 2010.
Harrell, John. Personal correspondence with the author. April 24, 2010.

Hendrix, Steve. "'Where There's A Will...': Staunton, Va., bets on Shakespeare." *Washington Post*, October 10, 2001.

Jones, Joel. Review of *Richard II*. *Charlottesville Weekly*, September 24–30, 2002.

Kozusko, Matthew. Personal correspondence with the author. November 3, 2009.

Loehlin, James. Personal correspondence with the author. November 6, 2009.

Mendenhall, Martha. *Interview* at http://www.monkeyclaus.org/culture. Accessed May 7, 2010.

Menzer, Paul. Personal correspondence with the author. April 19, 2010.

McQuade, Thadd. Director's Notes for *Richard III*, produced by Shenandoah Shakespeare, 2002.

Pickett, Holly. Personal correspondence with the author. October 30, 2009.

Sommers, Pamela. 'Review of *The Comedy of Errors*'. *Washington Post*, July 13, 1992.

About the author

Jeremy Lopez is Associate Professor of English Literature at the University of Toronto and the theatre review editor for *Shakespeare Bulletin*. He is the author of *Theatrical Convention and Audience Response in Early Modern Drama* (Cambridge, 2003) and several articles on the works of Shakespeare and his contemporaries. He has directed and acted in numerous works of early modern drama, including Beaumont and Fletcher's *The Woman Hater*, Ben Jonson's *Every Man Out of his Humour*, and a two-man adaption of Shakespeare's *Macbeth*.

8
Greg Hicks

Ben Naylor

Prologue

Greg Hicks is, not unusually, upside down. Standing on his head against a wall, deep in concentration. The rest of the Royal Shakespeare Company ensemble are upright, rehearsing *King Lear*, in which Hicks will play the title role. In his solitary inversion Hicks is seeking Nothing: physicalising a Zen paradox on the ego which he has earlier invoked in discussion.

Inversion and paradox are at the heart of Hicks' work. Despite a career in which he has played almost all Shakespeare's major tragic heroes (with the notable exception of Hamlet), his remains a relatively unfamiliar face to those other than theatre habitués; he has appeared on our screens comparatively little. He has often been masked, literally, to his widest audiences: on stage, as the leading actor in the worldwide tour of John Barton's ten-hour epic *Tantalus*, directed by Peter Hall; and as Dionysus in Hall's 2002 "homecoming" NT production of Euripides' *Bacchai*, which played to 15,000 at Epidavros. He is likewise masked in probably the most-printed picture of him, as Orestes on the cover of the ubiquitous revised edition of Phyllis Hartnoll's *The Theatre: A Concise History*; the four-hour production (again, Peter Hall for the NT) was also filmed and broadcast by the UK TV station Channel 4 in 1982 – complete with masks.

And despite Hicks' association, from almost the beginning of his career, with the UK's two major national theatrical institutions, he has been no stranger to controversy. He originated the role of Marban, the victim of the famous rape in Brenton's *The Romans in Britain*, for which indiscretion Mary Whitehouse initiated legal proceedings against director Michael Bogdanov; Hicks, masked by nudity, woad and a wig, is not easily to be recognised in photos of the scene of the crime.

It is with paradox in mind that I shall seek to interpret the work of this complex and fascinating actor. Critical responses to his performances have shown awareness of, if not always sensitivity to, his duality and ambiguity. He is often called a "physical" actor – "mannered" to some – but his interpretations are described in psychological terms: "intense", "sardonic", "bitter", "haughty". "Inside-out" actor or "outside-in"? Has concentration on the outer engendered a failure to perceive – or to reveal – the inner?

This binary division is, however, too essentially reductive to describe acting of the daring and precision Hicks often produces; rather, the coactive *dualism* of inner effort and outer action is richly present and observable in his work. In the terms of the Zen paradox: that everything both implies and depends upon its opposite.

I

Greg Hicks is, perhaps unsurprisingly to the astrologically inclined, a Gemini, ever divided and in duality: like Autolycus, "littered under Mercury". Born 27 May 1953, an only child in a lower middle-class Jewish family in the East Midlands (Leicester), his father was a relocated East-End market-trader, family name Godetsky, his mother a rural Rutlander and convert to Judaism. There was no local synagogue and few Jews; the backdrop to Hicks' childhood was the Friends' Meeting House the tiny local Liberal Jewish community hired for services. Given both the ethno-religious imperative, and the sense of outsider-ness, it is perhaps also unsurprising that his first stage role, at prep school aged 11, was Shylock.

Hicks speaks frequently of his "lapsed" Jewishness; reaching adulthood, he vacillated between Rabbinical college and drama school. The latter won out. Though he's played Jewish characters only twice professionally (Jesus in Berkoff's *Messiah* and Roy Cohn in Kushner's *Angels in America*), director David Farr, a frequent collaborator since 2003, nonetheless attributes some of the strength of their working relationship to shared perceptions moulded by Jewish upbringing (*personal interview*, 13/1/10, *and passim*).

There is also a vestigial trace of the Jewish discursive tradition in the style of Hicks' approach to text. At the table of a rehearsal room, spectacles perched on nose, pen jabbing pedantically at his script as he questions the meaning of a line, there is yet something Rabbinical about him: his inquiring intellect probing textual detail, then free-wheeling associatively, the style of his semantic and philosophical debate distinctly Talmudic.

Hicks' cerebral instincts welcome paradox and duality; he seeks their physical expression in *butoh* and *capoeira*. In headstands and swinging kicks, in agonisingly slow walking, he finds form through which to embody the relationship between these "inners" and "outers": this reflexivity of inner effort and outer action, each affecting and being affected in turn by the shifting of the other. Perhaps butoh and capoeira are now his religions.

Capoeira exists in the interstices of dance and martial arts, associated with slave communities in Brazil and dating back at least two centuries. Its precise origins and relationship to slavery are the subject of some scholarly debate. In the romantic view of its history, it is a martial art practised by slaves to resist their masters, disguised in the form of dance. Its signature kicks have been attributed to the shackling of the hands of its originators. Certainly it was banned for many years in Brazil and practice was a criminal offence; it gained respectability in the second half of the 20th century as an art form, and exploded in popularity around the world towards the millennium. A *roda*, the clapping, swaying circle of capoeiristas with drums and *berinbaum* (a stringed percussion instrument resembling a longbow), is by now a familiar sight in British parks and public spaces, the dancers within the circle engaging in dazzling displays of acrobatic headstands, kicks and rhythmic sallies and retires with their opponents. The sparring is an intricate, improvised duel in dance, not without danger; the contact of whirling limbs and heads is a genuine risk.

Hicks has practised capoeira since the mid-1990s, travelling to Brazil to study the form, and incorporating it extensively into his acting work. In his dressing-room before performance he stretches and exercises to a recording of the rhythmic *toqué* of the *batería* and *berinbaum*. In rehearsals for *Bacchai* at the National in 2002, Hicks would spar with fellow cast-member Chuk Iwuji during breaks. They brought capoeira to the on-stage relationship (and the fights) between their characters in *Coriolanus* in 2004, in which Iwuji played Aufidius to Hicks' Coriolanus. It appears too in less obvious contexts: upon the first entry of Kathryn Hunter as the Fool in *King Lear* (2010), Hicks gave out a lazy wheeling kick, Hunter ducking with the suggestion of a practised greeting routine between them; he used it also for a short solo dance, alone on the vast Olivier stage, at his first entry as Dionysus in *Bacchai* (2002), before donning the vast golden bull mask of the player-god.

Hicks is keen to pass on his enthusiasm. He performed in a full capoeira "version" of *Bacchai* (*In Blood*) at the Arcola Theatre in 2009, playing Gordilho (this time the Penthean role). During the run of *In Blood*, he led a capoeira workshop for acting students with his teacher, Mestre da Silva, and has since introduced capoeira classes at the RSC.

Butoh is, in Hicks' work, the symbiotic partner of capoeira. Where capoeira is free-flow and quick, butoh is bound, viscid, sustained. Deriving from Japanese Noh, yet also subverting tradition, butoh appeared in Japan after World War II, associated with anti-authoritarian protest and with the experience of the atomic bombs. White-faced performers are moved, as if by outside force rather than personal volition, sometimes with extreme slowness in tortuous and anguished positions, or like jerky, unwilling puppets subject to the manipulation of some giant hand.

Like capoeira, Hicks has introduced butoh to his colleagues and to companies he's worked with, often with his teacher, Marie-Gabrielle Rotie. He drew very consciously – and visually – on the form for his spectral, more-haunted-than-haunting Ghost in *Hamlet* (2004). The Ghost appeared, not armoured cap-a-pé but painted white and near-naked, in the manner of the members of Sankai Juku, one of the most famous butoh companies. He moved with elaborate and exaggerated slowness, dragging a giant sword, eyes rolling up in his head.

It may be that in his work with these two disciplines Hicks proves to be a more influential theatrical figure than the ephemerality of performance affords. He has brought movement forms at the fringes of the British theatrical consciousness onto its major classical stages, experimenting with them both as training and performance tools. Rather than invoking a traditional "acting" system (Stanislavski or the Method, for example), Hicks is a tireless missionary for butoh and capoeira, referring to them in almost every recent interview; more quietly but equally insistent, he introduces them to his fellow actors, though he makes no particular claims to being a teacher of either, rather facilitating their teaching by others.

Why should these two particular movement forms have so influenced him? Both are related to disguise, to the mask; both are born of frustration and tragedy; both are anti-establishment, subversive, anti-authoritarian; both are philosophical. Yet in each is also, crucially, ingrained a deep vein of anarchic, iconoclastic humour: in the jerky human puppets of butoh, in the held-breath near-misses of capoeira, we have the opportunity to experience the constant possibility of failure, and to laugh at it nervously.

II

Hicks' ability to make his dualities exist on stage – to inhabit them in the moment – is a great part of his appeal and charisma as a performer. Many of his choices seem to live equally on either side of the scales of truth; these complex, "double" details are also inevitably rooted in the style of his textual approach. In Act II scene ii of *Julius Caesar* (as Caesar, RSC 2009), Hicks would achieve a robust laugh from the audience on, "How foolish do your fears seem now, Calpurnia? / I am ashamed I did yield to them" – not a line which might appear comic on the page. His delivery, which clearly acknowledged the audience without addressing them directly, at once suggested the bombastic self-regard of the dictator, and a proleptic, foreknowing irony.

A more prosaic comic ambiguity appeared in his turn as Dr Caius in *Merry Wives* (2003) (a rare foray into Shakespearean comedy). The French Doctor's repeated expostulation, "By Gar!" was pitched by the actor equidistantly between a florid imprecation – "By God" – and the more earthy oath: "Bugger!" One was led by these two words (or one) to imagine Caius' difficulties learning English: back-story sketched with great economy of means.

What unites both these choices is the actor's willingness for the audience to infer layered, and even contradictory, meanings from his presence. Timing is key here; there can be, as in both examples above, a "catch-up" effect, meanings read consecutively, which tends to elicit a laugh; or they can be simultaneous, an emotional body blow. In IV.iii of *Julius Caesar* (2002), Hicks as Brutus responded to Cassius' (Tim Piggott-Smith) nagging insistence that he had not denied gold with a crushingly inhabited and massively present reading of a two-word line. Working ferociously against emotion – this is the scene in which Brutus carries around the knowledge of Portia's death silently – Hicks went about a quotidian sequence of business, washing his hands and face, taut as a wire with repressed grief and fury. As Cassius' petulant self-justification reached unbearable stridency – "I denied you not!" – Hicks paused fractionally before exploding the water in the washing-bowl with one hand, his arm outstretched with vicious speed to Cassius: "Y' DID!" Piggott-Smith reeled from the sheet of water coming at him. In one moment Hicks was an admonitory, exasperated parent and a misunderstood child.

On that vocal note: the "Y'" for "You" (and "Yer" for "Your") is a distinctive characteristic in Hicks' sharp tenor voice, as is his orotund "O". Indeed, "O" is a sound – and an expostulation – he seems to revel in enunciating and inflecting. His "O" is grand, visceral; it's also flattened, demotic, East Midlands:

"*YooooUuw Common Cry of Curs…I Could a Tale unfOwOld…OooooowWoh! Reason Not the Need!…Hooouuwwl! Ha-Ooouuuwwwl…!*"

Hicks is conscious of how he uses his voice. He is conscious of his vowels; he is conscious of his alliteration of consonants. His characteristic stretching of the first half of the verse line, and then coiling the latter half back, whip-like, is conscious. He is conscious of the Midland twang in his accent, which he keeps even in aristocratic parts; many actors of his generation would not do so, rather – perhaps *un*consciously – heightening their "Shakespearean" accents.

For some, his style is too conscious; and Hicks is commensurately *self*-conscious about it:

> "Not everybody likes the way I do things, I quite understand that. I have a very particular style which some people find really..." he stops and thinks carefully about the next word "...shite. They see it as too studied, too mannered, too presented."
>
> (*The Guardian*, 10/10/05)

This "physical" actor, then, is also one of our "greatest verse-speakers". Hicks is conscious of both the notion of theatrical style, and of his own style; the relationship of style to truth is the great conundrum of the post-Stanislavskian actor. Hicks' stylisation, and his consciousness of it, creates a crucial effect: that of the character being aware of his own stylised self, and the untruths that self-awareness entails. In other words, the great Shakespearean gift: irony.

This irony has led critics on occasion to see his performances as detached, with the actor standing at a remove from the character. His vocal pyrotechnics can be interpreted as mannerisms, and his choices are dismissed by some as "tricks" – perhaps the dirtiest word in the post-Stanislavskian lexicon. These criticisms are injudicious, often unfair. They miss the richness of Hicks' dualities, interpret only the superficies of his performance, and neglect both the intensity with which he inhabits character and situation, and the thought he puts into his craft. But there's also sometimes confusion as to what kind of actor he is, a difficulty in "reading" him, which may derive from another particular ambiguity in his work: that of his age, and where to place him in the theatrical continuum.

III

"Just so you all know," director David Farr announces on the first day of rehearsals for *King Lear*, "Greg will be, er, made to look, er..."

"Not the stripling that he is?" somebody suggests.

"Yes, made to look...old."

At 56, Hicks' torso has the defined musculature of a 30-year-old, and is bared frequently both in performance and rehearsal. He seems a much younger actor than he is. Few actors fresh out of drama school could match his headstands. Indeed, he's been nervous about being an overly youthful Lear; one of his first decisions about the character is to age his voice, deepening to a baritone rasp. He's still haunted by the offhand comment of one of his drama school tutors more than three decades before: "You'll never get anywhere with a voice like that." He refers to this often: one suspects he takes it (and perhaps it was meant) more as a challenge than an admonition.

Hicks' drama school, the Rose Bruford College of Speech and Drama, was founded in 1950, and was a newish and still radical institution when he attended. Bruford, a renowned voice teacher, had been a student of Elsie Fogerty at Central, steeped in the verse-speaking tradition of Poel. Her school combined this tradition with the principles of Stanislavski, and was thus one of the first in the UK to marry the "English tradition" and Russian actor training.

Hicks trained at Bruford in the early 70s: the Manson family; Black September; Vietnam; Nixon's resignation; the Yom Kippur War; the industrial actions and escalation of the Troubles under Heath's Tory government (the college being in Heath's own constituency of Bexley); decimalisation; and entry into the European Economic Community (EEC). A time too of great theatrical events, a time to be a young actor: Brook and Hughes' *Orghast* at Persepolis; the opening of the Bouffes du Nord; Olivier's final stage appearance; Peter Hall taking over as Director of the National; the publication of Uta Hagen's *Respect for Acting*; the end of censorship; the infant fringe booming; the foundation of Glasgow Citizens Theatre by Giles Havergal, Robert David MacDonald and Philip Prowse, who would become a career-long friend, mentor and collaborator.

Indeed, Hicks' career trajectory since that time might be seen in terms of a series of lengthy collaborations with a few directors: respectively Bogdanov, Prowse, Hall and, more recently, Farr.

The influence on him of each of the three theatrical elders has been significant: Bogdanov political, daring and relentlessly iconoclastic; Prowse an aesthete and demotic polymath; the magisterial Hall's rationality, precision and principle; all three in different ways radical. However, Bogdanov directed him only twice in Shakespeare (out of seven productions together); Hall also twice – as Aufidius to Ian McKellen's Coriolanus at the NT in 1984 and as Edgar at the Old Vic in 1997 – out of 13 collaborations; Prowse never (eight productions). This is in contrast to his more recent collaboration with Farr: in four productions, three Shakespearean leads and one Marlovian.

Statistically at least, it is in this mature period and this collaboration that Hicks has found his stature as a Shakespearean, though his apprenticeship in the 70s and 80s – working with Nunn, Barton, Dexter and Bogdanov on Shakespeare, with Hall on the *Oresteia*, with Mike Alfreds on Chekhov's *Cherry Orchard* – was an enviable continuation of the training begun at Rose Bruford.

With this as a backdrop, the range of Hicks' more recent collaborations is striking. He shows considerable trust in his juniors, placing his reputation in the hands of up-and-coming directors in experimental and small-scale work; he collaborates with writers and dancers; he seeks to pass on his craft in classes and workshops. He is of both the generation of rep and of the generation of the fringe, and perhaps he is caught between them.

IV

In this section, I turn to Hicks' Shakespearean performances since 2002, all at the RSC. Since then, his status as one of the UK's leading classical actors has been confirmed both in castings and critical responses. Contextually, one should note the startling array of non-Shakespearean roles he has undertaken since 2000. His parallel theatre career is almost unique in its breadth, from the tiniest of spaces to the grandest, from the most modern to the most ancient, from Apollonian temples to Orphean underworlds.

Touring internationally in Peter Hall's ten-hour masked production of John Barton's Trojan War cycle, *Tantalus*, Hicks received great acclaim in the roles of Priam, Agamemnon and Menelaus. He worked with Hall again – masked once more – in 2002 as Dionysus in *Bacchai* at the NT. With the title role in Hall's *Oresteia* (1980) and Tiresias in *The Oedipus Plays* (1996) behind him, it's reasonable to say that his reputation as a Greek mask actor is unique in the UK. Unmasked, he played Jesus in Berkoff's *Messiah* and Roy Cohn in Kushner's *Angels in America*, and the title role in Farr's production of *Tamburlaine the Great*. At East London's arty, grungy Arcola, he played Dr Stockmann in Ibsen's *An Enemy of the People* and Gordilho in *In Blood*. He returned to work with Colin Teevan (adapter of *Bacchai*), on *Missing Persons*, a one-man show weaving Greek myth, the IRA and football, performed at Edinburgh and in London's 80-seat Trafalgar Studios 2.

Despite this eclecticism, Hicks is very strongly associated with the RSC. He's been described as an "RSC Megalith" (*The Guardian*, 10/10/09, an interview about playing Tamburlaine), and in the same interview as an "RSC stalwart"; the latter phrase crops up elsewhere, for instance in the reviews of *Missing Persons* in both the *Sunday Times* and the *Evening Standard*. Indeed, "RSC stalwart" is a phrase that seems to fit Hicks in particular; it is a martial honorific with a 17th-century ring. It also implies that the RSC is a challenge – or burden. It almost follows his name. *You know…Greg Hicks, the RSC stalwart.*

To be accurate, Hicks is called an RSC stalwart mostly when he isn't at the RSC. It gives a stamp of the RSC's authority to his fringe exploits, and perhaps also ensures name recognition for this actor who still carries such a degree of anonymity.

In 2002, 16 years after his last – and only "juve" – RSC lead (when he was an unlikely cast-change takeover from Sean Bean's Romeo), Hicks played Brutus for the company in a production directed by Ed Hall. Despite the more familiar face of Tim Piggott-Smith as Cassius, the centrality of Hicks' Brutus in this version was clear. In a sequence of great beauty at the end of II.i Brutus, left alone on stage, stared into the garden pool as the forthcoming murder of Caesar appeared in shadow play on a red-lit cyc behind him. With a horrified slashing movement, Hicks struck the water into a glittering sheet, dispelling the vision (prefiguring the washing bowl moment in IV.iii, as described in II above) and framing the central action of the play simply, as Brutus' phantasma.

Hicks' troubled and intelligent Brutus was played with great inner intensity, contained by a measured, sustained, but almost desperate, outer control. The production, whose style hinted equally at ancient Rome and Mussolini's Italy, supported a performance in which Brutus' self-control seemed a natural, effortful reaction to a police state. His Coriolanus of 2003, in his first collaboration with David Farr, was a different beast: quick-tempo, sudden and mobile. In contrast to the adamantine self-discipline of Brutus, Hicks' Coriolanus was a man vibrating with the possibility of explosion or meltdown. In the Gown of Humility scene (II.iii), exasperated by his own nervousness at public speaking, his insistent mocking of the citizens' "voices" was the mask of a fearful man; his exultation at news of impending war in I.i was its necessary underlying opposite. The "Samurai" Japanese-styled production made the duality of the central character seem deeply aligned with that of his world. Hicks' Brutus exerted control over himself. His Coriolanus was by contrast controlled by his world – until he discovered that it was elsewhere.

The setting of *Coriolanus* naturally fitted both Hicks' practice of butoh and his love of the films of Kurosawa (from which he frequently draws inspiration). In his working relationship with Chuk Iwuji, it was an outlet for his capoeira. Butoh and capoeira became, in this highly physical characterisation, expressions of the relationship between control and self-abandonment; the movement of the hooded exile of the play's second half hinted at the more extreme butoh stylisation of the Ghost the following year. The synchrony of passions and part clearly worked: Hicks was nominated for the Olivier (Best Actor) and received a Critics' Circle Award (Best Shakespearean Performance).

In rep with Coriolanus, he was performing in a casting as unusual as the pairing of plays: Dr Caius in *The Merry Wives of Windsor*, directed by Rachel Kavanaugh. There was thought behind the pairing. Aside from sharing a name, the two characters were both irascible and self-regarding – and in their self-regard ridiculous.

Hicks spoke at the time (in an interview in the *SOLT Official London Theatre Guide*, 13 June 2003) of the psychologically "healthy" opportunity of performing tragedy and comedy simultaneously; he seems to get few opportunities to do the latter. He alludes frequently in interviews to psychological health; it seems at times a grail, at times a gift. In a recent interview – ominously titled *What playing King Lear does to an actor* – he said, with a typical mix of self-awareness and self-consciousness:

> "Are you having fun?" someone said to me the other day. Of course it would be indulgent for me to say, "No, I'm suffering for my art." That's not the case. But I wouldn't say I'm having fun. It's too difficult for that.
>
> (*Financial Times*, 26/2/2010)

The ghoulish butoh ghost in *Hamlet* (Michael Boyd, 2004) was perhaps the nadir of suffering: pure white, skeletally pathetic, grim as a soul in torment should be. However, Hicks found comic equilibrium here in doubling: a very funny Gravedigger, and a restrained and graciously formal Player King, recalling the Ghost through physical echoes in each. A great ensemble performance, and one which hints at the underlying reasons for his search for comedy in even the darkest roles. This quest for equilibrium seems to drive more of Hicks' work than is necessarily obvious from his performances.

After considerable acclaim for his Ghost – a part which does not always attract either praise or censure – *Macbeth* (2004) had Hicks' name all over it, the next step in his Hamletless ascent through Shakespeare's tragic *cursus honorum*. However, the production and his performance were generally received either coolly or disappointedly, as if it were too obvious that Hicks was a "perfect" Macbeth for that to be the case in fact. True to form, though, he found the humour in this blackest play:

> [Hicks] has some wonderful riffs when he inflects Macbeth's later soliloquies with a "this is all so beyond a joke, it's a joke" tone of exhausted, punch-drunk irony.
>
> (*The Independent*, 23/3/2004)

Macbeth was the termination of three consecutive years at the RSC, unbroken other than by a short engagement in Berkoff's *Messiah* at the Old Vic. In interviews after he left the company, Hicks spoke of a desire to leave theatre itself behind for a time. This was not to be; the following year saw *Missing Persons* and *Tamburlaine*, in which he found, once more in an unremittingly and narcisistically negative protagonist, a bleak ridiculousness. He went on to shows in Liverpool and at the West Yorkshire Playhouse (another tragic clown: the title role in *Don Quixote*), and three small-scale productions at the Arcola.

Hicks returned to the RSC in 2009, from stalwart, perhaps, to elder statesman. A three-year contract signalling the RSC's return under Michael Boyd's leadership to a long-term ensemble: fourteen plays including *King Lear*, international touring, and the resumption of his collaboration with David Farr.

In the opening production of the "long ensemble", Hicks played Leontes in *The Winter's Tale*. Conceived by director Farr as the first stage in a progression to the Lear planned for 2010, Hicks' Leontes, in Farr's words, was a "domestic" hero, rather than a tragic one. In a production visually reminiscent of Arthur Rackham and Gothic Victoriana, the diseased jealousy of Leontes was a madness of symbolic, fairytale proportion in the mind – again in Farr's words – of "a quiet man".

Farr, himself quite a quiet man, felt that Leontes presented a particular challenge for Hicks, pushing the actor to "soften…I think that's linked to listening", in playing a character noteworthy for his incapacity to listen. This note, from Hicks' closest current collaborator in a distinguished line of them, appears to acknowledge that the intensity of the actor's focus can seem intimidating and introspective to those around him.

Farr's open, gentle intelligence, and his understated directorial presence, are interesting foils for Hicks. They both share a quick inner tempo; but when, at work, Hicks can seem obsessive and intent, Farr fizzes lightly. In rehearsal Hicks holds a vast circle of attention; Farr is naturally intimate in his interactions, using little personal space, vocal volume or physical weight. While Hicks' inspiration seems to strike from louring thunderclouds, Farr's ideas generate with the quality of a Van de Graaf: busy, local, surprising even to their originator. Farr in rehearsal beams with enthusiasm at everything, as if pleasantly surprised to be making theatre; Hicks smiles seldom while working (when he does it's a dramatic event). Farr's fingers and knees jiggle, he mouths lines as actors speak them; Hicks seems always to be imposing – though only just – an iron physical self-discipline, suppressing the nerves.

They are, perhaps, unlikely fellow journeyers in some ways; in others naturally contending and yielding partners in collaboration. Farr speaks of "framing Greg in a way he's comfortable with; he becomes a collaborator in terms of the vision of the piece". Their intense creative relationship has engendered some of Hicks' best performances, in visually arresting, memorable productions. Is there a cost? It might seem to some that Farr's creative process in their work together is too predicated on his lead actor, though that censure may derive from the twin, though perhaps paradoxical, British obsessions with ensembles and directorial hegemony.

Hicks as a leading stage actor can carry a redolence of an earlier generation of stars, yet directors turn to him in collaborations of emotional and creative intensity, often over many years. Much as he is high-status in a rehearsal room (even from its physical fringes and while standing on his head) he seems to find it easy to plug directly into the directorial vision of another. He evinces no personal interest in "crossing the House" to direct, and yet, in rehearsal, it is clear that Hicks is acutely aware of his relationship to the cosmos of the production, attuned to it rather than controlling it – which is most of what a director requires. I've never heard him in rehearsal refuse to try something out; he never says that he's not "feeling it", never blocks an idea, offers many. Indeed, he sniffs out huge ideas, hunts them down, runs them to ground, and then, Laocoön-like, grapples openly and physically with them.

During the first three months of 2010, I was able to observe Hicks, Farr and the RSC company in rehearsal for *King Lear*; I devote the final section of this essay to those rehearsals. Inevitably, my focus is still on Hicks as Lear. However, I should record here the great satisfaction, and inspiration, of observing the work of Kathryn Hunter (the Fool), Kelly Hunter (Goneril), Darrell D'Silva (Kent), Katy Stephens (Regan), Geoffrey Freshwater (Gloucester), and the rest of the company, and thank them all for their openness in allowing a stranger with a notebook to intrude upon their rehearsal room. I hope that my abstract and brief chronicle might mirror theirs. Where it diverts, it is a very personal impression I record. Inevitably, there were many memorable moments; the following is just a smattering of snapshots which give a sense – no more – of Greg Hicks at work.

V

Mid-November 2009, RSC rehearsal room in Clapham

Greg Hicks has made a lot of choices. Read-through etiquette is something on which there is some division among actors. Still, a broad consensus seems to exist: that it is best *not* to act in a read-through. It's perhaps unclear what might be meant by "acting", when the 30-or-so-strong company, actors and creatives, are sitting around a quadrangle of tables, reading aloud. Highlighter pens have done their work: now pencils hang above scripts, little Damoclean swords ready to fall on choices.

To my eyes, "acting" in these circumstances means "making choices": adding details of behaviour or inflection to the text. Whether in Darrell D'Silva's Rotherham mumble, Geoff Freshwater's rich, smoky boom, Kathryn Hunter's treacly sing-song or Kelly Hunter's diffident, throwaway tones, the majority of the company definitively chooses *not* to act, to read the text with nugatory inflection. It avoids imposition, preferring discovery. It leaves the text neutral, a blank canvas, and it negates the possibility of being judged.

If most avoid judgement, Hicks seems to seek it. His reading, seated on the director's right hand, is rich with choices. I wonder: how many will remain in performance? Is he opening up ideas or closing options down?

There's virtuosity to the textual details, and they're attached to obvious moments: every iconic line, every famous coinage, every character crux is given a firm "reading". Hicks is carefully attaching carabiners to the rock-face or mountain to which the part is so often compared, at those sheer places where so many actors before him have dug in their own. He laughs chummily to the court before "Nothing will come of nothing"; fires "Peace Kent" from his characteristic pistol-like point; yelps houndishly on "O reason not the need"; belabours "I am a man more sinned against…" with Vulcanic hammer-blows of irony; drops to a hollow whisper for "unaccommodated man". Only the storm scene (III.ii) signally remains uninflected and underplayed. Perhaps only these most visceral and elemental words resist choices until rehearsed physically.

There's a comic choice too, hidden in a line which seems both to demand humour and reel from it.

> No, you unnatural hags
> I will have such revenges on you both ...
> That all the world shall – I will do such things –

At this point a glance of senile confusion, the introspective muddle of age –

> What they are yet I know not –

Lear collects himself at the caesura, and goes back on a strident offensive:

> —but they shall be
> The terrors of the earth...

Everybody laughs. It's a typical Hicks moment: the acute, self-observed human frailty buried in a landslide of rhetoric.

Mid-December (raining outside)

Rehearsing the storm scene (III.ii), and the mood itself is turbid. As the scene is read, Hicks works unconsciously at the ring on his finger – wringing it. Darrell D'Silva (Kent) and the aptly named James Gale (Gentleman and Hicks' understudy) seem restless; movement director Anne Yee inward and thoughtful; Farr higher tempo than usual, as if time is oppressing him.

Are these internal storms an inverse pathetic fallacy? Discussing the text around the busily laden rehearsal room table (papers, editions of the play, coffee cups, water bottles), Hicks speaks of the storm as "the twisted, fertile landscape of my imagination" and focuses on the possibility of a "skeleton in the cupboard" of Lear's family – has the king "fucked his daughters"? Farr replies gently: "I would be loath to suggest so much."

Hicks worries immediately at the reference to Lear being bare-headed, trying to find a place in the text when he might cast off a putative headpiece, proposing: "Fool, I shall go mad." It's the first strong idea he's attached to a particular moment in this scene, though it's an odd choice, practical rather than interpretative. He's seeing the actuality of playing the part, no longer the idea, trying to feed a rope of psychophysical detail through the textual carabiners, and there's a latent sense of this scene as a character summit.

There seems to be a degree of avoidance in the unusually scattered discussion, and transference in the tension. When the scene is finally played on its feet, there's a lot of imprecise "weather acting" going on. Hands clinging to sides, faces in rictus grins of cold, leaning against the non-existent wind: too much acting, not enough imagination supporting it. Everyone seems unsatisfied, the frustration of laborious inertia.

In response, Yee leads an exercise in which Hicks stands, his legs held in place by the diminutive Hunter and the burly D'Silva, torso buffeted by Gale behind him, declaiming the great set-piece speeches, "Blow, winds…" and "Let the great gods…". He bends and elongates the vowels as his weight is shifted by this physicalised storm; he seems almost to vomit the words "ingrateful man". Hunter's lithely sympathetic, sad Fool, clinging to Hicks' ankles, seems animistic, a familiar or totem. D'Silva, almost aggressively pragmatic, screws up his eyes to the lashing elements: he plays the given circumstances, the storm real to his Kent, no figment of Lear's imagination but of the actor's own. The "weather acting" now looks like a blasted truth.

It's a very powerful exercise to watch, unlinear and non-literal. The effect seems to radiate from Hicks to the other actors centrifugally, transforming their own imaginative responses.

Early January

Round 2: having passed once through the play, roughly chronologically, the company are now, after the Christmas break, rehearsing each scene again. In a standard rehearsal schedule, the second assay at a scene is usually expected to be a "fixing" rehearsal: if not to carve the detail of the scene in stone, at least to hew the shape.

So we are returning to Act I, scene i. As Farr explains changes to the set to the company, Hicks is in the opposite corner of the room, upside down.

Lear's first entry remains as in early rehearsals. On Gloucester's "the King is coming!" the court bows towards the central entrance upstage; Lear will appear downstage behind them, through the audience, to their dawning consternation. When first rehearsed, Hicks was testing the court's expectations, leaving a lengthy silence before walking to sit in his throne for "Meantime we shall express…" The timing of his pause is remarkably similar to before, but now he is mocking his courtiers in complicity with Hunter's Fool. The laugh spreads nervously around the court. Hicks laughs again, this time mocking them through high-status self-mockery, on "…while We / Unburdened crawl toward death."

But the mockery is also vain; as always, ironic and layered. This Lear wants, in Hicks' gloss, "a public display, and I want it to be appreciated". The jocularity of his invitations to his daughters to stand on wooden boxes and declare their love for him, like contestants on a Medieval gameshow, heightens the awful mortification of Cordelia's rejection on "Nothing, my Lord". Hicks mouths "Nothing will come of nothing" to her, trying to snatch a moment of impossible intimacy after the bombast of the set-up. At her insistence, he attempts to seize back his dignity, casting rueful, embarrassed smiles to his courtiers, expecting the like in response.

It's very funny, a little grotesque. As the company run the opening again, Kathryn Hunter adds a jaunty "Evenin' all" to the Fool's entrance, to the confusion of the court. The consequent versions of the scene are progressively weirder, and all differently detailed. A strong sense emerges of Lear's different attitude to his daughters: husbandly towards Goneril; almost overtly sexual towards Regan (is Hicks still imagining a skeleton in the cupboard?); beaming with the pride of a young father for his toddler at Cordelia. His rage at Kent's admonition erupts into a violent impulse which his age cannot sustain: Hicks draws a sword, but stumbles. With each iteration of the scene, the details and the character are shifting perceptibly into something richer and stranger, which offers an answer to my read-through question: Hicks wasn't closing options down, but sniffing out opportunities to hunt.

Throughout rehearsal, Hicks has been working hard at the details of ageing, exploring different centres of balance, different tempos, using different muscle groups. Ageing can be an actor's nightmare: there is a risk of losing energy, of playing a lethargic negative quality. By the end of this day Hicks' age-playing has found its will-to-youth, its energy. An arcing rope has been strung between the carabiners of details and choices; and between his two generations.

Acting theory often considers narrative – in various terminologies – in terms of arcs. A character has an arc in a play, in a scene, in a single line. The arc of this day's rehearsal is a familiar, quotidian one for Hicks as for many actors: fear is annihilated by work, by the rehearsal room's permissiveness of failure.

If this day is a line, this production a scene in his career – perhaps late in the third or early in the fourth act – and if the daily arc is a microcosm of the whole – then perhaps, I wonder, at this apogee of his career, he has found some equilibrium.

After rehearsals finish that day, Greg does seem relaxed. I ask him, "Are you having fun?"

He responds: "Fun?…ummm…I don't…"

After a pause, indistinctly: "Know." Or maybe he just says, "No."

Epilogue

At the performance of *King Lear* I attended in preparation for this essay, I was sitting among people who might be thought of as the RSC's classic demographic: at the upper ends of middle-age, middle-class, middle-England; if not the backbone of British theatre, at least one of its load-bearing spokes, the unsung, off-stage "RSC stalwarts". A comfortable conversation was taking place in front of me as two such spectators, apparently strangers, exchanged with quiet cordiality their feelings anticipating this monolithic tragedy of age and of ego:

FIRST RSC STALWART:	(*Politely, turning to her neighbour*) So, how d'you feel about *Lear*?
SECOND RSC STALWART:	Well, we came to see Greg Hicks, really – he's always very good.
FIRST RSC STALWART:	Oh, yes? (*With apparent mild embarrassment, turning to face the stage*) Oh, yes, always. *Pause* It'll be interesting, *Lear*.

There is still this air of anonymity. If I told people I was writing about Greg: *Who's he, again? What's he been in?* Yet he reaches out performatively to a wide audience: the RSC stalwarts, the cognoscenti, the Fringe make-do-and-menders, the experimental theatre wing, the citizens of the global theatre, the mystics, the acting students, the scholars. He reaches out also in speaking about his craft (few British actors are as willing to buck the public's distaste and discuss what they do in interviews with the same frankness as he does), and in passing on his disciplines and enthusiasms in workshops and studios. These are the public "outers" of his work: one senses that the corresponding "inners" are engaged in a serious, deeply personal, sometimes introspective search. Maybe Greg's right: maybe fun isn't part of it.

The storm on the heath is tonight, in performance, not a physical but a literal one. Hicks stands on a platform raised from the stage; to an apocalyptic soundscape and flashing lights the set collapses behind him and rain sluices down from the high ceiling of the Courtyard Theatre. It's a moment both banal and grandiose; I miss the muscular intensity of the rehearsal exercise. As technology evokes the reduction of Lear's world, Hicks looks, as his face inclines back into the light and water, very much like a man taking a shower after a hard day's work. It might be almost funny. *Lear's taking a shower.* But the shower, after all, is a contemporary icon of daily redemption, and Greg looks a bit like he might actually be at peace.

If the storm is baptismal, what follows is more surprising: the madness Hicks plays after it does look very much like fun. Or perhaps, it would be better to talk – and to have asked him – about 'playfulness'. Hicks' mad Lear, hopping about after Charles Aitken's Dürer-esque Poor Tom, is the most playful I've seen him: innocent, curious, easily amused, unweathered: in madness, for once the ironic distance is annihilated; though it must perforce emerge again, in the fugue and coda of Lear's return to the world as it is. For Shakespeare and for Hicks, awareness *is* ironic.

The madness of Hicks' Lear is the awareness of duality temporarily suspended, and it seems terribly seductive. It is typically ambiguous of Hicks to discover that for him, unaccommodatedness – the inversion of the reality of which we are aware, the Zen Nothing – consists of playfulness.

*

A final rehearsal snapshot. Discussing Lear's inner life, the notion that the Fool is Lear's therapist, and the speech: "Let me not be mad, not mad, sweet heaven! Keep me in temper: I would not be mad!" (I.v):

GREG HICKS:	"Fuuuuucck!" is going on underneath, the Fool is circumnavigating that "Fuuuuucck!", stimulating it.
KATHRYN HUNTER:	Do I leave him alone?...maybe he has to be alone?
HICKS:	Yup, that's it.
HUNTER:	So in terms of therapy, you can be led, but you have to do the last bit on your own...
HICKS:	Yes. You have to do the last bit on your own. *(He guffaws.)* *Pause*
HUNTER:	But what does he *fear* about madness?
HICKS:	Well, I mean, what do we all fear about madness?

Selected chronology

1976	Balthazar *Romeo and Juliet* Trevor Nunn/RSC
1976	Watch *Much Ado* John Barton/RSC
1976	Seyton *Macbeth* Trevor Nunn/RSC
1979	Silvius *As You Like It* John Dexter/NT
1982	Lorenzo *The Spanish Tragedy (Kyd)* Michael Bogdanov/NT
1983	Malcolm *Macbeth* Michael Bogdanov/NT
1984	Aufidius *Coriolanus* Peter Hall/NT
1985	Antonio *The Duchess of Malfi (Webster)* Philip Prowse/NT
1986	Romeo *Romeo and Juliet* Michael Bogdanov/RSC
1997	Edgar *King Lear* Peter Hall/Old Vic
2002	Brutus *Julius Caesar* Ed Hall/RSC
2003	Coriolanus *Coriolanus* David Farr/RSC
2003	Dr Caius *The Merry Wives of Windsor* Rachel Kavanaugh/RSC
2004	Ghost/Player King/Gravedigger *Hamlet* Michael Boyd/RSC
2004	Macbeth *Macbeth* Dominic Cooke/RSC
2005	Tamburlaine *Tamburlaine the Great (Marlowe)* David Farr/BOV/Barbican
2009	Leontes *The Winter's Tale* David Farr/RSC
2009	Julius Caesar *Julius Caesar* Lucy Bailey/RSC
2010	Lear *King Lear* David Farr/RSC
2010	Soothsayer *Antony and Cleopatra* Michael Boyd/RSC

About the author

Ben Naylor is a director and acting teacher. Currently Lecturer in Acting at the Central School of Speech and Drama, he studied Ancient History and Theology at Durham University and Magdalen College, Oxford, and acting with Reuven Adiv, John Beschizza and James Kemp at Drama Centre. Since 2000 he has directed numerous productions of plays by Shakespeare and his contemporaries; taught acting and theatre history in drama schools, studios and universities in the UK and abroad; and acted on film.

9
Rory Kinnear

Paul Prescott

I

> The actor is onstage to communicate the play to the audience. That is the beginning and the end of his and her job. To do so the actor needs a strong voice, superb diction, a supple, well-proportioned body, and a rudimentary understanding of the play.
>
> David Mamet (1999), 9

> The fluency of Shakespeare's movements, the subtle interpenetration of thought and emotion, the tangled web of motives, the mingling of the heroic with the familiar, the presence of constant verisimilitude under exceptional and exaggerated conditions, all demand great flexibility of conception and expression in the actor, great sympathy of imagination, nicety of observation, and variety of mimetic power. In these Charles Kean is wholly deficient.
>
> G.H. Lewes (1875), 16

What is Shakespearean acting? Does it require distinct equipment? How is Shakespearean acting any different than acting *per se*? Is the alpha and omega of a Shakespearean actor's job to 'communicate the play to the audience'? And what might that mean? Is it sufficient to have merely 'a rudimentary understanding' of the play you are in, or does Shakespearean playing, as Lewes insisted, demand 'great flexibility of conception [and] nicety of observation'? And what of emotion and motivation? According to Mamet's anti-Method polemic *True and False* (1999), the quest for a character's back-story and inner emotional life is a con foisted on the student of acting by vainglorious quacks. Yet for Lewes, writing before Stanislavsky (let alone the Method), the 'tangled web of motives' must be untangled if the actor is to do justice to Shakespeare (and distinguish his own efforts from those of Charles Kean.) Lewes may also call for 'constant verisimilitude' – but verisimilar to what? This piece cannot hope to answer these questions, but they and the epigraphs from which they spring might be borne in mind as terms of reference throughout this account of one actor's Shakespeare.

II

I first became aware of Rory Kinnear a few minutes into an undergraduate production of *Ghetto* at the Oxford Playhouse in 1996. I had some weeks earlier considered auditioning for the part of Kittel, the SS commander, but had failed to show up and was now curious to see how the occupant of the leather boots would fare. Rumour was that the role now belonged to a gifted first-year but nothing quite prepared for Kinnear-Kittel's first entrance, upstage centre and all cylinders immediately firing. An overgrown and dangerous boy in uniform, his immediate dominance of the space gave the apt impression of one man lynching a crowd. The clear, well-supported baritone voice sailed downstage and filled the theatre. There was something Marlovian about the entrance and the acting: it was large, imperious and histrionic, but remained on the right side of bombast. Unnervingly, enviably, this all seemed to be achieved by the late teenager without undue strain. Much of the power of this first entrance was a function of the part – Kittel *must* dominate, mark his territory – but the playing also served notice that here was an actor of uncommon presence and charisma.

In the following year, these first impressions were confirmed at close range when Kinnear and I acted in the same company for two undergraduate productions of *Volpone* and *The Taming of the Shrew* (Kinnear played the Fox and the Tamer). The sense of amplification, scale and confidence was, I could now observe, consistent across his acting. But other qualities quickly became apparent: the ludic invention during rehearsals, the roving, penetrating intelligence, and the desire – ebullient, perhaps incorrigible – to entertain the onlooker. In Mamet's provocatively spare formulation, Kinnear was already doing the job of an actor: he was in possession of a strong voice, superb diction, an athletic body and was certainly adept at communicating the play to the audience.

Fast-forward thirteen years, through the lifespan of the New Labour governments, from spring 1997 to the summer of 2010: Kinnear is now, at the time of writing, poised to play Hamlet at the National Theatre under Nicholas Hytner's direction. It is an honour bestowed on a British actor roughly once every decade and he will follow Peter O'Toole (1963), Albert Finney (1975–6), Daniel Day-Lewis / Ian Charleson (1989), and Simon Russell Beale (2000) in offering a Hamlet that will capture the form and pressure of its historical moment. On 9 December 2010, Kinnear's Hamlet will be transmitted live to cinemas across the world making his the most widely seen Shakespearean stage performance of the year, perhaps even of the century so far.

This chapter starts by joining the dots between the promising student actor of the mid-1990s and the performer who is now routinely described as one of the most exciting actors of his generation. It draws on eye-witness accounts – my own and others – of Kinnear's performances; it has also been substantially informed by a series of interviews conducted as he played the role of Angelo and prepared the role of Hamlet in the first half of 2010 (all quotations of Kinnear are taken from these interviews). These experiences offer windows into one contemporary actor's approach to a classical text; they are also his most detailed and distinctive contribution to Shakespearean theatre to date. *To date*: unlike most of the actors profiled in this volume, Kinnear has nearly all of the great Shakespearean roles stretched out in *front* of him. This, then, is a snapshot of an actor in midflight, an actor working hard, inventively and intelligently, to define his own Shakespeare.

III

Kinnear's path into the acting profession is relatively well trodden. Like many British actors and directors of the last fifty years, he studied an Arts subject (English Literature) at a good university (Oxford) before attending drama school (The London Academy of Music and Dramatic Art – L.A.M.D.A.), finding an agent and entering the world of work in his early twenties. In the first decade of his career, he has juggled stage and television work, with occasional forays into film. In the years 2005–9, for example, he spent almost exactly half each year on stage, the other half working in television.

Kinnear has mixed feelings about the value of an English Literature degree for his career. On the one hand, the experience of analysing dense texts is 'probably quantifiable' when it comes to preparing a classical role and is certainly useful in the first week of Shakespearean rehearsal which many directors choose to spend sitting round a table paraphrasing and elucidating the text. On the other hand, an ability to comprehend the texts by no means automatically transfers into an ability to perform them. It is drama school, then, that tends to have a defining influence on the young actor. Kinnear believes that L.A.M.D.A. both fitted his personality when he entered ('wholehearted but utterly ramshackle') and cultivated what he describes as a 'purist, philosophical approach to acting'. At university, he had relied on having an 'easy command of the stage, an easy command technically' and as a result had 'lapsed into giving "star" performances'. L.A.M.D.A. corrected this. His teachers, already confident that he would find work as an actor when he graduated, pushed him to 'keep working on the insides' of his characters. He would only improve, they insisted, if he was 'interested enough in mining for the truth'. This approach owes much to the work not only (and inevitably) of Stanislavsky, but also to the formative influence in British drama schools of practitioners like Michel Saint-Denis, himself inspired by the work of his uncle, Jacques Copeau: 'No *affectation* of any kind whatsoever, whether of the body, the mind, or the voice. What we are seeking is headlong harmony' (1970, 219). It is an approach which also promotes ensemble playing as 'the most complete and most exquisite joy in the theatre' (1970, 221) and in which individual performances are of value only to the extent that they contribute to the overall effect of a piece:

> Some people still love acting that demonstrates, that eulogizes the actor, but I don't. L.A.M.D.A. helped me to start looking out for what styles of acting meant the most to me, what moved me, what I enjoyed: it honed my sensibilities.

While Kinnear is clear on the value of formal training, his emphasis repeatedly returns to the unassailable benefits of learning on the job, the value of sheer experience. 'One has to work instinctively and that instinct only kicks in when working with other people and when performing the part.' On leaving L.A.M.D.A., Kinnear secured stage work as Konstantin (Northampton) and Caliban (Plymouth and touring); the latter, as far as I can tell, is the only performance for which he has received anything less than widespread critical approval. Some critics thought him miscast;

one claimed that he was at war with the verse and failed Shakespeare's poetry, an accusation often levelled at interesting actors (cf. Kean, Olivier) at the beginning of their careers. Kinnear subsequently signed for fourteen months with the Royal Shakespeare Company, playing Tranio in paired productions of *The Taming of the Shrew* and Fletcher's *The Tamer Tamed*, and 1st Gentleman and Caius Lucius in *Cymbeline*. His reflections on playing both Tranios are revealing: 'I grew to like Shakespeare's Tranio. I felt I found a heart to the part.' The role is the second longest in the play and drives the subplot, but requires creativity if the audience is going to invest much interest. Kinnear's performance balanced comic technique (his first tottering entrance in his master's too-tight shoes was beautifully executed pantomime) with an emotional undertow:

> He falls in love with playing the master; there was also the suggestion that there was this fledgling romance between Tranio and Bianca, but they always knew it would be unfulfilled because of their different statuses.

Fletcher's Tranio, on the other hand, he found 'pretty thin – it was just about trying to dupe somebody. There was not really any heart to be found there.' This need to find depth beneath the surface, a hinterland (or 'heart') to the character is of course common to all but the most alienated or alienating of actors. The quest for objectives, subtexts, back-stories and emotional arcs are staples of a Stanislavsky-based mimetic 'emotionalist' approach. As in the comparison between Shakespeare and Fletcher here, many actors relish playing Shakespeare – just as most audiences love watching it – for the richness of the characterization and the uncanny illusion of widespread individuality conjured in successfully naturalistic productions. Post-modernism might have announced the death of the character at roughly the same time as it attempted to annihilate the author, but both character and author are still alive and well in the mainstream theatre and are 'part of the *lingua franca* of our theatre, the set of assumptions that allow theatre artists to tell a story and for audiences to understand and to experience the story they are telling' (Mazer 2010, 359).

Kinnear speaks warmly of his experience in *Cymbeline*, the third of his productions with the R.S.C. in 2003–4. He relished 'the creative ethic' of Dominic Cooke's rehearsal process – 'a big room of props, we devised our own costumes: everything was up for grabs' – but also found his relatively small roles deeply instructive on a technical level. It is the 1st Gentleman who is charged with the taxing opening exposition of the play. There is no imperative to look for heart or subtext here, just the challenge of plunging the audience into dense late-Shakespearean exposition and bringing them out, safe and wiser, on the other side. Experimenting with different ways of 'using the verse to lift and point and suggest' was the most instructive experience of his season in the company.

On leaving the R.S.C., Kinnear played Laertes in Trevor Nunn's modern-dress, consciously youthful 2004 production of *Hamlet* at the Old Vic starring Ben Whishaw. Kinnear was praised for finding an unaccustomed range of hues in the character: '[Laertes] is bashful at court, sheepish with his father, dangerous in rebellion and the visceral shrieks he makes when he jumps into Ophelia's grave are the most unnerving strokes in this production' (Taylor, *Independent*). The actor of

Laertes has a notoriously long time offstage and Kinnear's stormy, keyed-up re-entry into this production might have hinted at an intense backstage process. We might remember Richard Flecknoe's report that Burbage 'so wholly transform[ed] himself into his part [...] as he never (not so much as in the "Tyring House") assum'd himself again until the Play was done.' But then Burbage never had to play Laertes. The run of *Hamlet* coincided with the European football championships and Kinnear would typically leave the stage in 1.3 (off to 'France'), get changed, walk the ten minutes from the Old Vic back to his flat, cook some dinner, watch a game, then stroll back to the theatre in time to lead the rebellion and avenge his father's death. He is generally 'very keen not to add to the lustre or the mystique of the process of acting' and this anecdote functions to remind us that acting is sometimes as much a 'mystery' in the early modern sense of a highly skilful or technical operation in a trade as it is the inexplicable workings of a capricious theatrical deity.

After Laertes, it would be another six years before Kinnear returned to Shakespeare. In these years he made the quantum leap from supporting actor to leading man, a leap that, by definition, most actors never make. (We should never forget that all of the actors featured in this volume are statistical freaks.) Under the direction of some of the UK's leading stage directors, he continued to play damaged sons – Michael in the stage adaptation of *Festen*, Piotyr in Gorky's *Philistines* – while his television work included suspicious loners, costumed aristocrats, and a young Dennis Thatcher. But his breakout stage performance came as Sir Fopling Flutter in Nicholas Hytner's garishly *au courrant* 2007 production of *The Man of Mode*. The role was not only an almost bespoke vehicle for Kinnear's skills (comedic, improvisational, musical), it also invited him to confront a distinct theatrical type – the Restoration fop – and rewire its settings. Critics noted a revelatory and unexpected pathos. The central psychological insight: that the posturing, the innumerable affectations, the collage of designer labels through which Sir Fopling assembled his identity were all attempts to win affection and approval, commodities in short supply in Etherage's hyper-materialistic London. The performance was awarded an Olivier for Best Supporting Actor and confirmed Kinnear's place near the top of National Theatre's caste/casting system.

IV

It was during the run of *The Man of Mode* in 2007 that Kinnear was unexpectedly called into Nicholas Hytner's office. The Artistic Director of the National Theatre proceeded to make one concrete and one speculative offer: Vindice in *The Revenger's Tragedy* in the 2008 season, and then, 'in the longer term', would Kinnear be interested in playing Hamlet? The National *Hamlet* was notionally planned for the 2009 season but was rapidly postponed following the news that both Jude Law and David Tennant would be playing the part in high-profile productions for the Donmar Warehouse and the R.S.C. respectively. The production would finally open in October 2010, three years after that initial conversation, and six years since Kinnear had appeared as Laertes in Trevor Nunn's production. When Angelo has greatness thrust upon him in the opening scene of *Measure for Measure*, his first response is to question his preparedness: 'Let there be some more test made of my metal / Before so noble and so great a figure / Be stamped upon it' (1.1.48–50). Analogously, with Hamlet on the near horizon, Kinnear looked around for some middle-distance Shakespearean role in which to work himself back in to the distinct challenges of the playwright.

At the beginning of the rehearsal process, what most attracted him to Angelo was the evolution of the character both during and between scenes. Other actors he had seen in the role had played the obvious and unavoidable crises of self ('What's this? What's this?' [2.2.168ff.]) but had not, as far as he could remember, differentiated between these selves. The role reconfigures on each appearance:

> What's nice about the part is that he gets a lot of changes on stage. You have to create your character at the beginning of the show – who he is, where he's come from, what job he does, his position in the court, friends (presumably not a lot) – and then you have to imagine the twenty-four hours after coming to power, how he's gone about changing things, how he's rubbing up against the old guard, how they're eventually deferring to him. And then you have these crises moments: finding yourself allured to somebody and then (I think unwittingly) finding yourself demanding…

The process Kinnear is describing here is one he calls 'Writing the Script'. It is based on the assumption that Shakespeare's characters are designed to resemble real people and that part of the actor's task is, in Lewes's words, to present 'constant verisimilitude under exceptional and exaggerated conditions'. To do this, you need to know/invent the character's background and what has happened in his life between each stage appearance. If Kinnear is playing characters located in a specific historical moment (e.g. Mitia in the Soviet Russia of *Burnt by the Sun*) he will undertake extensive research through wider reading, but for the modern-dress, modern-day Shakespeare performances of 2010 he is tending to work solely from the production's edited text of Shakespeare. ('There's so much there for you already.') When his teachers at L.A.M.D.A. had insisted that he keep working 'on the insides', it was this type of process they had in mind. 'Writing the Script' is a largely cerebral exercise for Kinnear:

> It's about thinking. Thinking moment to moment about what the character is thinking and to at all times know what's going on inside. And that when you're rehearsing, when you're performing (mainly when you're rehearsing), to have this otherness that's looking at your thoughts, looking at what's going on inside. Because you can say lines and people will believe you, but to avoid being generalized, to avoid it being parroted, the way that things will change is if you keep on looking for the holes in your performance, the ways you're gliding over stuff that you don't understand, the places where you've yet to make a decision.

Working on Angelo's insides in this fashion led to a performance dense with detail and nuance, one in which sheer interpretive intelligence was everywhere apparent.

Costume and appearance ('seeming, seeming!' [2.4.150]) were crucial in charting the changes. After the first week of rehearsal, each actor spoke to designer Lez

Brotherston; for Angelo, they discussed a dark suit, 'with overtones of piety' but Kinnear wanted to start more obscurely and less formally. His first entrance, minutes into the play, thus presented us with a flustered figure, jacketless, sleeves rolled up on an unfashionably beige shirt, evidently at the end or beginning of a punishing workaholic's shift. He was unangelically bearded and wore glasses for reading – a result of 'the "Guess Who?" approach to characterization', he jokes, referencing the children's game in which you deduce your opponent's chosen character by eliminating key facial features ('Glasses?' 'Yes'. 'Beard?' 'Yes'.) On the first preview, the effect was capped by the addition of a maroon tank-top, but this was soon dropped after a friend pointed out that this made the later costume changes seem like the stock soap-opera scene in which the hitherto plain girl removes her glasses, lets down her hair and transforms into a stunner. In effect, the tank-top was over-coding, tipping the appearance towards caricature, and would have to go. But Kinnear saw textual prompting for some transformation:

> Look at the lines in the opening soliloquy in 2.4: 'Could I with boot change for an idle plume': 'How often does thou with thy case, thy habit' [2.4.11–13] – it just felt like he'd changed himself in some way and that he was recognizing it. I wanted to materialize that change after meeting her.

Aptly for a play concerned with signs and signification, reviewers offered various decodings of the opening outfit and demeanour: a geography teacher, a Liberal Democrat councillor, a Stasi bureaucrat, and a refugee from a David Lodge campus comedy. (For the record, the appearance was indeed modelled on institutional figures from Kinnear's past, an unguessable hybrid of a former teacher and of a teenage classmate notorious for his ability to refrain from self-abuse.) The keynote of unpreparedness was sustained throughout the opening scenes: when Escalus expressed his uncertainty about his exact role (1.1.76ff) in the new administration, Angelo's ''Tis so with me' = 'me too; if you're confused, imagine how I feel.' Escalus ended the scene by offering to 'wait upon your honour' and Kinnear registered how extraordinary the title sounded with a self-deprecating, uncomfortable laugh and a shooing away gesture with his hand. The net effect of these individual readings was that the audience tangibly sympathized with this sudden putting on. The decisions taken in these first few minutes laid the groundwork for the rest of a performance in which this Angelo would almost always be on the back foot and struggling to adjust to external and internal pressures. The fact of these struggles did not vary from performance to performance; the reading of the part was a settled one. What did, of course, vary was the fashion (the intensity, the colouration, the tone and texture) with which these struggles were felt, processed and communicated in Kinnear's performance.

'Writing the script' for Angelo meant treating the descriptions offered by other characters with some scepticism. In 1.3, we hear the Duke's description of Angelo ('Lord Angelo is precise, [...] scarce confesses / That his blood flows [1.3.50–52]); in the following scene, we have Lucio's portrait of 'a man whose blood / Is very snow-broth; one who never feels / The wanton stings and motions of the sense' (1.4.56–58). Kinnear's main innovation was to take everything said about the character as unreliable: 'People talk about Angelo a lot, but nobody knows him.' Other actors in the part, especially in the opening scenes, have correlated far more closely to these descriptions (Ian Richardson's Angelo probably *did* urinate congealed ice). Kinnear's character was not the product of a sea-maid or two stock-fishes (3.1.371–72), he was the product of male-dominated institutions, the offspring of a public school and PricewaterhouseCoopers. In 2.1, sitting behind his desk, checking his watch while Pompey et al last out the night in Russia, his posture curved forward in impatience – he hadn't met Isabella yet, but there was nevertheless a sense of coiled energy, a series of hints that he was the uncomfortable inhabitant of a very nervous system. The blood readily mustered to his heart: 'Go to; let that be mine' (2.2.12) was a bad-tempered explosion at the Provost. The eventual discovery of his capacity for love was reminiscent of the small cardiacal tremor felt by Nabokov's Pnin: 'The repulsive automaton [his heart] he lodged had developed a consciousness of its own and not only was grossly alive but was causing him pain and panic' (2010, 13).

It is a good maxim for the performer that 'the character does not know what type of play he's in'. And this uncertainty is doubly apt for the actor in *Measure for Measure*, which is a play that barely knows what kind of play it's in. 'Pain and panic' are, of course, laughing matters. One of the most distinctive choices in this performance came in Kinnear's by-play in the moments before the second meeting with Isabella in 2.4. On his entrance in this scene, the first thing you noticed was the costume – a contemporary if not flashy suit with dark tie; the geek-to-chic translation was not too startling but effected the change Kinnear had sourced in the text. Before a word was spoken, he undertook to prepare the room for her arrival, primping the space in jittery bursts of energy – this was situational comedy and the audience responded as such. He attempted to pray, failed, then began his short soliloquy. A servant announced Isabella's arrival then exited to fetch her; alone again, Angelo's 'Oh heavens' (2.4.19) was delivered in a quasi-falsetto and with a slight pause before the rest of the line: the crisis again drew laughter. After the headline announcement 'Why does the blood thus muster to my heart–?', the ensuing several lines might as well have been spoken in Old Norse – nobody in the audience, I would hazard, heard a word of the stuff about the 'foolish throngs' and the 'well-wish'd king': our attention was entirely fixed on the speaker's fumbling and surprising attempt, hunched over his desk and without the aid of a mirror, to insert a pair of contact lenses. The act of vanity was strangely winning (perhaps 'mingling the heroic with the familiar' [Lewes]?) and offered a standout moment of business, pounced on by every reviewer seeking a handy synecdoche for the whole performance. It caused Kinnear some soul-searching. Was the moment 'truthful'? Perhaps not. But then again:

> It says a lot about the character in just that action. And also are the lines that it's covering, are they really that rewarding psychologically? That's why I wanted something there – those lines, I thought, might need some more colour. I'm always aware business shouldn't be for business's sake, but felt that it might actually add something.

In his defence, he might have cited Henry Irving's assertion that 'by-play [...] is of the very essence of true art. It is more than anything else significant of the extent to which the actor has identified with the character he represents' (2009, 31). In return, a purist might object that such additions villainously distract from what Hamlet calls 'some necessary question of the play' (3.2.42–43). But what *is* the necessity of these lines? If certain lines feel extraneous or bland, the actor has at least five options: 1) cut them; 2) discover/invent the reason why the playwright put them there (not that this will always help make them playable); 3) make them somehow psychologically rewarding; 4) cover them in business; 5) speak them clearly and/or beautifully and forget about psychology. In a less conservative production, the lines would simply have been cut and the ritual undergone in silence. Of the four remaining, the last option is generally the least attractive for Kinnear:

> What you can't do as a Shakespearean actor (and which I'm guilty of at times) is think, 'As long as people understand me, as long as I'm sharing the language with people, that it's so rich I don't need to do anymore.'

At stake in these and other choices are the dynamics of the actor-audience relationship; for Kinnear, a gifted comedian, such moments of by-play might unbalance a performance, even, momentarily, an entire production. The laughter in 2.4 was not a surprise – in rehearsals he had begun to think through parallels with that other inadvertently entertaining puritan, Malvolio – but throughout the run 'it was always a bit of a fight to subdue that response because you mustn't let them totally give into you. You have a responsibility for them to be both attracted and repulsed in equal measure.' Measure for measure indeed. It is exactly the thrill of this kind of tight-rope walking, this affective push-and-pull, that keeps actors returning to work in live theatre.

I have dwelt on this episode because it compacts key questions about the authority of the text and the liberty of the actor while also grounding some of Kinnear's characteristic inventiveness in a concrete passage of playing. This was only the most obvious example of him finding his own quirks and niches in a production that generally steered clear of risk or innovation. Cast as he was in a naturalistic, modern-dress but formally conservative production, Kinnear's task was to create a plausible psychological portrait of the meltdown of a contemporary bureaucrat. That his acting had clarity and legibility is evinced by the consensus among critics, all of whom faithfully decoded and approved of the actor's reading of the character. In reflecting on the universally warm response to the production as a whole, Kinnear noted, somewhat wistfully, that 'a really good production, especially of a classic text, should have one or two slag-offs [negative reviews]. Like *Revenger's Tragedy* – that polarized people's opinions. If you're following a line of thought passionately, then it's quite likely you're going to offend someone else's view of it.'

He would soon be given another chance to polarize opinion.

V

At the time of writing (late August 2010) Kinnear is two weeks into rehearsals for *Hamlet* at the National Theatre. The opening preview is five weeks away. He has spent one week in rehearsals with the cast, eight days before that in fencing practice and roughly three years before that knowing that he would play the role. Hamlet has been kicking about the margins of his daily thoughts for months: now, finally, the character, the words, the production are at the centre of his waking and working life. And nearly everything is up for grabs.

He is wrestling, in a relaxed fashion, with the question of originality. 'Today I came up with an idea – what if Polonius's line "Look whe'er he has not turned his colour, and has tears in 's eyes" [2.2.521–22] describes *Hamlet*'s reaction to the Player King's speech and not the Player King himself?' He knew that, in all likelihood, Shakespeare intended the description to refer to the Player King but found his new reading more exciting. He then discovered that 'his' reading dated back at least to the early nineteenth century. This does not mean that the idea will be abandoned, merely that it may lose a little of its bounce, feel a little shop-soiled and harder to sell. Kinnear comments:

> I get excited about having ideas. I didn't go to see David Tennant or Jude Law because if they'd had a good idea that I'd had as well, it sort of *halves* it. You'd be playing the moment hand-in-hand with another actor.

He says this with good humour, but like many classical actors Kinnear has the fretful task of navigating between hoary tradition and wilful eccentricity, the Scylla of cliché and the Charybdis of perversity. Two weeks in, he has arrived at a calm, fall-of-a-sparrow-y reconciliation: 'Every choice I make will have been made before, but the collection will be original.'

Certain interpretive choices have indeed been made. Clare Higgins (Gertrude) and he discussed the relationship between mother and son almost a year before rehearsals began. The conclusion: there will be no place for Freud in the relationship and certainly no funny business in the closet. How could this decision be arrived at without rehearsal? Higgins has played Gertrude before, so her aversion to a Freudian reading might (I presume) derive from her work on that production. But for Kinnear the resistance to Freud could be traced to two different sources. First, he had a generalized sense of How-the-Closet-Scene-is-Usually-Played derived in part from productions he had seen and as much from 'an imagined sense of how people have *probably* done this scene'. Simultaneously, the private study of the scene yields new insights:

> What I first noticed was how dense the language is; it's quite often played in a flurry of pushing and pulling but you never get the language. Freud gets in the way of the language.

Despite this realization, when he first played the scene in rehearsals a week ago he ended up in just such a noisy blur of diffuse emotion, as if, perhaps, exorcising the histrionic imprecision of that phantom production. It confirmed his instinct: 'The scene went for nothing. It will be much more powerful when he's really trying to talk to his mother.' Fail again, fail better.

Initial responses such as these – many of them having emerged in a series of preparatory discussions over the previous year – are now helping to structure the opening phase of rehearsals. The cast needs something to hang on to and these working hypotheses provide a series of base camps through the play. Any single hypothesis can be abandoned over the next four weeks should it start to prove obstructive, even if that hypothesis is widely cherished ('Kill your babies', Hitchcock reminded us). The company is currently going through a phase of collective reorientation:

> You have a map of the play in your mind when you come into rehearsals and then you realize that somebody else has themselves drawn a completely different map. We're at the stage now where we're putting each other's maps over each other and trying to realign the contours.

'What country, friends, is this?' The question has already been answered in part by Hytner's decision to set *Hamlet* in the present day and by Vikki Mortimer's model set of reconfigurable walls and semi-abstract spaces.

Kinnear's work on 'writing the script' for Hamlet, providing that character with a credible psychological journey through the play, is already yielding some boldly theatrical ideas. The decision has been made (based on Ophelia's testimony and with due awareness of Shakespeare's haziness on such matters) that three months pass between the encounter with the Ghost and the next time we see Hamlet in 2.1. 'Writing the script' demands that Kinnear become an expert in what happens in those three months. The central insight is both simple and extremely suggestive:

> The antic disposition must become so *boring* to keep up. Three months of having to bay at the moon whenever anyone comes into the room. There's a performed level of madness, then there's a level of depression, wakefulness, fretfulness that is his true personality. You know from acting experience that playing a tragic role is exhausting. I'm usually quite good at cutting off, but I remember coming out of the run of *Festen* – that other Danish incest play! – and being absolutely wiped out.

Hamlet spends three months tricking his body into going through something, deceiving his own nervous system. This is an actor's insight. Having hit on this idea, how can it be made legible to an audience? How to show this long-term loss of mirth and the schizoid and exhausting oscillation between performed madness and actual depression? At present, the production is experimenting with Kinnear's suggestion that 2.1 should be set in Hamlet's bedroom – a mattress on the floor, his trunk from university, ashtrays, a chaotic rug – simple, portable props affording an immediate view into the clutter of his mind. The environment not only solves a problem by marking the passage of time and showing us Hamlet alone in a dumbshow that denotes him truly (1.2.83), it also creates new opportunities. There's a knock at the door and in come Rosencrantz and Guildenstern – 'They've known each other from the ages of 4–18, gone their separate ways' – and their entrance into this fuggy room will, in a very English (and playable) way, be of some embarrassment to the prince.

'Writing the script' for Hamlet is proving more straightforward than it was for Vindice, the post-Hamletian protagonist of *The Revenger's Tragedy* whom Kinnear played two years previously on the same stage. With Vindice, the script Kinnear wrote was 'five times as long' as Middleton's:

> I think I made the mistake of trying to make it as psychologically credible as possible. And I don't think that play is too bothered with that. I could have played it for each scene without an over-arching journey – as a portrayal of a bereaved and vengeful man it's exciting and entertaining but doesn't really hold together.

Filling the gaps between scenes led to some contortions:

> Vindice met his brother in a safe house and that's where he gave him the costume – okay. But then who made the skull? And when did he make the dress for the skull? It seemed to me he'd always been at court, but maybe he went out to the *safe house* again. That safe house was revisited in my mind offstage a lot!

The Hamlet of Acts I–IV is proving somewhat easier to account for, largely because he rarely leaves the stage, although joining the dots from his exit to England and reappearance in the graveyard will provide more of a challenge (when were pirates last active in the North Sea?).

But it is a challenge Kinnear savours. He is enjoying himself. Actors return to the stage for the thrill of live performance but it is also the deep pleasures of the rehearsal process that distinguishes stage work from the other media of their profession. Theatre – and Shakespeare in particular – offers the addictive kick of problem-solving. I ask if it bothers him that Hamlet only mentions his father's murder a couple of times in the closet scene. On the contrary: 'The fact that Hamlet *avoids* talking about the murder is one of the fun things about Shakespeare.'

VI

In Act V, at the burial of Ophelia, Hamlet shares the stage with a Priest and a Clown. Hamlet himself is both – he is the play's official voice, its mediating conscience and its resident puritan, but he also, clown-like, keeps derailing the 'necessary question of the play' with speculation, unbusiness-like dilations, riddles, quibbles and evasions. There is something of both professions, too, in every classical actor; not that the Priest and the Clown are locked in a schematic Jekyll-and-Hyde battle for the soul of the actor, more that they are approximate metaphors for two simultaneous and dialectical impulses. In the processes and performances of Rory Kinnear's Shakespeare we can witness the generative power of this dialectic. What is priestly? There are the hours of private study with the text and the centrality of the exegetical power of thought to interpretation. He is not an iambic fundamentalist or a Folio fetishist, yet there is a clear recognition of the authority of the text and a commitment to honouring authorial intention, however conceived. He also has a purist's aversion to topical conceptual productions of Shakespeare in which, as he puts it, 'The butter of Shakespeare is dolloped onto the hot potato of the present.' What is clown-like? The occasional, strategic and wholly healthy preference for theatrical effect over putative authorial intention; the relish with which he invents and performs extra-textual moments of character-revealing by-play; the high-wire direct connection with the audience; the love of company. In the light of this dialectic, 'Writing the script' is a revealing phrase in that it conflates playwright and actor – Shakespeare's text is one thing, the actor's script another: together they author the performance – and recognizes the bifold authorities of Shakespearean acting. Kinnear, himself a talented creative writer, reflects:

> I guess for writers, which is where we tend to start in this country, they want to see their arc and their narrative adhered to and what they probably get the most reward out of, if that is done, is seeing the characters that other people create to fulfil that arc. The job and the joyfulness of being an actor is that as long as there is that arc, as long as you're serving what you take to be the author's intentions, there's always that license to add, embellish, and to make more entertaining, to make more affecting.

There, bound in a nutshell, in that oscillation between adherence and licence, between serving the author and meeting the audience, is the in/finite space of Shakespearean acting.

Much is to be decided in the next five weeks before the opening preview of *Hamlet*, but one thing is already certain: Kinnear's talents, training, background and temperament will fuse with the resident genius of the role and the result will be something moving, funny and, yes, original. It will demonstrate, once again, why an actor might want a piece of – might want to possess and be possessed by – Shakespeare.

Chronology

1999–2001	Trained at the London Academy of Music and Dramatic Art
2002	Konstantin, *The Seagull*, dir. Simon Godwin at Theatre Royal, Northampton; Caliban, *The Tempest*, dir. Patrick Mason at Theatre Royal, Plymouth (and touring)
2003–4	Tranio, *The Taming of the Shrew* and *The Tamer Tamed*, dir. Greg Doran; First Lord / Caius Lucius, *Cymbeline*, dir. Dominic Cooke at the Royal Shakespeare Company
2004	Laertes, *Hamlet*, dir. Trevor Nunn at The Old Vic
2004–5	Michael, *Festen*, dir. Rufus Norris, West End, 2nd cast
2005–6	Mortimer, *Mary Stuart*, dir. Michael Grandage, Donmar Warehouse and West End
2007	Sir Fopling Flutter, *The Man of Mode*, dir. Nicholas Hytner, Olivier Theatre; Pyotr, *Philistines*, dir. Howard Davies, Lyttelton Theatre; Ian Charleson Award for *Man of Mode* and *Philistines*
2008	Vindice, *The Revenger's Tragedy*, dir. Melly Still, at the Olivier Theatre; Olivier Award for Best Supporting Actor for *Man of Mode*
2009	Mitia, *Burnt by the Sun*, dir. Howard Davies at the Lyttelton Theatre
2010	Angelo, *Measure for Measure*, dir. Michael Attenborough at the Almeida; Hamlet, *Hamlet*, dir. Nicholas Hytner at the National Theatre

Bibliography

Copeau, Jacques (1970) 'Notes on the Actor' [1955]. Repr. in *Actors on Acting: The theories, techniques, and practices of the great actors of all times as told in their own words*, ed. Toby Cole and Helen Krich Chinoy. Revised ed. New York: Crown.

Irving, Henry (2009) 'The Art of Acting' [1885]. Repr. in *The Drama (Illustrated Edition)*. Teddington: The Echo Library.

Lewes, G.H. (1875) *On Actors and the Art of Acting*. London: Smith, Elder and Co.

Mamet, David (1999) *True and False: Heresy and Common Sense for the Actor*. London: Vintage.

Mazer, Cary (2010) 'Echoes: Shakespeare, the reviewer and the theatre historian, revisited'. *Shakespeare* 6 (3): 357–63.

Nabokov, V.V. (2010) *Pnin* [1957]. London: Penguin Classics.

Shakespeare, William (2005) *The Oxford Shakespeare Complete Works*. Ed. Stanley Wells, Gary Taylor et al. 2nd ed. Oxford: Clarendon Press.

About the author

Paul Prescott is Associate Professor of English at the University of Warwick and has acted and taught Shakespeare in Britain, America, China, Japan and Australia. He writes on arts criticism, creative pedagogy, theatre history and contemporary Shakespearean performance and his publications include *Richard III* (Palgrave Shakespeare Handbooks), introductions to the New Penguin *Hamlet* and *Coriolanus* and chapters in the *New Cambridge Companion to Shakespeare* (2010), *The Routledge Companion to Directors' Shakespeare* (2008), and the *Blackwell Companion to Shakespeare and Performance* (2007). Future projects include a study of Sam Wanamaker and a monograph, *Reviewing Shakespeare*.

10
Kevin Kline
Donald McManus

American actor Kevin Kline's success has been built on an iconoclastic personality in a nation that historically follows fashion and has been ruled by market forces. He has managed to maintain a film career as a top box office draw playing dashing leading men, primarily in the high comedy genre, while simultaneously dedicating himself to performing the great roles of the classical repertoire on stage. He has played Hamlet twice, Richard III, Henry V, Lear and Falstaff and has brought his classical acting reputation to the screen playing Bottom and Jacques in popular film adaptations of *A Midsummer Night's Dream* and *As You Like It*.

Class distinctions have long divided American audiences. A stigma of elitism has been attached to any actor who seems to emulate British style, and cinema-influenced natural delivery and behaviour have served as indicators of unaffected, American-style performance. Linguistic idiosyncrasies, actor training and native repertoire have all conspired to inhibit the development of first rate classical actors in the USA, leaving Kline to give great performances in less great productions. When American actors seemed to get verse reading right they appeared false, but if they played in their native dialect they seemed out of tune with the text.

Kline's Hamlet in 1990 was one of those rare moments in American theatre when a contemporary sensibility and aggressively modern technique combine in an actor who commands both mass audience appeal and respect for Shakespeare's poetic vision. It was the second time he played the role, and by directing the production himself he hoped to focus the interpretation more clearly, replacing directorial flourishes with simplicity of presentation and clarity in vocal delivery. During an interview I had with him in 2010 (from which all otherwise unattributed quotes here are taken), Kline reflected on his approach to staging the play. He told set designer Robin Wagner to give him 'a bare stage with only the minimal bits of furniture—and then get rid of those too'. He described his directorial style as 'old-fashioned actor management' in which he surrounded himself with like-minded actors who wanted to focus on the words; he told them 'we don't need a director, we can do this ourselves'.

This Hamlet was a test case of sorts for the limits of the American realist tradition of acting in Shakespeare. From Kline's first entrance, his Hamlet was an emotional wreck. His intensity of feeling was so strong that even in repose, when listening to another actor's lines, he seemed on the edge of a breakdown. No sooner had he spoken the lines 'the fruitful river of the eye' to Gertrude in the wedding scene, than his eyes began to brim with tears. There was no scene in the play where he backed away from the emotional commitment of that first image of mourning, guilt and resentment, drawing from the fruitful river of tears again and again to build a complex set of emotional extremes.

It was a remarkably brave performance in which his psyche seemed laid bare. If audiences rejected this Hamlet they rejected the emotional life of the actor himself. Even in scenes where Kline used his considerable comic talent to great effect, Hamlet's fragility and suicidal depression remained on display. Indeed, the comic moments, such as when engaging with Polonius over double meanings of words or parrying Claudius's queries about the whereabouts of Polonius's dead body, maintained the antic disposition of clinically observable manic-depressives. It was an interpretation rooted in mental instability: not the cliché, literary madness of gothic novels or received notions of the renaissance world view, but rather the kind of depression that most of the audience would recognise and have some personal experience of as individuals. He was a tangible, convincingly distraught Hamlet whose suffering seemed familiar despite his princely status and introspective poetic tangents.

Kline's strategy to create a constantly suffering central character demanded the audience's empathy. This was a marked contrast from his first performance of Hamlet directed by Liviu Ciulei. In that version Kline had decided he wanted to play each soliloquy in a 'presentational style, directly addressing the audience'. Later he was studying production stills of himself delivering some of the big speeches, and he thought it looked as if he was lecturing the audience. He became convinced that 'explaining the words rather than saying them' had cut the audience off from the inner life of the character. When he remounted the play, his approach to the soliloquies was radically altered and it affected the entire performance.

This was not a dry, self-centred, intellectual Hamlet. He was a sensitive, passionate, wronged man whose damaged greatness was the core of the tragedy. Although Kline's performance was consistent with an American tradition of intense emotional commitment to character, it was also technically very precise. His approach to the 'To be or not to be' soliloquy was almost akin to a textbook reading of the lines as metre, except that the tone was so hushed and steeped in stream-of-consciousness that the audience had to lean forward to make sure they could hear the over-familiar words. He entered entirely into his own thoughts, with no awareness of Claudius and Polonius in the previous scene or Ophelia's proximity in the next. No doubt was left that this was a genuine consideration of suicide as an option, with sorrow at the realisation that he didn't have the courage to take that step. He shared both parts of this pain with the audience, the despair followed by the frustration, equally. His tears of release on 'to die, to sleep' were almost enough to make one forget rhetoric and believe that suicide was a good choice, while his realisation that suicide had no guarantee of release seemed so spontaneous that a sensitive viewer almost felt guilty for being privy to such private confessions.

It is always a problem for actors to create the illusion that they do not know what they will say next or what thought will come next, but in set pieces like 'To be or not to be' where the audience also knows the lines, delivering a spontaneous reading is even more difficult. Kline's preparation for Hamlet focused almost exclusively on the problem of spontaneity. He wanted to avoid a pre-meditated or scheming quality in each of his readings and reactions. Above all he wanted his Hamlet to be fresh and to appear as if each moment genuinely followed upon the last. Where another actor might be tempted to 'kick the ball ahead of him' as Joan Littlewood used to complain, Kline obsessively guarded against such strategising in rehearsal, concentrating on each individual beat as complete and independent. His approach was centred on the words and the effect the words had on him in rehearsal. By moving from word to word and religiously avoiding generalities or preconceptions, trusting his personal reactions to the text, he was confident that he could appear as a present and living character as opposed to satisfying a given interpretation. In fact he consciously avoided specific interpretive notions based on the Oedipal complex or 'Hamlet as an intellectual and therefore unable to make decisions or act impulsively' (Guskin 2003: 155).

Kline performed an elaborate pantomime with his knife as he seemed about to seize the moment to kill Claudius at prayer. As he had done in the 'To be or not to be' soliloquy, he managed to externalise interior monologue, in this case adding physical action by encroaching dangerously on Claudius's space and threatening his ear with the point of his blade. In the closet scene with Gertrude, he balanced extreme physical action, throwing her across the stage and wrenching back her head, with equally compelling images of a child who seemed to want to nestle at his mother's breast. At his most violent, Kline's Hamlet never lost the audience's sympathy because his rash acts never seemed part of a generalised plan.

Throughout his performance, Kline cleverly balanced Hamlet's tendency to analyse and intellectualise with scenes of open-hearted guilelessness. Hamlet's treatment of Ophelia can create a barrier for the audience's compassion if he seems to privilege his suffering by belittling her feelings. When Ophelia entered after the soliloquy in Act III, i, Hamlet approached her with unguarded love and ingenuous affection. Kline made it clear that it was only after she delivers an incriminating line reading on 'I have remembrances of yours, that I have longed long to redeliver' that he turned from welcoming lover to betrayed one. A similar strategy was used for Hamlet's first interaction with Rosencrantz and Guildenstern. Kline, who emphasised Hamlet's insomnia throughout the play, was sleeping when they entered and startled him into wakefulness, whereupon he spontaneously expressed his love and affection for his two friends. Only much later in the scene did he start to play a suspicious character with superior wit calculating how to foil their treachery. This Hamlet was only cruel when circumstances conspired to bring out that side of his character.

The balance between honest soul and intellectual schemer had its corollary in Kline's use of simple commitment to stage action and manic theatricality. Where Shakespeare has Hamlet enter in Act II scene ii reading a book, Kline entered actually reading a book; he didn't pretend to read a book or use a book as a pre-meditated prop to catch up Polonius. Yet once the dialogue began and Hamlet called Polonius a fishmonger, the book was transformed into a prop and eventually the pages were torn out, licked and pasted on Polonius's forehead. At one point Hamlet sat reading, Marcel Marceau style, in a non-existent mime chair, while he turned the pages saying 'words, words…words'. The artifice of these manic moments was effective precisely because the initial image of the scene was always so simple and direct.

Of all Shakespeare's great tragic characters, Hamlet was the closest to Kline's persona in the mind of his audience, serving as a test of his ability to live up to his promise as a leading man capable of succeeding in the most challenging roles. If Kline's Hamlet was a charming yet tortured manic-depressive whose recognisable symptoms enhanced the audience's empathy, his first starring screen role was as a similar character in *Sophie's Choice*. In that film he played a psychologically disturbed, yet attractive and engaging young man who brought about the destruction of the eponymous heroine in a double suicide but somehow maintained the audience's sympathy. The tightrope act of flirting with the absurd while implying the familiar has become Kline's most recognisable and consistent attribute, although it has produced contrasting results in his stage and screen work.

Throughout his career, Kline has traded on the cachet of having played classical roles in the 'legitimate theatre' to bring a larger than life quality to film acting, while simultaneously trading on his A-list film star status to bring a large audience to Shakespeare. As a stage actor he has sometimes been criticised for being subtle to a fault, while his success as a film star was based on over-the-top, overtly theatrical performances in such films as *Sophie's Choice* (1982), *A Fish Called Wanda* (1988), and *Dave* (1993). Film director Alan J. Pakula (1928–98) cast him in *Sophie's Choice*, his first film role and one that established all his trademark qualities, because he had seen him as the Pirate King in *The Pirates of Penzance*. Pakula was attracted by what he called Kline's 'fatal glamour', which in his mind matched the tragic attraction of the character Nathan in the novel *Sophie's Choice*. The actor's 'fatal glamour' was tempered with what Pakula called a great life-force and fun about him. An attractive, tragic quality combined with an irrational sense of humour and theatrical unpredictability were the ingredients that made Kline an apparently obvious Hamlet. Even when Kline played King Lear in 2007, critics continued to gauge the actor's performance in the context of the screen persona he had established twenty years earlier: 'Nobody who's seen *Sophie's Choice* should doubt that Kline can unleash an old-school freak-out when an unbalanced character demands it' (*New York* 7/3/07: 70). I asked him about the stress of balancing the two careers and Kline insisted that he has never made an acting choice based on the audience's perception of him from his films: 'You want to be the character you need to be that night and not think about what the audience expects from you.' He acknowledges that a lot of the audience is drawn to the theatre because they know him from movies but the different context of the play makes any previous experience irrelevant.

At times the screen and stage careers have merged when he played classical roles in film adaptations. A nineteenth-century Italianate setting for *A Midsummer Night's Dream* (1999) drastically cut Shakespeare's text and included questionable performances by popular film and television actors, but also provided a vehicle for Kline's delicately nuanced interpretation of Bottom. He presented a wistful, almost self-indulgently tragic clown in scenes that showed Bottom's unhappy home life. It was a loving portrayal of a simple man with an artist's soul at odds with his environment. Bottom the weaver had an excellent tailor, and Kline looked Byronic in a white three piece suit and bow-tie declaiming each character's lines at the first meeting of the rude mechanicals, until waifs in the crowd drenched him in red wine. Director Michael Hoffman hoped that having a romantic leading man as Bottom would add poignancy to the scenes of mock-tragic acting, but the strategy backfired when the comedy in Bottom's big scene as Pyramus seemed strained, particularly next to a naturalistic, weepy performance from American actor Sam Rockwell as Flute. Kline was most effective in the internal, reflective moments such as his speech about dreams after waking without the ass ears, or the aggressive and absurd love scenes with Titania, played by Michelle Pfeiffer. This Bottom actually seemed to seduce his fairy queen and the passion ignited between the two unlikely lovers was sustained through the denouement. The film received mixed reviews, but that didn't prevent British actor-director Kenneth Branagh from casting Kline as Jacques in his ill-conceived film version of *As You Like It* (2006) inexplicably set in Japan. Despite an exceptionally interior and effective 'seven ages of man' reading, Kline's Jacques was almost indistinguishable from his Bottom. While it seemed inspired to bring an introspective, thoughtful Bottom to the screen, those same qualities are standard Jacques material and what had appeared as subtlety in *Dream* seemed like slovenliness in *As You Like It*. Nevertheless Kline's Jacques was the most engaging performance in an otherwise perverse film adaptation.

Kevin Kline was born in St. Louis Missouri in 1947. His mother, of Irish-American descent, and his father, a secular Jew, raised him in a liberal, free-thinking environment and encouraged him to have an open mind philosophically and develop a well-rounded skill-set academically. He got his first acting experience at The Priori, a Catholic boys school run by Benedictine monks where he excelled in music, French and Latin but was otherwise a mediocre student. His father Bob Kline had studied classical singing and flirted with a career in opera before becoming a businessman. Kline inherited his father's interest in music and became proficient enough at piano to be admitted to Indiana University as a music student before becoming obsessed with acting and switching his major in the late 1960s. His talent for music and ear for rhythm would become essential tools in his performance technique.

He was among the first cohort of acting students at the Juilliard School of Music in 1970, when John Houseman (1902–88) was director of the fledgling drama division. Kline and his Juilliard colleagues were forged into a professional unit after graduating and continued under Houseman's direction as 'The City Center Acting Company'. Kline stayed with what became simply 'The Acting Company' until 1976, touring the country in performances of classical repertoire that included works by Sheridan, Congreve, and Molière as well as Shakespeare. Repertory companies of any kind were rare in that period of American theatre, and a company made up entirely of young recent graduates performing strictly classical plays was unheard of.

As first director of Juilliard's drama division, Houseman hoped to train a younger generation of actors to have the conviction to perform Shakespeare in unaffected American inflections without aping British masters. He hoped to use Juilliard to correct 'the ever widening chasm between the classic and realistic schools of performance in this country' (Houseman 1979: 30). Kline was cast as Charles Surface in Sheridan's *The School for Scandal*, the first of many classical roles he would play as a company member, and the first play to be presented by the Juilliard repertory company. It was an enormous critical success prompting Mel Gussow to pour forth his enthusiasm for the production and the entire 'Acting Company' project in the *Times*: 'Anyone worried about the future of the American theatre should have seen the new Juilliard Acting Company in action' (Houseman 1983: 452). The success of *The School for Scandal* assured the pre-eminence of the new drama division on the horizon of conservatory programmes in the United States.

Kline subsequently became a protégé of American director and impresario Joseph Papp (1921–91), founder, artistic director and motivating force behind New York's Public Theatre, and the mastermind behind the presentation of free Shakespeare in Central Park to a mass audience. Kline's first job in New York was playing minor characters in an extravagant, marathon production of Shakespeare's history plays, conceived as an all-night publicity event to raise money for the constantly struggling company. He joined The New York Shakespeare Company at the Delacorte Theatre in Central Park in 1970 and played mostly minor roles, gradually rising to star as the Pirate King in *The Pirates of Penzance*, which became a genuine hit for the festival, enjoying a long run in a Broadway house after initial success in the park.

The relationship between Papp and Kline grew over many years. 'He was not the disciplinarian I expected him to be, he was more like a nagging conscience, or a kind of forceful paternal figure I did not have in my life: a demanding father' (Epstein 1994: 423). Well before Papp died, *New York Times* critic Frank Rich had declared Kline the usurper of his artistic father's place: 'With all due respect to Joseph Papp, it's now Kevin Kline who really rules the New York Shakespeare Festival's annual alfresco outings in Central Park. Mr. Kline is our king for all summers—or, at least, three of the last five' (*New York Times* 6/7/84 C3:1). This fulsome praise, crowning Kline as America's king of classical acting is all the more striking because he had yet to play Hamlet and Lear. Rich's implication that the metaphorical burden of American-style Shakespeare performance was passed from Papp to Kline in the manner of a regal inheritance was valid. At his mentor's death in 1991, Kline took over as associate producer of the American Shakespeare Festival.

Kline's first encounter with live Shakespeare was at a performance of *King Lear* and he remembers it as being incomprehensible with the actors using a phoney 'phaw, phaw' voice that turned him off. 'When I was introduced to Shakespeare in High School I didn't really understand it and it was frustrating and then I was afraid of it and then I hated it. It was as an actor that I found my way into Shakespeare' (Jacoby 2002). While associate director of the festival, Kline brought Peter Hall and John Barton over from England to hold workshops with American actors. He wanted to expose the younger members of the company to the idea that 'the problems of speaking Shakespeare are the same for Americans and Brits'.

Although he sees himself as part of a modern, natural trend in performance, he has continually been praised for his ability to evoke the past and even the image of Broadway's lost generation of actors. He won a Tony award for playing the role originally played by John Barrymore in *On The Twentieth Century*, another Tony for playing the Pirate King, was cast as Douglas Fairbanks in the film *Chaplin*, and when a film was being produced based on the life of Cole Porter, Kline was chosen to play the composer in *De-Lovely* (2004). As his career blossomed, Kevin became strangely separated from his peers in a way that indicated he was a star on the one hand, but somehow a throwback on the other. When he first played Hamlet in 1986, Mel Gussow's positive notice of Kline dismissed the supporting cast, and Frank Rich had a similar response, praising the star but giving a scathing report of almost every other performer. The more Kline's career grew, the more he was praised in contradistinction to the perceived limitations of his American colleagues. His persona developed as an outsider, a rhetorical actor who seemed to belong to past epochs surrounded by hopelessly contemporary American actors with no poetry in their voice or soul.

Kline's contradictory tendency to give a startlingly original presentation of one character and an almost self-indulgently understated reading of another may be evidence of his relationship with acting coach and long time friend Harold Guskin. Although Joseph Papp and John Houseman were significant figures in Kline's development, neither were teachers who worked closely with him on acting technique, whereas Guskin had a direct effect especially in his approach to text. Guskin encouraged and reinforced Kline's ideas about speaking classical texts in a way that was consistent with American rhythms and speech patterns. His association with Guskin began when Kline was still a student at Indiana University. He and some fellow undergraduate acting students who had formed a small acting company sought more intense and challenging direction for their work and asked Guskin to coach them. Kline's entire approach to character and text was transformed by the serendipitous meeting, and the two men have maintained a close working relationship ever since. He turned to Guskin for help with auditions and even suggestions on approaches to roles during his formative years, and continued to use him as a sounding board while in rehearsals and during long runs well after he had become an established leading player.

Guskin's approach is derived from the Stanislavsky system, but is a radical departure from most other American theories of method acting. 'My debt to Stanislavsky and the many other great acting teachers I discovered in my early reading is enormous. But any theory or analysis puts the actor in his mind not his instinct' (Guskin 2003: xix). Assuming that an actor already possesses basic technique and the intangible qualities that define talent, Guskin encourages his students (mostly established stage, screen and television performers) to learn how to 'lift words off the page' without the pre-meditated, logical through-line of action and carefully planned, concrete objectives that are the core of most Stanislavsky-based processes. Guskin is opposed to actors who 'interpret' a role in an effort to put a personal stamp on a performance. 'Critics and audiences may analyze the performance afterwards and praise or fault our "interpretation," but we as actors must not interpret. We must give ourselves—including our intellect—over to the role, and let the text take us where it will' (Guskin 2003: 156). Guskin urges actors to trust the words themselves, free of interpretation or even cognition. If the actor will '*just say it*, the line will be full' (Guskin 2003: 10). The ultimate goal of the technique, captured in the title of his book *How to Stop Acting* (with a forward written by Kevin Kline), is to let actors 'become the character and about a way not to act' (Guskin 2003: xx). Kline was Guskin's first and most important pupil. He coached the future star while still an undergraduate, prodding him to take personal responsibility for his performances. Recalling their earliest sessions Kline explains how Guskin took him line by line through the scenes. Guskin would ask: What does this line mean to you? And Kline would respond with frustration: 'Who cares what it means to me? What's the right way to say it? Up until that point, I would look at a line and say "How would Olivier or Brando deliver it?" just as a painter would say "How would Velasquez paint this?" or a musician would say, "How would Horowitz play this?"' (Guskin 2003: xxi). Eventually he completely changed his approach, however: 'Where I once would have written "ideas" in the margin of a script I now found myself writing over and over again *Trust yourself, trust yourself*' (Guskin 2003: xxii). According to Guskin, 'Kevin's acting began to become totally instinctive in a personal way that would become his signature style' (Guskin 2003: xxii).

Despite Guskin's anti-intellectual rhetoric that seems to privilege spontaneity over analysis, he also proposes a 'use of the negative' when faced with one of the great parts from the classical repertoire. According to Guskin, an actor must consciously differentiate a performance from the audience's collective memory of other actors: 'It is necessary for the actor to approach such roles from the negative, saying to himself "anything but what I remember from that particular performance"' (Guskin 2003: 157). Kline's performance as Henry V in 1984 was structured around a negative reaction to Laurence Olivier's 1944 film. Olivier's portrayal of Henry made a great impression on Kline and he self-consciously determined to contrast his reading in rhythm and overall structure from the well-received and widely seen film version. Where Olivier seemed to have no doubt, Kline filled the hero with uncertainty. Sir Laurence built the 'Crispin's day' speech into a patriotic, war-time cry of histrionic defiance. He paused after 'He would not die in that man's company / That fears his fellowship to die with us' (*Henry V*, IV: 3: 41–42) where he drove home his point by reminding the men that the day was 'the feast of Crispian'. After the pause his voice grew to the inevitable crescendo as the final cheer of the troops drowned out the last word of his cry of St. Crispin's day. Kline reminded his audience of Olivier's reading at the beginning by raising his voice line by line until he got to the exact same point in the text where Olivier had paused in the film, 'That fears his fellowship to die with us.' And then he stopped and completely dropped the bravura acting style and went in the opposite direction, bringing his voice down dramatically as if he had just realized that it was the feast of St. Crispin for the first time. From that point, as he described how the future generations would look on this day, he got more and more personal, emotional and quiet. The effect was not lost on audiences and critics. *Times* critic Frank Rich was completely won over by Kline and Guskin's 'negative strategy' to performing Henry: 'In the spellbinding St. Crispin's Day oration, Mr. Kline rouses his tattered, outnumbered soldiers to their cause in tones more inspirational than rhetorically chauvinistic; Henry seems to choke back tears of affection for his men on the word happy' (*New York Times* 6/7/84: C3: 1).

Even much later in his career critics still looked to his performances to find a reading markedly unlike what they may have seen before. Hilton Als' reception of Kline's Lear in 2007 is an excellent example. While critics were divided in their response to this *Lear*, Als is unambiguous in his praise of Kline's ability to give a performance that is against the traditional grain, claiming that he usurped the traditional reading of the role by 'bringing Lear down a notch' (*The New Yorker* 19/3/07: 144). British director Jonathan Miller's production of *Lear*, starring Christopher Plummer in 2004 (originally produced at the Stratford Festival in Canada, 2002) looms large when considering Kline's king. The Miller/Plummer *Lear* was praised for its subtle, family sized scope, which self-consciously avoided the grand, tragic sweep that has often sunk even the most promising performances. Kline's Lear coming so soon after Plummer's was received as a competition of underplaying. Audiences and critics weren't sure what to make of this tendency to back away from Shakespeare's greatest challenges: 'Somehow Kline—ruminating on madness, forever inclining to the comic—over and over gives the impression that he's showing us what it might be like if he played King Lear' (*New York* 7/3/07: 70).

Kevin's Lear was further complicated by incidental music written by Broadway composer Stephen Sondheim. Sondheim's score was atypically minimalistic but had the odd quality of up-staging the title character. Sondheim's legions of fans came to *Lear* anticipating great things but were only slightly rewarded by hearing the composer's sporadic attempt at counterpoint to Shakespeare. Still more problematic was the direction of James Lepine, another Broadway legend associated primarily with the musical theatre whose successful career has been largely due to his partnership with Sondheim. As a result, the *mise en scène* was calculated to accentuate the aural subtleties of the performance. It was an interesting reading of the tragedy, full of discreet nuances, but came across as just that: a reading, as opposed to a major production that gave Kline full scope to play perhaps the most challenging role of his life. In his overview of the highlights of the 2007 New York season, Charles Isherwood linked Kline's acting style to the British tradition that Kline had spent much of his formative years trying to avoid, saying, 'Mr. Kline is a cerebral actor more in the classic British mold than the emotive American one, and while many of Lear's speeches were beautifully handled, the performance lacked a core of intense feeling' (*New York Times* 1/1/08: E1). Kline had evolved an approach that had ironically landed him 'in the classic British mold' associated with academic, finely crafted and tasteful character readings. Hilton Als used the word 'literary' in a positive sense in his response to *Lear*, betraying his preference for a subtle, intelligent reading over a possibly messy, if visceral, performance. Als links a 'distinctly literary' interpretation with 'internalization,' implying that the performance was more true and emotionally rooted than previous, grandstanding Lears, rather than 'less emotive and American' as Isherwood complains. These contradictory responses were more the result of Lepine's idiosyncratic direction than Kline's actual performance of Lear. According to Kline, Sondheim summed up the critical reaction to *Lear* by saying, 'When we gave them green they wanted orange, when we gave them orange they wanted to see green.' I asked Kline if he was planning a return to Lear in the future and he said no, but added: 'If I do it again it won't be to please the *New York Times*.' One can only hope that Kline will accept the challenge of playing Lear again, as he did so brilliantly with Hamlet, in order to place his subtle readings in a more dynamic setting and give audiences another chance to assess his contribution to the legacy.

What had been critically received as underplaying in Lear, was actually evidence of a matured technique for speaking Shakespeare's text. Kline's whole career has been dedicated to finding a way to deliver verse in a clear and unaffected manner while honoring the poetry and relishing the sheer elation and emotional power of words. A distinct, if subtle, change in his approach has developed over the years. His rhythm has relaxed markedly with the stresses becoming less emphatic even in histrionic scenes. He has come to the conclusion that rules concerning scansion and breathing are mostly irrelevant. He is impatient with discussions of feminine endings of verse lines and whether or not to breathe at commas. As an example he refers to the 'hollow crown' speech from Richard II:

> The audience doesn't respond to pauses and rhythms. It is the words themselves that are important. I have become fascinated with Shakespeare's use of monosyllables and his placement of one word in a series to create antithesis. 'I live with bread like you, feel want, / Taste grief, need friends: subjected thus, / How can you say to me, I am a king?' (*Richard II*, III, ii, 175–78). The only word over one syllable is 'subjected' so its multiple other meanings (as king he has subjects but feels subjected etc.) are emphasized by its placement with the shorter words.

This approach to text places the emphasis on Shakespeare's specific choices from word to word with extra sensitivity to syntax rather than obsessive attention to metre and notions of rhythm and breathing.

Kline was given the opportunity to demonstrate the sophistication of his technique when he played Falstaff in a combined version of the two parts of *Henry IV* in 2003. Director Jack O'Brien took an almost scholarly approach to preparing the play, choosing to subvert literary critic and Yale professor Harold Bloom's vision of Falstaff as Dionysian truth teller. Kline told me that he quite admires Bloom's analysis of Falstaff, just as he admired Olivier's films of *Hamlet* and *Henry V*, but O'Brien here used Bloom as a kind of foil to audience expectations, comparable to Guskin's 'negative approach' but in this case employed in the dramaturgical realm. Instead of planning a role to contrast another actor, this Falstaff was organised as an intellectual retort to an academic interpretation.

New Yorker columnist Adam Gopnik arranged a meeting between Kline and American Shakespeare scholar and Harvard Professor Stephen Greenblatt. 'They had a lively and happy talk, though of course ultimately the kinds of things that preoccupy Steve and the like—who might have been the model for Falstaff, Lords of Misrule, Oldcastle and Falstaff—aren't of much help to an actor. It's certainly the case that Kevin has an appetite for scholarship, and for reading about his roles, that in my experience is unique in an actor of his gifts' (Gopnik, personal communication 2010). Indeed, Kline maintains that academic ideas interest and inspire him but are limited in their practicability because 'you can't play an idea'. Nevertheless, the fact that he met with a Harvard professor while preparing for a role that was, at least partly, conceived to challenge the suppositions of a Yale professor, indicates a willingness to embrace theoretical questions in his performances that goes against the anti-intellectual grain of American theatre practice.

As Falstaff, Kline got to exercise his many disparate and contradictory impulses—comic, reflective, intelligent, spontaneous, charming and repulsive—but where these same qualities had seemed an extension of his screen persona with Hamlet, the fat knight provided a distinct mask that served to distance the performance. Director O'Brien insisted that the fattening of Kline for Falstaff simply brought out an unacknowledged natural quality of his star actor. 'Kevin's a big guy, extremely tall, and when you pad him out he's huge, not just fat, not just a joke thing.

Oddly, what it's allowed him to do is evolve an extremely intimate real person, that isn't just a funny madman coming out. It's coming out of Kevin. It's just a Kevin you haven't seen' (*New York Times* 9/11/03: 2: 1). Kline had always been a very physical actor, whether tumbling and flying as the Pirate King or providing an athletic fencing clinic in *Hamlet*, but his physicality was less of an addition to the American lexicon of technique than his approach to text. Creating a larger than life Falstaff who bore no resemblance to any of his previous performances on stage or screen released his physical, playful side, giving him license to explore linguistic subtlety more than ever.

Although American audiences have been anticipating Kevin Kline's Prospero in a great production of *The Tempest*, he chose to follow Lear and Falstaff with *Cyrano de Bergerac* instead. His discovery of the liberating nature of Falstaff's bulk led him to seek another physical mask, this time the absurd nose, to obscure his matinee-idol features. His Cyrano was subdued and textured, balancing broad physical comedy and intellectually challenging, sub-textual readings. It was a restatement of the principles he had explored with Falstaff and Lear, but Rostand's bloated alexandrines, however brilliantly delivered, only whet the appetite for the next foray into Shakespeare's blank verse.

Chronology

Title role, *King Richard III*, New York Shakespeare Festival, 1983
Title role, *Henry V*, New York Shakespeare Festival, 1984
Title role, *Hamlet*, New York Shakespeare Festival, 1986
Benedick, *Much Ado about Nothing*, New York Shakespeare Festival, 1988
Title role, *Hamlet* (also directed), New York Shakespeare Festival, 1990
Duke, *Measure for Measure*, New York Shakespeare Festival, 1993
Falstaff, *Henry IV*, Lincoln Center, 2003–4
Title role, *King Lear*, Public Theater, 2007

Roles in films based on Shakespeare plays

Bottom, *A Midsummer Night's Dream* (1999)
Jacques, *As You Like It* (2006)

Bibliography

Epstein, Helen (1994) *Joe Papp: An American Life*, Boston: Little, Brown & Co.
Guskin, Howard (2003) *How to Stop Acting*, New York: Faber and Faber.
Houseman, John (1979) *Final Dress*, New York: Simon and Schuster.
Jacoby, Oren (2002) *The Shakespeare Sessions with John Barton Featuring Sir Peter Hall*, DVD, Applause Theatre & Cinema Books.
Personal interview with Kline, conducted by the author, Sept. 23, 2010.

About the author

Donald McManus is Assistant Professor of Theatre Studies at Emory University and Resident Artist at Theatre Emory in Atlanta, Georgia. He has worked professionally as an actor, director, musician and clown in Canada, the USA, Asia and Europe. His book *No Kidding! Clown as Protagonist in Twentieth-century Theater* was a CHOICE award winning Outstanding Academic Title in 2004. Dr. McManus wrote the chapter on Giorgio Strehler in *The Routledge Companion to Directors' Shakespeare.*

11
Adrian Lester

Jonathan Holmes

Such is their centrality to English-speaking culture that, in performance, all Shakespeare plays become history plays, though that history is rarely made as those involved would wish. Actors engaging with this canon of work find themselves negotiating a wide range of historical influences, and engaging with an unusually complex mesh of personal and cultural experience.

Appropriately, then, the approach of most actors to their work revolves around a conscious investigation of different forms of memory and history. Over the past century there has developed a tradition, largely inaugurated by Stanislavski, of bringing the actor's own life to the process of rehearsing and playing a part on stage or screen, and for most actors it is now the case that this latter use of experience dominates all else. The actor Harriet Walter, in one of the pithiest articulations of this mesh of experience, writes that 'acting is what I do with who I am', (Walter, 1999, frontispiece) while the subject of this essay, Adrian Lester, grounds his whole acting process, from preparation through rehearsal into performance, in a dialogue with an extensive series of parallel systems of experience.

Lester has appeared in only three Shakespeare productions on stage, yet each has been a landmark event in the history of staging those plays. The parts played, too, represent an unconventional sequence in the career of an actor: Rosalind in Cheek by Jowl's touring *As You Like It* (1991 & 1994) directed by Declan Donnellan, and the title roles in *Hamlet* (Bouffes du Nord, 2001) directed by Peter Brook, and *Henry V* (National Theatre, 2003) directed by Nicholas Hytner. In discussing this trajectory in interview, it becomes clear that for Lester in particular the experience of playing Rosalind at the age of 22 continues to influence his subsequent approach to Shakespeare, and in particular to the notion of character.

After being cast in Donnellan's all-male production, Lester began quite logically by addressing the issue of gender difference: 'I started off thinking I was playing a woman, so I began researching how a woman would walk and move.' Very rapidly, however, he found this approach deficient:

> There was a paradox in what I was doing, which was about playing 'woman'; I was being more and more general in an attempt to be particular. As I rehearsed it suddenly clicked that all this was ridiculous, because I was trying to displace myself to play some idea of 'woman', whereas from the

> start I should have been playing Rosalind, this individual, a Rosalind who happened to be my height, my shape, with my voice.

The initial attempt to play gender in a non-specific manner in fact drew him away from any notion of nuanced characterisation and towards cliché, 'because most of the things that make men, men and women, women are guidelines and assumptions set out in society'. The result was that he risked playing a stereotype, a camp cartoon of femininity. Realising this, Lester stopped trying to play gender in some broadly essentialist way, and instead made the cultural associations surrounding gender difference his subject. He began to focus on the social assumptions made about the character in the script, and on those made about himself as a male performer, and to construct his performance in the gap between the two:

> In the text she's quiet, under-confident, the poor cousin at court who finds release in the forest. So then I thought, well, she's tall (because I'm tall) she's got a low voice and a flat chest (because so do I); she's a 20-year-old girl who had suddenly shot up in height and who now is trying so hard to be smaller.

Lester's Rosalind was a Rosalind who had suddenly to contend with looking like Adrian Lester, and had 'to adopt all of these coping mechanisms to do with her-my body'. The comedy inherent in this surprised approach to characterisation of course fits perfectly with the character's experience in the text, as she is suddenly forced into another gender identity in a very different world. It also has the sophisticated benefit of stressing the constructed nature of gender to begin with; Rosalind's femininity is as constructed as her later, performed, masculinity, and a cause of equally as much bewilderment, as she is constantly surprised by the 'subconscious responses to society's unwritten laws' she sees in herself and others.

Lester was aided in his interpretation by the costuming Nick Ormerod designed for the production; eclectically period, it allowed for simple and clear denotations of gender and class, which in turn gave space for cast and audience together to construct their own independent sense of the characters as they appeared. In choosing to crop his hair close to his head and not to wear a wig, Lester immediately made it clear that easy readings of gender and sexuality would be resisted by his Rosalind, that he would allow the narrative of the play to determine his gender at pertinent moments. Consequently, for him the production became 'genderless; I lost sight of me and him [Orlando, played in the original production by Patrick Toomey] as male actors, or me female and him male as characters'. The idea of gender came from the text and from narrative necessity; it was never at the forefront of any fixed notions of characterisation.

This breakthrough as an actor also lead to Lester seeing the notion of character itself somewhat differently. In glossing Rosalind, Lester remarks that 'people form understandings about themselves and their world, and then something happens and breaks that, and they find they've formed these assumptions simply to disguise the madness underneath'. The fiction of stability and continuity that Rosalind happily jettisons in Arden began to be reflected in Lester's own rejection of the more formal aspects of Stanislavskian consistency:

> There is no such thing as character, in the sense of a defined individual at a single point that is me or you or Rosalind or Hamlet; character for me is a collection of understandings and emotions and assumptions.

Playing the fractured role of Rosalind, especially as a male actor, made it impossible to maintain notions of character as something stable that developed rationally over the course of a play. Instead, he began to embrace 'everything non-linear', understanding that the text and his physical presence would supply the continuity necessary for character recognition, and that it was the audience's job, not his, to find the links between the character's scenes: 'Trying to make the audience believe something is a futile exercise; my job is to make me believe it.'

More than this, the understanding that gender exists only as it is performed led Lester to make the same discovery with the idea of character: Rosalind exists only as it is performed by him, and beyond this there is no personality. This places any actor in the position of paradoxically taking the cues for characterisation from a text that contains no character. The whole process depends on a complicit understanding between actor and audience that a particular performer's body will anchor an interpretive process that otherwise could easily spiral beyond any useful limits. Lester intuitively understood that the audience read Shakespeare in performance by not reading him at all, but by reading the body of an intercessory exegete – the actor.

The noteworthy aspect of this shift in one actor's perspective on his work is its clear relationship to, and suggestion by, the ideas within the text he was playing: by the end of rehearsal, Rosalind was in a sense playing Adrian, rather than the other way around. A text that explores the notion of fluid gender, class and sexual identities led to its performer also jettisoning conventionally stable ideas of such concepts. Not only his idea of what made up this particular character, but also his understanding of character itself, and of his role as an actor altered as a result of the experience of playing this part. It's not unusual for actors to have a fairly fixed group of strategies for dealing with a role; such was the impact of this experience, however, that Lester rejected almost all of these in favour of an aptly Shakespearean mobility of characterisation.

This flexibility was born of his attention to a constantly shifting text. One of the notable lexical features of *As You Like It* is the recurrence of the word 'if', which is used more often than in almost any other Shakespeare play (97 times; the record for any of the 38 scripts is 110). It is deployed both frequently and centrally to emphasise the mutability of identity over time and space, as well as in the more provisional, playacting, sense of 'as if'. 'Much virtue in if', as Touchstone remarks in act five, scene four, as there is indeed an ethical dimension to transformation in the play: the more a character shifts, alters and re-invents him/herself, the more virtuous they become. As Rosalind states:

> I'll have no father, if you be not he:
> I'll have no husband, if you be not he:
> Nor ne'er wed woman, if you be not she.
>
> (V, IV, 118–20.)

Relationships and the ethics of their behaviour in this play are grounded not on a fixity of belief, but on an openness to experience and metamorphosis. Such a perspective spills over into performance strategies themselves, as Lester's account of altering his own conception of acting in order to play Rosalind demonstrates.

The emphasis on experience, mainly physical in this instance, leads to this ethical consideration of behaviour, found in the detail of a character's self-expression. As Lester says, 'The line is a tool to change something.' The change occurs on the level of expression and personality, and also in the context of the political world of the play, in the alterations taking place within parallel court societies, clearly defined class hierarchies, and norms of sexual behaviour and gender boundaries. Rosalind's re-invention brings her into contact with all manner of taboos regarding social and sexual behaviour, same-sex romance and cross-class interaction, which are negotiated, too, by this actor at the level of public performance. The results are an invention of experience for audiences that has a palpable political dimension, even as it ranges out of the actor's personal control: 'It's the ability to change, and to hear yourself change, and then to change again because of that change.'

Of course, nowhere in the canon is this interplay of politics, identity, theatricality and experience explored in more depth than it is in *Hamlet*. Peter Brook's production of 2001 was a radical re-invention of the text, which was cut considerably and significantly re-ordered, with a multi-ethnic cast including both Lester and, as Horatio, his erstwhile Orlando from the 1994 Cheek by Jowl tour, Scott Handy.

Hamlet's views on the relationship between experience, ethics and performance are famous:

> I have heard
> That guilty creatures sitting at a play
> Have, by the very cunning of a scene,
> Been struck so to the soul that presently
> They have proclaim'd their malefactions.
>
> (II, II, 584–88)

The argument here is that if the experience of performance is sufficiently akin to actual lived experience for its audience, then a powerfully ethical response will be called forth. The structure of this relationship is avowedly neo-platonic: the mimetic act, the creation of a parallel reality, brings about a fuller understanding of the equivalence of everyday reality. But whereas for Plato in book three of *The Republic* this equivalence was dangerous, distracting the audience from their moral identities, for Shakespeare it has the opposite effect, leading to an enhanced sense of an auditor's ethical self. Again, as with Rosalind, Hamlet's transformative acts are virtuous in their intent; the more layers of mimetic action, or 'madness', are imposed, the purer the self-awareness of the character, and the more likely it is within the narrative that truth will be revealed. Reality lies within inconstancy and transformation, not in fixity and permanence. As Lester says, 'That's how Hamlet fits into the world of the play – he doesn't fit. That's how he fits.' Shakespeare in this play not only acknowledges the veridical equivalence of theatre with everyday reality, he predicates the very construction of his play on agreement that this is the case – and not in the abstract, but in the material actuality of performance. *Hamlet* simply does not work if you believe art to be a lesser reflection of reality; you have to accept the two to be of an equal order of experience.

Brook's direction of the play explored this ethical dimension of metamorphosis above all others. The narrative aspects of the play were stripped back to a minimum, while contrary to the *fin de siècle* theatrical norm, the visual elements of the production were designed to comment on the action as little as possible, restricted essentially to basic lighting, functional costume, and props used in a variety of non-naturalistic ways. Lester recalls that the essence of Brook's direction was 'as soon as we knew what we were doing, we were told not to do it'. The theatrical-historical strand of influence was countermanded as much as possible: 'If he [Brook] recognised the shape of anything we did, or if it seemed to derive from a tradition of performing this play, then we threw it out.' Just as Hamlet rejects Polonius's pedantic generic taxonomy, Brook and Lester rejected the traditions of playing this play. The intention was to deny the least instructive layer of experience for this script in order to focus all the more on those emerging from the text and from the context of each unique performance. One group of ghosts, the memories of previous Hamlets, were dismissed: in this sense it was the antithesis of Kenneth Branagh's 1996 film of the play. The film was uncut, uncritical and populated with generations of actors known for their Hamlets; Brook's production was dynamic, dystopian and filled with many actors who had never played Shakespeare before.

Yet Brook's assault on the tropes of Hamlet-memory did not extend to an attack on theatricality itself; rather this production located itself in a very different, un-English series of traditions, encapsulated by the casting of the actors playing the players – the distinguished Japanese actor and teacher Yoshi Oida, and the avant-garde Anglo-Indian dancer Akram Khan. Such a move away from the English tradition towards those of other cultures is itself typical of Brook, and is indicative not only of an ambitious desire to discard the tired patterns of English theatre history, but also to author the play anew as Peter Brook's *The Tragedy of Hamlet* (to give it its full performance tile). The position of the central actor in such a tussle of influence and authority is inevitably challenging, but Lester revelled in the opportunities it provided:

> Hamlet himself rejects any answer he's heard before, and is essentially not of the world of the play; he's a renaissance man in a medieval world, and I was a twentieth-century man in a renaissance play. Always there's an element of this play that's not of the play; in this instance it was me.

The result was liberating:

> Actors often feel daunted by previous interpretations of the role, but I didn't because none of them looked like me. When I played Hamlet, I didn't feel Olivier's Hamlet or Branagh's Hamlet; the audience did. And so I was able to play off their memories by doing something different. It's like a jazz standard; they know the tune, and so I can jazz in and out of it in counterpoint with their preconceptions.

This is a highly sophisticated understanding of the performance potential of this role. By deploying his own difference as a black actor from the classic English Shakespearean tradition in juxtaposition with the audience's knowledge of aspects of that tradition, the result was a performance that played on convention to create an entirely apt characterisation, one that was changeable, unpredictable and dangerous, often involving direct, unplanned interaction with auditors. As Lester says, 'Yes, it's a play, but actually it's not, because we will use you.' Experience within the world of the play is not of a different ontological order to that without it, and audiences are not protected by a magic 'fourth wall'. Everyone is in it together, an understanding that is both profoundly ethical and reflected in Hamlet's own understanding of the workings of mimesis in his own theatrical experiments.

Lester continually emphasised the liveness of the performance, taking to heart Brook's maxim to try never to repeat an action. Entrances and exits were improvised, blocking never fixed, the audience never out of bounds. On one occasion, noticing an audience member following the play with her own edition, Lester strode into the audience, took the script from her, and played the rest of the scene by reading from it. Such deliberate metatheatricality fits perfectly within the mimetic world of this play, not just by playing a tricksy metatheatrical game but also through its result, which was to implicate that audience member in the onward progress of the action. This was especially so in this instance, as because of the heavily trimmed script, Lester's reading restored dialogue that had been cut, causing other cast members to have to read from the same edition to keep up.

This is an event that could only happen live, and only with the sanction of a production committed to improvised action. The retention of narrative and conceptual sophistication in such a moment is only possible through the reality of audience experience; its participation in an aesthetic act that is of equal empirical value to everyday behaviour (something that perhaps comes close to a definition of live performance). It implies too a characterisation open to the acknowledgement of its own fictional status; the understanding that Lester is an actor playing a character playing multiple roles. As he says: 'Character is simply how you react…something the audience does, not me.' Willing to be entirely open to shifting input from both audience and company, Lester's Hamlet was decentred and constantly changing, never where or who he was assumed to be. Every audience caused him to vary some detail of the performance; a line would be directed at a particular spectator, or an exit would change to take him by a row of school children. Often a line's inflection would alter interpretation on a macro level, deciding, for example, how 'mad' Hamlet was on certain nights. In this way, constantly changing actions altered the performance as a whole to a greater or lesser extent, making it unrepeatable and dynamic. For students of a landmark production, this is an essential marker of the collaboration between text, director and actor that is lost, inevitably, in the otherwise fine film made of the production for television.

The constant displacement of characterisation onto the audience ascribed to it an authorial responsibility usually absent from mainstream Shakespearean performances, where auditors are encouraged to be passive, consumers of a product rather than real interlocutors. In an interesting comparison, the Royal Shakespeare Company production of this play that ran contemporaneously in Stratford and London with

Samuel West in the title role featured a similar metatheatrical moment. During a London performance, a US student replied to Hamlet's enquiry 'Am I a coward?' (*Hamlet*, II, II, 564). 'Yes!' he yelled in reply. West himself later recalled himself 'thrilled' with the moment:

> It was the 'rogue and peasant slave' speech. I said, 'Am I coward?' And someone yelled out, 'Yes!' The next line was, 'Who calls me villain?' And he said, 'Me! Last row of the circle, don't know the seat number!' Stage management met me in the wings and said, 'Are you all right?' I said, 'It's the best thing that's ever happened to me!'
>
> (Interview in *The Times*, 18.10.08)

As he implies, representatives of the RSC were less delighted, however, and the gregarious student was threatened with expulsion from the theatre, while ushers were subsequently warned to be extra-vigilant for future demonstrations of audience misbehaviour. Commercial, large-scale Shakespeare companies need their customers to be obedient and silent. As a footnote to this incident, it is also worth observing the intriguing echo of past theatrical history contained within it. David Warner, playing Hamlet in Peter Hall's famous 1965 production, was also challenged at the same moment in the 'rogue and peasant slave' soliloquy as Samuel West; he too found the subsequent lines curiously suited to continuing the dialogue.

These examples reflect of course to a text deliberately written to operate with a maximum of mimetic potential; they also point to the ethical dimension of such strategies. Having audience members involved in the action changes the nature of performance; it becomes, however temporarily, a dialogue, a two-way process. This in turn makes us recall once again that theatre is a political act, one in which the narrative experience for all present in the room is equivalent (if not identical). Instead of receiving passively what is served up, there is always the potential for individuals to discover the possibility of questioning and altering their relationship with the play. This is what alarmed the RSC officials, and what excited West and Lester about the possibilities of the role. For Lester, in a studio space and on the same physical level as his audience, the potential for engagement and transformation was huge. The 'as if' aspects of his job became significant and powerful. It was a dialectical performance, with character fluidly constructed as each performance went along, not fixed and confined by a previous rehearsal contract or by the traditions of theatre history. Brook's *Hamlet*, like his celebrated *A Midsummer Night's Dream*, was both an attempt to stamp his own authority upon a text and also a successful experiment in allowing the meaning of that text to proliferate to a greater degree than before (ironically, partly by cutting it dramatically). In performance, Brook's *Hamlet* became Lester's Hamlet, and increasingly and disconcertingly an audience's *Hamlet*.

The resonances of this endeavour chime not only with the tropes and strategies of the script but also with its wider philosophical context. Lester's performance satisfied the formal structure of neo-platonic performance while undermining the traditional politics of its outcome. The potential for theatrical mimesis to affect the audience's relationship with the play was exploited to the full, but rather than pulling back from actual engagement, as the RSC stewards preferred their man to do, Lester encouraged the extension of performance into the regular life experience of the auditors. This final, inclusive layer of mimetic action therefore touched on the ethical positions of all concerned, and marked the moment when the triangular structure of mimesis, experience and ethical response was completed. This, a working-class black actor controlling audience and cast response to the text central to Western drama, was a profoundly effective political act.

Lester's careful use of his own identity and experience as an actor became more explicitly ideological in his performance as Henry V two years later at the National Theatre, in a production directed by the newly installed artistic director, Nicholas Hytner. Coming just two years after David Oyelowo drew criticism from the right-wing British press for being the first black actor to play an English king in a major Shakespeare production (Henry VI at the RSC), Lester as Henry V was a potentially controversial piece of casting. As he dryly remarks: 'I don't feel my skin when I'm acting. But the audience sometimes does.' After his dreadlocked Hamlet, he was close-cropped and cautious as the king, his race both ignored and also used for occasional pointed effect, such as when touring the camp in disguise on the night before Agincourt. When challenged by Pistol for his name he replied, as in the text, 'Le Roi', but this time with a West Indian accent, punning not only on the character's royal identity but also on the English stereotype of men of West Indian descent often being called Leroy. Once again, as with both Rosalind and Hamlet, this was a performance that both masked Lester's own identity and drew attention to it for intelligent metatheatrical effect.

The production connected even more emphatically with current political events than this instance suggests, however. With a modern dress, militaristic design by Tim Hatley (including a drivable Land Rover) and a heightened sense of the perils of mounting a debilitating foreign invasion on questionable grounds, *Henry V* opened less than two months after the UK/US-led invasion of Iraq in March 2003. As part of Hytner's inaugural season as artistic director of the National theatre, and playing on the theatre's vast Olivier stage, named of course after the most famous wartime Henry V of all, this was Shakespeare as explicit political commentary. The layers of memory and experience available to audiences were densely packed. Recollections of Olivier, the NT's first artistic director and the near-legendary leader of English theatre, playing the king as filmic propaganda in 1944 were strong. They merged with the most famous modern interpretation: Kenneth Branagh's deliberately minor-key response in the year of European ideological collapse in 1989. Most of all, connections between rhetorically adept and telegenic leaders leading a weary and ambivalent army to war were hard to miss, while Lester's expanding sense of private ambiguity at Henry's task seemed to throw the fervent confidence of Tony Blair into even greater relief.

Lester's preparation for this role relied to a large degree on research, 'historical research, interviews with politicians, and combat training'. This took him into more conventional Stanislavskian territory than his two previous roles had done, and the characterisation he formulated had a more structured base. This fitted well with the clear and managed agenda of the production as a whole, though Lester also found ways of preventing it from foreclosing the kind of opportunities for fluency and transformation that had distinguished his Rosalind and his Hamlet. He began with a recognition of the theatrical nature of politics: 'It's that thing about politicians; they're not actually insincere, they just believe everything they say at the time they're saying it.' The result was a vision of the character as 'a succession of masks; his own face, a face for the army, a face for the public with microphone and camera'. The continuity between them was supplied by the character's job: 'He's a king. That's what he does. That's who he is.' The role played by the character once again determined the role played by the actor, who located his characterisation not only in internal psychology, but also on the demands made by the responsibilities of leadership, on the throne and in the field, on this man's responses to the world. This Henry was continually re-inventing himself at every new occurrence; his personality was defined by the needs of the hour.

The king's inability to be psychologically constant in his relationships with others was redressed by an intense physicality of characterisation. Lester and some of the other actors playing soldiers trained for a short time with the British Army, a strategy popular at the time due partly to the success of the WWII television series *Band of Brothers*, which required its large company of mostly British actors to do the same. An experienced and able dancer himself, this emphasis on a tough bodily characterisation enabled Lester to push this element of his work further than in previous roles. His Henry was always on the move, always exerting himself to a greater degree than other characters, always leading from the front. Lester placed his body under additional strain by opting to run aslant a severely raked stage, and he requested the volume of the sound design be increased to put his voice under more stress. 'I've rarely chosen to push myself so hard in a Shakespearean role, to make life difficult for myself deliberately by choosing to be nearly drowned out by the sound and crippled by the set. But it was necessary, so that the audience could see the strain was real, not just acting. That I was really struggling, and therefore so was Henry.' The king's struggle was conveyed through that of the actor; once again, Lester is using his very real experience onstage to tell the character's story. Moreover, the politics of Henry's development as a king were embodied, felt physically, and as with his previous performances it was Lester's body that became the principal signifier of his character, rather than a part-hidden psychology. And, again, a connection with the audience was essential: 'I also asked for the house lights to be left slightly up, so I could see and talk directly to the audience.' As ever, the principal relationship established in performance is with his auditors, who are once again given room to determine the boundaries of Lester's characterisation.

Interestingly, the complexity of this interpretation was lessened by the connections made with the invasion of Iraq. Perhaps unfairly, this was a production that unexpectedly suffered precisely because of its juxtaposition with the extensively reported nature of modern warfare. Footage of real soldiers preparing for or recovering from battle was screened hourly at the time on television news programmes, and only served to highlight the unreality of the depiction of battle onstage at the National Theatre, functional vehicles notwithstanding. The emphatically naturalistic design unexpectedly emphasised the gap between staged and actual battle experience, and the explicit nature of the political dimension to this production therefore began to detract somewhat from its potency. The fictional world built by Hytner and Hatley was so watertight, it refused the kind of ambiguity and plurality of interpretation encouraged by Donnellan and Brook, and because the production became so clearly pertinent to an actual situation, there was a paradoxical risk that the audience would be distanced from it by a sense, not wholly merited, that the theatrical world was in competition with daily reality. The result was ideologically punchy and yet curiously mimetically deficient, a closing down for the audience of interpretive possibility that ultimately threatened to reduce the play to a footnote to superordinate experience.

Throughout a decade of playing a unique combination of Shakespearean roles in very different productions by forceful English directors, Adrian Lester has gradually built an approach to characterisation notable for its complexity and originality. This approach is distinguished most of all by its incorporation of audience knowledge and response, its physicality, and its reliance on varied levels of experience above all. It starts from a thoughtful understanding of the cultural place of Shakespeare, and a willingness and ability to play on that to produce fluid and ever-changing interpretations of varied roles.

Lester's work demonstrates that performances of Shakespeare that inhabit and emphasise the dynamic between individuals in the room, and which underline the relationship between performers and audience through the lived experience of a fluid and unorthodox characterisation, are capable of a remarkable power and political force precisely because it is the uniqueness of live performance that carries the burden of textual and bodily signification. In contrast, productions that strive to replicate the innocence of silent reading, that place the emphasis on narrative and upon the fractured fictional world it fosters, tend to retreat from full theatricality into a passive poetics redolent of the non-live and the anti-aesthetic. To these productions, all audiences are alike, blank pages on which interpretation will be imprinted. The reality, as ever, is more complex and less clean than such assumptions allow. Theatre, and Shakespearean theatre above all, is a weave of real, lived experience, the complicit construction of a communal and complex world by all those actually present temporarily together in the same space. 'The Murder of Gonzago' is of interest to Hamlet not just because of its narrative of betrayal, but chiefly because of the potential of its effect upon the audience; not because of its artifice, but because of the unique and entirely real moment of its individual performance. What distinguishes fully realised live performance from other artforms is the manner in which the plurality of influences impacting on an audience adopt an unavoidably ethical dimension: we can be made to react to other actual bodies in a space. Or, as Adrian Lester puts it, 'Yes, it's a play, but actually it's not, because we will use you.'

Chronology

Born in Birmingham in 1968.

1991, revived 1994	Rosalind in *As You Like It*, directed by Declan Donnellan and designed by Nick Ormerod, Cheek by Jowl world tour.
2000	Dumaine in *Love's Labours Lost* (film), directed by Kenneth Branagh, Miramax.

2001	Hamlet in *The Tragedy of Hamlet*, directed by Peter Brook, Bouffes du Nord and tour.
2003	Henry V in *Henry V*, directed by Nicholas Hytner, National Theatre.
2006	Oliver in *As You Like It* (film), directed by Kenneth Branagh, BBC Films.

Bibliography

Interview with Adrian Lester conducted by Jonathan Holmes, 2 December 2008 in London.
Brecht, Bertolt (1984) *Brecht on Theatre*, ed. & trans. John Willet, Hill & Wang.
Drakakis, John, ed. (1985) *Alternative Shakespeares*, Routledge.
Plato (1955) *The Republic*, ed. & trans. Desmond Lee, Penguin.
Stanislavski, Konstanstin (2008) *An Actor's Work*, trans. Jean Benedetti, Routledge.
Walter, Harriet (1999) *Other People's Shoes*, Viking.

Author biography

Jonathan Holmes is a writer and director, and was formerly Senior Lecturer in Drama at Royal Holloway, University of London. His books include *Merely Players?* (Routledge, 2004), and *Refiguring Mimesis* (with Adrian Streete, UHP, 2005), and he has written articles for *Shakespeare Survey*, *Modern Poetry in Translation*, *The Guardian*, *The Independent*, *The Times* and *The London Evening Standard* among others. In 2005 he recovered and premiered several songs by John Donne at St. Paul's Cathedral.

For his theatre company Jericho House he has written and directed *Fallujah* (ICA, 2007, published by Constable), *Katrina* (Young Vic, 2009, published by Methuen), and *Into Thy Hands* (Wilton's Music Hall, 2011, forthcoming), and directed *Orpheus Behind the Wire* (Bond & Henze, South Bank Centre, 2008) and *The Tempest* (Barbican, 2011 & Middle East tour). His feature documentary *Perpetual Peace* premiered at the South Africa International Film Festival in 2010. His next book, *What's the Point of Art?* will be published in 2012.

www.jerichohouse.org.uk.

12
Sir Ian McKellen

Peter Holland

1 Raw data

What defines the Shakespeare actor? Perhaps it is no more than a list of roles. A list of McKellen's professional Shakespeare roles appears at the end of this article (p. 157). By decades, it adds up to seven in the 1950s, nine in the 1960s, seven in the 1970s, two in the 1980s, three in the 1990s and one since the millennium.

A list maps out a framework, a territory that was first taken as given to the young actor and then carefully chosen by the star. The last few choices have not been surprising. McKellen had played Aufidius in Tyrone Guthrie's production of *Coriolanus* at Nottingham Playhouse in 1963 and discussed playing Coriolanus himself with Adrian Noble for the RSC in 1984 but, instead, McKellen chose to play it at the National Theatre, working again with Peter Hall who had directed him so successfully as Salieri in *Amadeus* on Broadway in 1980. After the brilliance of Macbeth at The Other Place in Stratford in 1976, directed by Trevor Nunn, the chance to play Iago in Nunn's *Othello* in 1989 was not an opportunity to be missed. Kent to Brian Cox's King Lear was the consequence of cross-casting the company at the National Theatre to be able to tour *King Lear* and *Richard III* (Cox playing Buckingham to McKellen's Richard III). And McKellen was bound to play King Lear sooner or later, returning, again, to work with Trevor Nunn, the director who gave him the Shakespearean space he needed. As he acknowledges ('Exclusive Interview' on the *King Lear* DVD), there is little left beyond supporting cameos of the kind he is not interested in playing, not even a return to Justice Shallow whom he played in 1959 in Cambridge to excited reviews in the national press. The map of McKellen's Shakespeare career, considered in simple list form, may be complete.

2 A speech

If lists and the mechanics of casting do not reveal the nature and quality of a Shakespeare actor's work, then perhaps a close analysis, a 'thick' description of one speech will help to find something of that elusive quality. Here is McKellen as Macbeth in 5.5.16–27, Macbeth's last soliloquy, in Trevor Nunn's production for the RSC (originally on stage in The Other Place and then filmed for Thames Television in 1978, broadcast 1979), a description from my watching the television performance.

The hair is slicked back as hard as can be, plastered to the head, leaving the forehead high and clear and the face particularly naked. He is still intent on his right hand which has been the focus of his definition of himself as someone who can no longer feel fear (9–15). This has not been the response of someone surprised to find that he actually is still capable of being afraid as if the cry of women had awakened a feeling against which he had assumed, on good evidence, he was now inured. Instead, it has simply confirmed the absolute assurance that one emotion at least has been evacuated from his system or controlled within it: 'I have almost forgot the taste of fear' (9) is precisely 'almost' but not quite completely, and yet the awareness of 'the taste' is not really disturbing, not marking a breach in the carapace he has built around his feelings. He has checked the hairs on the back of his hand and seen that they are not raised. But the recollection of the past, 'I have supped full with horrors' (13), has brought his hand to his throat as a mark of the level of his total engorgement with past engagements with the 'dire' and the 'slaughterous' in his thinking – full right up to here. There is something almost smug and urbane here, certainly aware of his superiority to those lesser beings who still have to undergo the human experiences of such trivializing and disturbing emotions. The voice is level and tightly controlled, a sign of that arrogant power that he now confidently senses in himself, and a slight smile plays across his mouth.

Macbeth has been looking out, not at the camera though prepared to let his eye glance at it in passing. He is profoundly disconnected from others, so that the Doctor (not Seyton in this production), who had identified the 'cry of women' (8) as the source of the strange sound, heard as a low and continuous moaning or keening, not a sudden outburst, is behind his left shoulder and, while the Doctor has looked at his back, Macbeth has barely moved his head and never seen the speaker. Now, Seyton arrives to bring news, not to report on the meaning of the cry (for, with the reassignment of line 8, he enters not in response to a previously assigned mission but coming from another space, the space outside the production's circle within which the action always plays). Again the other person is behind Macbeth's left shoulder; again Macbeth senses his presence but does not turn to acknowledge him. Macbeth is finishing putting on his right glove, flexing his hand inside it, pushing down between his fingers. Seyton's line is slow, respectful, nervous, saddened: 'The Queen, my lord, is dead' (16). And, once spoken, he moves back and exits even before Macbeth has begun to respond.

'She should have died hereafter' is almost matter-of-fact, a statement about the inevitability of death – 'she would have died sometime' – and rather less about a preference – 'it would have been better if she had died sometime later'. The last vowel, 'hereaft*er*', is elongated and, as his head smoothly turns on the syllable towards where Seyton should still be, he realizes, noting it with a slight moment of discomfort pointed up by a little jerk of the head, that the messenger is no longer there. Now he can turn back to look straight at camera, as firmly engaging the viewer with the possibility of seeing him think as he had refused it for the earlier speech. 'There would have been a time for such a word' is still smoothly, almost cynically in control and, rather than any pause at the line-end, he runs on to 'Tomorrow': that would have been a better day, far better than now and as good as any other, on which she might have died.

But the word 'Tomorrow' induces a pause and something that really is as terrifying as the old cliché of a glimpse into the abyss ought to be. Now there is a sense of what 'Tomorrow' leads to: another tomorrow and then another, each one more meaningless than the previous, each as predictable but therefore more frightening in their emptiness and inevitability. The five words of the line take a slow twelve seconds, across long pauses, with each syllable firm as the face registers the awfulness of the march of day after day. The triviality of the 'petty pace' moves us all, Macbeth himself included, on 'from day to day' and the next word, again 'to', seems to be about to repeat 'day' ('day to day to day', as it were, as if repeating the trio of 'Tomorrow, and tomorrow, and tomorrow') but then moves on to a possibility of ending, the absolute end of time itself, the last act of recording that time itself can make.

Now, as he invokes the past (having pointedly gone from 'tomorrow' through 'to day' to 'yesterdays'), the image conjures up the mouldering sepulchre, 'dusty' with the signs of deaths long past. If there was a quaver in the voice on 'day to day', there is none now. Instead, again, only an assurance of the truth of what he knows, knows so well that it is ridiculous that anyone could not know it. He both is one of those 'fools' who have seen in the light shone by the past that death is the only future and, at the same time, knows himself to be superior to those who have not grasped this inevitability. Both in the group and above it, his knowledge is comfortless for him. Sharp final consonants on 'Out, out' move us on from 'lighted' to the 'brief candle', the former the way the past illumines the road, the latter now life itself. The 'walking shadow' leads inexorably to the performer, the actor that the word *shadow* suggests. 'And then is heard no more' is spoken through a sighing exhalation that makes the absence of memory, the closure of death as an act of silencing (and of course as the ending of breathing), into something momentarily melancholy. Breathing out so strongly makes us aware of breath itself, of the act we do without any consciousness but whose absence is the sign of the end of our time.

Then the urbane cynicism surfaces again with the image of the 'idiot' telling his 'tale', again the sharpness of the final 't' of 'idiot' marking the assuredness of Macbeth's knowing. The curve of 'told by an idiot' is almost a sung phrase, moving neatly down the scale, mocking as he does so. 'Signifying' seems to portend that there will be something that has meaning and the upwards movement of tone on the word promises a positive that, after another substantial pause, leads to a dissyllable, almost two words ('nuh-thing'), a sound of complete desolation, a nullity that stretches as far as eye can see or intelligence know, an unending vista of negativity. The eye both looks at the camera (and hence at us) and at the same time gazes nowhere, lost permanently as if, had the sound of footsteps not broken the moment, Macbeth would have been fixed in this look forever, until his own death and beyond, in the contemplation of the 'nothing' that is the only truth he now knows. Finally the camera pulls back from the extreme close-up (nothing in the frame but Macbeth's face) to show the arrival of Seyton and Macbeth can break his meditation.

The whole speech is remarkably slow in pace, a slowness all the more remarkable for being on television, a medium that does not like speech to move at this speed. The absence of much camera movement allows for an unremitting focus on the space and, as it were, implicitly on the mind that is constructing the thought. Here we can see 'the mind's construction in the face' (1.4.12) but also in the exactness of the voice: each sound, each syllable and each word, let alone the rhythm of each line, precisely charted with a clarity and with a definition that goes beyond making audible the structure of syllable or word and makes that definition into the source of meaning. The actor is achieving an exactness that is one of absolute craft. Yet I do not listen and watch with an awareness of the craft as overly foregrounded; I am conscious of the technique – of, for instance, the way in which McKellen chooses to pitch certain words with a distinctness that separates them from the flow of the language – but the consciousness is not in itself an intrusion, only an awareness that he is doing this in order to make me understand precisely what he understands Macbeth/Shakespeare to be meaning, sound by sound. The whole has a coherence that is not static, for the dynamic movement of the thought through the speech is always apparent, but it is undoubtedly connected and shaped towards its conclusion. With hindsight I am aware of it as an echo (in reverse time) of the 'Credo' that Boito wrote for Iago in Verdi's *Otello*. But where Verdi's Iago laughs, McKellen's Macbeth stares.

3 An analysis

I had drafted this account of the speech before I watched McKellen in the filmed version of *Acting Shakespeare* analysing at length exactly the same speech. It was while he was at the RSC in 1976, playing Macbeth, Romeo and Leontes, that he was invited to create a one-man show for the Edinburgh Festival in 1977. *Acting Shakespeare* was so successful that McKellen would go on touring it until 1990, including playing it across the United States of America from February to October 1987. It was taped in November 1981 in 'a brief version'. McKellen distinguished his aim from, for example, John Gielgud's equally long-running 'Ages of Man', premiered at the 1957 Edinburgh Festival. Where Gielgud's show was no more than an anthology of Shakespeare excerpts, *Acting Shakespeare* was intended to include anecdote, gossip and information about early modern staging as well as allowing McKellen to 'confide how an actor copes with the dense language and point out what is helpful about its rhythms and structure', comments that appear on his carefully maintained official website.

The one substantial exploration of the movement of a speech that justifies this intention is 'Tomorrow and tomorrow and tomorrow' from *Macbeth*, a minutely detailed description of how the images, the rhythm, the semantics and the thought work, and how it is possible to track all these facets through the speech. If the performance that follows the anatomizing has little of the intensity of the film of *Macbeth*, it aims to show how all the thinking creates the connective tissue and determination of vocal colour, rhythm and pitch that the analysis has demonstrated to be thought through by the actor.

Act 2 of *Acting Shakespeare* has mocked Gielgud as a style to be totally rejected in favour of the modern that is McKellen himself. As he turns to the 'secrets I unlocked when I was preparing Macbeth', those secrets that the verse shows that defines how the actor should play, he first gives the speech in what he claims as early modern sounds. This stab at original pronunciation (OP) is in effect a tribute to John Barton who had often toyed with such possibilities, another of McKellen's many echoes of his Cambridge undergraduate theatre experiences. Here McKellen's voice covers a geographical diversity that is magnificently inauthentic, mixing Warwickshire and Geordie, Scots and Somerset in ways that Barton would never have permitted, let alone more recent explorers of OP like David Crystal (See Crystal 2002, Crystal 2005 and Crystal's website). It's a performer's turn, a moment of trick before the surprising and impressive intensity with which he then unpicks the speech, word by word, moment by moment, laying bare his construction of thought that precedes the speaking.

The analysis of the speech begins with a definition of space and audience connection: in the tight intimacy of The Other Place, McKellen began by 'fix[ing] someone in the audience with my eye and said "There would have been a time for such a word"' (my transcriptions from the DVD release). 'Time' becomes, for McKellen, the key word in the speech. But what word is Macbeth defining as 'such a word'? 'The Queen, dead, died'? But McKellen argues that the 'tripping' rhythm of the line, 'like the ticking of a clock', leads on to 'Tomorrow', the word that Macbeth is aware of being about to consider. The repetitions of 'tomorrow' make the word lose all meaning, 'as life is beginning to lose its meaning for Macbeth'. 'Creeps in' defines the arrival not as 'grandiloquent' but as 'mean', 'as there is something mean about life for Macbeth'. What records time ('syllable of recorded time') is 'clocks and bells' and McKellen therefore finds a pun: 'sylla-bell', something he punches home when he performs the speech in *Acting Shakespeare* but which cannot be heard when he played Macbeth for the RSC. The temporal cycle of 'Tomorrow' and 'to day' is completed by 'yesterdays', 'the full complex of time', a system that Macbeth is part of, offering it as something that necessarily includes and binds us: 'not only that he is but we are: "all *our* yesterdays"'. So Shakespeare and Macbeth draw the audience into the speech.

The 'fools' are those who 'creep…with petty pace', the 'village idiot[s]' whom he will soon define. The 'brief candle' is 'a penny candle,…the cheapest thing in your house'. 'Walking shadow' is linked to the lowest kind of actor, a 'walking gentleman' who plays as cast. Macbeth makes life into something 'despicable', it is like an actor: 'What? Life is like an actor, says Macbeth who is being played by McKellen who is an actor? Life is like me?' The awareness of the pointlessness of strutting and fretting is 'McKellen's predicament' but it also mocks the audience that watches such a poor thing as acting. The tale is not a grand, romantic narrative but one told by an 'idiot', mumbled as the idiot 'creeps' along and it leads to 'nothing'. Nothing is 'the blackest, blankest word in the English language, conveying the total emptiness of Macbeth's vision and Macbeth's future and Macbeth's hope'.

The aim of all this thinking through is to avoid 'some generalized despair': 'it must be as particular as that analysis' so that it can all be filtered through body and voice in performance. McKellen is aware, even as he rejects the label, that the analysis can sound like a 'university lecture'. But I also hear in it the kind of unpicking of the structures of Shakespearean verse that John Barton taught actors at the RSC, explaining at great length how verse form and syntax operate and how an actor might reveal both the abstract skeleton and the complexly immediate fleshing that colours every fragment of the details of the passage. Behind Barton also stands George Rylands (1902–99), always known as 'Dadie', fellow of King's College from 1927, who had directed recordings of all Shakespeare's plays for Argo records, and was a revered guru for Barton, McKellen and many generations of Cambridge student actors.

But also influencing the way in which McKellen defines the processes of the speech is 'Practical Criticism', the centrepiece of academic study in English at Cambridge, the close reading of poetry in ways often forcedly separated from historical and other contextual possibilities – texts in class were usually presented without identification of the author. McKellen the student seems, in his engaging exploration of the speech to the audience at *Acting Shakespeare*, to have turned briefly into McKellen the professor, as easy in his chair as a Cambridge don in a supervision with a student.

4 A role

If that starts to suggest that McKellen's approach to a Shakespeare role depends on intellectual examination, the cerebral work of academic analysis dominating anything else in the process of preparing the playing, then that would be far from the truth of McKellen's method. His Iago (RSC, 1989, directed by Trevor Nunn) exemplifies his refusal of the conventional dictates of scholarship in favour of a psychological realism found, substantively, as much within himself as beyond it. Coleridgean dictates of 'motiveless malignity' are, for McKellen, effectively unplayable:

> Within his confessional asides, Iago makes his motives clear. I wouldn't have known how to play the critical cliché of the man as the embodiment of all evil. So I played the jealous husband who suspects 'the lustful Moor hath leaped into my seat' and can urge his boss to 'beware of jealousy' because he himself is a victim of it.
>
> (McKellen in 2003, quoted on his website)

McKellen found the explanations that Iago offers for his actions not a smokescreen to disguise something more profound and aberrant but instead entirely satisfactory accounts of Iago's own sense of his motives – and what was adequate for Iago had to be at the centre of this actor's playing of the part. Sexual jealousy over Emilia was not here to be, as, say, it had been when Olivier played Iago to Richardson's Othello in 1937, a transposition of a repressed homosexual desire for Othello himself but instead a direct result of the nature of Iago's marriage, his own sexuality and the ways in which he both expresses it and fears it. If there is no apparent reason for Iago's belief that Othello has had sex with Emilia, then that was itself the point: jealousy does not need to find an adequacy of cause, any more for Iago than for Othello.

There is a further aspect of McKellen's method of preparation that is crucial. Work on the text – but not research around the text – is supplemented by the definition of models who function as the basis for the physicalization of the performance. So, for example, McKellen found something of the Dalai Lama in Richard II, of John McEnroe in Coriolanus and of Moshe Dayan, John F. Kennedy and Mohammed Ali in Macbeth. In no sense did this mean that the Shakespeare roles looked like these other figures, nor did it suggest that the audience should see and accept the parallels. In working on Macbeth, he started by trying to think of generals who had gone into politics but then realized that 'Macbeth is the glory of the world, he's the golden boy'. And the 'modern parallel' for that was Ali: 'so I asked myself what it would be like if he were to decide to be President of the USA' (McKellen in Barton 1984, 184).

Perhaps the envy and jealousy of Iago came, as McKellen claimed, from his own experience: his long-term relationship with Sean Mathias which ended not long before he played Iago was soured by the imbalance between McKellen's success and Mathias' comparative failure. Perhaps too, his Iago drew something from an ex-soldier who drilled McKellen and others for a school gymnastics display (Barratt 2005, 161).

What McKellen achieved was, though, not a solo effort. It depended crucially on two other people. The first was Nunn not only as a director with whom McKellen felt confident but also because Nunn's new approach to Shakespeare was defined by a kind of hyper-realism within which the minutiae of McKellen's action would find place. If Iago was not to be an abstracted evil but an inhabited individual, then the props-laden style in which Nunn now directed would richly support him. So, as the Duke and senators discussed the threat of invasion at a table covered in papers while they filled glasses of whisky from decanters and filled the room (and the theatre) with smoke from their cigars, the materials of the set provided Iago with materials for his actions. As he talked with Roderigo, he was scanning official documents left on the table and, as he exited after his soliloquy at the scene's end, he opened the Duke's cigar-box, took out three cigars and put them into the breast-pocket of his uniform. Significantly, the cigars were not pinched for him to smoke, for Iago always smoked tiny roll-ups kept in a small tin along with matches that he carried with them. Instead, the cigars reappeared in Cyprus in 2.1, handed out to the waiting and drenched officers as an act of ingratiation, a sign of the way that Iago would always be life and soul of any gathering.

The second major contribution was from Zoë Wanamaker whose incisive, revisionary exploration of Emilia was the necessary counterpart, creating a marriage that would horrifically parallel the one of Othello and Desdemona. Wanamaker had researched Emilia as a battered wife, a woman whose desire for her husband was still strong in spite of his treatment of her. Two moments, in the performance, two kisses, fixed the relationship. The first was Iago's response to the passionate kiss between Desdemona and Othello reunited in Cyprus, a couple whose sexual excitement seemed to shut out everyone else on stage. McKellen circled round them, watching them intently, curious perhaps but also oddly thrilled by it so that as he came up to Emilia he twisted her head to take a long, intense, brutal and empty kiss, half-eying the other couple as he did so. As he broke, we knew how desperately Emilia wanted that kiss and yet how humiliating it was and, in her own half-look at Othello and Desdemona, still locked in their embrace, she showed she understood the reason for her own kiss.

The second was at the start of the second half. The interval had been put in mid-scene (at 3.3.293), as Othello and Desdemona left for dinner with 'the generous islanders' (284). The dropped napkin stayed on stage throughout the break, becoming an object I found myself mesmerized by when I settled again in my seat after the interval. The second half began with Emilia contentedly smoking a pipe, spotting the napkin, taking it for Iago. In response to getting it, Iago pulled Emilia onto his lap and, again, kissed her brutally, lengthily, unlovingly. Her response showed her abject joy in the moment. He broke the kiss as suddenly as he began it and began smoking her pipe which somehow, unnoticed, he had gathered up in the moment. After her exit, his elaborate relighting of it, sucking on it to build the flame, seemed a much more pleasurable, exciting event for him than the kiss. He had given Emilia her reward as if he had thrown his bitch a bone.

The perfect non-commissioned officer, McKellen's Iago was in every sense buttoned up. Alone among the soldiers he wore his uniform jacket always done up to the neck. His straight back was almost a parody of the cliché of the ramrod posture, and he frequently marched off stage, after pulling himself to attention, thumbs down the trouser seam, chin in, shoulders back, 'the obedient, uncomplaining, efficient cog in the military machine' (Smallwood 1990, 113). But there was a tactile closeness to others that worked against his intentions: his willingness to touch, cradle, stroke (in turn Roderigo, Cassio, Othello and, strikingly often, Desdemona) seemed almost tender.

On the arrival at Cyprus and again after Othello has called Desdemona a whore, Iago's comforting cuddle is almost a class transgression, certainly something intense enough from his perspective to prove that 'I do love her too', clearly 'Not out of absolute lust' but not only 'to diet my revenge' either (2.1.290–91). After Cassio has lost his position and vomited up his drink, Iago tidies the messroom where the scene has been set, washes out the sick-bowl, puts Cassio to bed, carefully tucking his blanket around him, and then sits on the bed to turn to us and ask 'what's he then that says I play the villain[?]' (2.3.327), Cassio's arm twitching at one point across him, something that, like those cigars, Iago stores away for future use: 'I lay with Cassio lately' he tells Othello later (3.3.418). Most endearingly – and that is not a word one often uses in connection with Iago – he bandaged the wounded Roderigo's head, swiftly and knowledgeably, a technique probably learned on the battlefield, but then arranged the tufts of Roderigo's hair that stuck up above the bandage, toying with them as he did so and admiring his own handiwork.

Against the upper-class, received pronounciation tones of Cassio, Roderigo and Desdemona, Iago spoke with the flat, northern vowels of McKellen's own background, the sounds he had taught himself to displace as an actor but which now returned to define the working-class NCO who had no place other than as servant to these upper-class masters. This was the career soldier, happy in the company of other soldiers, not because he needed male company but precisely because they were soldiers, happy too to sit beside his general as the ADC feeding him papers to sign. Iago was the perfect insider, whose own inside was invisible and left him painfully the outsider. The explosive vision of interiority was rare but, when it came, devastating: he almost screamed 'I hate the Moor' (1.3.278), with a volume and passion and violence that was totally unexpected and which were no sooner uttered than they could be repressed back, buttoned up again.

At the end, Iago did indeed do what Lodovico ordered: 'Look on the tragic loading of this bed' (5.2.373). He walked up to the bedrail and looked down on the two corpses in their closeness and embrace with a complete lack of satisfaction or even comprehension. It had been done as he had wanted it done but there was no smirk of pleasure, no secretive delight, only a knowledge both of his own accomplishment and the meaningless of that achievement. The blankness of the look was something often seen throughout: his furrowed brow raised his eyes wider open but any twinkling in them was simply for the benefit of others. The look was no window towards interiority but instead powerfully reminiscent of Olivier's performance as Archie Rice in Osborne's *The Entertainer*, the man who knows that the eyes are dead.

5 The problem of art

I have suggested earlier that there is a precision in McKellen's acting, a visible calculation of what effect is wanted and how best to achieve it. There is a brilliance of execution that is viscerally thrilling, superbly intelligent and always driven by the play, not by an enforced interpretation. He has, deservedly, won numerous awards for his Shakespeare roles. His Iago, for instance, won him both the Evening Standard and the London Critics' Circle awards as best actor, his Macbeth won the Plays and Players' London Theatre Critics award, Coriolanus the Evening Standard award and Richard III the SWET award. But this seems the right moment to insert the 'and yet…' concerns.

In summing up her account of McKellen's Iago, the critical sharpness of Joy Leslie Gibson is finely perceptive:

> Yes, great acting. But again of a heartless character, and again we see only too well how the effects are obtained. McKellen showed once more that he has all the technical gifts, but lacks the art that conceals art. But, having said that, it was a gifted, towering performance…
>
> (Gibson 1986, 155)

The heartlessness is inherent in the role and I cannot quite see why it is ground for doubt. But the recognition of the visibility of the effects is striking, the way in which the calculation is McKellen's even more than it is Iago's, the technique that is determined to draw attention to itself in order to be admired, the tricks – almost the tricksiness – that are dazzling but with precisely a dazzle that can obscure as well as illuminate. Whenever Iago carefully takes another cigarette from the tin, selects a match, lights it and puffs on the little fragment of tobacco, McKellen's display often pulled focus from the other actor on stage, showing off a theatrical virtuosity that says less about Iago than about the performer. At worst this is upstaging. At best it is part of the way in which the small hand-props work to provide an objectification of the character's interiority, externalized through the object.

Part of what makes McKellen so excitingly risky on stage is bound up with this possibility of using his undoubtedly charismatic presence to pull the audience into an undeviating focus on him. And this, in turn, is the result of the frequent –

indeed, usual – lack of others in the cast able to match up to him. The outstanding quality of his Macbeth, for instance, is directly related to the quality and equality of Dench as his wife. Zoë Wanamaker's Emilia is never overwhelmed by his Iago and, as the reviews indicate, his Romeo (RSC, 1976) was fully matched by Francesca Annis's Juliet. But often McKellen can make the rest of the company look over-parted so that, in his *King Lear*, only Frances Barber as Goneril seems able to hold the stage with him. Such undercasting allows him to indulge his delight in tricks without opposition.

McKellen is well aware of how such tricks work, seeing them as belonging to theatre. Sometimes, the device is no more than the necessary response to the limitations of a particular production. As Henry V at Ipswich early in his career, working with a small cast left Henry's army even more meagre than usual:

> We had very few soldiers. So I imagined that the army were in the audience and I knelt down at the front of the stage and whispered, 'Once more unto the breach, dear friends, once more / Or close the wall up with our English dead.' I was able to get just as much passion into that and bravado and patriotism by whispering as I could by shouting. In fact I think I got more because it felt more real.
>
> (McKellen website)

This move to the real and away from something that might be emptily oratorical is a repeated movement in his practice.

At other moments, though, the effect risks dominance. As Richard III, for instance, McKellen and Richard Eyre, who directed the National Theatre production, developed an extensive piece of stage business during the wooing of Lady Anne. Reading Richard's statement, as he offers her his sword, 'Which if thou please to hide in this true breast…/ I lay it naked to the deadly stroke' (1.2.163–65), as Shakespeare's indication that this was 'the one and only time when undressing is in order',

> I removed hat, gloves, greatcoat, Sam Browne's trappings, jacket and undid the collarless shirt to give Lady Anne a glimpse of the naked flesh that was so close to the spine's deformity and was hers to explore.
>
> (McKellen 1996, 82)

He then used the soliloquy at the scene's end as a time to 'put everything back on as quickly as I could, single-handed, meanwhile talking to the audience. Then I marched off to a score or two of tailors' ([1996], 86). Crowl found the effect one of 'bravura physicality', so that 'Anne, like the audience, was completely disarmed by the slick force of will revealed by such a performance' (Crowl [1997], 54). McKellen, for his part, was 'nightly aware that this was an actor's trick, mine as much as Richard's' and therefore 'was almost relieved when [Richard Loncraine] didn't want me to repeat it in the film', so that, of the business of putting the clothes back on, 'all that survives of this cheeky theatricality is the final wriggling-on of his leather glove' (McKellen [1996], 82, 86).

McKellen's move towards being willing to play the role was based on his perception that Richard's 'inner moral turpitude' is not given outward expression by his physical deformity but rather 'that Richard's wickedness is an outcome of other people's disaffection with his physique' so that this man has been subject to 'verbal and emotional abuse which from infancy has formed [his] character and behaviour' (McKellen 1996, 22). As always, McKellen resists the abstract symbolism – here of Richard as derived from the Vice figure of morality plays – in favour of 'what actors discover, that Shakespeare fleshed-out those types and made them human' (McKellen 1996, 22).

Of course the controlled investigation of the humanity of the characters he plays is central and excess is a sign for him of a weakness in technique. At one performance of *Richard III*, as Brian Cox noted in his diary,

> Ian at the news of Edward's death staggers and I say, 'Can I get you anything?' and he said, 'No, I'm just overacting.'
>
> (Cox 1992, 162)

But, more seriously, it can lead McKellen to be unable to chart something a character reaches that is simply outside his construction of the human. It is one thing to bring Richard III back from the abstraction of absolute evil but Lear in the storm and in madness poses a different problem that McKellen did not resolve. It is striking that as the mad Lear McKellen frequently loses his characteristic clarity. Lines are often mumbled and inaudible (not only because of the sound effects of the storm) and there is no progress and interconnection of irrational thought, the leaps of the mind that other Lears have found and shown. Whatever kinds of perception about, say, justice and whatever fascinated horror of sexuality Lear may reach in this sequence is, quite simply, beyond McKellen. It is only in the return to the representation of a more conventional psychology in the reunion with Cordelia that McKellen returns, too, to the emotional power he has at the start. From there to the end is as moving as almost any Lear I have seen (I except Olivier's creation of a man somehow already beyond the moment of death). But there is a gaping hole in the middle of the character's progress.

6 Verse and voice

McKellen is unusual in his combination of psychological studies of his characters with a Peter Hall-like obsession with verse-speaking. Sometimes the creation of back-story, however helpful to the actor, can seem odd when described. He wore two wedding rings as Lear because he saw Cordelia as the child of Lear's second wife, the love of Lear's life, dead in childbirth. Cordelia had therefore been brought up by Lear and now, at the moment of the play, looked to McKellen's Lear the same as her mother at the moment of her death. I don't see how an audience would have grasped ('read') any of this and perhaps it does not matter. More difficult, because more thematic than biographical, was McKellen's sense, shared by Nunn, of Lear's particular connection with the 'numinous' ('Exclusive Interview' on the *King Lear* DVD), a concept that produced the opening sequence of Lear as priest-king in Russian Orthodox vestments blessing the court. For McKellen it was this link with the gods that was 'all th'addition to a king' (1.1.136) and he gestured towards the heavens on the word *addition*. This seems both an odd reading of the phrase and something he does not manage to communicate in performance.

I have been pointing to weaknesses and I need to add to the list the irritation that some feel with the mannerisms in McKellen's voice. On the one hand there is the concern for fine verse-speaking. Hence, the day before the film of *Richard III* began rehearsals, McKellen wrote a long letter to Richard Loncraine, the director:

> but now I thought I should sit down and try
> to clarify what blank verse means to me;
> and thereby re-assure your doubting heart.
>
> (McKellen 1996, 31)

lines about which he teasingly points out: 'And yet, of course, they're written in blank verse!' (the letter is reprinted in McKellen 1996, 31–35). McKellen matches this with a willingness to change the odd word, always preserving the rhythm of the blank verse line, in the interests of making sure the audience is not confused by opaque archaisms, so 'presently' always becomes 'instantly'.

He could be irritated by the failure of training and experience to provide other actors with the same necessary tools for speaking Shakespeare's verse. The first month of rehearsals for *Coriolanus* was largely spent on 'teaching the company the basic rules of verse-speaking':

> It was, I think, a pity that that kind of work hadn't happened before rehearsals, because too much time was spent on it...But if you cast a play with people who aren't used to blank verse – Peter Hall had to give them a quick course...
>
> (Bedford 1992, 142)

McKellen's respect for verse is something not always shared by his contemporaries, even among those who are part of the Cambridge network. Above all, he has defined it as something which requires immense work from the actor and then must not be noticed as such by the audience. As he commented to John Barton, 'We don't want [the audience], as they're sitting through a play, to be aware of all this work that we've done' (Barton 1984, 45).

But, on the other hand, McKellen can also twist words into strange sounds. Benedict Nightingale's *New Statesman* review of McKellen's Coriolanus voices the dislike of such tricks most vociferously. It was headlined 'Booyaahayaaee':

> McKellen...has just been heard transforming the simple sentence 'Come I too late?' into 'Caahm Ai too laiyate?'. And so it goes on, insistently displaying its dissatisfaction with vowels as they are used by patricians and plebians...At the point of death the word 'boy' becomes a weird gurgling wail of 'booyaahayaaee'. In fact, there are times when one feels that

> Mr McKellen's tongue has invented a new tongue, or at least a new regional accent: a blend of melodic throb and euphonius whinny, mainly to be found on upmarket stages in and out of the metropolis.
>
> (Quoted in Gibson 1986, 145)

It is, of course, grotesquely unfair but it is also unusual for a critic to perform this kind of anatomical surgery on the speaking of a native English speaker – non-anglophone actors in Shakespeare are regularly pilloried in such terms. Nightingale was alone in his dislike, most critics reserving their venom for Hall's treatment of the audience-as-on-stage-crowd. Insofar as it is at all justified, it points to McKellen stretching his voice's resources at climactic moments, trying to find something to match the exceptional in Shakespeare. His voice is comparatively narrow in range of register and volume and such moments, especially Coriolanus' cry of 'Boy?' (5.6.117), demand sounds he cannot naturally reach. It is precisely the inability to achieve the large-scale grandeur that has meant that so many of his finest Shakespeare roles were in smaller venues (for example, The Other Place) and transferred successfully to filming for television.

7 An inconclusive conclusion

I return to my list and am struck afresh by the superb successes and the infrequency of failure. Leontes (1976) and Prospero (1999) were unusual in the widespread agreement that he had failed. *The Winter's Tale* suffered, in McKellen's view, from having three directors (Barton, Nunn and Barry Kyle). He had not really wanted ever to play Prospero and most reviews shared Smallwood's assessment of it as 'an eccentric but fascinating reading', carefully documenting in his account McKellen's performance of 'a profoundly weary, disillusioned Prospero, crotchety and aloof and slightly dotty':

> Weary old fuddy-duddy, his old brain more or less permanently troubled, was what we were mostly offered here – along with a virtuoso command of Shakespearian versespeaking. This was a Prospero one couldn't stop listening to – partly because some of the phrasing was so wilful that total attention was essential to stay abreast of meaning.

And, again, the technique was admired and very visible:

> But the sudden little spurts, the musicality with which certain phrases were slowed or speeded, language orchestrated as much as spoken, the apparent throwaway nonchalance that was in fact so precisely calculated, the mixture of the conversational and the majestic, the sheer bravura brilliance of technique unashamedly on display, were a constant source of fascination.
>
> (Smallwood 2000, 267)

Among roles that have rarely continued to figure as foregrounded parts in his Shakespeare line, the clip (available on his website) of McKellen's Sir Toby Belch in the RSC's 1978 small-scale tour shows a revisionary brilliance in this tweedy country gentleman, an intelligent man of whimsicality, sorrowfully aware that he was wasting his life. McKellen's reputation was not built on Shakespeare's comic characters but this briefly shows what he chose not to pursue. And in the performances that are now the stuff of theatre legend – Richard II, Romeo, Hamlet, Coriolanus, Iago, Richard III and what I unhesitatingly identify as the greatest Macbeth I have seen – the faults and problems pale away beside the pleasures, the energy, the craft, the verse-control, the intellectual and emotional exploration, the imagination and, not least, the unfiltered transmission to the audience of the sheer excitement of watching a great actor in a great Shakespeare role.

Selected chronology (professional roles)

1962	Belgrade, Coventry: Claudio (*Much Ado About Nothing*)
1963	Arts Theatre, Ipswich: Henry V (*Henry V*)
	Nottingham Playhouse: Aufidius (*Coriolanus*)
1964	Nottingham Playhouse: Sir Thomas More (*Sir Thomas More*)
1965	National Theatre: Claudio (*Much Ado About Nothing*)
1968	Prospect Theatre Company: Richard II (*Richard II*)
1971	Prospect Theatre Company: Hamlet (*Hamlet*)
1974	Actors' Company: Edgar (*King Lear*)
1975	Royal Shakespeare Company: Bastard (*King John*)
1976	Royal Shakespeare Company: Romeo (*Romeo and Juliet*), Leontes (*The Winter's Tale*), Macbeth (*Macbeth*)
1978	Royal Shakespeare Company: Sir Toby Belch (*Twelfth Night*)
1984	National Theatre: Coriolanus (*Coriolanus*)
1989	Royal Shakespeare Company: Iago (*Othello*)
1990	National Theatre: Kent (*King Lear*), Richard III (*Richard III*)
1999	West Yorkshire Playhouse: Prospero (*The Tempest*)
2007	Royal Shakespeare Company: King Lear (*King Lear*)

Bibliography

Barratt, Mark (2005) *Ian McKellen: An Unofficial Biography* London: Virgin Books.

Barton, John (1984) *Playing Shakespeare* London: Methuen.

Bedford, Kristina (1992) *'Coriolanus' at the National: 'Th'Interpretation of the Time'* London: Associated University Presses.

Cox, Brian (1992) *The Lear Diaries* London: Methuen.

Crowl, Samuel (1997) 'Changing Colors Like the Chameleon: Ian McKellen's *Richard III* from Stage to Film', *Post Script* 17, 53–63.

Crystal, David (2002) *Shakespeare's Words* London: Penguin Books.

——*Pronouncing Shakespeare: The Globe Experiment* (Cambridge: Cambridge University Press, 2005).

Gibson, Joy Leslie (1986) *Ian McKellen: A Biography*, London: George Weidenfeld and Nicolson.

Kliman, Bernice W. (1992) *Macbeth* Manchester: Manchester University Press.

McKellen, Ian (1996) *William Shakespeare's 'Richard III': A Screenplay*, London: Doubleday.
Smallwood, Robert (1990) 'Shakespeare at Stratford-upon Avon, 1989 (Part I)', *Shakespeare Quarterly* 41, 101–14.
——(2000) 'Shakespeare Performances in England, 1999' *Shakespeare Survey* 53, Cambridge: Cambridge University Press, 244–73.

Websites

David Crystal, 'Shakespeare's Words': www.shakespearewords.com
Sir Ian McKellen Official Website: www.mckellen.com

DVD releases

Acting Shakespeare (E1 Entertainment, 2009).
King Lear (Metrodome Distribution, 2008).
Macbeth (Fremantle Media, 2004).
Marlowe, *Edward II* (Warner Home Video, 2009).
Othello (Metrodome Distribution, 2003).
Richard III (MGM Home Entertainment, 2000).

About the author

Peter Holland has, since 2002, been McMeel Family Professor in Shakespeare Studies in the Department of Film, Television, and Theatre at the University of Notre Dame. Educated at Cambridge, he was Judith E. Wilson Reader in Drama in the Faculty of English there. From 1997 to 2002 he was Director of the Shakespeare Institute, Stratford-upon-Avon, and Professor of Shakespeare Studies at the University of Birmingham. He is editor of *Shakespeare Survey* and co-editor of *Great Shakespeareans* and *Oxford Shakespeare Topics*. He is the author and editor of many books, including *English Shakespeares* (Cambridge, 1997). He has been a Governor of the Royal Shakespeare Company and a regular broadcaster for the BBC. He has been watching Ian McKellen on stage and screen with delight ever since seeing him as Marlowe's Edward II in 1970.

13
Marcello Magni
Stephen Purcell

Elizabethan clown and fool roles have often been seen as a sort of concession to popular taste: an unfortunate necessity which poetic drama just about managed to accommodate. Philip Sidney's *Apologie for Poetry* famously decried plays which 'thrust in clowns by head and shoulders, to play a part in majestical matters', and this set the tone for a great deal of theatrical criticism which followed: Samuel Taylor Coleridge, for example, suggested in 1818 that *Macbeth*'s Porter sequence was probably 'written for the mob by some other hand, perhaps with Shakespeare's consent' (1907: 377), while in 1910, Ronald Bayne argued in the *Cambridge History of English Literature* that the Elizabethan clown 'was a discordant and incalculable element in the play, and hindered the development of artistic drama' (1910: 313–14).

More recently, however, critics have begun to reassess the role played by clowns in Shakespeare's plays. In his influential study *Shakespeare's Clown*, David Wiles takes issue with 'an established critical discourse which isolates a game from a play, sport from theatre, clown acts from deep or significant art' (1987: 167). Analysing Shakespeare's clown and fool roles within their historical contexts, with detailed reference to the actors who played them, Wiles makes the case for an understanding of the Shakespearean clown as 'game-maker', arguing that 'the clown performed *with*, and not *to*, an audience constructed as equals' (1987: 179).

A similar understanding of clowning as 'game' is what underpins the work of one of the most prolific performers of Shakespeare's clown and fool roles in Britain today. Marcello Magni's first question on approaching such a role is simply, 'What's the *game* that Shakespeare is creating?' Thus, for example, when he played Launcelot Gobbo at Shakespeare's Globe in 1998, the game in his scene with Ralph Watson's Old Gobbo became 'trying to make my father totally mad in trying to find where I was':

> How I can make it difficult for him to find me? How can I make my voice come from all different directions? How can I confuse him? How can I make the development of my play become bigger and bigger, wilder and wilder, nastier and nastier?
>
> (Interview, June 2010)

Magni took Launcelot's desire to 'try confusions' (2.2.34) with his blind father very literally, mimicking a dog, a cat, and a horse, and brought the sequence to a climax by climbing one of the Globe's pillars and spraying his father (and the audience) with half-chewed pieces of apple. For *Shakespeare Survey*'s Richard Proudfoot, the sequence 'transformed the often dull (or cut) scene with his blind father into a comic high point' (1999: 220) and 'displayed the theatrical dynamic that so easily made the clown the dominant figure in Elizabethan acting companies' (1999: 219).

Magni is perhaps known better for his physical theatre work than his Shakespearean performances. Born in Bergamo, he studied at Bologna University before moving to Paris and training at the renowned École Internationale de Théâtre Jacques Lecoq. There and elsewhere, he trained in mime, clowning and physical theatre with such practitioners as Philippe Gaulier, Pierre Byland and Yves LeBreton. Upon graduating from Lecoq's school, he moved to London and co-founded Complicite (then called Théâtre de Complicité) with Annabel Arden and Simon McBurney, and in 1985 they won the Perrier Comedy Award for their clown show *More Bigger Snacks Now*. Their first foray into Shakespeare – 1992's *The Winter's Tale*, in which Magni played Autolycus – was also Magni's Shakespearean debut. He would go on to play the Fool in Helena Kaut-Howson's *King Lear* (Leicester Haymarket and Young Vic, 1997) before being invited to join the company at Shakespeare's Globe by Mark Rylance in 1998. His performances there included Launcelot Gobbo in *The Merchant of Venice* (1998), both Dromios in *The Comedy of Errors* (1999), and various roles in *Pericles* (2005). More recently, he played Roderigo in *Othello* for the Royal Shakespeare Company (2009).

It is worth noting that the majority of Magni's Shakespearean performances have resulted in some way from his long-term collaboration with the actor and director Kathryn Hunter (his partner in both his personal and his professional life). Hunter directed him in three of the productions discussed here (*The Comedy of Errors*, *Pericles* and *Othello*), and performed alongside him in a further two (*The Winter's Tale* and *King Lear*). In an interview with the *Independent*, Magni explained that Hunter was 'very strong in the interpretation of the text, while my formation leads me more towards the images, the physicality of the presentation' (2 March 1997). This complementary double-act has often seen Magni work alongside Hunter as movement director (as on *The Comedy of Errors*, *Pericles* and *Othello*), as well as bringing his physical expertise to a variety of Shakespearean roles – not all of them comic – in her productions.

Play as physical game

Magni invariably characterizes himself as a physical (rather than primarily textual) performer; he always interprets his characters 'from a physical point of view', setting out 'to understand what the physical situation is'. The concept of 'game' is central to this. He explains that 'the release of the physical expression of the situation must be performed with pleasure':

> That's what I mean by 'the play'. In French, it means 'to play' when you are on stage: *jouer*, *le jeu*. I understand theatre like that.
>
> (Interview, June 2010)

This model of acting is derived from Magni's training in the methods of Jacques Lecoq, whose writing makes much of the various meanings contained in the words *jouer* and *le jeu*. For Lecoq, 'game', 'playing', 'acting' and 'performance' are collided with a stress on the importance of 'playfulness'.

For Magni, the 'game' is the physical manifestation of his character's situation. Sometimes it takes the form of illustration: when, for example, he performed Dromio's horrified description of Nell the kitchen wench in *The Comedy of Errors* (3.2.90–152), he mimed it grotesquely, swimming in her imaginary sweat and illustrating her 'spherical' body by puffing out his own. Later on, as Dromio attempted to exert emotional pressure on Adriana, the line 'Will you send him, mistress, redemption?' (4.2.46) was followed up with a fast-paced mime of Antipholus's predicted suffering and execution, and the subsequent departure of his soul towards heaven.

Sometimes the 'game' is a more literal one. In 2.2 of *The Comedy of Errors*, the long string of puns following 'There's no time for a man to recover his hair that grows bald by nature' (2.2.72) was punctuated by a sort of tennis match between Antipholus and Dromio. Several reviews characterized this as an attempt 'to take our attention away from a patch of dull dialogue' (*The Times*, 7 June 1999) or as having 'overshadow[ed] the speech it is meant to illustrate' (*Evening Standard*, 4 June 1999), but the sequence was not as disconnected from the text as these comments suggest. Magni stresses that it grew out of a very close reading of the text, and was an attempt to physicalize the dynamics of the scene:

> The image I had at that moment was that I was sending something back violently, with the energy of wanting to defend myself.
>
> (Interview, September 2010)

As Susannah Clapp's review points out, the 'battling motion' began, after 'a few deft returns', to emphasize the 'rhythm and vehemence' of the lines (*Observer*, 13 June 1999).

Magni's game-playing is almost always about physicalizing an emotional or interpersonal dynamic. He explains:

> There must be always, in the relationship of a play, a certain *tactic*. In life we are like that: we charm, we entice. I see it in a playful way, like a game. So then I have to put it physically on stage. I have to find the dynamic of that play. Either it's attraction – pulling – or it's pushing, it's rejection. And then there are many different variations on doing that – searching, hunting. They're all physical expressions.
>
> (Interview, June 2010)

This is another application of Lecoq, who taught that 'everything a person does in their life can be reduced to two essential actions: "to pull" and "to push"':

> We do nothing else! These actions include the passive 'I am pulled' and 'I am pushed' and the reflexive 'I pull myself' and 'I push myself' and can go in many different directions: forwards, to one side or the other, backwards, diagonally, etc.
>
> (Lecoq 2002: 84)

An expression of love, hunger, or desire, then, might involve 'pulling' physically; rejection, disgust, or hatred might be a 'push'; one might resist something by refusing to be pulled, or acquiesce by allowing oneself to be. Dramatic conflict, of course, will always involve some sort of unreconciled tension between pulling and pushing.

A straightforward example can be found in Launcelot Gobbo's monologue about the conscience and the fiend (2.2.1–29). Magni would mime being pulled diagonally in two directions, shushing an imaginary character each way before speaking. Mimicking 'the fiend', he would kneel, miming horns, while his 'conscience' was upright and weightless; 'Budge!' and 'Budge not!' (2.2.18) became a frenetic physical repeat of the introductory mime as Launcelot was pulled towards each character with increasing pace. In Magni's performance, Launcelot's indecision as to which direction to take became a virtuosic physical performance of a clown almost literally pulling himself apart.

Magni identified a similar physical tension in the dynamic between Lear and his Fool. Lear begins by calling for his Fool – certainly a 'pull' – and greets him as 'my pretty knave' (1.4.95) – another 'pull'. But within a few lines, Lear takes umbrage at the Fool's satirical remarks, and warns, 'Take heed, sirrah – the whip' (1.4.109) – a 'push'. He alternates between pushing ('A bitter fool', 1.4.134) and pulling ('Teach me', 1.4.137) for the rest of the scene. Magni explains:

> It's almost as if the King says, 'I want my Fool close to me. – Careful! I'm going to hit you! – Come here. – Careful!' It's like this game in which physically you're being asked to get close – and then you say too much, and then you are whipped – and then you try again to get close. It's between the King inviting, and saying, 'Careful! I'm going to hit you!'
>
> (Interview, June 2010)

Magni describes the physical dynamic as 'like a constant elastic': 'How close can he be, and not be caught? And at the same time, he's asked to get closer' (Interview, June 2010).

Magni's Fool became more intimate with Kathryn Hunter's Lear over the course of the play. In the scene on the heath, for example, he made use of the physical dynamic between himself and the diminutive Hunter:

> The King could not hold me – but I could hold the King. So in the storm, Kathryn leaned on me – I held her up like she was a fallen tree. She went up the scaffolding and I caught her when she was falling. So it was a very different relationship: I was like the bodyguard, the bouncer, the friend, the companion.
>
> (Interview, June 2010)

The production featured several moments of poignant tenderness between Lear and the Fool. At one point, the two performed a soft-shoe shuffle together; at another, the Fool cowered in the shadows while Lear railed against his daughters, and according to *The Times*, 'the expression on his face [told] you how well he [could] read the future' (4 July 1997). The physical became an extension of the poetic, mirroring and elaborating its tensions and its dynamics.

Physical eloquence

Magni emphasizes the importance of 'physical language'. He has frequently spoken of the English theatre's reluctance to embrace the physical, suggesting in 1993, for example, that 'English theatre has forgotten how to be big' (*The Times*, 12 January), or expressing his alarm in 1996 that movement classes and warm-ups were not compulsory at the RSC (*Observer*, 10 November). Upon his arrival at Shakespeare's Globe in 1998, he found many of the company insufficiently physical in their approach, relying on the language to do everything for them. He felt a further kind of 'eloquence' was required:

> What is the physical language that matches your situation? We have to prepare people to be eloquent in this way too....Frequently we say, 'go to the end of the line', but we don't say enough 'go to the end of your physical expression or gesture'.
>
> (Bessel 1999: 26–27)

In rehearsal, Magni will spend a huge proportion of his time working physically. Rehearsing *The Winter's Tale* in 1992, Complicite would turn to text work only at around 4pm, after a long day of physical rehearsal (a process based on ensemble movement work is the norm for Complicite). In 1998, Magni would sit, move and write as Launcelot Gobbo even when he was not working on his scenes for *The Merchant of Venice* (Globe Education 1998). The following year, he found it useful to take on the physicality of particular animals when developing his roles (a monkey and a fish for Dromios of Ephesus and Syracuse respectively), and to find objects which externalized particular character traits (worry beads for the put-upon Dromio of Ephesus, and a handkerchief for his brother – a visitor in a hot climate) (Globe Education 1999). His *Pericles* rehearsal notes describe his characters in similarly visual terms: King Simonides was to be 'quite round and positive and jovial', Helicanus 'a straight person – like a flag or a strong point of reference', while Boult, the brothel doorkeeper, was 'always on the move': 'he's a lightning bolt, dashing from place to place' (Globe Education 2005).

Magni's work at Shakespeare's Globe has often been a response to the demands of the space itself. 'I love that theatre,' he explains, 'because it requires you to perform in a different way':

> You can't hide. You are seen by everyone: you're seen 360 degrees, in all directions. You work in the daylight....It's a requirement of the space to be physical in your dialogue, contact, movement. You can't be 'looked at' – you are 'looking at', and they look at you. It's two ways. You have to call upon focus. The focus is not given to you by lights, so you have to go and *present* yourself.
>
> (Interview, May 2004)

He has described movement at the Globe as 'like editing on stage', in that performers need to move their bodies to shift focus in the same way that modern film-makers use cameras. Calling the building 'an actor-athlete's space', he stresses the importance of physical warm-ups (Bessel 1999: 26). Magni himself likes to be 'alert like a cat' during a show, and in order to achieve this state for his Globe performances he would spend 40 minutes running and stretching, warm up his voice, and then play 'a kind of volleyball' with the company in the theatre yard (Globe Education 2005).

Magni's time at the Globe also had a great influence on his delivery of Shakespeare's text:

> Mark Rylance loves the robustness of the language, and I thought, 'Yeah, I'm a physical performer, I understand that. I understand how I have to be robust with my way of speaking: I have to *find* different words, I have to hit them, I have to liberate them, I have to explode them, I have to make them soft or delicate.'
>
> (Interview, June 2010)

Magni is keen to emphasize that speech is not independent of the body; he points out that the term 'physical theatre' ought to be tautological, since '*all* theatre is physical'. 'When you use your body as well as you use your voice,' he argues, '*then* you have magical theatre' (Interview, September 2010).

Commedia dell'arte

An important factor in Magni's performance style is his background in *commedia dell'arte*. He trained in the traditional Italian form with the expert Antonio Fava, and has performed extensively in the work of what he describes as 'a wide spectrum of commedia writers': Molière, Marivaux, Goldoni and Ruzante.

Commedia dell'arte originated in the carnivals and marketplaces of medieval Italy, and the period described by John Rudlin as its 'golden one' (1994: 1) was roughly contemporaneous with the Elizabethan era in England. Performed in public spaces on temporary platforms, commedia was a form of masked, semi-improvised comedy which relied heavily on physical display. Its stock characters included Arlecchino – better known in English as 'Harlequin' – who was one of the low-status servant characters, or *zanni*. Magni has specialized in this role in particular.

Magni was initially invited to join the company of *The Merchant of Venice* at the Globe because of his *commedia* background. The production's director, Richard Olivier, was keen to emphasize the play's Venetian carnival setting, and hired Magni to perform a commedia-like prologue and intervals between the play's five acts. As Magni explains,

> at the carnival of Venice, it must be that there are people performing commedia in the streets of Venice. Therefore there must be an Arlecchino, there must be a *zanni*.
>
> (Interview, May 2004)

Magni played a masked, Arlecchino-like character for these interludes. He would enter the stage ringing a bell at the beginning and end of each interval, announcing the interval length in a variety of languages. Magni would spend these interludes engaging in physical comedy (the bell would get 'stuck' to his hand), making a pantomime of falling in love with audience members, posing for photographs and stealing handbags. He would interact with people standing in the yard, seated in the galleries, waiting outside the theatre, or even outside in the street. Frequently, he would drag a female playgoer onto the stage and behind the discovery space's curtain, from which would emanate some highly suggestive noises.

He played Launcelot Gobbo without a mask, but the sense that his Arlecchino character was an extension of Launcelot – or vice versa – was marked. An itinerant worker from the Italian countryside, always on the lookout for food, drink and sex (and keen to avoid having to do any work), Arlecchino shares many characteristics with the clown in Shakespeare's play. Magni describes him thus:

> Cheeky, charming, trying to survive, trying to please. The servant is terrified, or is eager to get the job, or is terribly hungry, or wants to waste a lot of time in order not to work.
>
> (Interview, May 2004)

When Magni played the Dromios in *The Comedy of Errors* the following year, he found that they too were characters 'in the spirit of commedia'; Kathryn Hunter noted in the programme that they were 'classic harlequin, or clown, characters' (Neill 1999).

Magni has found an understanding of commedia useful not only in the direct parallels, but also in a broader sense. He uses the commedia concept of *lazzi* (*lazzo* in the singular form) to describe a particular kind of comic physical storytelling. When playing Boult in *Pericles*, for example, he carried around a small door bolt, using it to mime the action of unbolting a door, and adding vocal sound effects as he opened and closed the mimed door ('*squeeeeak*…SLAM!'). This short movement sequence – or *lazzo* – was repeated, faster and more frenetically, as the performance progressed. Magni explains that it was a physicalization of Boult's role in the play:

> We understand 'gag', but not so many people understand *lazzo*. A gag is: I fall on the table once with my head, and I get hurt. The *lazzo* could be what I did with Boult and the bolt at the door. I developed it. The gag stays where it is. A *lazzo* is something that is also connected to your emotional state. So I wanted to give him a sense of: 'I am controlling this house. I am the boss at the door.' *Lazzo* is like taps of your emotional journey – comically.
>
> (Interview, June 2010)

The bolt was not the only *lazzo* in the production. Though King Simonides is hardly a typical clown role – indeed, Magni's clowning was generally much more understated in this part – the scene in which Simonides 'dissembles' his disapproval of his daughter's marriage provided one of the production's most slapstick moments. In Magni's performance, Simonides' playful deception was just as much of a 'game' as

Launcelot Gobbo's had been: upon the line 'Thou liest like a traitor' (9.47), both Simonides and Pericles threw off their jackets, shoes and socks, and engaged in a farcical wrestling match, complete with tweaks of nipples and noses and attempts to steady themselves by grabbing hold of audience members. Some critics complained that the sequence demolished any sense of subtlety: Benedict Nightingale, for example, wondered how 'loss, grief and other matters of the heart' could 'exist in such circumstances' (*The Times*, 6 June 2005). But the scene was a comic rendering of a very real human emotion (protective paternal love), providing a kind of parodic foreshadowing of the play's final scenes. As Magni explains, 'Simonides loves his daughter and although the fight is fun, it is hard for him to give her away' (Globe Education 2005).

In this sense, one can see this sort of physical joke as much more than a simple attempt to make an audience laugh; rather, it provides a comic picture of the character's situation in the play at that given point, and may well provide resonances beyond it. Several critics commented on the effectiveness of a moment in *King Lear* when Magni found inspiration for a much darker joke in the text's wordplay:

FOOL. Nuncle, give me an egg, and I'll give thee two crowns.
LEAR. What two crowns shall they be?
FOOL. Why, after I have cut the egg i'th' middle, and eat up the meat, the two crowns of the egg.

(1.4.138–42)

Sticking the broken eggshells into his eyes in a gruesome parody of Lear's wild staring, the moment became, in the words of Michael Coveney, 'a Beckettian image of blindness' (*Observer*, 2 March 1997).

Spontaneity and play

One of the more controversial aspects of Magni's Shakespearean performances – as far as press reviewers are concerned, at least – is his tendency to depart from the Shakespearean text. This was certainly evident in his very first Shakespearean role. Aware of the need for a textual specialist when staging *The Winter's Tale*, Théâtre de Complicité invited the experienced classical director Annie Castledine to collaborate with them on the production as Associate Director. It was Castledine who first suggested that Magni, who was having difficulty with the complexities of Autolycus's language, should speak his lines in Italian. Magni explains:

> I was not at all good in English, so a lot of the text was cut: the entire first introduction, 'When daffodils begin to peer,' and all that....She [Castledine] said, 'Start in Italian, and then translate it into English, into correct Shakespearean English.' So every phrase was broken up – first in Italian, then in translation.
>
> (Interview, June 2010)

Magni's first few translations were, in fact, very loose – Peter Holland reports that 'I have served Prince Florizel, and in my time wore three-pile' (4.3.13–14), for example, became a brag about an 'Armani suit' (1997: 125). As the sequence went on, however, Magni started to 'translate' his Italian lines into ever-more perfect Shakespearean ones.

Magni continued to elaborate on his lines in later productions. In *The Merchant of Venice*, his Launcelot Gobbo monologue became an inspired piece of audience interaction, involving playgoers very directly in the 'game'. Concluding that 'to run away from the Jew I should be ruled by the fiend, who, saving your reverence, is the very devil himself' (2.2.22–24), he turned to the audience to ask for their help:

> What should I do, huh? [*Pause. To a groundling*:] What should I do? [*Pause.*] PLEASE HELP! [*Mimics nonchalant pose of groundling. Audience laughter.*]

He then solicited responses from the playgoers in the yard, who would call out a variety of solutions. He continued:

> You're confused, huh? Please, okay, hands up for the fiend! [*Hands go up in the yard.*] One, two, three – hold it, hold it...[*He tries frantically to count hundreds of hands.*] Hold it, hold it!...Nobody in the galleries, huh? Thanks very much! [*Laughter.*] That's because you're all rich, you are! [*Laughter.*] Hands up for the conscience, please! [*Pointing at gallery.*] Ah, now, there! [*Playful booing from yard.*]
>
> (Transcribed from video recording)

In true *commedia dell'arte* style, he made much of an imagined social distinction between the audience members in the yard (working-class, likely to resent a miserly boss) and those in the galleries (bourgeois, likely to sympathize with the employer). It was a comic provocation which continued to echo as the play progressed, and the themes of commerce and class difference took on a darker tone.

Magni's priorities are clear – it is theatrical function, not text, which has precedence. He stated as much very clearly in an interview with *Theatre Annual* in 2000:

> In *Winter's Tale* we tried to be faithful to the story, but we were not scared, in the case of the clown, to select what was important in order to convey what is a clown for the 90s....If the text doesn't convey what is required, chuck it. Otherwise you are a parrot, not an interpreter. Many times I think that actors don't go to the level of thinking they are regiving birth to the text.
>
> (Wade 2000: 75)

But Magni's apparent iconoclasm might not be as radical as it seems. As David Wiles points out, all of the roles thought to have been played by Shakespeare's clown Will Kemp allow space for improvisation, containing 'at least one short scene in which he speaks directly to the audience':

> This monologue is normally placed at the end of a scene, and thus seems to provide a format within which the clown may extemporise without risk to the rhythm of the play or direction of the narrative.
>
> (1987: 107)

Various contemporary sources suggest that Kemp was indeed a gifted improviser (see Purcell 2009: 67–69). But even if such improvisation did not take place (and we must remember that unscripted performance on the Elizabethan stage would have bordered on the illegal), Shakespeare's clown and fool roles are very often scripted *as if* they are improvising. As Wiles points out in his discussion of Launcelot Gobbo (though he could be referring to any number of Shakespeare's clowns), 'the fact that the clown speaks in prose when most of the play is in verse creates the illusion of spontaneity' (1987: 9). Often, this scripted improvisation takes the form of a game: Autolycus extemporizes in order to fool the Shepherd and his son (4.4.715–831); Touchstone dupes the residents of the Forest of Arden throughout *As You Like It*; Feste plays a nasty game with Malvolio by dressing up as 'Sir Topas' (*Twelfth Night*, 4.2); we have already explored Launcelot Gobbo's deception of his father, and there are many further examples.

Critical resistance to Magni's performances, however, has often focused on his willingness to abandon the text. Paul Taylor's review of *The Winter's Tale*, for example – conceding that Magni's performance was 'very funny' – argued that the constant ad-libbing betrayed an 'insufficient trust in the play' (*Independent*, 4 April 1992). In the first of many reviews which would take a dim view of Magni's Shakespearean performances, Benedict Nightingale found the same production's clowning 'dreadfully witless' and 'incomprehensible' (*The Times*, 4 April 1992). The *Evening Standard*'s Michael Arditti perhaps summed up the bias of many such critics in his review: 'while undeniably entertaining,' he noted, 'this is of limited appeal to one brought up on the poetical realist style and liberal humanist philosophy of the RSC and Trevor Nunn' (8 April 1992).

Shakespeare Survey's Robert Smallwood articulated similar concerns in his review of *The Comedy of Errors*, arguing that the production had 'sold out…to the lowest common denominator of groundling taste':

> Marcello Magni is undoubtedly a very accomplished mime artist, but as a Shakespearean actor he is not an easy taste to acquire.…To cast in a role for which the basic requirement is sharpness and dexterity in verbal repartee an actor whose command of spoken English is at best precarious is openly to declare that one's primary interest is not in the play's verbal texture.
>
> (2000: 261)

Leaving aside the issue of Magni's spoken English (which is hardly 'precarious'), Smallwood was probably correct in identifying that the production's interest was not primarily in 'verbal texture'. But to assume that a Shakespearean clown's primary interest even *should* be in the subtleties of wordplay is to misunderstand what a clown is for, and how such roles work dramaturgically.

Locus and *platea*

Annie Castledine found the critical reaction to Complicite's *The Winter's Tale* 'disappointing but not unnerving', and suggested that it had been largely misunderstood: far from being a silly trivialization of the play, she argues, it was a 'highly serious' production which took a fundamentally Brechtian approach to its source. The idea, she says, was that it should be impossible for the audience to sustain any one response to the play, switching (as does the text itself) between comedy and tragedy, engagement and distance. Magni's controversial performance choices were, she explains, based on Autolycus's function in the play: 'it's important that the audience take him straight to their hearts' (Interview, May 2006). Magni himself describes Autolycus as the 'unwitting catalyst' of the play's happy ending, and stresses the dramatic importance of making the audience laugh with the character – even if it is at the expense of the text itself (Interview, September 2010).

Lois Potter touched on the dramaturgical function of the clown in her account of the Globe's *The Merchant of Venice*. Before the play started, a black-robed choir sang an Italian madrigal on the Globe's stage; at the same time, Magni's Arlecchino was in the yard with a chaotic group of masked commedia performers, singing loudly and banging drums. Potter read this as a battle between Carnival and Lent, foreshadowing the contrast between Gratiano and Antonio in the play's first scene:

> High and popular culture, initially separated as neatly as in Robert Weimann's *locus* and *platea*, were now competing for the same space and for our attention. It was both funny and embarrassing; we weren't sure whether we really wanted to participate in this attempted sabotage of high art.
>
> (Potter 1999: 75)

But in Weimann's theory as it applies to the Elizabethan theatre, in fact, *locus* and *platea* were not 'neatly separated' at all. For Weimann, Shakespeare's drama staged an interplay between these two very different modes of performance inherited from medieval theatre: one the one hand, the *locus*, which was the site of heightened drama, generally in verse and featuring high-status characters; on the other, the *platea*, a 'theatrical dimension of the real world' which encompassed direct address, audience interaction, vernacular prose, and clowning (1987: 76). But neither was staged in its purest form: 'between these extremes,' explains Weimann, 'lay the broad and very flexible range of dramatic possibilities so skillfully developed by the popular Renaissance dramatist' (1987: 212). Thus, for example, Lear's 'grandiose and rhetorical' speeches are tempered in the very same scenes by the 'simple, everyday speech' of the Fool (1987: 216). The result, for Weimann, is a 'dual perspective' which encompasses 'conflicting views of experience' (1987: 243).

Clowns are not isolated from the rest of the play – they may be 'discordant elements', but they bring a perspective to the play which has a relationship with its other dramatic elements. In a 1998 article titled 'Send out the clowns at the Globe', Benedict Nightingale complained that

> Magni continues to run amok in *The Merchant*, doing horse impressions, miming death throes, and I don't know what.
>
> (*The Times*, 3 August 1998)

In response, Mark Rylance defended Magni's performance on the grounds that he was 'doing exactly what the text suggests, which is to play tricks on his near-blind father':

> The play is a comedy, and Magni's role is to play the clown. I really was not convinced last weekend that this action hindered or coarsened the audience's judgment of the situation in which Shylock finds himself.
>
> (*The Times*, 14 August 1998)

The point is arguable. On the one hand, the audience were much more inclined to laughter after the Gobbo scene than they had been before it, and their mirth persisted even into the trial scene, where Gratiano's anti-Semitic insults and the Duke's instruction that Shylock must 'presently become a Christian' (4.1.384) were met with laughter. On the other, it is somewhat patronizing to audiences to assume that their laughter renders them incapable of switching to any other mode of reception, or of registering moral ambiguity. As Dominic Cavendish's review pointed out,

> Far from rendering our responses insincere, this universal role-playing charges the atmosphere with ambivalent emotion.
>
> (*Independent*, 1 June 1998)

The audience were not asked simply to side with the clown. Even at its most benign, the comedy had a distinctly nasty edge to it, and several playgoers audibly sympathized with Old Gobbo as Launcelot lied to the old man about his son's death. Potter identified the moment when Magni's Launcelot kicked his blind father's cane away as 'the epitome of carnivalesque behaviour', suggesting that it highlighted the extent to which the play 'gets a lot of its laughs from cruelty' (1999: 75).

There were moments in *Pericles* when the comedy reached a kind of breaking-point. Hannah Betts, condemning the production as 'ghastly', complained that

> when presented with the prospect of a virgin being about to be raped by a blunt instrument, the audience falls about laughing – not edgy, uncomfortable laughter, but great guffaws of hilarity as the child-like victim cowers centre stage.
>
> (*The Times*, 11 June 2005)

Betts seems to have watched a very different performance from the one videotaped for the Globe's archives. Certainly, the gruesome reality of Boult's attempted rape was abundantly clear, as he unrolled a rusty toolkit and promised that Marina would be 'ploughed' (19.170). But the laughs were laughs of horror, and at times, they stopped entirely. Most powerful was a horribly invasive clowning sequence in which Boult and the Bawd examined Marina (16.54–56), prompting much audience laughter, which culminated in a horrified silence:

BAWD. Boult, take you the marks of her, the colour of her hair –
BOULT. [*peering under her skirt*] Natural.
BAWD. Complexion –
BOULT. [*sniffing her armpit*] Fresh.
BAWD. Height –
BOULT. [*squeezing her breasts*] Pert.
BAWD. Her age –

BOULT. [*kissing her*] Underage.
BAWD. With warrant of her – [*Bawd grabs Marina's crotch as Marina screams*] – virginity.

(Transcribed from video recording)

Here, comedy veered suddenly into something else. The silence was all the more intense because of the noisy enjoyment which had preceded it: its sudden change of tone was, perhaps, *locus* and *platea* interplay at its most dramatically effective.

Laughing and crying

Magni's most recent Shakespearean role (at the time of writing) was significantly different from any of those which have been discussed above. When Kathryn Hunter was casting her production of *Othello* for the Royal Shakespeare Company, Magni asked her for 'a challenge':

> I said, 'Iago!' And she said, 'No, they will kill you.' [*laughs*] And I understood, because you have to be an expert in the language. I love that character: he's terrible, he's horrible, he's fantastic. But linguistically, I would have no defence whatsoever from anyone saying, 'You're not up to the level of the language.'
>
> (Interview, June 2010)

The compromise upon which they settled was Roderigo: a role within Magni's linguistic capabilities, but one which would challenge him as a dramatic actor.

Magni set out to take his character seriously. 'I didn't want to be a clown at all,' he explains. 'He's not a clown. He's in love, he's desperately in love.' Thus, Roderigo's first appearance was a suicide attempt from a Venetian bridge; his final one, an attempt to shoot Michael Gould's Iago with a gun:

> I tried to be truly overwhelmed, to be emotionally distraught. I made him terribly, terribly angry.... Psychologically, I tried to connect every moment of the text to some kind of echo of a moment in life in which I had seen or felt that kind of emotion, in somebody else, or in me.
>
> (Interview, June 2010)

Magni notes that while this was a significant shift in his approach, however, it was not a complete departure: 'I always have an image of a person, so in a way I always work psychologically.'

His performance was still very physical, of course. His Roderigo hung from the bridge for most of the first scene, as Iago attempted to rescue him:

> I wanted to give the picture of the emotion. I didn't simply say 'I am terribly sad', or whatever. That's why in the final scene I took the gun, and I menaced him [Iago] like I was doing a hold-up, so to speak. And maybe in English theatre this is seen as extreme, but for me, that's how I see theatre. I see theatre in a picture.
>
> (Interview, June 2010)

One might wonder whether Magni's external, picture-led approach was somewhat at odds with his attempts at emotional memory. His performance was widely interpreted as comic: Lyn Gardner's review, for example, describes his Roderigo as 'a complete buffoon' (*The Guardian*, 7 February 2009), and he often provoked laughter in performance. Magni felt that since Roderigo would not be '*au fait* with weapons', his gun would discharge accidentally, but that 'when he finally tries to use a gun, he does it seriously'. 'But people misunderstood it,' he explains:

> They thought I wanted to be funny....I wanted to touch the audience. If I didn't, maybe I still have to learn a lot in playing those kinds of characters.
> (Interview, June 2010)

Whether 'funny' and 'touching' are mutually exclusive, of course, is open to debate: readers who have seen Magni's work with Complicite may well suspect that a clown of his calibre is more than capable of achieving both at once.

Magni recently visited the vocal coach Kristin Linklater, and worked with her on the role of King Lear. 'It gave me an enormous satisfaction,' he says; 'my dream would be to play Lear'. He and Hunter plan to return to the play, in fact, after Hunter's own performance as the Fool in David Farr's 2010 RSC production. It might strike one as odd that a performer so widely associated with clown roles hopes to undertake such a serious part, but Magni does not think so:

> As a performer you always want to touch both extremes: to be on one level, comic, and then in another moment, very, very human and touching. And in Shakespeare – I've found that in moments, he's very funny, and then in moments, extremely painful. As a dramatist, his range is huge, the variety of emotion is fantastic, and you only have to have the courage sometimes to go further. My irritation is that sometimes I can't, but I know I see Kathryn, Mark Rylance, other actors, and you go, and you cry. You laugh, and you cry.
> (Interview, June 2010)

In most of Shakespeare's plays, one can identify a shifting dynamic between tragedy and comedy, the beautiful and the grotesque, engagement and distance, illusion and self-reflexivity. Clowning, as Magni's career has shown, can play a resonant and powerful role in that dynamic. Whether an approach based in clowning can span its full range must be open to question – but it is a question that Magni's work will surely continue to explore. After all, if any of Shakespeare's plays blurs the line separating tragic protagonist and fool, it is *King Lear*.

Selected chronology

1981–82	Trained at L'École Internationale de Théâtre Jacques Lecoq, Paris.
1983	Formed Théâtre de Complicité with Annabel Arden and Simon McBurney.

1984	Won the Perrier Comedy Award for *More Bigger Snacks Now*.
1992	Autolycus / Mariner / Gaoler in *The Winter's Tale* (dir. Annabel Arden, Théâtre de Complicité, international tour).
1996	Co-directed *Everyman* for the Royal Shakespeare Company with Kathryn Hunter (The Other Place, Stratford-upon-Avon, and BAM, New York).
1997	Fool in *King Lear* (dir. Helena Kaut-Howson, Leicester Haymarket and Young Vic).
1998	Launcelot Gobbo in *The Merchant of Venice* (dir. Richard Olivier, Shakespeare's Globe).
1999	Dromio of Syracuse / Dromio of Ephesus in *The Comedy of Errors* (dir. Kathryn Hunter, Shakespeare's Globe).
2003	One-man show *Arlecchino* (dir. Jos Houben & Kathryn Hunter, BAC) and Master of Comedic Play on *The Taming of the Shrew* (dir. Phyllida Lloyd, Shakespeare's Globe).
2005	Master of Physical Play and Helicanus / Simonides / Boult in *Pericles* (dir. Kathryn Hunter, Shakespeare's Globe).
2009	Movement Director and Roderigo in *Othello* (dir. Kathryn Hunter, Royal Shakespeare Company, UK tour).

Bibliography

Bayne, Ronald (1910) 'Lesser Elizabethan Dramatists' in Ward, A. W. & Waller, A. R. [eds] *The Cambridge History of English Literature, Volume V: The Drama to 1642, Part One*, Cambridge: Cambridge University Press, 309–35.

Bessel, Jaq (1999) 'Interview with Marcello Magni' in *Globe Research Bulletin 15a: Interviews with the White Company*, <http://www.rdg.ac.uk/globe/research/1999/1999WhiteBulletin.htm>. Accessed 30 June 2010.

Coleridge, Samuel Taylor (1907) *Lectures and Notes on Shakespeare*, London: George Bell & Sons.

Globe Education (1998) 'Launcelot Gobbo', rehearsal notes, <http://www.globelink.org/resourcecentre/themerchantofvenice/launcelotgobbo/>. Accessed 30 June 2010.

——(1999) 'Dromio of Syracuse – Dromio of Ephesus', rehearsal notes, <http://www.globelink.org/resourcecentre/comedyoferrors/dromioofsyracusedromioofephesus/>. Accessed 30 June 2010.

——(2005) 'Helicanus – Simonides – Bolt', rehearsal notes, <http://www.globelink.org/resourcecentre/pericles/helicanus/siminides/bolt/>. Accessed 30 June 2010.

Holland, Peter (1997) *English Shakespeares: Shakespeare on the English Stage in the 1990s*, Cambridge: Cambridge University Press.

Lecoq, Jacques (2002) *The Moving Body: Teaching Creative Theatre*, London: Methuen.

Neill, Heather (1999) 'Master pieces', interview with Kathryn Hunter in programme for *The Comedy of Errors*, Shakespeare's Globe.

Potter, Lois (1999) 'A Stage Where Every Man Must Play a Part?', *Shakespeare Quarterly*, 50:1, 74–86.

Proudfoot, Richard (1999) 'The 1998 Globe Season', *Shakespeare Survey* 52, 215–28.

Purcell, Stephen (2009) *Popular Shakespeare: Simulation and Subversion on the Modern Stage*, Basingstoke: Palgrave Macmillan.

Rudlin, John (1994) *Commedia dell'Arte: An Actor's Handbook*, London: Routledge.
Smallwood, Robert (2000) 'Shakespeare Performances in England, 1999', *Shakespeare Survey* 53, 244–73.
Wade, Alan (2000) 'A *Theatre Annual* Interview with Theatre de Complicite's Lilo Baur and Marcello Magni', *Theatre Annual* 53, 69–78.
Weimann, Robert (1987) *Shakespeare and the Popular Tradition in the Theater: Studies in the Social Dimension of Dramatic Form and Function*, Baltimore/London: Johns Hopkins University Press.
Wiles, David (1987) *Shakespeare's Clown: Actor and Text in the Elizabethan Playhouse*, Cambridge: Cambridge University Press.
Personal Interviews conducted by the author: Annie Castledine, May 2006; Marcello Magni, May 2004, June 2010, September 2010.

Video recordings

The Comedy of Errors (Shakespeare's Globe, 1999). Recorded 19 August.
The Merchant of Venice (Shakespeare's Globe, 1998). Recorded 8 July.
Pericles (Shakespeare's Globe, 2005). Recorded 2 June.

About the author

Stephen Purcell is a lecturer in English and Performance at Southampton Solent University, UK. His research interests include Shakespeare in popular culture, comedy, and contemporary theatre. He is the author of the book *Popular Shakespeare: Simulation and Subversion on the Modern Stage* (Palgrave, 2009) and of several articles on Shakespeare in contemporary performance. He also directs for The Pantaloons, an open-air theatre company who 'aim to recapture an aspect of Shakespeare's drama which the modern naturalistic theatre has lost: the riotous energy of the clown'.

14
Patrice Naiambana

Darren Tunstall

A group of British acting students enter a dance studio. They are met by an imposing man in his late forties playing an African talking drum. He sings phrases to them and they respond by singing them back to him. As this call-and-response game develops, he gives them to understand that they should stand alongside him in a block and copy his dancing. Within the space of a few minutes, the group is stamping out a rhythm with their feet, chanting in an unfamiliar language, improvising with their bodies in a spirit of growing exhilaration. As the game changes and the group are invited to sit in a circle, I realise that not a word has yet been spoken by the man – everything has been communicated through music, rhythmic movement and discreet gesture. Now the man begins to tell the group (in English) a story of the birth and upbringing of a great African warrior. It is some time before it dawns on the group that the storyteller is talking about Othello. He leads the group into the plot of the play, provoking them into responding with simple questions such as, 'Why can't I marry Desdemona? Why don't we just go and talk to her father?' and so on. What we are all witnessing – in the music and dance, the storytelling, the creation of a mythic genealogy for a hero, the eliciting of response through audience provocation, the physical and verbal openness to improvisational possibilities – is an example of the kind of approach to Shakespearean performance that might be taken by a griot.

For some years, Patrice Naiambana has been working to develop what he calls a performance aesthetic that connects Shakespeare – in particular, *Othello* – with the methods of the griot. Emerging out of a bardic tradition some time between the twelfth and fourteenth centuries in West Africa, the griot (the word is thought to be of Franco-Portuguese derivation) was a key figure in the formation of dynastic empires among peoples such as the Wolof, Bambara, Fulbe, Soninke and others inhabiting the Malinke cultural field. The griot, who would be born into, and trained by, a 'griot family', would act as an attendant to the warlords, kings, and (later) to Islamic scholars; he – and, in more recent times, she – would be tasked with the maintenance of family genealogies and histories through such forms as praise-songs and storytelling during social rituals. In return for their services the griot would usually receive valuable gifts such as food, horses, or clothes (or indeed slaves). In a society reliant upon oral transmission, these highly skilled 'Masters of the Word' became guarantors of cultural continuity. While elites found in the stories, speeches and music of the griot an opportunity to legitimise their own power, the relationship between griot and patron was always complex, since the griot could at times make use of their special status (as 'one who does not work') to remind the chief of their obligations to the wider community. With the encroachments of Islamisation, followed by Colonialism, and finally modern Westernisation, the griot's status and functions naturally changed. As Colonialism dissolved the context of patronage in which the performance of the griot held social meaning, one alternative route for young boys of griot families was to enter the white man's schools and, from there, to gain power over former rulers by joining the colonial administration as clerks, while others set aside their ancestral heritage to enter into trade (Panzacchi 1994). In more recent times, the impact of broadcast media has created new spaces in which griot praise songs once again have taken on a contested status within the context of political representation and legitimacy (Schulz 1997).

Patrice sees in the performative mode of the contemporary griot a template for his own practice, one that can be deployed within a Shakespearean production not merely by 'playing the character as a griot' but, more productively, by 'adopting the methods of the griot'. In fact, when the function of actor and storyteller become blended, as when he played Gower in *Pericles* at the Globe Theatre, the distinction between the two becomes to a considerable extent nonexistent. This is an important point for Patrice, sensitive as he is to the accusation of denying the authority of the text:

> When we were doing *Pericles* I proposed this to Kathryn, before she offered me Gower…We had two workshops, and then I did Gower, and she said, 'Can you do it like that?' So I did. I went and found a griot instrument. I told Mark Rylance. Mark was OK with this griot coming off the text, and then straight back into the verse. So that was me taking on a role that was pushing my research…So that was a good platform, and I did it as an African but still Shakespeare was in the frame, and that was very important for me, because I sometimes feel that it goes, 'Well, yes, but he's not really doing Shakespeare.' People still said that, but I was like, no, it's very Shakespearean, the use of what was happening, I was coming off the text, then straight back on.
>
> (Interview with the author, 5 November 2009: hereinafter 'Interview')

Essentially, Patrice keeps Shakespeare 'in the frame' by imagining him also as a kind of griot, 'in the way he combines history, proverbs, major canonical texts, his drive to what's happening now – that's what griots do' (Interview). This is how the Shakespearean text speaks to him – with a hybrid, politically attuned, epic-storytelling voice; in the Western European theatre, perhaps the nearest equivalent to the griot approach would be found in the theatrical adaptability and political cunning of the Brechtian performer, as well as in Brecht's own method of treating the Shakespearean text as raw material to be worked over. Since it assumes that the actor has the right, at least from time to time, to speak words on the stage not actually written by the Bard, this method can be something of an irritant to audiences and critics who may wish to insist on what they believe to be Shakespeare's intentions. Yet the critic Paul Taylor responded warmly to Patrice's 'outrageously charming and wily African story-teller who delights in departing from his brief to josh the punters about everything from the anti-snob nature of the Globe ("if you want 'art' go to a museum") to their memory of the highly episodic plot' (*The Independent*, 6 June 2005). Beyond the immediate pleasures or irritations of this mode of acting, the griot stands as a reminder of the sheer power of stories such as *Pericles* to bind a community, or to change people's lives. It is easy in our postmodern culture to fall into cynicism about the tired conventions of narrative, but the belief that performers can, and do, effect significant, even lasting, transformations in themselves and others through their engagement with dramatic stories can still offer shape, meaning and dignity to a profession that often seems chaotically unpredictable and subject to exploitation. It is, by way of example, a griot mentality that has led Patrice to create workshop-based projects such as his 'Gospel of Othello', which seeks to create opportunities for different sorts of artists to work together with him on shared histories, using the play as a provocation for debate. The workshops have a flexible, open-ended format. In one incarnation, during a break while filming *Schweitzer* in South Africa, Patrice decided to visit a small village where he gathered a group of teenage schoolchildren, taught them the story of *Othello*, and rehearsed their improvised version of it. This version was then performed to the village later in the same day, accompanied by a DJ who brought along some sound equipment and a troupe of Zulu dancers who arrived by chance. It is a testimony to Patrice's formidable energy and commitment that this impromptu performance should have become a moment of communal affirmation.

Born in Ghana – with a father from Sierra Leone who nonetheless held a British passport and worked for the RAF, and a mother hailing from Bermuda – Patrice Naiambana was, as he says, 'brought up in different places' (Interview). He embodies what could be described as a diasporic identity. In the pan-African movement for Black solidarity in the 1950s, the notion of an African diaspora emerged as a description of the dispersal of people native to sub-Saharan Africa across the globe. Here, the argument for a common diasporic experience tended to draw upon a biological idea of 'blackness' coupled with an insistence upon common experiences of racial discrimination; later, it moved towards a recognition of the shared significance of those parts of African culture that had survived the scattering of communities. In the 1980s and 90s the terms of argument shifted again, now towards the reconfiguration of diaspora as 'hybridity', which suggests the possibility of a blending of cultural histories that can survive without making use of nostalgic illusions about one's roots. Thus, while the term can encompass a wide range of possible meanings, the concept of the African diaspora has always pointed not only to particular groups of people, but also to a sense of identity that somehow transcends national borders. Patrice's background seems to encapsulate that paradoxical relationship between a group identification with one's (lost) home and a shifting individuality that resists labelling.

Much of Patrice's work over the last two decades can be seen as an attempt to relate his sense of himself as a diasporic performer to the challenges of multiculturalism. New Labour's multiculturalist policy has come under fire in recent years, not least for a perceived failure to give sufficient value to cultural signifiers of 'Britishness'. For Patrice, though, the problem with some current manifestations of multiculturalism, at least in the performing arts, is not that they deny the validity of the host culture, but that, quite simply, they are not multicultural in any authentic sense. To be meaningful, the agenda must be founded upon a genuine effort at inclusivity:

> But when you start talking about inclusivity, be sure that what you're including me into is not any kind of, 'Why yes, we're alright now, you can come and play Henry VI,' because you're not really including me – because if you're including me, you need to be able to take my lens, like I've taken yours. There needs to be reciprocity in inclusivity. Any move of so-called inclusivity that doesn't have that is not inclusivity. It's inclusivity *in your image*. The progress that is being made is made on your terms. Which is not really progress, actually.
>
> (Interview)

To understand the 'lens' he is referring to, we need to dig deeper into his background. As a young man, it had been his intention to train as an actor in the UK:

> Because of empire and everything, Britain sits at the crossroads of so many things – geographic and cultural locations. So that's why I came: I thought I could learn and I could be useful…I tried to go to Rose Bruford but I couldn't afford it. I had to leave after six weeks. I was working at MacDonald's Marble Arch at night, and I couldn't sustain myself for three years…And I suddenly realised, because I'd spent fully seven years in Sierra Leone before I commenced this adventure, I was already into an organic way of performing, of music, movement, storytelling. Tabule Teatr, who I apprenticed with, that's what everybody did – you all had to do that.
>
> (Interview)

The Tabule Experimental Theatre was founded in Freetown in 1968 by Raymond Ayodele ('Dele') Charley (1948–94). From the start it was committed to the creation of a Krio theatre. The term 'Krio' refers to both an ethnic group (descendants of freed slaves from Britain, the USA and the West Indies) and a *lingua franca*, which makes hybrid use of Yoruba, Nova Scotian English, French, Spanish and Portuguese among other languages, and is spoken by most of the population as either a first or second language in Sierra Leone; as the first 'Western' black community in Africa, the great majority of Krios are Christians. Krio theatre began to flourish after Sierra Leone was granted independence in 1961, and owed much to the innovations of Thomas Decker, who translated *Julius Caesar* into Krio in 1964, and whose early experiments were then extended by Dele Charley among others. 'Tabule Theatre was very good, they'd come out to LIFT, they had some international experience…We did *Merchant of Venice* in Krio, blank verse, we did *Macbeth*' (Interview).

Then a chance meeting with the actress Glenna Foster Jones led to an offer of work on a British Council theatre project:

> But I wasn't thinking 'actor'. I was just left with this experience that stories could be something that could help deal with all these questions I'd been asking – you know, 'Why was Africa like this?' – all this stuff…It grew out of that kind of impetus and it stayed with me ever since. I've never looked for a role. I've never said, 'Oh, I must play Lear.' It's always started from what needs to be addressed in terms of story.
>
> (Interview)

From the outset of his career, then, Patrice connected an idea of himself as an African storyteller with his evident drive for self-determination, a drive which in practice has meant attempting to put himself in a position to make performance choices which do not efface his diasporic identity – including choices that favour any notion of 'correct' Shakespearean acting. Patrice is as mindful as anyone of Shakespeare's continuing pervasive influence far beyond England. More, though, than the undeniable cultural cache of a global brand called 'Shakespeare', there is surely something else in the plays (and *Othello* in particular) that speaks to an artist-performer like Patrice, who seeks recognition for both himself and his culture on terms of his own choosing. Perhaps the peculiar challenges of performing Shakespeare – of discovering through one's body and voice a relationship to those dense and demanding words – can still confront an actor with his or her own image. Looking at the work Patrice did with Tabule, Shakespeare, it seems, was never far from that process of discovering his performative self.

Patrice's sensitivity to the criticism of his extra-textual improvisations with Gower at the Globe Theatre suggest an anxiety about legitimacy that has haunted the black Shakespearean performer working in the Anglo-American theatre, and indeed reminds us that it has never really been clear when the questioning of an actor's training and competence to handle sophisticated Shakespearean text shades into downright racism.

Two figures from the Anglo-American tradition have been enormously influential upon Patrice. His Othello for the Royal Shakespeare Company took its place in a tradition of black actors essaying the role that begins properly with the American Ira Aldridge. Aldridge had been associated with William Brown's African Grove Theater (established around 1820) since the age of about fifteen. The first occasion that Aldridge stepped out as Othello was in London, where he took over from Edmund Kean, who had collapsed on stage; Aldridge was advertised to the public as 'The Celebrated Mr Keene, the African Tragedian'. Aldridge's remarkable (and remarkably successful) story marks the beginning of a racially inflected discourse about the identification of actor with role by both commentators and, on occasion, by the actors themselves. It seemed at times with Aldridge that the only way in which his talent could be given the recognition it deserved was through the backhanded compliment of describing him as a 'natural': that is, by suggesting that Aldridge was not acting at all – he *was* Othello, and thus was highly credible in the role. At the same time, Aldridge attempted to distance his own performance from the conflation of 'natural' with 'savage' that accrued around white actors such as Edmund Kean, Spranger Barry and Tomasso Salvini, all of whose displays of histrionic passion in the role did much to cement their reputations as star performers. Aldridge achieved this distance – part of a concerted effort to establish his status as a classical actor by deploying Othello's nobility – at an ironic cost: he was accused by critics of being too restrained. In the history of *Othello* performance criticism this then becomes a significant strand: white Othellos are frequently praised for their supposedly primal emotional ferocity, while black Othellos are accused of having too much self-control (see Marks 2001).

Along with Aldridge, for Patrice a crucial model of the committed black artist is Paul Robeson, who spent a very considerable part of his career performing Othello.

Kathryn Hunter's debut production as director for the RSC (she is rather better known in the UK as a performer, who rose to prominence through her work for Theatre de Complicite) was used as an occasion for marking the fiftieth anniversary of Robeson's appearing at Stratford in the role: on tour, the production was accompanied by an exhibition entitled 'A Slave's Son at Stratford', celebrating Robeson's life and work. In performing the role, Robeson was looking for a way to speak to and of the black American experience; a key context for him was the continued prohibition on miscegenation – the racial-sexual narrative that has haunted the play's reception throughout its history – in several American states at the time. Robeson played the part (the only Shakespeare role he ever did play) in three different productions between 1930 and 1959. His influence became inescapable. He was a role model for a generation of black actors, while his political force was critical in the gradual rejection of the part of Othello as a viable proposition for white actors: it was, quite simply, increasingly embarrassing to black up for the part after Robeson. While that fact may seem like a kind of progress towards taking the role 'seriously', it is also a consequence of the peculiar theatrical history of the play, in which, as I have suggested, a debate opened up about the identity of the character that continues to disturb modern productions. Earle Hyman, who played Othello twice in the 1950s, declared Robeson to be the best Othello because 'He did not have to act' (quoted in Potter [2002], p132). Such statements of course raise as many questions as they answer: in what sense, for example, can it be possible for any actor, black or white, to perform Othello without acting? In any case, just how 'natural' was Robeson, really? When interviewed by the press, he would sometimes assume a naive attitude in relation to the performance of Shakespeare. But to what extent was this itself a performance intended to ward off criticism? It is just such a cultural awkwardness around the figure of Othello that, I think, provokes Patrice into a seemingly revisionist attitude towards multiculturalism:

> You can black up, I can white up. No problem...I'm not one of those people who say, 'You can't; I'm all offended.' It's imagination, it's art. It depends on why you're doing the thing. If you're doing it to take the piss out of me, then why? But if you're doing it for a constructive reason, and it's going to help all of us – Shakespeare is much more about, 'What do you think of this? What do you think of that?'
>
> (Interview)

In fact, during our discussions Patrice suggested to me that he would be interested to see – indeed work with – a blacked-up actor playing Othello: blackness as a theatrical construct rather than an inescapable biological fact. Robeson, of course, saw Othello's tragedy in the fact that he is 'sooty black'; an outsider, Othello is hyper-sensitive to his status in Venetian society and thus 'feels dishonour more deeply' (*New York Times*, 18 May 1930). The character's jealousy, being a matter of ultimately uncontrollable and thus 'savage' emotions, was subordinated to a concept of 'nobility' that was both more engaged with the political context and revealing of the actor's anxiety to be accepted as a truly Shakespearean performer. The influence of this view of the part (which can be traced back to Aldridge) could be registered in Patrice's

Othello but with an ironic twist: the performance made clear that Othello's sense of honour has an irreducibly social motive – it was tied to the need to belong to a world that prizes military honour. Without the necessary recognition from one's social context, all of the constructions of Othello as the noble Moor, the man whom passion could not shake, were then in danger of losing their meaning.

Curiously, when discussing his acting in interview, Patrice also tended to make use of the same tactic of modesty we witness with other black performers of Othello: he is not, he would say, a proper actor, he is not trained in Shakespearean verse-speaking, and so on. It is still more telling to note how this is also a tactic that Othello himself deploys in the play:

> Rude am I in my speech,
> And little blessed with the soft phrase of peace...
> And little of this great world can I speak
> More than pertains to feats of broil and battle;
> And therefore little shall I grace my cause
> In speaking for myself...
>
> (*Othello*, 1.3.82–90)

Given that Othello proceeds very soon after saying that to speak with great eloquence on the subject of wooing Desdemona, once we recognise the rhetorical strategy behind his assertion of modesty, we are tuned in to what Martin Orkin calls Othello's 'extraordinary ability in negotiating, appropriating, *playing* this world' (Orkin 2005, p38) – a survival skill of the exile, as Patrice knows:

> He's a man trying, and exiled people always do their best to survive. This thing of how calm he is, look how calm he is when he says, 'Put up your bright swords'...What else are you going to do? He uses his authority, but it's quite outrageous what's happening to him. You have to be proud, you rely on arrogance, you rely on those things. You rely on your charisma when you go into places where you know you don't have power anyway.
>
> (Interview)

Under the corrosive influence of Iago, Othello's sense of self is drastically eroded, premised as it is upon both his capacity to 'play' the world he moves in and his reliance upon Desdemona as a bulwark against the chaotic feeling of isolation; now, the rhetorical game of false modesty turns in a rather more painful inward direction: 'Haply, for I am black/And have not those soft parts of conversation/That chamberers have' (*Othello*, 3.3.266–67). His collapse can then be seen as due to the impossibility of maintaining a coherent sense of self not as a black man but simply as a human being with a history of enforced 'existential deviation', as Frantz Fanon would have said.

> You know what people need to understand? That the default position of humanity is not whiteness...If it's going to be instructive, we have to see [Othello] as an exile. And I believe that Shakespeare understood it. And his audience probably would have understood it in a way that we don't.
>
> (Interview)

Given a context in which one accepts there is no default position of humanity of whatever complexion, Patrice opts to describe himself as bi-cultural. In reality, this has meant offering two versions of his acting self to a director: one of them attuned to that blended British tradition of psychological realism and an idea of classical performance that imposes self-restraint upon the actor's body so as to focus almost entirely upon the actor's vocal delivery of the text (what used to be derogatively called 'acting from the neck up'); the other, the singing, dancing, physically expressive African storyteller – the 'griot self'. But in my view the most interesting thing about watching a performance by Patrice is the degree to which one can perceive a 'blended' quality in his acting, where these separate cultural influences intersect in the use of body and voice, so that Patrice can be seen as standing between two modes of representation without finally privileging one over the other. For example, in the opening sequence of the RSC production Patrice presented an Othello who offered himself to his new bride through the gesture of a fluttering hand-on-heart motion that accompanied a love song. Such movement recalls the practice within some African dances of articulating everyday gestural behaviour (here, putting your hand on your heart to demonstrate sincerity) through rhythmic stylisation. Such a practice would hold a certain appeal for a director steeped, as Kathryn Hunter is, in the theatrical-gestural pedagogy of the French teacher Jacques Lecoq where, at the beginning of the actor's training, very basic actions such as pushing and pulling are broken down into constituent parts and re-articulated before being put to use, often in a relatively stylised form, in the embodiment of the text. This method overturns the traditional approach to rehearsal in which the actors are required to produce intellectual work on the text through discussion before getting to their feet. The intellectual work on the text is still to be done, but after the actor has discovered what his or her body 'thinks' of the text.

During rehearsals for the production, Patrice persuaded Kathryn that group warm-ups should be conducted to the music of Fela Kuti. One can also, of course, interpret this as an attempt to counter the feeling of isolation that can crush the black performer of Othello – and at times Patrice himself did and does feel quite alone in his journey:

> I think the mysteriousness of Othello is important – as a leader, an exile, someone who is solitary. The isolation. The fact that you don't really know – they say he's noble, but is he?...I see a man who's in exile. Exile is one of the saddest fates. The man's a mercenary, what's noble about that? Wars, these sorts of things, they may ennoble you but they leave scars which can be opened, and Shakespeare gives us a clue about that when he says, 'when I love thee not, / Chaos is come again.'
>
> (Interview)

Once again, it seems hard for black performers of Othello to avoid feeling contaminated by the character's harrowing predicament. Yet the feeling of being apart from one's colleagues is not unique to Othello: it can be an equally lonely business playing, say, Hamlet or Coriolanus. Here, it is further exacerbated by a difficulty in knowing how to make sense of Othello's verbal display – the so-called

'Othello music', a quality of suspiciously rhetorical self-consciousness that has often been detected in his language. The language is perhaps another tactic in Othello's attempt to overcome his alienation from Venetian society; Patrice, for his own part, in rehearsal appealed to communal feelings evoked by ritual dance and song. In fact, when we discussed the rehearsals, Patrice expressed his surprise to me that, in his experience, British productions tend not to make much use of music as part of the group creative process. At the Tabule Theatre in Freetown, such an absence would have been unthinkable. At the same time, again testifying to that quest for a blended, bi-cultural approach, during his preparations for the role Patrice had planned to visit a psychiatrist in character, following the intuition that Othello undergoes a kind of mental breakdown. While for logistical reasons the visit did not take place, he nonetheless sought to develop a sense of Othello's brittle inner life by developing a physical vocabulary deriving from both Griot performance style and from everyday conventions of gesture; neither mode in isolation being the 'authentic' Othello present to us on stage, together they offered a gestural correlative of the exile's predicament. In his opening scenes, when Othello is most fully the storyteller of his own past, Patrice tended to implicate the audience in his gestures, which were frequently (and here we must make use of expressions from gesture theory) Open Hand Palm Up movements, during moments when the situation called for judgement, as here:

> If you do find me foul in her report,
> The trust, the office I do hold of you
> Not only take away, but let your sentence
> Even fall upon my life.
>
> (*Othello*, 1.3.118–21)

He also – not surprisingly for a storyteller – made significant use of Illustrators (visual supporting messages, usually performed subconsciously), as when, in speaking of 'my boyish days' (1.3.132) he pictured his height as a boy for us. A very conventional gesture for us, of course, and this is partly the point: what could be seen as merely a storyteller's method of picturing with the body becomes, in this pressurising context, a rather more painfully self-conscious appeal to a recognisable (if not necessarily shared) body language. This was made clearer still when, in relating his encounters with the Anthropophagi, he mimed gnawing comically at a human bone, presumably in an attempt to distance himself from the stereotypical racist image of blacks as cannibals. The effect of this crudely literal joke was however a kind of embarrassed silence among the group, in a scene that had been choreographed to exclude Othello from an authoritative position from which to tell his story at the centre of the stage. This was reinforced by the choice to show the gesture from a subjective viewpoint – Othello as cannibal – a sort of forced error of identification that one could not imagine any other character in the play making; by contrast, the 'boyish' gesture was, as it usually is in conversation, from an observer's viewpoint since it is performed with a nostalgic sense of distance from the subject. This switching between subjective and objective viewpoints was indicative of Othello's shifting struggle to affirm his status in the scene, and cut against his overall posture of a self-possessed, high-ranking warrior exhibiting the 'classical authority', signified by bodily restraint, of his fellow Venetians.

As the play progressed, and Othello won over his judges, his awkwardness was transferred to particular moments in the charting of his relationship with Desdemona (Natalia Tena), as when he handed her a gift of a musical instrument fashioned from an old petrol can – an object that, in her eagerness to please him by validating his cultural past, she appeared to have no idea what to do with. This exemplified also the movement away from Open Hand and Illustrator gestures, related as they are to an internal impulse provoked by textual imagery, towards a more pronounced attempt to disclose character dynamic through the use of so-called Adaptors – objects like a hat, a whip, a gun, a small white Bible – that are external to the text's image structures, along with movements directed in towards the face and body as opposed to out towards other characters and the audience. In folk psychology Adaptors often appear as more revealing of subtext than hand movements that may be being controlled by the speaker, rather as Freudian slips of the tongue are sometimes thought to be more telling than chosen words. In any case, here they served not only to suggest a shift away from 'declarative storytelling' into 'psychological realism' but to substitute for the 'imagistic' motions that had marked his storytelling mode. In addition to this adjustment, from the critical turning point of Act 3 Scene 3 Patrice began to use a greater number of aggressive Deictics (pointing gestures), Open Hand Palm Down motions (indicating an effort at domination) and Baton gestures, that beat out the vocal stress patterns of the text as if, in this case, attempting to stamp out the chaos enveloping from both within and without, to re-discover or re-assert an authority that was under attack; consistent with these choices, Patrice almost never used Open Hand Palm Up gestures directly to Iago; when he did so, as during ''Tis not to make me jealous / To say my wife is fair' (3.3.186–87), he included the audience in the movement as if, again, making an appeal to our judgement.

As the second half of the performance unfolded, Patrice's gestural language became increasingly fragmented and angular. During his 'Farewell the tranquil mind' speech (3.3.347 ff), his knees suddenly buckled as if he were a Pantalone figure from the commedia dell'arte, and on 'O blood, blood, blood' (3.3.451) he crabbed bizarrely across the front of the stage like a Zulu warrior readying for war, a move that, later in the tour at the Liverpool Playhouse, had developed into a ritual of slashing his own wrist: as before, we witnessed one gestural language colliding with another to produce a 'hybridised' Othello, a kind of psychologised griot. In the final scenes of the play, he seemed at times like a traumatised child, unable to escape the nightmare of his own inner collapse. The result was variously provocative, moving, grotesque – and, at times, not wholly satisfying, since it was obliged to operate within a scenographic territory that referenced the 1950s, which tended to limit the provocations of the performance by drawing a historical boundary line around it. The production did, though, call into question just what it means to be a 'noble' black man in a white society, not least by the appearance on stage of a small golliwog that Patrice had found in a street market and brought in to rehearsals. Coincidentally, as the tour began, journalist Carol Thatcher was denounced for referring to a tennis player as a 'golliwog' in a BBC green room – a fact which reduced the audience at the Warwick Arts Centre to a charged silence whenever the golliwog made its appearance. At the

Liverpool Playhouse a few weeks later, since the scandal had died down, the audience felt more comfortable laughing at the uses made of this troubling object.

The director's background in a continental European tradition inspired by Lecoq, and given great impetus in this country by the popularity of Theatre de Complicite, should be seen as instrumental in the attempt to create a strongly 'embodied' acting style in the production. It was Kathryn Hunter and Marcello Magni (her partner and collaborator on *Othello*) who spotted Patrice in the early 1990s and responded to his determination to bring his cultural training and heritage, his diasporic identity, into his performance choices. The Lecoq tradition has always allowed for a kind of multiculturalism by default; it encourages students to learn about cultures, and to discover resonances between cultures, rather than imposing a particular stylistic approach on them. While no doubt reflecting his own artistic tastes, under the stewardship of Michael Boyd the RSC has moved towards embracing models of performance, such as those that derive from Lecoq's training system, that are more likely to speak to new audiences: hence the opportunity given to an artist like Hunter – and, increasingly, others like her – to direct and act at Stratford. Lecoq-trained actors tend to see themselves as artist–creators as well as actors; they will often seek out a feeling of ownership of, or responsibility for, the entire performance in some way. Inevitably within a large structure like the RSC, with its particular history, this can create tensions and frustrations. For example, a certain devaluing of bodily expressiveness can still arise, as revealed in this anecdote of Patrice's experience of playing in Boyd's Histories cycle:

> At the end of *Henry VI*, just before Warwick comes out in part three, I was standing there; I was going 'Let's go to Parliament to get the King'; the drums were going like this – badaboom ba boom boom – Johnny [Slinger] was the only one moving. Johnny was the only one going, 'Well I'm hearing music, I'm gonna do this!' I said to him afterwards, 'That's African theatre.' But I started out doing that...How long it takes. Twenty years, come to the RSC, one white actor's going like this, and everyone's going, 'It's fantastic!'... But you black man there, you go and bring in your movement – 'Ah well, that's what they do.'
>
> (Interview)

Patrice's evident frustrations remind us that it is not a matter of dressing up a production or a character to look 'African'; what is at stake is a set of basic physical and verbal choices revealing how the actor intends, or is expected, to come across on stage. Since Ira Aldridge, stage representations of Othello have tended to be caught between an unwillingness to countenance both white impersonations of the black man and histrionic behaviour from black performers (since that might call up the stereotype of the emotionally hysterical savage). Taking the 'diasporic view', as Patrice continues to try to do, may help us to sidestep the dilemma altogether. Or at least it may help to connect the play more productively to some of our current global traumas. For what Patrice's work ultimately insists on is the question of Shakespeare's *usefulness* for our context – a perhaps scandalous question to some, in the Brechtian sense in which I intend (and it is worth recalling here that Brecht considered even Josef Stalin to have had his uses). Nevertheless, Shakespeare does continue to prove extremely useful to artists like Patrice, in their commitment to the ideals of self-determination and the transformative potential of art.

Chronology

Born Ghana 1962.

1996–97	Friar Francis in *Much Ado about Nothing*, directed by Michael Boyd. Royal Shakespeare Theatre, Stratford-upon-Avon.
1997	Caius Lucius and Jupiter in *Cymbeline*, directed by Adrian Noble. Royal Shakespeare Theatre, Stratford-upon-Avon and Theatre Royal, Plymouth.
1997	Don Andrea in *The Spanish Tragedy*, directed by Michael Boyd. Swan Theatre, Stratford-upon-Avon.
1998–2002	Aslan in *The Lion, Witch and the Wardrobe* at Royal Shakespeare Theatre, directed by Adrian Noble, Stratford-upon-Avon, Barbican Theatre, London and Sadler's Wells, London.
2000	Gower in *Pericles*, directed by James Roose-Evans. Ludlow Festival, Ludlow Castle.
2001	Oberon in *A Midsummer Night's Dream*, directed by Richard Hayhow. Shysters Theatre Company, Belgrade Theatre, Coventry.
2005	Gower in *Pericles*, Prince of Tyre, directed by Kathryn Hunter. Globe Theatre, London.
2006–8	Earl of Warwick in *Henry VI Parts 1, 2 and 3*, directed by Michael Boyd. Courtyard Theatre, Stratford-upon-Avon.
2007	The Elder in *Highlander: The Source*, dir. Brett Leonard (film).
2007	Ghost of Warwick in *Richard III*, directed by Michael Boyd. Courtyard Theatre, Stratford-upon-Avon.
2007–8	Earl of Warwick in *Henry IV Part 2*, directed by Richard Twyman (Associate Director Michael Boyd). Courtyard Theatre, Stratford-upon-Avon.
2007–8	Earl of Warwick in *Henry V*, directed by Michael Boyd (Associate Director Richard Twyman). Courtyard Theatre, Stratford-upon-Avon.
2009	Louis Ngouta in *Albert Schweitzer*, dir. Gavin Millar (film).
2009	Othello in *Othello*, directed by Kathryn Hunter. Warwick Arts Centre, Hackney Empire (London), Northern Stage (Newcastle-upon-Tyne), Oxford Playhouse and Liverpool Playhouse.

TV work includes *Black and Blue*, *Belly*, *In Exile*, *Doc Martin and the Legend of the Cloutie*, *Absolute Power*, *Judge John Deed*, *Casualty*, *Silent Witness*, *Nina and the Neurons*, *Torchwood*.

Under the banner of his company Tribal Soul, Patrice has performed his one-man show *The Man who Committed Thought* on many occasions in different locations.

Bibliography

Barthelemy, Anthony Gerard (1987) *Black Face Maligned Race: The Representation of Blacks in English Drama from Shakespeare to Southerne*. Louisiana: Louisiana State University Press.

D'Amico, Jack (1991) *The Moor in English Renaissance Drama*. Florida: University of South Florida Press.

Hall, Kim F., ed. (2007) *Othello: Texts and Contexts*. Boston and New York: Bedford/St Martin's.

Hankey, Julie (1987) *Plays in Performance: 'Othello': William Shakespeare*. Bristol: Bristol Classical Press.

Hill, Errol (1984) *Shakespeare in Sable: A History of Black Shakespearean Actors*. Amherst, Mass.: University of Massachusetts Press.

Jones, Eldred (1965) *Othello's Countrymen: The African in English Renaissance Drama*. London: Oxford University Press for Fourah Bay College, University of Sierra Leone.

Kaul, Mythili, ed. (1997) *Othello: New Essays by Black Writers*. Washington D.C.: Howard University Press.

Kolin, Philip, ed. (2002) *Othello: New Critical Essays*. London and New York: Routledge.

Loomba, Ania and Orkin, Martin, eds. (1998) *Post-colonial Shakespeares*. London and New York: Routledge.

Marks, Elise (2001) '"Othello/me": Racial drag and the Pleasures of Boundary-Crossing with *Othello*', *Comparative Drama* 35.

Neill, Michael, ed. (2006) *The Oxford Shakespeare: Othello*. Oxford: Oxford University Press.

Okri, Ben (1997) 'Leaping out of Shakespeare's Terror', in *A Way of Being Free*. London: Phoenix House.

Orkin, Martin (2005) *Local Shakespeares: Proximations and Power*. Abingdon and New York: Routledge.

Panzacchi, Cornelia (1994) 'The Livelihoods of Traditional Griots in Modern Senegal', *Africa* 64:2.

Potter, Lois (2002) *Shakespeare in Performance: Othello*. Manchester and New York: Manchester University Press.

Schulz, Dorothea (1997) 'Praise without enchantment: Griots, broadcast media, and the politics of tradition in Mali', *Africa Today* 44:4.

Thompson, Ayanna, ed. (2006) *Colorblind Shakespeare: New Perspectives on Race and Performance*. New York: Routledge.

Vaughan, Virginia Mason (1994) *Othello: A Contextual History*. Cambridge: Cambridge University Press.

About the author

Darren Tunstall read English at Cambridge before working as an actor, director and writer for more than twenty years. He has taught at several drama schools in the UK and is now a lecturer on the BA (Hons) Acting course at the University of Central Lancashire. He is currently preparing material for a book, *Shakespeare in Practice: Gesture*, to be published by Palgrave Macmillan in 2013, and continues to direct for the theatre.

15
Vanessa Redgrave

John F. Deeney

Born on 30 January 1937, Vanessa Redgrave's entry into this world was transformed, almost immediately, into a piece of theatre. Her father, the actor Michael Redgrave, was playing Laertes to Laurence Olivier's Hamlet at the Old Vic Theatre in London. News of the birth had reached the theatre before the end of the performance. Following the curtain call Olivier turned to the audience and declared, 'Ladies and gentleman, tonight a great actress has been born, Laertes has a daughter' (Redgrave 1991: 1). Olivier's quick-witted theatricalisation of the newborn infant would prove to foretell only part of the story. In a career that has spanned more than fifty years, Vanessa Redgrave would not only emerge as one of the most accomplished, versatile and celebrated British actors of the period, but alongside the development of her acting career has been a deep, continuous and frequently high-profile and controversial commitment to a range of political and humanitarian causes. This chapter does not seek to establish a trouble-free reciprocal relationship between 'actor' and 'activist'. Rather, this discussion will focus on how Redgrave's acting practice demonstrates particular forms of engagement with Shakespeare's texts that are enlightened by particular methodological approaches, and through which her own sense of agency and political sensibility has been allowed to reveal itself.

Vanessa Redgrave's inclusion in this companion seems entirely fitting. Her performance as Rosalind in *As You Like It* for the newly-formed Royal Shakespeare Company (RSC) in 1961 would come to be regarded as a defining theatrical moment, not only in terms of embodying an invigorating sense of modernity in Shakespearian performance, but also in ways that resonated strongly with the 'freedoms' demanded by embryonic forms of political and cultural radicalism. Redgrave's most recent Shakespearian venture, in 2000, was of comparable significance in its endeavour to challenge both theatrical and critical histories; as Prospero in *The Tempest* at the newly reconstructed Globe Theatre in London, she sought less to conquer one of the great male Shakespearian roles, but redefine the character's very function within the play. However, during the intervening forty years Redgrave's engagement with Shakespeare in the theatre has fluctuated considerably. There was, for example, a break of ten years, from the early 1960s, before she played Viola in *Twelfth Night*, Cleopatra and Lady Macbeth in quick succession. More than a decade would then elapse before she offered new incarnations of Cleopatra and Katherine in *The Taming of the Shrew*, the latter she had previously played at the RSC in 1961. Yet another decade would pass by before Redgrave returned to Shakespeare, again to the role of Cleopatra, but this time in three productions which she also directed. It may be tempting to explain this pattern in terms of the unpredictable *modus operandi* of the acting profession and the comparatively limited opportunities afforded women players. Indeed, Redgrave's autobiography details extensively the juggling demands of work, motherhood and financial security. To many readers she will be most familiar as a film and television actor, not least perhaps as a supporting player in Hollywood blockbusters such as *Mission Impossible* (1996) and *Deep Impact* (1998). A survey of her Shakespearian résumé also reveals significant absences; Beatrice in *Much Ado About Nothing*, Isabella in *Measure for Measure*, Lear's daughters and Portia in *The Merchant of Venice*, all well within her reach, are just some of the roles that have been passed by. Equally, and this is of particular significance, since the early 1960s Redgrave has not performed in any Shakespeare at the RSC and has yet to be engaged for such a purpose by the British National Theatre (NT), although she has made appearances in Euripides, Ibsen and Chekhov for both companies. This uncoupling from the RSC and NT has also meant that Redgrave did not collaborate with some of the leading post-war British directors of Shakespeare. She worked with Peter Hall and Tyrone Guthrie at the Shakespeare Memorial Theatre in the late 1950s, but was persistently missing from the cast lists of directors such as Peter Book, John Barton, Trevor Nunn and Terry Hands. One can only speculate if Redgrave was the solo architect of such absences, or whether her presence on various political platforms, including an attempt in the 1970s to politicise the actors' union Equity, negatively affected her employability. What remains clear is that, as her career has progressed, Redgrave has proved highly resourceful in forging the means through which she and like-minded individuals could interrogate the challenges and possibilities that Shakespeare's texts present for the modern actor. This has not only meant sidestepping mainstream theatre institutions such as the RSC and NT, but also their embedded working practices. This has made possible what she regards as a corner-stone to her acting practice – the ability 'to play a part more than once' (Ibid: 95). We can see this most particularly in her numerous returns to the role of Cleopatra. What, to the outsider, may appear as an obsession is for Redgrave a steadfast demand on the imaginative and intellectual resources of both the actor and her audience.

There is no doubt that Redgrave's emergence as a professional actor in 1958 was profoundly shaped by the theatrical dynasty into which she was born. Her father Michael Redgrave made a huge impression on British theatre and film during the 1930s, 40s and 50s. Initially regarded as something of a matinee idol, Michael Redgrave would spend much of the early 1950s working at the Shakespeare Memorial Theatre in Stratford, playing leading roles such as Antony, Hamlet and King Lear. Accompanied to Stratford during school holidays by her mother, the actor Rachel Kempson, and siblings Corin and Lynn, both of whom would also follow in their parents' footsteps, Vanessa Redgrave's formative and frequent encounters with Shakespeare in both rehearsal and performance represented a unique opportunity, not least to develop a critical eye. Her recollections of this period are fascinating in the way that she continuously distinguishes the actor's work within a production's *mise en scène*; she writes of her father's performance as Shylock in *The Merchant of Venice* (1953) in terms of its success in overcoming the implied 'anti-Semitism' of the production (Ibid: 43). As we shall see in more detail later, Redgrave's concerns here do not simply represent a form of political critique, they endeavour to champion an ethical mutual responsibility between actor and director, text and context.

Acting was not Redgrave's first choice of profession. During her childhood and teens she attended the Ballet Rambert School in London, but her original wish to become a ballerina was thwarted by accelerated teenage growth that took her to a peak height of almost six foot. Michael Redgrave had originally steered his daughter into ballet training, and although Redgrave was now intent on entering drama school, her father thought she would have a more successful career in the theatre if she trained for musical comedy (Ibid: 52). She was determined to put her unfashionable physique to the test, and in 1955 succeeded in gaining a place at the Central School of Speech and Drama. Although she makes little direct reference to her encounters with Shakespeare at drama school, the training regime that was provided clearly presented a predicament:

> Speech therapy was one of the courses provided...We did hours of consonant and vowel practice with [a] bone prop between our teeth. I found concentrating entirely on technique limiting. Weeks spent listening to sounds and correcting them, with no work on a scene or a situation from a play, on subject or character, made students nervous. My own voice strangled with self-consciousness...The mime classes were still of the old school, 'pretend you have a tea-cup and saucer in your hand'...
>
> (Ibid: 53)

The dilemma was not so much 'technique' in and of itself, but the means by which technical training might facilitate the fuller development of her acting practice. It is instructive here to compare her observations on drama school to the rigours of ballet training:

> I became aware of the significance of physical movement and physical space, of extension and relations of bodies in space. Aware also of tempo, and that while music may have a certain regular beat, the form of the movement will sometimes take a different, longer tempo than the beat that sustained it. While in my daily life I was round-shouldered and stooping, so much taller than my friends and self-conscious about my height, in class I stretched upwards and ceased to think about myself.
>
> (Ibid: 37)

The young Redgrave clearly had an evolving ability to distinguish between 'technique' as a means of freeing the actor from 'self-consciousness', as opposed to being a way of acquiring a set of performance skills. She also found an antidote to the restrictive practices of her drama school training as a pupil of the influential Hungarian singing teacher Jani Strasser. Strasser alerted Redgrave to the need to begin – initially through physical exercises – by removing tension from the body and voice. His teaching methods were geared not to producing a note-perfect sound, which would incite the pupil to listen to – and therefore correct – the sounds she was making, but rather to be fully receptive to the 'what' and 'why' of the song, to work 'in the moment' of performance itself (Ibid: 50–51).

It is significant how Redgrave draws substantially off her experiences of training in the media of song and dance to reflect on the development of her acting practice. Her awareness of the limitations of the training at the Central School was further substantiated by her father. In his book *The Actor's Ways and Means* (1953) Michael Redgrave presented a ground-breaking investigation into the significance of twentieth-century developments in actor training in Europe, Russia and the USA. Michael Redgrave had worked with the influential French director Michel Saint-Denis at the Old Vic Theatre Company in the late 1940s. It was also through the London Theatre Centre and subsequently the Young Vic Theatre School that Saint-Denis sought, along with collaborators such as Glen Byam-Shaw and George Devine, to inculcate acting students with – what were at the time in Britain – relatively unfamiliar training practices, including those of Copeau, Stanislavski and Meyerhold. Although Saint-Denis was to exert considerable influence on British theatre practice, his enterprise was brought to an abrupt halt in 1952 with the withdrawal of government funding. Redgrave's lamentations over the absence of such wide-reaching forms of training for herself were particularly influenced by her budding fascination with the acting theories of Konstantin Stanislavski. The acting student could not comprehend why Stanislavski was not on the syllabus at Central. His *An Actor Prepares* represented not only 'the first analysis of a method of work with which an actor can overcome the problems that arise in the course of developing a part', it was founded 'upon objective processes in nature and society as the source for all development in art' (Ibid: 74–75).

It is perhaps difficult to reconcile Redgrave's seemingly debilitating years as an acting student with her early career successes in Shakespeare. Whilst it may be tempting to explain this away by her theatrically privileged upbringing or, even more sceptically, as innate talent, one must acknowledge here Redgrave's developing interrogation of her acting practice together with the evolving sense of her own agency. Significantly, her reflections on training do not reserve any extended space for approaching Shakespeare. She bypasses, for example, the unique demands placed on the actor by the formal challenges of speaking blank verse. This can be partly explained by her student fascination with Stanislavski, if only this was initially through his writings. Redgrave's querying of 'technique' in her drama school training she clearly associates with an aggregated (emotional, physical, vocal, etc.) form of obstruction, geared primarily towards producing certain predetermined 'effects' in performance. Conversely, the Stanislavski 'system' represents not 'technique' *per se*, but the key to unlocking the actor's imagination and physical, emotional and psychological awareness (Ibid). It is useful here to note the similarities with Redgrave's observations about her Ballet Rambert training and vocal tutoring under Jani Strasser. She also places particular value on Stanislavski's demand for 'research and study of the historical circumstances, customs and social life of the play and its characters' as a precursor for any rehearsal process (Ibid: 168). Most importantly, the Stanislavski system provides the actor with an ethical basis for her work:

> The more the actor is engaged in trying to change the conditions of his or her life, to grasp the meaning of problems and to analyse them, the more, in the course of rehearsal and performance, impressions will emerge. In further rehearsal and thinking these will become definite notions, which seem to have their own life. In fact they *do* have their own life. They reflect all that is essential now [in the theatre and contemporary life] and all that was essential then [in the play and the context of its writing] in the clearest and most advanced form.
>
> Every actor knows such moments, when it seems that someone else has taken possession of him. It is the union of the conscious with the unconscious. The problem is that everyone knows it when it happens, but artists spend most of their lives trying to understand *how* it happens, especially when they run into difficulties.
>
> The actors will be surprised and look at each other with excitement. Suddenly the atmosphere of rehearsal becomes charged. All will know, even if few or none can understand how it happens, that from somewhere a living truth has convinced them and made them convince each other and has taken shape in the thought and action of the characters.
>
> (Ibid: 168–69)

This passage from Redgrave's autobiography is worth quoting at length, not simply because it further highlights the seriousness with which she takes her craft, but also due to the number of important questions it raises in her approach to playing a role. In Redgrave's estimation, what can be deduced about the relationship between the actor and the text here? The actor appears not to exist to *serve* the authority of the text and its author as some meagre interpretative artist, but then neither is such authority simply transferred onto the performer. Can we therefore infer that Redgrave is promoting an ideal in which the two exist in some kind of undisputed equilibrium? These are critical questions in the rehearsal and performance of Shakespeare, not simply because of the arresting literary, historical and cultural value that his plays carry, but also because of the burden of their performance histories, something likely to be felt by any actor approaching the texts. Furthermore, the conjoining of Shakespeare with Stanislavski is beset with potential difficulties. As Jonathan Holmes points out, the introduction of Stanislavski's work into twentieth-century actor training – with its particular emphases on 'psychological consistency in characterization', achieved through the 'formulation of a through-line of action, or psychological arc', underpinned by the use of techniques such as 'emotion memory' and the establishment 'of a full back story to the character's actions' – might offer the actor a functional vocabulary, but is this sufficient for approaching the prodigy of Shakespearian character composition (Holmes 2004: 18–19)? If dramatic realism, with its emphasis on determinism and social environment, works to contain and shape the actions of character, then in Shakespeare's open dramatic form characters appear 'to exist not only within but outside the dramatic narratives that give them life' (Fuchs 1996: 24). We need to be cognisant here, as Redgrave certainly is, that the actor's use of Stanislavski does not have to be by any means indiscriminate. Indeed, Redgrave seems primarily inspired by the 'social roots' of his system, those 'objective processes in nature and society' (Redgrave 1991: 75).

When adjectives such as 'natural', 'sunny' and 'radiant' were invoked in reviews of *As You Like It* to describe Redgrave's performance as Rosalind in 1961, we come up against, even in the early twenty-first century, an irksome problem. Theatre scholarship, let alone journalism, has not yet succeeded in developing a language to discuss performance in an illuminating fashion. Whilst actor training has become increasingly technical, discussions of acting in general tend to be set in a critical theory context. But what was it exactly that critics in 1961 were responding to? As Penny Gay points out, many reviewers were besotted by Redgrave's performance, as though they had 'been forced to recognise that the part of Rosalind is there to be filled out by an actress who can put into it her own sense of what it is to be a young woman "fathom deep" in love' (Gay 1994: 55). The critic of the *Birmingham Mail* went as far to suggest that maybe Redgrave was 'not playing fair to Shakespeare to turn his Rosalind into a twentieth-century gamin, fantasticated Bisto kid, a terror of the lower fifth' (quoted in Ibid). We might therefore deduce from this that Michael Elliott's production was at least partly conceived as a launch-pad for Redgrave, in which the actor was given free-reign to impose her 'personal style' and 'presence' onto the role of Rosalind (Ibid). Her performance did not simply surprise commentators; it also seemed to relegate initial concerns about characterisation and the appropriateness – or otherwise – of the actor's choices. In a more discerning commentary on the production Robert Speaight observed how the actor rightly resisted the temptation to play Rosalind with such amazement at 'the things she has to say that she forgets to whom she is saying them'. Rather, 'Redgrave was so passionately concerned about *what she was doing* that the words sprang to her lips with the spontaneity of a mountain stream' (Speaight 1961: 433; my emphasis). What we have here is an example of a performance art that seeks to meet the challenge of 'character' in Shakespeare, and particularly in relation to a Stanislavskian shaped practice. Speaight's phrase, 'what she was doing', does not refer simply to Redgrave's physical animation of Rosalind, the score of physical actions that, together, signify a meaningful and coherent stage 'character' – for example, the reproduction of masculine manners when disguised as Ganymede in Arden. Rather, Redgrave's 'doing' was clearly concerned with the 'actions' of Rosalind in the broadest sense possible, or, in Stanislavskian discourse, understanding what it is that propels the character through the action of the play. In relation to this, Holmes observes how the musings of Shakespearian actors as diverse as Michael Redgrave and Antony Sher points to 'a distinct understanding of mimesis in order to compose their onstage selves, both as actors and characters' (Holmes 2004: 9). Whether consciously employing Stanislavski or not, Holmes argues that a particular pattern is discernible in the rehearsal and performance of Shakespeare, in which 'identity [becomes] pluralised… while remaining unfixed and "impermanent"' (Ibid).

The critical acclaim that Redgrave received for Rosalind should not be viewed in isolation from the originality and accomplishments of Michael Elliott's production. In an unusual move for the time, Elliott broke with etiquette and had one interval rather than two. Also, a 'movement director', Litz Pisk, was employed for the first time at Stratford. The production's designer, Richard Negri, dispensed with pictorial representation and created 'a single, stylised huge tree placed on a steepish rising mound' (Gay 1994: 57). The production not only emphasised the violence and tension underlining the banishment to Arden, it critiqued dominant views around identity and sexuality; for example, 'the killing of the deer became a crucial symbolic set-piece which acted as a critique of naive pastoralism', and Orlando (played by Ian Bannen) suggested repressed bisexuality in the presence of Ganymede (Ibid: 57–58). As Gay observes, the production was 'the first theatrically self-conscious reading of the play' at Stratford, 'recognising the court-country opposition as a metaphor enabling exploration of the human psyche in its social construction' (Ibid: 59).

However, we cannot fully appreciate the significance of Redgrave's performance as Rosalind simply in terms of a 'reading' of the role that responded positively to a directorial concept. As has been argued above, her performance, and this is also evidenced in the 1963 BBC television film of the production, was constantly characterised by an alert moment-to-moment playing of the text, not only in the dialogue but also in the long speeches. Her 'naturalness' or 'spontaneity' – better words to use here might be 'flexibility' and 'responsiveness' – should not be presumed as givens, but rather the result of a determination to root her practice in a physical, vocal, emotional and intellectual openness to its playing possibilities. There was also a distinct physical improvisatory quality to her performance, notably during the forest scenes as Ganymede in her exchanges with Orlando. As Gay observes, the actor's eschewing of 'ladylike behaviour' emphasised 'a character thrown on her own resources when exiled by an authoritarian state' (Gay 1994: 55). Redgrave's vision of Rosalind, particularly in terms of the cross-dressing, clearly succeeded in addressing the gender challenge of the role that had previously troubled actors such as Margaret Leighton and Peggy Ashcroft (Ibid: 50–54). It is instructive here to consider her account of preparing for Rosalind. She refers to listening to a recording of Edith Evans and Michael Redgrave playing a scene from *As You Like It*; Evans, Redgrave asserts, provided an 'Ordnance Survey of the Forest Of Arden' and so she set about memorising her predecessor's tempo and phrasing. She also read large quantities of Elizabethan prose, and particularly latched on to the story of Dick Whittington, which offered 'the nearest window into the actual vocabulary and style of speaking in everyday life in the late sixteenth century' (Redgrave 1991: 93). However, shortly before the production's opening the director Michael Elliott reprimanded Redgrave for refusing to 'give *all*' of herself to 'the play, the actors and the audience' (Ibid). She states that Elliott made her realise that she was 'cautiously trying to control' her performance, 'to get it right' (Ibid: 94). It might be tempting to view Elliott's wake-up call as a criticism of the actor's part-Stanislavskian preparation for playing Rosalind, as though her 'research' had resulted in a constrained form of playing in rehearsal aimed at achieving a certain level of mimetic realism. More pertinently, it reveals how Redgrave, at the age of twenty-four, was able to comprehend the constituents of a mature, integrated and embodied acting practice.

It was during the run of *As You Like It* that Redgrave also became a politically active figure. Over the subsequent decades she would journey from pacifism to Marxism and Trotskyism, and become a leading member of the Workers' Revolutionary Party (WRP). In 1974 she stood as a UK parliamentary candidate for the WRP, and in 1977 made a controversial documentary film, *The Palestinians*, about the consequences of Israeli occupation of the Palestinian territories. Redgrave perceives a direct connection between her 'leap as an actress' in *As You Like It* and this 'leap into political life' (Redgrave 1991: 95). Commentators have also identified a verifiable connection between Redgrave 'the actor' and Redgrave 'the activist'. For example, 'she reinterpreted Kate in the *Shrew* [1986] as a plutocrat's daughter emotionally deformed by wealth' (Howard 2007: 149). *Antony and Cleopatra* (1973) was set in the 1930s, and Redgrave was encouraged by her director (and former husband), Tony Richardson, to think of Hollywood stars such as Bette Davis and Joan Crawford. She recalls playing the scene when Cleopatra learns of Antony's marriage to Octavia 'as if she was very, very drunk' (Redgrave 2002: 45). The production has been viewed as 'a cartoon of American imperialism' (Howard 2007: 149). For Redgrave's third outing as Cleopatra in 1995, which she also directed, the play became 'a study of multi-cultural crisis and possibility' (Ibid). Influenced in part by the actor's involvement in the political crisis in the Balkans, this *Antony and Cleopatra* had a multi-ethnic cast, 'a Republic that was being torn apart by political factions' (Redgrave 2002: 46). In such attempts to perceive 'the political' in Redgrave's work, it is pertinent to note how commentators, including the actor herself, have frequent recourse to a production's conceptual premise as distinct from the actor's practice. In fact, a curious blind-spot is discernible around this particular inter-relationship. Tony Howard observes how, in certain film roles, Redgrave's acting manifests both 'immersion and conviction', also illustrated by a faculty for 'condensing the character's experience into one *gest*' (Howard 2007: 149). The Brechtian invocation here suggests a tacit self-awareness on Redgrave's part for adopting techniques that disclose the contingent social and political meaning of a role. Is this reconcilable with her endorsement of Stanislavski? The ideal of achieving a 'living truth' is a particular motif in Redgrave's reflections on acting. Arguably, this aligns her with Stanislavski's indebtedness to Romanticism, 'that art is a special privileged form of human activity, and that the spectator as well as the actor must "identify" with the role' (Leach 2004: 49). However, another aspect concerning the influence of Romanticism on Stanislavski's work, 'that one must travel through the particular to reach the universal', is especially relevant here (Ibid). Redgrave's acting practice – and, indeed, her political radicalism – is informed by this Romantic quest for 'truth', but it is through her attendance to 'the particular' that she casts revealing light on playing Shakespeare.

Redgrave's fascination with the role of Cleopatra, particularly during the 1990s, represents her most resourceful and productive engagement with Shakespeare to date. Between 1995 and 1997 she played the role three times in productions which she also directed, in both Europe and the USA. These were not three entirely individuated productions, but denoted more of an extended interrogation into *Antony and Cleopatra*. The play was initially produced under the auspices of the Moving Theatre Company (MTC) – inaugurated in 1993 and spearheaded by Redgrave and her brother Corin – an ensemble which aimed to be 'activist and international in its scope' (Greenwald 1997: 86). In taking on the role of both actor and director, she not only released herself from the potential of directorial conceptual impositions, and yet neither was her choice to direct geared solely towards envisioning an international actor-centred ensemble.

Informed by extensive research, and drawing off sources that included Epicurus, Lucretius, Plutarch and Lytton Strachey's *Elizabeth and Essex: A Tragic History* (1928), Redgrave formed a view of the play – her ruminations were subsequently published in a short book – which sought to locate *Antony and Cleopatra* within the historical conditions of both its narrative and composition. For Redgrave, 'Cleopatra and Antony, by virtue of their birth, their times, and their circumstances, were obliged to think of their personal lives in a way that was inextricable from political and economic necessities' (Redgrave 2002: 55). Most significantly, her conception of the Egyptian queen was influenced by readings of Elizabethan texts – including letters, speeches and poems – that suggested a strong association between Shakespeare's Cleopatra and the historical figure of Elizabeth I:

> ...as soon as I began to think of the equally legendary Queen Elizabeth, desired and hated by every prince of Europe, Catholic or Protestant, the Gloriana, the Cynthia, the Cybele, to all the earls and dukes of her court, then I could begin to touch, to feel and, most importantly, to hear the authentic voice of Shakespeare's Cleopatra.
>
> (Ibid: 50)

Furthermore, Strachey's *Elizabeth and Essex* provided the actor's key to 'the inner organism, the inner architecture of [the] role':

> The complex psychology of the lady, 'wrinkled deep in time', the doubts, the fears, the hesitations, the confidence, the tempests of wrath, and the longing for infinite adoration are all there.
>
> (Ibid)

What is edifying about these observations is not so much the scholarly authority – or otherwise – of Redgrave's analysis, but how her practice as an actor yet again reveals itself. The 'authentic voice' of Cleopatra, that *true*, *essential* thing of Shakespeare's creation, can only be accessed by the actor determining, in Stanislavskian language, the 'given circumstances' of both the play and the character. Something of a paradox thus arises. How might one reconcile the concern for discovering the 'authentic voice' of Cleopatra with Redgrave's historico-political research imperative, a decidedly *interpretative* and therefore contingent act? Are we perhaps seeing here a conflict between the functions of actor and director?

In discussing her own productions of *Antony and Cleopatra*, Redgrave is keen to stress its Jacobean authorship (c. 1603–7). The play 'is a homage to [the] vanished world [of Elizabeth I], and the greeting of a world that was new, frightening and must have seemed unrecognizable' (Ibid: 58). Each of her three productions not only used Jacobean costuming, the evolving scenographic motif was one of decay and detritus. Redgrave the director is equally keen to emphasise how a multi-ethnic cast, including a black Antony and Enobarbus, and a Vietnamese Charmian, emphasised the play's political contemporaneity (Ibid: 45–46). Little in this commentary suggests *how* Redgrave the actor worked inside the theatrical frame provided by Redgrave the director. Furthermore, critical reception was predominantly negative:

> ...she [Redgrave] struck viewers as imperious and testy rather than quixotic and volatile; her conception of the play and its rubble-strewn set came across as a muddle of deglamorising comment on colonial adventurism and

> the squalor underlying the overinflated reputations of great historical figures. No erotic feeling seemed to ignite the passionless relationship of Redgrave and her leading man...
>
> (Bevington 2005: 76)

Such observations also suggest how Redgrave was seeking to challenge received wisdom and re-vision the play and the role of Cleopatra for the late twentieth century. Interestingly, the production's failure amongst British reviewers was not repeated when, in 1996, it was developed and presented in repertory with *Julius Caesar* – directed by Corin Redgrave – at the Alley Theatre in Houston, Texas. Reviewers celebrated both Redgrave's directorial premise and her conception of Cleopatra. Dressed in Jacobean male attire and 'brilliantly red hair' (a clear reference to Elizabeth I), Redgrave's Cleopatra was both 'purposeful' and 'masculine', defined by the ability to play 'against type, often comically' (Greenwald 1997: 87, 89). For example, she played the speech, 'O happy horse, to bear the weight of Antony' (1.5.21) as 'wickedly erotic' (Ibid: 90). It was in Cleopatra's death scene that Redgrave's skill as both actor and director particularly communicated itself:

> After the Soothsayer brought her the asp, she kissed him sensually to thank him for his pains. It signalled her mental state as she was prepared to die: her encounter with the asp was, in effect, foreplay to her union with Antony in death...Her attendants, Charmian and Iris, draped her in a rich golden cloth, placed a crown upon her head and, later, a death mask on her face. Finally, Charmian set a grinning skull in her lap...Throughout this ritual transformation Redgrave superbly intoned Cleopatra's final speeches with an erotic joy, giggling like an adolescent in anticipation of a sexual tryst... The queen's was anything but a stony, tragic death meant to evoke tears in the manner of *Romeo and Juliet*; rather, it was an enviable escape from this 'baser life' into a better world, free from the machinations of political game-playing and earthly vanity. The finale that reunited the lovers in death was aligned more with the ancient *komos* of comedy than with the *agon* of tragedy; indeed, it was *gamos*, that joyful union of the sexes which concludes so many classical comedies.
>
> (Ibid)

Greenwald's description and reading of Redgrave's performance provides a valuable insight into her acting practice. When the actor writes of the 'authentic voice' of Cleopatra, is she not more accurately referring to the means by which the actor can identify for herself the reason for any action (here, Cleopatra's suicide), including those activities which prompt it (the kissing of the Soothsayer is a good example of this)? Again, we seem to be entering Stanislavskian territory here; indeed, Greenwald's observation of Redgrave's 'purposeful' Cleopatra is reminiscent of Speaight's comment about 'what she was doing' when playing Rosalind, that this is a practice rooted in 'taking action' and not simply 'acting' (see Leach 2004: 38).

It is not only in Redgrave's attention to the specific or 'the particular' that she uncovers insights, both performative and political, into the modern actor's approach to Shakespeare. Her preoccupation with Cleopatra also suggests an exacting concern for the very medium of theatre and its representational efficacy. In relation to this, Phyllis Rackin observes how the role of Cleopatra, like that of Rosalind, 'demonstrates the beneficent power of theatrical performance' (Rackin 2005: 85). In a discussion that encompasses the boy actors and transvestite performances of the Elizabethan and Jacobean theatres, Rackin argues that, '[e]ven as [Cleopatra] exemplifies those failings for which the enemies of theatre denounced the players, she also exemplifies the attractions for which the players were admired', and that Cleopatra 'is arguably Shakespeare's most profound and powerful exploration of the ambivalence of the player's craft' (Ibid). As a woman inhabiting a role originally composed for a boy player, it is instructive to note how Redgrave's performance as Cleopatra was marked as 'masculine'. Partly facilitated by her physical demeanour and vocal dexterity, her male costuming of Cleopatra reinforced the idea that Redgrave was cognisant of this dimension to the play. Although the actor/director seemed far from intent on forging a contemporary feminist reading of Cleopatra, this self-awareness of the operation of the gender/performance matrix and its destabilising potential was more fully evident in the actor's most recent theatrical encounter with Shakespeare.

In undertaking the role of Prospero in *The Tempest* in 2000 at the reconstructed open air Globe Theatre in London, Redgrave was not only opening up the possibilities of cross-gender performance, she was also taking on the weight of theatrical history. As a defining role in the Shakespearian canon and regarded as a test of any great actor, she had not only to contend with 'the benign magus of romanticised theatrical and critical tradition', but also 'Shakespeare himself, present through the reconstruction of his "original" theatre and through his identification with Prospero' (Klett 2009: 88). The director, Lenka Udovicki, offered a Balkan-themed production, emphasising exile rather than colonialism and imperialism – the penchant of many modern interpretations of *The Tempest* (Ibid: 105). But it was Redgrave's performance that prompted the most surprise. This was a Prospero that 'was neither "masculine" nor "feminine", but rather a watchful parent to both Miranda and Ariel' (Gay 2004: 172). Redgrave's costuming signified masculinity, but she made no attempt to disguise her own gender:

> ...by showing the audience continuously through her performance that she was effectually playing herself, Redgrave demonstrated how a particular body can exist in the tension between binary oppositions [masculine and feminine] – and hence challenge and unsettle them. By giving an understated performance and allowing audience sympathy to reside primarily with Caliban, Ariel and Miranda, Redgrave refused to comply with the expectations of many theatre reviewers, who wanted a performance that would bolster Shakespearian authority and English national identity.
>
> (Klett 2009: 89)

This otherwise insightful reading is somewhat underpinned by the supposition that audiences are hard-wired not to contest the conventions of theatrical illusion, and that actors and directors have to work especially hard to disrupt such conventions. The architecture of the Globe Theatre certainly encourages modern audience to be self-aware in the act of spectating, to fully accept the fiction of 'the play' before them. Standing as a groundling amongst the tourists, my own memory of this production is certainly not one of a bravura performance by Redgrave. I recall saying to a friend accompanying me to the performance how unfortunate it was that she had not played Brecht's great female roles: Mother Courage, Pelagea Vlassova in *The Mother*, Shen Te in *The Good Person of Szechuan*. I perceived Redgrave's 'playing herself' as something approaching an 'alienation effect', not simply in terms of the performance and deconstruction of gender, but as an anti-theatrical intervention in which our very ideas of 'acting' and 'performance', particularly within the environment of the Globe Theatre, are put to the test. But rather than making the familiar strange, I think now that Redgrave was making the strange familiar. There was a *seeming* effortlessness and economy to this Prospero, a fearless, almost prosaic, directness that particularly found its apotheosis in her delivery of the epilogue. As John Russell Brown reminds us, the epilogue invites the audience 'to accept the wisest character, with the play itself, as an image of any imperfect human performance, including their own' (Brown 1968: 250). *The Tempest* provides one of the most useful gateways to understanding what it is that ultimately propels Redgrave's acting of Shakespeare. The actor who inhabits his texts must acknowledge the theatre, without relegating its imaginative possibilities, as a place of resemblance and correspondence between actor and audience, of similitude rather than verisimilitude.

Vanessa Redgrave's performances of Shakespeare offer a unique insight into the possibilities of playing his roles in the modern theatre. Whilst her political views, however controversial, appear transparent and assertive, as an actor she continues to prove a curiously difficult figure to quantify. Over the past twenty years, she has cast herself as something of an outsider as a Shakespearian actor, working against expectation, and creating the conditions through which she can exert her own agency. She now readily embraces Hollywood – out of financial necessity – and this might well be regarded as irreconcilable with her politics. Conversely, Shakespeare functions in her career as a territory something akin to a laboratory. We can see this most readily in her investigations into *Antony and Cleopatra*. What emerges most clearly in this discussion is how Redgrave's performances of Shakespeare are anchored in an understanding of acting not simply as a representational or interpretative art form but as a *productive* craft. Through whatever critical lens we may wish to view Redgrave's work, our cognisance of this is foundational to a more complete appreciation of her playing of Shakespeare. In the actor's own words we find a simple yet shrewd assessment of the challenge:

> In the present day when impressions, images and sound-bites dominate the media, when 'effect' is all that counts…'cause' is feverishly neglected as too time-consuming and therefore non-productive, and consequently 'thinking' likewise…
>
> (Redgrave 1995: viii)

Chronology

1961–62 Rosalind, *As You Like It*, Royal Shakespeare Company (RSC), Stratford-upon-Avon and London

1961–62	Katherine, *The Taming of the Shrew*, RSC, London
1973	Cleopatra, *Antony and Cleopatra*, Bankside Globe, London
1986	Cleopatra, *Antony and Cleopatra*, Theatre Clwyd, Mold and Haymarket Theatre, London
1986	Katherine, *The Taming of the Shrew*, Theatre Clwyd, Mold and Haymarket Theatre, London
1995	Cleopatra, *Antony and Cleopatra*, Riverside Studios, London, UK and European tour
1996	Cleopatra, *Antony and Cleopatra*, Alley Theatre, Houston
1997	Cleopatra, *Antony and Cleopatra*, Public Theater, New York
2000	Prospero, *The Tempest*, The Globe Theatre, London

Bibliography

Bevington, David (ed.) (2005) *Antony and Cleopatra*, Cambridge: Cambridge University Press.

Brown, John Russell (1968 [1957]) *Shakespeare and his Comedies*, London: Methuen and Co. Ltd.

Fuchs, Elinor (1996) *The Death of Character: Perspectives on Theater after Modernism*, Bloomington: Indiana University Press.

Gay, Penny (1994) *As She Likes It: Shakespeare's Unruly Women*, London: Routledge.

——(2004) 'Women and Shakespearian Performance', in Stanley Wells and Sarah Stanton (eds), *The Cambridge Companion to Shakespeare on Stage*, Cambridge: Cambridge University Press, pp. 155–73.

Greenwald, Michael L. (1997) '"An Enterprise of Great Pitch and Moment": *Julius Caesar* and *Antony and Cleopatra* at the Alley Theatre, 1996', *Shakespeare Quarterly*, 48(1), 84–90.

Holmes, Jonathan (2004) *Merely Players?: Actors' Accounts of Performing Shakespeare*, London: Routledge.

Howard, Tony (2007) 'Icons and Labourers: Some Political Actresses', in Maggie B. Gale and John Stokes (eds), *The Cambridge Companion to the Actress*, Cambridge: Cambridge University Press, pp. 134–53.

Klett, E. (2009) *Cross-Gender Shakespeare and English National Identity: Wearing the Codpiece*, New York: Palgrave Macmillan.

Leach, Robert (2004) *Makers of Modern Theatre: An Introduction*, London: Routledge.

Rackin, Phyllis (2005) *Shakespeare and Women*, Oxford: Oxford University Press.

Redgrave, Vanessa (1991) *An Autobiography*, London: Hutchinson.

——(1995) 'Introduction', in Michael Redgrave, *The Actor's Ways and Means*, London: Nick Hern Books, pp. vii–ix.

——(2002) *Actors on Shakespeare: Antony and Cleopatra*, London: Faber & Faber.

Speaight, Robert (1961) 'The Old Vic and Stratford-upon-Avon, 1960–61', *Shakespeare Quarterly*, 12/1, 425–41.

About the author

John F. Deeney is Senior Lecturer in Drama and Theatre at Manchester Metropolitan University, where he specialises in teaching acting and directing. He has worked extensively as a professional theatre director, with productions at Contact Theatre (Manchester), the Traverse Theatre (Edinburgh) and the Glasgow Citizens', ranging from Shakespeare (*Measure for Measure*) to contemporary drama (he directed the European premiere of Susan Sontag's *The Way We Live Now*). He is the editor of *Writing Live: An Investigation of the Relationship between Writing and Live Art* (1998) and co-editor, with Maggie B. Gale, of the *Routledge Drama Anthology: From Modernism to Contemporary Performance* (2010). He has authored numerous articles and chapters on contemporary drama and theatre, and his book on the playwright Mark Ravenhill for the Routledge Modern and Contemporary Dramatist series will be published in 2011. He has seen a number of productions featuring Vanessa Redgrave, including *The Tempest*. The author would like to thank Stephen D. Berwind and Maggie B. Gale for their feedback on early drafts of this chapter.

16
Pyotr Semak

Maria Shevtsova

Born in Ukraine in 1960, Pyotr Semak was admitted into the four-year acting class of Arkady Katsman and Lev Dodin at the National Institute of Theatre Music and Cinema in Leningrad, from which he graduated in 1983. Semak's successful entry into this prestigious school is noteworthy because its selection procedures in the 1970s were no less rigorous than they were in the 2000s. In 2005, for instance, Dodin, who had been left in charge after Katsman's death, auditioned some 2,500 people, whittling them down over four rounds until he selected twenty-six of them (Dodin in Shevtsova and Innes 2009: 42–43). The Institute was renamed the Academy of Theatre Arts after the dissolution of the Soviet Union in 1991.

On completing his course, Semak, together with a group from the same class, immediately joined the Maly Drama Theatre whose new artistic director, as of 1983, was Dodin. This commitment to continuity between an acting school and a theatre dedicated to the same principles was key to Konstantin Stanislavsky's work and distinguishes the Maly today from virtually all other companies in Russia. Most of them had fallen prey to the commercial imperative dominating the country since the collapse of communism, or else they simply wanted a change from established Russian practice, much of which had atrophied under the Soviet regime. School-theatre continuity is of fundamental importance for the Maly's organic approach to acting, and Semak's work on Shakespeare is inseparable from this approach, nurtured by Dodin and his team of teachers-collaborators not only in the school as such, but in the ongoing training that occurs within the company as the actors rehearse and perform (Shevtsova 2004: 36–60).

Semak's first role was Mikhaïl Pryaslin in *Brothers and Sisters* (1985), which was also the Maly's first production under Dodin's leadership. *Brothers and Sisters* was a six-hour long epic that focused on the hardships of villagers living in the Arkhangelsk region during the last years of the Second World War and the early post-war period. Its themes, starting with state control and the injustices perpetrated by it, were of the moment, chiming with the overhaul of structures, ideas, attitudes and expectations that underpinned Mikhaïl Gorbachev's reforms – perestroika and glasnost – from 1986 to 1988; this socio-political focus, combined with performances of an uncommon clarity, musicality, energy and humour, gave the production something like legendary status. Semak's role was seminal to his development as an actor and also to the company's fame, both national and international. The production has remained in the Maly's repertoire ever since.

Semak has never stopped playing Pryaslin. Having assumed the role when he was much the same age as his character, he brings to it, twenty-five years later, the benefits of the maturation process undergone by the production. Semak carries into it, as well, his experience of roles in other productions whose tones and colours wash over into the different parts he plays, modifying them, sometimes quite radically, over time. This kind of inter-influence is integral to the work of all the Maly actors and affects their dynamic within a given production as well as their relations with each other as a collective whole. The fact that the Maly is not only a repertory company, but also a permanent *ensemble* repertory company, is crucial and to be remembered in the discussion of Semak's Shakespeare roles that follows.

Semak's second major role was that of Stavrogin in *The Devils* (1991), devised from the novel by Dostoevsky. This was a part he had tried out in rehearsals for several years, along with many other company actors, until it became clear that it properly 'belonged' to him. Probing and developing roles before selection rather than straight-out casting is central to the Maly's working method and has an impact not only on how the actors act their own roles, but also on how they *connect* with other roles, and the experience gives them a more sharply defined sense of the work of their partners. Semak subsequently played Chepurny in *Chevengur* (1999), which, like *Brothers and Sisters* and *The Devils*, is a piece of Dodin's 'theatre of prose' (Shevtsova 2004: 63–100), devised from the novel by Andrey Platonov. He then played Doctor Rays in *Molly Sweeney* (2000), Astrov in *Uncle Vanya* (2003) and James Tyrone in *Long Day's Journey into Night* (2009).

Semak's Shakespeare roles are only two to date, but are significant in the Maly's history. The first was Leontes in *The Winter's Tale* (1997) directed by Declan Donnellan, the first production of Shakespeare ever undertaken by the company. The second was the titular role of *King Lear* directed by Dodin (2006), the first Shakespeare he had ever directed since his career began in the late 1960s, even though he had worked on Shakespeare plays with his students more than once. Dodin's second Shakespeare production was *Love's Labour's Lost* in 2008.

That Semak's roles in the space of more than two decades appear to be few should be understood in the Maly's repertory framework, where roles crafted by a given actor mature and change with this actor over time. The continual exploration of established parts and productions, characteristic of the Maly, means that actors incessantly regenerate their roles; it is a stimulus to growth that allows them to expand their creative possibilities rather than narrow them because of the restricted number of roles they play. The fact that Semak subscribes to the Maly ethos and absorbs its axioms in his work on Leontes and Lear will be clear as much in the performance details noted during the course of this chapter as in Semak's observations in interview with me on 18 February 2009, as cited later. (All translations from Russian are mine.)

The Winter's Tale was Declan Donnellan's first, and only, experience of working with the Maly. He and his partner-designer Nick Ormerod, both founders of Cheek by Jowl in 1981, saw *Brothers and Sisters* in 1986 and were completely 'blown away' by it (Donnellan interview, 30 December 1998). They cemented their friendship with Dodin and the Maly when Cheek by Jowl performed *Measure for Measure* and *As You Like It* in St Petersburg in the early 1990s. Opportunities to maintain this friendship arose when Cheek by Jowl and the Maly performed at the same international festivals. By the time they came to St Petersburg for *The Winter's Tale* in 1997, they felt that they knew the Maly actors well – well enough, it turned out, to cast them in one morning, to Donnellan's surprise, since he and Ormerod normally spent months establishing their cast (30 December 1998). Semak, for his part, observes that casting was painless because the 'whole thing' differed greatly from the Maly's prolonged experimentation, which always involved various actors rehearsing the same role either concurrently or successively (18 February 2009).

King Lear came late in Dodin's life as a director, mainly because he had previously felt that neither he nor the company was ready for this, perhaps the 'most powerful Shakespeare play' (Shevtsova and Innes 2009: 51). For Dodin, *King Lear*, like *Hamlet*, 'asks the most fundamental, the most substantial existential questions' and he was daunted by its immense scope (ibid.). When he finally broached it, he had several actors rehearse Lear right from the start, in accordance with Maly practice. They were Sergey Kuryshev, who plays Vanya to Semak's Astrov in *Uncle Vanya*, Igor Ivanov, who performs Serebryakov in *Uncle Vanya*, Aleksandr Zavyalov, who is an unexpectedly rustic Konstantin in *The Seagull* (2001) and Semak himself. Semak notes that consistent rehearsals lasted for only one year (although, with interruptions, the overall process lasted about three years) and, towards the end of this intensive period, the company's consensus was that the role was his.

In the meantime, Semak had tried out Edgar and Edmund whom Dodin felt he could have played on the stage, if he had been younger (Semak, 18 February 2009). Cutting across parts during the rehearsal period, as Semak did from Lear to Edgar and Edmund – and Kuryshev from Lear to Gloucester – is another typical Maly feature, based on Dodin's conviction that role-crossing provides actors with greater insight into the role that eventually becomes their own. This is so – here extrapolating from Dodin's commentary to actors in rehearsals – because, when getting into the skin – or under the skin – of another character, actors gain a greater understanding of the *relations* between characters. The primary importance of relational play is stressed at the Maly, over and above any notion of individual mastery over one particular role.

Donnellan stepped with confidence into this work ethic, work culture and ensemble discipline and unity, knowing he could draw on them fully for *The Winter's Tale*. Rehearsals followed Donnellan's pattern, usually starting with games. Many were like children's games, involving plenty of movement, as Semak recalls, and encouraging quick reflex actions; and there were exercises that focused attention on partners (Semak, 18 February 2009). The Maly actors were able to respond easily to such exercises because their training emphasised both physical and psychological work, the latter entailing not only close attention to their partners, but staying attentive to them. Semak also recalls how Donnellan employed études which, for Leontes, opened out a whole network of relations with his family, courtiers and army. Semak stresses that all the études were very precise, giving, as examples, the actors' use of military and other maps to conjure up Leontes's power and their discussions around the number of men and ships he could have had for battle to protect his kingdom or attack his foes.

All in all, Semak's account suggests points in common between Donnellan's rehearsals and those of the Maly. What differed between the two was, first of all, the short rehearsal period – a mere two months – imposed by the heavy commitments of both the Maly and Cheek by Jowl. Notwithstanding the companies' tight schedules, Semak and Donnellan agree, in their respective commentaries at a distance of ten years from each other, that a great deal was accomplished within the limited time at their disposal. The second significant difference concerns directorial method. Dodin, Semak notes affectionately, 'talks and talks' before actors try something out, and then he 'talks and talks' again (ibid.). Such talk, as the present writer can testify, generally works around a play (or a novel), raising questions tangentially related to it rather than interpreting it head on; textual interpretation, when it does occur – and it does – is less a matter of textual analysis or its variations in a 'literary criticism' vein and more of a speculative and philosophical one, elaborating imaginatively and emotionally on the words on the page.

Donnellan, although not silent, was far less philosophically inclined. In addition, he gave actors less leeway for conjecture than Dodin would do, partly because of the short rehearsal period and partly because, Semak surmises, of his cultural heritage. Unlike Dodin, Donnellan had grown up with Shakespeare and 'knew Shakespeare's culture – even as an Irishman'. (This was said with a smile.) As a consequence, he had 'a certain understanding' that allowed him to cut corners with the actors. Equally, this 'authority' prepared them to accept his decisions. Semak, for his part, had no difficulty in following Donnellan's lead, irrespective of his Maly training, which prescribes a method of slow fermentation and maximum actorly input into the evolution of a work. To Semak's questions about Leontes and his relations with other characters Donnellan would generally reply, 'Trust me, believe me, it is like this' or 'Believe me, we need this, just do it' (ibid.).

Semak did, indeed, trust Donnellan, as did the other actors, and this showed in their effortless adaptation to the idea of 'stakes' that is central to his rehearsals. The idea, it could be said, offered a more pragmatic, clear-cut and systematic way of doing things than the Maly's open-ended, organic approach. The actor's principal task, in Donnellan's schema, was to identify what was at stake at every given moment. As the stakes rose, so did the conflicts driving a character's actions, and they were always ambiguous, always divided, in one and the same instance. The positive and the negative in the impulse to action had to be played, 'incarnated' one might say, in the sequence of moments on the stage:

> It is not true that the actor cannot play two things at once. We are always playing two things at once. But these two things are highly specific and precisely opposed. We must play in doubles because there is always something to be lost and something to be won.
>
> (Donnellan 2002:71)

It could be deduced, from these words, that the actor's target is the play of tension between the loss and the gain necessarily embedded in every emotion, situation, and event. Furthermore, as can be surmised from Donnellan's discussion in its entirety, these stakes shift constantly. Regardless of their motility, the actor must grasp them in order to *perform*.

Semak by no means diminishes Donnellan's notion of 'stakes' but nor does he imply that the Maly actors mechanically applied it to their work on *The Winter's*

Tale. He found Donnellan's method of playing opposites useful for coming to grips with Leontes's inexplicable jealousy but he also referred to his personal experience – a device used by Maly actors to imagine their characters. He recollected his own irrational jealousy of a woman whom he had loved; how he spied on her and hounded her until he finally realised that his suspicions were unfounded. He struggled, as he had done in his own experience, with the sheer force of a mania that drove all else before it, propelling Leontes to accuse Hermione, dismiss Polixenes, and destroy his son and daughter in a torrential flow that seemed to have come from nowhere. Semak observed that he had to understand this somehow or he would not have been able to play the role at all.

Semak's account of how he worked on Leontes was brief, but he did state quite unequivocally that he found Leontes terrifying because he seemed to be driven by virulent needs that had to be met, no matter what the cost. Most terrifying of all, as can be paraphrased from Semak's remarks, was not their unstoppable force, but the fact that Leontes benefited from their release. It was as if Leontes had to expel whatever it was that had been triggered off so as to lay it to rest forever. The harm brought in its wake was a necessary condition of the freedom Leontes was to find. In Donnellan's terminology, the loss and the gain for Leontes were in perpetual tension at every moment. Semak did not echo Donnellan's words on the 'stakes', yet the idea seems to have merged in his thoughts about Leontes's harmful actions and their ultimately redeeming consequences. Semak did not attempt to rationalise Leontes's behaviour in psychological, psychoanalytical or moral terms. The most he could say was that 'these inexplicable things happen' (18 February 2009) as, indeed, they had happened to him personally. Vestiges of this thinking were to resurface in Semak's preparation of Lear, although he did not draw an explicit parallel between Lear and Leontes.

How Semak worked on Leontes is best gleaned from his performance, even though a spectator's subjective interaction with any given performance inevitably shapes his or her account of it. Perhaps the most striking feature of Semak's playing was his externalisation of Leontes's emotions in their raw state. This is especially pronounced in the first three Acts, where Donnellan's direction is palpable in the way Semak objectifies his character's passions, including jealousy, suspicion, violence and cruelty, offsetting them against the situations that distinguish scene from scene. Donnellan achieves his distancing effects by having actors concentrate on what is happening outside their characters, and Semak modifies this ploy in order to make Leontes humanly recognisable in otherwise improbable circumstances. While adapting Donnellan's 'out there' to the Maly's 'in here', which centres on internally motivated playing, Semak nevertheless performs for these first three acts in that virtually non-empathetic, crisp style that has become a hallmark of Donnellan's productions.

Donnellan structures these acts into three clear parts, coming very close to separating them off into discrete units. At least this is how they appear from Semak's performance, which seems to highlight the three faces of the same man, in succession: the man in his home, behaving senselessly, in Act I; the master of his house in Act II; and the supreme ruler of his kingdom in Act III. Act I sets the tone – or the highest 'stakes' – in scene ii, which involves Mamillius. Donnellan divides the scene into two sequences, thus giving Semak the opportunity to build up its impact while revealing that Leontes is possessed by something unknown, rather than being in possession of his faculties. The first sequence is Leontes's dialogue with Polixenese about Mamillius. (Here Leontes suddenly, and falsely, suspects that Mamillius is Polixenes's son.) The second is Leontes's attack on Mamillius, which is foregrounded spatially and isolated by light. It is also put into relief by the penumbra of the rest of the stage and by the remaining characters, who 'freeze', in profile, for the duration of the sequence. Put together, these two sequences give a comprehensive picture of violence, one that encompasses sinister confidence, paranoia (expressed in voice, gesture, glances), sheer brutality and blind fury, the latter exploding when Leontes confronts Mamilllius. Semak's grip on the boy's cheeks, almost pedantic articulation of syllables, and deliberate thrust and sway of his body are facts of violence, and it is to these facts, rather than to their reasons or ramifications, that Semak gives his concentrated attention.

In Act II, Semak-Leontes, the master of his house, is dressed in a silk gown over his suit and smokes and signs documents behind a desk covered in red cloth. The setting is functional, and the man in it is business-like. His speech and manner exude a self-confidence reminiscent not of the Russian upper classes but of the English ones, or at least of their cinema or television version: the image is so familiar that it verges on parody, whether intended or not. Semak gradually brings out into the open the aggression latent in this seemingly detached figure by taking care, at the same time, to show Leontes's domination over his retinue. Semak may well have remembered in his predominantly passive-aggressive play in this Act the terrifyingly unswerving Leontes whom he had imagined as he rehearsed.

In Act III, during the trial of Hermione (performed with moving simplicity by Natalia Akimova), Semak presents Leontes, the ruler of his kingdom. It is this ruler, rather than a husband or a father, who subjects his wife to his imperious scorn and who remains impervious to Hermione's dignified speech. The whole scene, where Hermione speaks on a platform through a microphone, suggests a show-trial, and creates, through its spatial arrangement as well as unimpassioned dialogue, a sense of distance between the event and its spectators, both on stage, as part of the performance, and offstage, as audience in the theatre. Semak accentuates that distance by being well to the side of the stage, where he watches and comments on the spectacle that he has set up. Observation is of such importance in this Act that its pivotal moment, when Leontes discovers the wrong he has done, cannot change mode fast enough to catch up with Semak's change of key. Here Semak's play is more inward-looking, quiet and reflective, presumably to avoid the danger of over-doing Leontes's change of heart by a more extroverted way of playing.

It is not until Act V that Donnellan's distancing mechanisms fall away. The reunion scene between Hermione, Leontes and their daughter is a scene of resolution and reconciliation in which the production's undercurrents of emotion well up, surge forward, and let go, in all their beauty. When the spectre of Mamillius enters, guided by the young woman playing Time, Leontes is on his knees, asking his son for forgiveness. Mamillius gently places his hand on his father's head, and walks out as silently as he had come in. The emotional impact of this silent scene is extraordinary and is sustained by the magnitude of Semak's emotion which, although held together, communicates itself by osmosis, viscerally, without needing to be externalised.

*

It is always difficult to ascertain, in any given performance, just how much comes from an actor and how much from the director. This is particularly difficult when the actor and the director collaborate in the fullest sense of the word. Such is the case of Semak and Dodin in a company where actors are nurtured to be co-authors of a production – that is, where their collaborative input is vital to the director's orchestration of the whole (Shevtsova, 2004: 36–60). None of this, moreover, happens according to a formula: there is no tool-kit either for Dodin or the Maly actors to use routinely, at will. This is important for understanding how *King Lear*, and Semak's Lear, were not tailored to a production plan or according to a director's 'vision', but grew out of long-term explorations in rehearsals. In addition, they drew on the common values of the company, which were established over a longer term still and were not only aesthetic, but also life values. All this ensured optimal conditions for the immersion that, although a general principle of the Maly, was taken to be indispensable for the challenges posed by Shakespeare.

Immersion, it is clear from Semak's observations, allowed the actors to try out various possible versions of *King Lear* some of which, as potentially dominant ones, were gradually abandoned, while others, even though they fell away, left traces, to a lesser or greater degree, of the work that had gone in to them. Semak takes as an example of rejected versions the company's attempts to see the play through contemporary politicians, particularly where the relationship between Lear and Gloucester was concerned. The latter provided a model of political cooperation, coupled with personal intimacy, of the kind to be found, according to Semak, between Presidents and their close advisers in the modern world, in the United States or Russia. John Kennedy and Bill Clinton came to mind, as did Vladimir Putin. The essential point for Semak was that Lear and Gloucester, as could be interpreted from Shakespeare's text, were 'very close' (18 February 2009) and their bond had to do with how they had lived and worked side by side, presumably for decades. Some of that intimacy between their characters, as played out by Semak and Kuryshev, survived in the relationship between them in the final version shown to the public.

As Semak and Kuryshev explored the intricacies of political relationships by using études, locating them in contexts derived from the wars and intrigues of the play rather than replicating the latter, they slowly whittled away the political dimensions of *King Lear*. This occurred, as well, when Kuryshev played Lear, indicating how symbiotic the exploratory process between them must have been. Their elision of politics accompanied a similar movement away from history, which came, in part, from the company's agreement that a historicised *King Lear* in a pre-medieval, medieval or even Renaissance political framework made no sense in today's quite different constellation, and the very idea of a jester in cap and bells seemed like the worst kind of cliché of supposedly historical accuracy. It came, as well, from Dodin's reflections on how impossible it was for them, today, really to imagine what it would be like to be a King, let alone fathom how he might carry out royal duties and rituals. Dodin, as Semak recalls, had noted that it was impossible to ask the Queen of England for permission to come and stay at Buckingham Palace to observe her in her daily rounds (ibid.). This kind of first-hand acquaintance or full-scale immersion in a specific environment, as had happened for example when the company travelled to Archangelsk to research *Brothers and Sisters*, was part of the Maly's usual preparatory process but was, in this instance, completely out of reach. As a consequence, so, too, was anything like a genuine understanding of modern royalty in relation to which an intelligible image of kingship could be constructed. To construe Lear's daughters as a King's daughters seemed equally unfeasible.

However, the disappearance of the political aspects of *King Lear* was also due to Semak's inability to grasp fully what kind of King his character was. He worked around the hypothesis that Lear may have been a benign 'tyrant', a leader with ideals for his country who had gone to great lengths to defend those ideals but was now satiated. He had achieved his goals by the time the play begins and now imagined that he could relinquish his responsibilities without causing damage or incurring blame. This view provided Semak with a motive for Lear's division of his kingdom, and his sense of Lear as a man of ideals stimulated him to seek a parallel in the world that he knew. Not surprisingly, he began to think of Gorbachev and the latter's plan for restructuring the Soviet Union – a radical turn around and upheaval which he and his generation of actors at the Maly had lived through directly. Semak's emphasis on how he sought tangible, concrete detail rooted, preferably, in experience is in keeping with how Maly actors begin to shape their characters.

While possible versions inspired by contemporary politics disappeared, others that had experimented with what might be called domestic themes left their mark on the production. Dodin referred in rehearsals to a story related by the filmmaker Sergey Paradjanov to David Borovsky, the stage designer of *King Lear*. Paradjanov, when in jail (he was imprisoned several times during the Soviet period for alleged homosexuality) encountered an old man from the Caucuses, who had repeatedly committed incest with his young daughter. After he had married her off, his daughter continued to return home secretly for sexual relations with her father. Eventually, her husband discovered them, and was shot by his father-in-law. The story had made enough of an impression on Dodin to come back into his thoughts when he and the actors were exploring the relations between Lear and his daughters. Goneril and Regan, Dodin suggested, could not have been purely arbitrary in their behaviour to their father, and the psychological realism at the heart of the Maly's work prompted a search for causes for it.

The hypothesis that Lear may have abused his daughters, not necessarily sexually but in some other way, became a main strand of their rehearsals, and études around this idea opened up several interpretative leads. Among them was one of a psychoanalytical nature, and it survived in the production in rather startling flashes. Goneril and Regan's relations with Edmund (Igor Seleznyov) are made explicitly sexual by Elizaveta Boyarskaya and Yelena Kalinina, who, at the time, were Dodin's students. He had incorporated four of his 2005 cohort into the company (thus also Darya Rumyantseva as Cordelia and Danila Kozlovsky as Edgar) on the grounds that they would benefit immensely from working with fully-fledged actors (Shevtsova and Innes 2009: 55). Each woman, in scenes involving Edmund, calls out the word 'Father' before she lies down on the floor beside Edmund-Seleznyov to suggest their coupling. The call is unexpected and seems contrived – perhaps even gratuitous in its reference. Yet, if it is meant as a sign of the unconscious speaking of a taboo (whether of an actual fact or a repressed desire), its significance becomes clear only when all aspects of Lear's harsh and possessive attitudes, as played by Semak, are taken into account. Sexual or not, Lear's control over his daughters is psychologically abusive, and the implication, as the production slowly accumulates its inferences and builds up its emotional force, is that Lear had been abusive in this way for many years before he divided his kingdom; that, in fact, he continues to be an abusive father, almost goading his daughters to turn against him.

A major consequence of this line of action was the development of a bond between the three sisters. Time and again the women's small gestures in the production imply warmth and solidarity between them. What the collective work between the actors makes clear is that moral judgments cannot be made: they can only be in flux because actions have a comprehensive genesis and explanation. It was Semak's task, as may be deduced from the production, to provide the actors and particularly Boyarskaya, Kalinina and Rumyantseva with cues to help them avoid stereotypical representations. Thus they did not separate Lear's daughters into 'good' Cordelia and 'bad' Goneril and Regan. Indeed, Rumyantseva's impertinent 'Nothing' right at the beginning has little to do with a conventionally 'good' or innocent daughter, and Boyarskaya's and Kalinina's manifest sympathy with Cordelia demonstrates from the outset that they were conceived in a complex way. Nor is Semak's father-patriarch a straightforward case of tyranny. His response to Cordelia booms out Lear's domination over his female household, in which, nevertheless, lies a certain care-worn resignation and, as well, something like a tension or struggle within himself. Semak compared what he thought might be Lear's inner debate to Hamlet's 'to be or not to be', and felt he could pursue this existential pathway in his playing (18 February 2009). 'To be or not to be' can, of course, be paraphrased as 'to do or not to do', which, in the light of Semak's reflections below, does not reduce in the slightest his perception of Lear in existential terms.

Placing Lear, during rehearsals, within a familial context took hold, guiding designer Borovsky to dress the character in a stark, white, short nightshirt until the scenes on the heath in Act III. Thus, from his very first appearance, Lear is a Lear-at-home – so much so that he even has his feet washed by a servant in a common white enamel basin of the kind to be to be found in any bathroom or kitchen. When asked where these images of Lear may have originated, Semak referred to a teacher visiting his Institute in the winter who was so absorbed in his thoughts that he forgot to put on his trousers: underneath his coat was long underwear that he must have mistaken for trousers (ibid.). The memory of that episode prompted him to see Lear as being so engrossed in his worries over whether to divide the kingdom or not that it no longer mattered to him whether he was dressed, half-dressed or undressed. Semak believed that drawing up a 'very human, very knowable' Lear right from the start would give both himself and spectators access to the extreme circumstances of the heath scenes in which the recognisably 'human' constantly risked being overwhelmed by what Semak described as the 'cosmic'. In Act III, Semak wears white long underwear and socks, Borovsky having taken his cue from Semak's memories of his student days. Semak, following Shakespeare to the letter, strips down naked, bullying Kent into doing the same.

Semak referred to this accessible Lear in his search for the motives behind Lear's decision to give his kingdom away, or as Dodin puts it: 'he gives it away *without* giving it away' (Shevtsova and Innes 2009: 54). However, having officially given it away, regardless of whatever his motives may have been, he finds himself without a home. Dodin and Semak, who carefully studied the collocations of 'house' and 'home' in Shakespeare's text, began to pull them together in their experiments during rehearsals. Slowly, their explorations of what it might be like to be homeless took form and began to emerge as a dominant motif of the nascent production. Once again, Semak drew on his personal experience. He remembered his grandmother, who, at one time, in the complexities of living conditions in the Soviet Union, no longer had anywhere to live. She went from daughter to daughter, complaining about the one to the other, like Lear, except that the solution to her predicament was nowhere near as drastic. While reflecting on his grandmother's situation and how it affected both her and his mother, Semak must surely have set into motion his 'affective memory', to use Stanislavsky's terminology, to give him insight into the emotional wellsprings of his part.

Filtering his vision of Lear through a domestic context helped Semak to formulate a series of questions regarding Lear's division of his kingdom: Was he embarrassed that he had lived to such a ripe old age and was still full of energy to rule? How anxious was he about his daughters' future and particularly about Cordelia, who was still unmarried? How troubled was he by the fact that he had no son to whom, by law, he would necessarily have left the entire kingdom, undivided? Was he afraid, if he showed the slightest weakness once he had divided the kingdom, that his entourage would take advantage of him? Would the division be seen as a sign of weakness? How would he live?

Semak did not find satisfactory answers to these and many more questions that arose for the rest of the play; and, as he observes: 'I don't think on the stage. *There* you have to play, not think, but I *do* think off stage' (18 February 2009). But such questions nurtured his playing, leading him to act Lear as a man whose unresolved dilemmas had brought him to the brink of madness. It is this Lear who opens the performance. He enters abruptly through the audience, from the side of the auditorium, suggesting, by both the place and manner of his entrance, that Lear has broken with protocol. His gaze is unfocused and his eyes, catching the light, are too bright. Nevertheless, he takes command of the space, addressing spectators as if he were running his own one-man show. He sits on the edge of the stage, still talking to them, and then clambers onto it, gesticulating to his Fool (Aleksey Devotchenko). The conversation between Lear and his foil, while funny, is patently daft. The Fool, a cabaret-style figure inspired by the radical Soviet actor-bard Vladimir Vysotsky, plays on a player piano below the stage, his music functioning like comments on his speech. Lear, then, is not driven mad by events. He *is* mad to start with (Shevtsova 2006: 251–56). Dodin notes that the actors 'had to gather this madness up from the very beginning' (Shevtsova and Innes 2009: 54), which meant that they had to start with a high point, or what Dodin calls a 'high jump' (ibid.), and keep going higher in Act III. Dodin was quite adamant that Lear 'should not be worn out or senile' at any stage (Dodin 2006: 86).

Senility is hardly the issue in Semak's virile rendition of madness in Act III whose scenes, however, are not constructed to be unmistakeably real. They are played, rather, on the edge of what can be taken to be real in one instant and, in another, to be surreal. It is precisely this strange, surreal quality that gives Lear's madness credibility. Nowhere is this more evident than in an invented scene in which Lear dances a minuet with his three daughters. He is in his underwear, without a shirt but with a black scarf draped around his neck whose ends he occasionally twirls as he dances. Lear's daughters are in identical stiff white dresses with high collars and with skirts held up by invisible hoops at the side: there is enough here to suggest Elizabethan dress, and it is the only 'historical' allusion in the entire production. Semak's delight in this loopy dance has a touch of child's play about it as it merges into Lear's dream, or fantasy, or hallucination, or flashback to the past. In all its formality, the scene momentarily breaks the austerity of the production as a whole. Yet even here, in this quasi-courtly vignette, the prevailing tone is 'human' rather than 'cosmic', to take up Semak's vocabulary once again.

The translation for the production was a new one by Dina Dodina, full of gritty street language for the Maly's purposes and as familiar and 'knowable' as Semak's image of Lear. What was often lost in the process, conspicuously in Acts III and IV, was the magnitude of Shakespeare's poetry, which opens up vistas of the 'cosmic' that Semak increasingly felt he wanted to convey as his years in the role progressed. That he has not yet managed to do so is probably bound up with the 'Everyman' direction the rehearsals took: such a *King Lear* may simply not be capable of soaring into the ether.

Dodin claimed in a press interview before the premiere of *King Lear* that the Maly translation offered the company the alternative that it had been looking for to the over-poetic quality (its 'poeticality', in Dodin's words) of the extant translation by Boris Pasternak (cited in Shevtsova 2006: 254). Semak, for his part, found Pasternak's translation 'overwrought' and, therefore, difficult for an actor to say. Dodina, the company's literary manager with responsibility for international liaison, was steeped in its ways. Consequently, her aim was not to come up with a perfect translation of Shakespeare's play as a piece of dramatic literature, but with a script that fell into step with the Maly's work as it unfolded in rehearsals. For this reason, Dodina frequently modified her translation so as to coordinate it with the actors' playing. In this respect, the evolution of the playscript was as organic as that of the production, the one folded into the other. Dodin's *King Lear*, while allowing Semak to discover his Shakespeare, is the Shakespeare of every participant in its making.

Bibliography

Dodin, Lev (2006) *Journey Without End: Reflections and Memoirs*. London: Tantalus Books.

Donnellan, Declan (1998) *Unpublished interview* with Maria Shevtsova.

——(2002) *The Actor and the Target*. London: Nick Hern Books.

Semak, Pyotr (2009) Unpublished interview with Maria Shevtsova (in Russian).

Shevtsova, Maria (2004) *Dodin and the Maly Drama Theatre: Process to Performance*. London and New York: Routledge.

——(2006) 'Lev Dodin and the Maly Drama Theatre: *Uncle Vanya* to *King Lear*', *New Theatre Quarterly* 22(3): 249–56.

Shevtsova, Maria and Christopher Innes (2009) *Directors/Directing: Conversations on Theatre*. Cambridge: Cambridge University Press.

About the aauthor

Maria Shevtsova is Professor of Drama and Theatre Arts at Goldsmiths, University of London. She is the author of numerous articles and chapters of collected volumes, contributing a chapter on Peter Brook to the *Routledge Companion to Directors' Shakespeare* ed. John Russell Brown (2008), pp. 16–36. Her books include *Theatre and Cultural Interaction* (1993), *Dodin and the Maly Drama Theatre: Process to Performance* (2004), *Robert Wilson* (2007), *Fifty Key Theatre Directors* (co-editor and contributor) (2005), *Jean Genet: Performance and Politics* (co-editor and contributor) (2007), *Directors/Directing: Conversations on Theatre* (with Christopher Innes) (2009) and *Sociology of Theatre and Performance* (2009). She has edited and contributed to the focus issues *Theatre and Interdisciplinarity* for *Theatre Research International* (2001) and *The Sociology of the Theatre* for *Contemporary Theatre Review* (2002). She is co-editor of *New Theatre Quarterly*.

17
Antony Sher
Martin White

At the beginning of the televised version of the Royal Shakespeare Company's (RSC) 1982 stage production of Bulgakov's *Molière*, Bulgakov (played by Sher) is woken in the night by a phone call from Stalin. In a tense scene, shot in black and white, Bulgakov treads his way carefully through a minefield of unpredictable shifts in his master's responses. As he puts the phone down, the film shifts abruptly into colour and cuts to backstage at the Palais Royale Theatre in seventeenth-century Paris, as a performance by the company led by the writer and actor, Molière (also played by Sher), comes to a close. Summoned back on stage by the King, Molière, in the role of Sganarelle – wearing a vast wig, gargantuan purple false nose with a giant wart and heavy make-up – improvises a eulogy to *his* master. For me, the juxtaposition of these two performances provides a metonym for Sher, who, as he has matured as a Shakespearean actor, has fused the virtuoso theatrical style – for which he was first singled out by reviewers and audiences – with what John Peter, writing of Sher's performance as Primo Levi, described as 'acting of the purest and most unostentatious kind, unadorned by self-pity or visible virtuosity' (*Sunday Times*, 29 January 2006). It is these qualities that define his acting: detailed nuances of gesture and vocal tone, physical and emotional energy matched by deep focus of concentration, the sense of an actor fully inhabiting the role, drawing on a well-spring of feeling, and the confident grasp of the blurred line between the humanity and grotesquerie of life. (These extracts can be viewed on YouTube.)

*

Antony Sher came to London from South Africa in 1968 with one ambition: to train as an actor. His first audition was for the Central School of Speech and Drama. Theatre schools require applicants to present a modern and a classical (usually Shakespeare) piece. Sher selected Mick from Pinter's *The Caretaker* followed by the more surprising choice of the ageing Cardinal Wolsey from Shakespeare's *Henry VIII*. Sher gives a glimpse of what his Wolsey might have been like, when he describes showing his prepared speeches to his cousin, the playwright and screen-writer Ronald Harwood, who

> sat very still, frozen almost, as, before him, this short bespectacled boy began to waddle round his study, arms hanging wide of the body – meant to indicate great girth, but perhaps more reminiscent of the Frankenstein

> monster – while speaking in low, wheezing tones tinged with a slight American accent.
>
> (Sher 2001, pp. 87–88)

Central turned him down, as, more brutally, did the Royal Academy of Dramatic Art, their rejection letter telling him that 'Not only have you failed this audition, and not only are we unable to contemplate auditioning you again, but we strongly urge you to seek a different career' (Ibid, p. 89). Refusing to be deterred, Sher was eventually accepted by the Webber-Douglas Academy, where he recalls he was barred from classes in singing (he is tone-deaf) but relished the classes in make-up, mime, improvisation and Speaking Shakespeare, where the training instilled in him two basic principles from which he has never deviated:

> You have to paraphrase every single word in every single speech, *translate* them into contemporary English; and then, when you've understood everything, get it back up to speed, like normal speech. We talk very fast, very deftly, and Shakespeare is easier to understand at this pace than when it's overemphasised.
>
> (Ibid, p. 107)

He discovered something else important about himself when, cast as Puck in a 'violent, funny, sexy' version of *A Midsummer Night's Dream*, devised by Steven Berkoff, one of his teachers ('strutting, snarling, grinning, half-human, half-creature'), Sher realised he

> could tap into a strange energy for the character and express myself forcefully through the same small body that seemed so inadequate back on the playing fields of Sea Point Boys' High.
>
> (Ibid, p. 107)

Gradually the elements that would come to shape and define him as a Shakespearian actor were emerging: a focus on form, feeling and energy in both spoken and physical performance; an awareness of how intelligence can feed emotion and vice-versa; the exhilaration of experimentation; an appreciation of the impact and importance of his heritage; and a desire to keep learning.

*

Webber-Douglas taught no rigid philosophy of acting. Indeed, one of the most lasting lessons Sher has learned is that the only rule in acting is that there isn't one: each part demands its own response. Nevertheless, he is adamant that he would still advise any young actor to go to drama school, to 'go and get the training, learn all they teach you and carry on learning through your career, because you will if you're lucky'. For Sher, learning-on-the-job has been sustained largely by his lengthy association with the RSC where:

> I suddenly found myself in a place where I was surrounded by great Shakespeareans who wanted to teach me: Cicely Berry [Head of Voice], [and directors] John Barton, Terry Hands, Adrian Noble – and then I ended up

> marrying one, which has been an extraordinary privilege because more than anyone Greg [Doran] has shown me that Shakespeare can be mine as much as anybody's.
> (Personal conversation with the author, 2009; all further unattributed quotes from Sher are taken from the transcripts of these conversations)

Given the extent of Sher's experience and success playing Shakespearean roles, this need for reassurance might seem strange. But at the start of his career he was almost cripplingly self-conscious – of his physique, his Jewishness, his (yet-to-be openly acknowledged) sexuality. Consequently, it is not so surprising that he saw acting – especially in Shakespeare – as something in which others, more physically and vocally blessed than he, would succeed:

> I'd always assumed classical theatre was the preserve of tall handsome honey-voiced British actors. When I was growing up and coming into the profession they all seemed to be of that mould: Redgrave, Olivier and Gielgud – that was what a classical actor was, it seemed to me.

When performing the lead role in Sartre's play *Kean* (Apollo, Shaftesbury Avenue), about the charismatic but troubled nineteenth-century Shakespearean actor, Sher wrote a piece for *The Guardian* (24 May 2007), noting that the subtitle of the play by Dumas on which Sartre based his own was 'Disorder and Genius', and suggesting that some of the most successful actors have a 'destructive force' in their lives on which they can draw. As he sets out with unsparing honesty in *Beside Myself* (a title which captures the close link between his acting and his own life), Sher has been in therapy for some twenty-five years. Of his decision to draw on his own 'demons' to create a role, he observes that:

> one has to be very careful about talking about this because it can sound very indulgent, but the more damaged you are the more you can put that into your work. And treading very, very carefully here, I think there is a wounded side to some of the acting that I like most. I've just read a biography of Marlon Brando, who's one of my heroes. I didn't really know anything about his life and I was amazed to find how unhappy he was and what a terrible childhood and terrible parents he'd had. And it kind of fell into place about why this person, who on the outside seemed so physically beautiful and talented, had something in his acting that moves me. In addition to the weight and power and danger, the astonishing thing that he brings to Don Corleone in *The Godfather* – which is possibly the greatest performance I know in any medium – is a sort of weird humanity and compassion. There's something broken in that man, something hurt, which is the most surprising element to bring to that part and which is what makes it sublime.

This statement seems to me central to understanding Sher's aims as an actor. From his earliest Shakespearean performances such as the Fool in *King Lear* (first at the Liverpool Everyman in 1972, then the RSC in 1982) and Richard III (RSC, 1984) he had been defined by his ability to bring to the stage an electrifying energy, a sense of unpredictability and danger. But for some, these performances, however brilliant, remained externalised, bravura displays rather than an expression of a character's psyche. While not wishing to lose that sense of the sheer joy of the physicality of acting, he increasingly sought ways to combine these detailed portrayals of the 'outside' of a character with humanity and compassion, drawing without self-censorship on the most intimate, often self-destructive experiences from his own life to find a 'sense memory' in which to root the performance.

Year of the two kings

In 1999, his performances for the RSC of Leontes (*The Winter's Tale*) and Macbeth, both directed by Greg Doran, marked, for many who had followed Sher's career, significant steps forward in his growing maturity as a major Shakespearean actor. Initially reluctant to play Leontes – believing it offered him no real challenge, being only another character who 'just keeps running round the stage shouting and snarling at people' (Sher 2001, p. 313) – he changed his mind when the suggestion was made that he should double Leontes with the comic role of Autolycus. Sher has himself tracked the reasons why he resolved before rehearsals-proper got under way to play only the King (Ibid, pp. 313–17), but his decision to step aside from the more flamboyant, theatrical role of Autolycus and concentrate on the emotionally damaged Leontes might perhaps reflect an unconscious desire to focus all his energies on a part that he would have to excavate to its core.

The performance retained the tightly controlled yet vibrant physical expressiveness that Sher has mastered. As Paul Taylor wrote, Leontes's 'spitting hatred':

> is the defence mechanism of a man who, through some sudden intuition of inadequacy, is running scared of his own life. You can see that in the tense, flinching way he can barely maintain his pose on stiff, judicious detestation in the presence of his accused spouse. When he backs away in a frenzy of sobbing and snarling from his new-born daughter, you can feel the tremendous attraction towards her that he is compelled to deny because of some cancerous sense of unworthiness, now perversely justified by his appalling actions.
>
> (*Independent*, 8 January 1999)

But as Robert Smallwood observed, there was another layer to the performance:

> It was a precisely charted psychological journey that Sher presented, brilliantly executed technically, but with the technique not…in any way diverting from the emotional power of the progress to disintegration and collapse, never allowing us to forget that there was another, a 'real', Leontes underneath this misery.
>
> (*Shakespeare Survey*, 53, 2000, p. 264)

A few months later, Sher played Macbeth in the smaller, more intimate space of the Swan Theatre at Stratford-upon-Avon, where he 'continued to develop the considerable extension of his range' revealed by his Leontes (Michael Dobson, *Shakespeare Survey*, 54, 2001, p. 252). As usual, and as he had with Leontes, his pre-performance research was imaginative and thorough (see below) and, as in *The Winter's Tale*, he was keen to develop nuanced relationships with other characters, and especially with Lady Macbeth, played by Harriet Walter. Together with Doran they investigated every little corner of the text, including the crucial question of whether or not the Macbeths have children. Their decision that they had had a child who died, and about whom they never spoke, underpinned their imagined relationship. One example must suffice of how this careful exploration paid dividends. In Act I scene vii, the actor playing Macbeth is faced with the problem of making a tricky U-turn: within the space of forty lines he must swing from 'We will proceed no further in this business' (I.vii.31) to 'I am settled, and bend up / Each corporal agent to this terrible feat' (80–81). At line 54, when Lady Macbeth reminds him 'I have given suck…', the scene immediately shifted ground. For Sher, the sudden mention of the baby, the obvious (though not in any sense manipulative) distress the recollection caused Lady Macbeth affected her husband – 'I suddenly needed to be on her side whatever the cost' (Sher 2001, p. 343) – solved the volte-face, found the tie between the characters and, in Walter's words, revealed 'the heart of Lady Macbeth' (Walter 2002, p. 32). John Peter described this as one of Sher's 'most profoundly thought-out performances, full of brutal power and subtle psychological perception' (*Sunday Times*, 21 November 1999), but its charged intimacy was thrown into thrilling relief by the retention of the actor's other distinctive qualities. 'Who can be wise, amazed, temperate and furious, / Loyal and neutral, in a moment?' (II.iii.108–9) Macbeth asks. And the answer might be Sher himself, moving sharply and cleanly from soul-searching to black comedy – ''Twas a rough night', he confided, the morning after despatching Duncan – or shifting the temperature on stage in the blink of an eye as he greeted his banquet guests affably one minute (III, iv), before threatening them individually the next, so making it clear in that moment that 'All pretence was over. An open reign of terror had begun.' (Walter 2002, p. 51)

Pre-rehearsal preparation and research

In 2009 the National Theatre mounted an exhibition of Sher's paintings and drawings, including a number of portraits of himself and other actors in various roles. Drawing plays a very significant part in the development of his roles, before and during the rehearsal period. For example, in *Year of the King* (significantly subtitled 'An Actor's Diary and Sketchbook'), he traces his work on Richard III (RSC, 1984) from the earliest negotiations with the RSC through to press night, showing how he uses sketches and more complete drawings to find a route to the character and give visual form to his developing thoughts, not just for his own benefit but also to share with director and designer. The first sketches – done before he had signed a contract or even knew for certain he would be offered the role – are of the character 'out there', including performances by other actors such the Georgian actor Ramaz Chkhikvadze for the Rustavelli company who had visited London in 1980, or – most difficult to eradicate from his mind – Laurence Olivier. Gradually, the drawings feature Sher himself more centrally, but still blended with these associations:

> The sunlight is weird at this time of the year – an insistent silver light. This morning as I shave it falls on the water and throws a strange light on my face. Instantly Richard III. I stare at him for a moment, then quickly fetch a sketchbook to put down what I've just seen. But it's a difficult drawing. And worst of all, the lips I have drawn are not my own, but Olivier's. Again that giant shadow falls across the landscape and I dart around trying to find some light of my own. My Richard is in its infancy; barely that, it is still struggling to take form, uncertain even *whether* to take form. And there's this fully formed, famously formed, infamous child murderer leaning over the cradle.
>
> (Sher 1984, pp. 37–38)

Once committed to play the part, his imagination starts to cast itself wider, reflected in a drawing (Reproduction Ibid, p. 76) that represents a 'melting pot' of his thoughts on how to fill an audience with pity and terror: a mix of Lion's Head mountain above Cape Town, the monster in *Frankenstein*, Klaus Kinski's eye, a harelip from J.M. Coetzee's *Michael K* (which he was reading at the time), as well as echoes of the original image of Charles Laughton as Quasimodo, with 'Brando's Godfather thrown in'. As he continues his search for Richard, more images present themselves: animals (lion, bull, boar, shark), the Kray twins, the mass murderers Neilson and Sutcliffe, and scenes and characters from his favourite film, Fellini's *Satyricon*. Gradually, however, one image comes to dominate, the image that would ultimately define the performance: the 'bottled spider' (Reproduction Ibid, p. 103). But only after all these ideas and images have faded does he accept that at last this Richard is his creation, not 'painted on top' (Ibid, p. 198) of others.

> Research is a wake-up call.…Research takes you back to the truth.
>
> (Sher 2001, p.143)

It is hardly surprising that Antony Sher should be so committed to research. His books have revealed with total honesty not only the actor's work on himself (to borrow a phrase from Stanislavsky) but tracked in great detail his work on the part (to borrow another). Though Sher takes note of director Max Stafford-Clark's view on research – 'never mind if it's interesting; is it useful' (Ibid, p. 321) – he believes it can open doors to the 'inside' of the character. Preparing to play Macbeth, for example, Sher met two real-life murderers who provided an insight into the actual physical act of murder 'that is very hard for anyone to imagine however well the part might be written':

> One murder was messy, almost an accident, and the man was completely haunted by it; the other was a tough guy who beat someone to a pulp so that his shoes were squelching with blood as he walked home and who didn't have a second thought about it. In a way, the first is like Macbeth, the other like Lady Macbeth. Now I don't know how you'd ever properly play that part without that being fed into you, and I came away from those interviews having learnt something that's immensely unsettling but simply

> makes you understand how people actually do that. And it's very important to Macbeth because Lady Macbeth is astonished at his feebleness, and indeed you think, 'Well this is someone who's "unseamed" Macdonwald "from the nave to th' chops" (*Macbeth*, I.ii.22) so why's he got this big problem about killing one old man in his house?' And then when he does do it he fucks it up and he brings the knives along which he wasn't supposed to. How is it this fantastic soldier, this butcher on the battlefield, has got such difficulty? And, of course, when you talk to real-life murderers you understand the incredible step that they have to take to do that taboo thing.

Interestingly enough, Sher uses an image from his art to explain what had happened to him in creating Macbeth: he had been unable to draw the character in his copy during rehearsal. It was the first time that had happened, but as he realised, 'His face isn't important. What lies behind it is. His brain.'

In 2001 he repeated on screen his role as Macbeth, again with Harriet Walter as Lady Macbeth and directed by Greg Doran. The key challenge director and cast set themselves was 'to make the experience of watching it in the theatre as live on film' (Bradby, Doran, Jackson 2005, p. 94), and to address the difficulty of matching the verbal density of the text on screen with its emphasis on the visual, where language is just one of a wide range of signifiers, not the most privileged as it was in Shakespeare's theatre. Sher's first experience of transferring a stage performance to the screen was filming the RSC stage production of *Tartuffe* for BBC television in 1984, when he confronted the issue of transposing stage acting to the screen (especially the small one), problems exacerbated for an actor like Sher who enjoys performing on a larger scale. As he wrote, after watching one of the scenes replayed on a monitor, 'I'm no longer sure I have successfully scaled down my performance. I thought I was going from the theatrical to the televisual, but might have taken a wrong turning and ended up with the operatic' (Sher 1984, p. 97). There were no such problems with *Macbeth*. By the time it came to filming, the company had performed the play in Stratford, London, Tokyo and America, and as a result (recalling his lessons as a student), 'we just knew it in a way that allows you to speak it on camera in a naturalistic way but still full of whatever you have to do to speak Shakespeare. After all the work of breaking it down into ordinary English and then getting it back up to speed you could put a camera really close and we could look like we were speaking.' Equally crucial was to try to recapture the unpredictable, dangerous atmosphere of the stage production. The solution was to film not in a studio but in a network of corridors in the cellars of the Roundhouse and then to shoot it like a documentary:

> Sometimes we wouldn't let the cameraman see a rehearsal at all. For example, the scene between Macbeth and Lady Macbeth after the murder of Duncan is all in short sentences, very panicky. And we filmed that on a back stairway and we threw the cameraman into the middle and Greg said to him try and catch what you can. The sequence lasts about ten minutes and the camera is not quite sure where we're going to go, and it has a terrific feel of that nightmarish exchange between them. So for me that's how you can do Shakespeare on film, and though it wouldn't suit all the plays it absolutely suits that one.

Rehearsal

Generally, however, the theatre's rehearsal process and the benefit and pleasure Sher derives from it is a significant factor in his preference for stage acting over screen, observing that during the shooting of the controversial television drama *God on Trial* (BBC 2, 2008) 'the atmosphere in the room just built up naturally, something I have only ever known to happen on stage before' (BBC press release, 27 August 2008). For Sher, the rehearsal period is a mix of careful deliberation and a willingness to respond to chance: in his account of rehearsing the Fool in *King Lear* (RSC, 1982), for example, he sets out in detail how frequently one abandoned idea can produce another, unexpected but ultimately more useful one (Sher 1988, pp. 151–65). In a sense, his rehearsal process mirrors his use of his drawings: sketches on a host of seemingly unrelated topics, some developed, others discarded. Sher admits he prefers directors who ask questions to those who seek answers. He feels especially stifled by directors who bring their own 'Theory of Acting' to the rehearsal room, and welcomes suggestions that he can shape in his own way rather than being presented with a more-or-less complete idea. Greg Doran, who has directed him more than anyone else in Shakespearean roles (*Woza Shakespeare!* provides an illuminating insight into their working relationship), observes that Sher 'soaks up direction like a sponge', and as I have seen for myself, he throws himself into improvisations and exercises. Notably, despite his thorough pre-rehearsal research, he unfailingly brings a complete openness to new ideas and interpretations from all around him. In *Year of the King* he recalls how at one rehearsal one of the young boys playing the princes in the Tower suggested Sher should change a move. It is possible another actor might have been amused, perhaps affronted by this apparent breach of protocol, but Sher recognised that the boy was right, and happily took the note. Rehearsals may also require the actor to polish up neglected skills or master new ones, and again Sher relishes these challenges. When he played Tamburlaine (RSC, 1992), for example, it was decided with the director, Terry Hands, that Sher would need to learn acrobatic skills to enable him to climb a rope to a point twenty feet above the stage, and then hang upside down while delivering the speech. Sher achieved it, but 'never stopped dreading that bloody rope. Each night as the scene approached I felt I had an appointment with fear coming up' (Sher 2001, p. 239).

Performance: playing Prospero

Although his professional career has been centred in the UK (he destroyed his South African passport in protest at the apartheid regime and now has British citizenship), his African background has remained a significant element in his work as an actor (as he first realised at Webber-Douglas) and writer (all his novels are wholly or partially set in South Africa). He has performed three plays in South Africa, two of them by Shakespeare, one a study of revenge, the other of forgiveness: *Titus Andronicus* (1995) and *The Tempest* (2008).

In 1994, he and Greg Doran were among a group of artists who visited Johannesburg to take part in a fortnight of workshops led by the Studio of the Royal National

Theatre, following which Sher proposed that he and Doran should try to stage a production of *Titus Andronicus* at the Market Theatre in Johannesburg. Richard Eyre believes that 'We can dress up in the clothes of other people, we can borrow the rituals of other societies, we can pillage the plays of other languages, but we must always do it in our own voices, not mimicking either the people we would like to be, or the people we feel we ought to be' (quoted in Sher & Doran 1996, pp. 117–18). Playing Titus brought Sher face to face with these tensions, in a production that would become as much an analysis of his own identity as that of Titus. (Jonathan Holmes, '"A World Elsewhere": Shakespeare in South Africa', *Shakespeare Survey*, 55, 2002, p. 271–84). Embarrassed by his South African accent, he had worked hard while at Webber-Douglas to disguise it, but as a result, although he sounded English 'lost my relationship with my own voice' (Sher & Doran 1996, p. 13). *Titus* offered an opportunity to restore that link. Sher's father grew up speaking with a strong Afrikaans accent, and Sher chose that as the basis for Titus:

> The accent feels like a gift. It's allowing me to do things with my voice, which more typically, as an actor, I do with my body. It gives me new muscles. It lets me flip through the air. Or rest on the earth. Or sink into it. ...The R sound is fantastic. It allows you to claw through certain words, possessing them, or the opposite.
>
> (Ibid, p. 117)

He began the performances in a state of excited anticipation:

> Stepping out on to the Market stage is an overwhelming moment for me. And Shakespeare, who seems to write all things for all men, allows me to say, 'Cometh Andronicus, bound with laurel boughs / To re-salute his country with his tears.'
>
> (Sher 2001, p. 264)

However, the decision to perform in local accents provoked widespread criticism of the production and despite many appreciative reviews it played to half empty houses.

> What startled me about the reception to *Titus* was that they didn't like home-grown Shakespeare: they wanted Shakespeare to be British and posh, what we would call old-fashioned. It was a sort of colonial hangover. They were obsessed by the fact that Shakespeare had to be beautiful and noble. We even had opposition from the cast: I remember one actor would not stop using the word 'noble'.

In 2008 he returned to South Africa to play Prospero at the Baxter Theatre Centre in Cape Town, a production that transferred the following year to the RSC's temporary Courtyard Theatre in Stratford-upon-Avon, followed by a tour of the UK. He considers the character of Prospero – with its 'deep dark melancholy' – to be the most complex he has played. That assessment, especially viewed in the specific context in which he created and first performed the role, provides a perfect example of the interaction between his art, his personal beliefs and his political convictions that has characterised his approach not just to Shakespeare but to *all* his work.

The director, Janice Honeyman – a former schoolmate of Sher's who had directed him in Fugard's *Hello and Goodbye* (RSC) – had first broached the idea of an 'African' *Tempest* in 2000. Honeyman reasoned that a 'colonial depiction of the play… where the assertion of one culture over another is a strong theme', in a staging which drew on 'images from animistic and ancestral traditions from various parts of Africa…would capture the same sense of immediacy that the play had when first written', and 'find an equivalent application of [Shakespeare's] message' that is 'familiar, identifiable and pertinent to our own audiences' (RSC programme). A decade after *Titus*, Sher was confident to play the part using his own, now very English accent, which, set against the predominantly South African accents of the rest of the cast, underlined Prospero's 'difference'.

Sher had been offered the part before by the RSC and turned it down, convinced that a 'lyrical voice' (epitomised for him by Derek Jacobi who he'd seen in Ron Daniels's 1983 production) was essential. Now, however, he felt ready to play it:

> because I was more comfortable in my voice and with speaking Shakespeare after years and years of doing it, but also because there is something about the anger and frustration of the character that intrigued me. There's such a rage in this man, and his power itself is insecure.

The potent mix of art and politics within an African setting not only resulted in an exhilarating and revelatory rehearsal process, but also provided an answer to one of the play's recurrent challenges in contemporary European productions – the magic:

> In Europe, magic has just become a form of entertainment, whereas in African society it's still a very real, powerful and potentially dangerous force, which is exactly what the play needs. Shakespeare's audience would have been like African society, taking these things very seriously and regarding them as real powers. And how do we simulate that or even feel that in a modern production? In rehearsals in Cape Town we came to the moment when Prospero summons Ariel. Now in a British rehearsal room, you'd come against that problem, and then you'd look round and say, 'So right, what are we going to do?' But in Cape Town, when I asked that, ten people stood up and said 'Oh well, it's by clapping or drumming', or whatever. For them, it's a completely simple straightforward question of how they would summon the ancestors, which is part of what traditional healing involves in South Africa. So I felt this special strength, this weapon that we had up our sleeve, so that we could do the magic in a way that was so real to the people on stage that it would be real to the audience.

It also prompted new insights to relationships within the play:

> In the colonial context of our setting, the two slaves – Caliban and Ariel – are black. I remember the first time John Kani and I rehearsed the first encounter of Prospero and Caliban (I.ii). Having both lived under apartheid,

> in obviously very different positions of power, we both understood these two people, their violent hatred of one another, which would be hard to come to terms with if you were working with British company. But almost more interesting was what it did with Ariel, because while under apartheid there'd been this violent hatred between the races, there could also at times be a love, absolutely in the context of master servant, but an affection that was real for both parties, and we wanted that for Ariel and Prospero. Prospero adores him and finds it impossible to contemplate giving him up, which underscores the very poignant parting.

This affection gave rise to how Sher played the moment of Ariel's liberation. Prospero ritually washed away the markings made in white clay that had covered Ariel's body, an act mirroring the African ceremony of circumcision that symbolises a youth's entry into manhood. Its specific significance as a rite of passage would be unlikely to be recognised by a British audience, but for Sher the moment was another example of how stage action derived from a truth provides him with a firm footing in performance, while the gentleness with which he carried it out – in marked contrast to the brutality of much of his behaviour towards his servants – embodied what he perceived as a profound element in Prospero's feelings towards Ariel:

> Whenever I read those scenes prior to doing them, I felt a kind of sexual crackle, and so for me it was very much a sort of *Death in Venice* moment – the old man with the beautiful younger man – an attraction which is, of course, in Prospero's imagination only.

These explorations in rehearsal provided the foundations for him to create a complex and deeply human performance of Prospero as a man both vulnerable and violent, tender and severe, contradictions reflected in the grubby colonial linen suit worn beneath his ragged, shell-covered magician's robe. And this superb performance (Sher considers it among his best, placing it above Richard III), was borne along by his complete command of the language and the verse: for example, his delivery of the great speech in Act V, 'Ye elves of hills' (for him, 'the absolute heart of the part'), was one of the most thrilling moments I have enjoyed in the theatre, exemplifying GB Shaw's view that Shakespeare should be played 'on the line and to the line, with the utterance and acting simultaneous, inseparable, and in fact identical'. And nowhere was Sher's trademark intensity of feeling more acute than as the play moved to its end and Prospero struggled to find forgiveness in, and for, himself. Many reviewers commented on the unique, revelatory interpretation where Sher played the closing couplet ('As you from crimes would pardoned be, / Let your indulgence set me free', V. i.337–38) not, as is usual, to the audience, but to Caliban. Significantly, this was Sher's own interpretation: 'Just as Prospero can't say a kind or gentle word about Caliban, it works the other way round as well, so it seemed equally important to let Caliban *not* take his revenge, which he could do.' And so the production was brought to a close with a final, moving plea for truth and reconciliation.

*

How does Sher sum up the demands Shakespeare makes of the actor?

> To play Shakespeare you need a variety of resources. You need enormous technical ease to phrase, shape and finally breathe the language like normal speech. You need great curiosity about human beings. You need to become so fascinated by our strange behaviour that you believe you're perceiving it for the first time – like Shakespeare did, I think – and feel compelled to tell the truth about us. So you have to be raw as hell and supremely skilled. You must be able both to grunt and echo, murmur and sing. You must be Marlon Brando and Placido Domingo in the same body. It's difficult.
>
> (Sher 2001, pp. 328–29)

Selected chronology

1949	Born Cape Town, South Africa, to a family of Lithuanian Jewish descent.
1968–71	Trained at the Webber-Douglas Academy of Dramatic Art.
1972	Fool, *King Lear*, Shakespeare (Liverpool Everyman).
1982	Joined the Royal Shakespeare Company (he is now an Associate Artist).
1982	Fool, *King Lear*, Shakespeare (RSC); Tartuffe (Molière; trans. Christopher Hampton).
1984	Richard III, Shakespeare (RSC).
1984	Won Olivier Best Actor award for his performances as Richard III and Arnold in Harvey Fierstein's *Torch Song Trilogy*.
1987	Vindice, *The Revenger's Tragedy*, Malvolio, *Twelfth Night*, Shylock, *The Merchant of Venice*, Shakespeare (RSC).
1995	Titus Andronicus, Shakespeare (Market Theatre, Johannesburg/ National Theatre).
1997	Cyrano de Bergerac (de Rostand; RSC); Stanley Spencer, *Stanley*, Pam Gems (National Theatre; Olivier Award for Best Actor).
1999	Leontes, *The Winter's Tale*; Macbeth, Shakespeare (RSC).
2000	Knighted for his services to acting and writing.
2002	Emperor Domitian, *The Roman Actor*, Massinger; Malevole, *The Malcontent* Marston (RSC).
2004	Iago, *Othello*, Shakespeare (RSC).
2008	Prospero, *The Tempest*, Shakespeare (Baxter Theatre, Cape Town; RSC).

Screen roles include *The History Man* (BBC 1981), Disraeli in *Mrs Brown* (1997; *Evening Standard* Peter Sellers Film Award), J.G. Ballard's *Home* (BBC 2003) and *God on Trial* (BBC 2008). He has written three plays (*ID*, *Primo* and *The Giant*), and four highly successful novels; he is also an accomplished artist and illustrator. In 2005 he directed Fraser Grace's *Breakfast With Mugabe*.

Bibliography

Bradbury, David; Greg Doran, Russell Jackson (2005) 'Gestures that Speak: Spectators who Listen', in *Shakespeare, Language and the Stage*, eds. Lynette Hunter and Peter Lichtenfels, Arden Shakespeare, Thomson Learning. pp. 89–107.

Sher, Antony (1984) *Year of the King*.
——(1988) 'The Fool in *King Lear*', *Players of Shakespeare 2*, Russell Jackson and Robert Smallwood, eds. Cambridge University Press, pp. 151–65.
——(1989) *Characters: Paintings, Drawings and Sketches*, Nick Hern Books.
——(2001) *Beside Myself: An Actor's Life*, revised and updated 2009. Nick Hern Books.
——(2005) *Primo Time*. Nick Hern Books.
Sher, Antony & Doran, Gregory (1996) *Woza Shakespeare!* Methuen.
Walter, Harriet (2002) *Actors on Shakespeare: Macbeth*. Faber & Faber.
White, Martin (2007) 'Interview with Antony Sher' in Martin White, ed., *The Roman Actor*. Revels Plays, Manchester University Press.

Plus personal conversations with the actor during 2009. I am very grateful to Antony Sher for the time he has given and interest he has shown in the preparation and writing of this chapter.

About the author

Martin White is Foundation Chair of Drama and Professor of Theatre at the University of Bristol, UK. He has published extensively as an editor, critic and theatre historian. Recent publications include 'Trevor Nunn' in *Directors' Shakespeare* (2008), the volume on *A Midsummer Night's Dream* for The Shakespeare Handbooks series, the Revels Plays edition of Massinger's *The Roman Actor* (2007) and *The Chamber of Demonstrations* (2009), an interactive DVD exploring the theatre practices of the Jacobean indoor playhouses utilising a full-scale reconstructed stage and auditorium lit by candles. He is currently preparing a book-length study of Ford's *'Tis Pity She's a Whore* in the new strand of The Shakespeare Handbooks, and the new Revels Plays edition of Jonson's *Bartholomew Fair*. White has directed around forty plays at his university. He works mainly on the less well-known plays and playwrights of the early modern period. He worked closely with Antony Sher on the RSC 2002 Swan season, in which Sher played Domitian and Malevole, and was the Season Consultant for the RSC 2005 Swan season. He also acts as an adviser to Shakespeare's Globe in London.

18
Jonathan Slinger

Phillip Breen

The British theatre critic Quentin Letts wrote in the Daily Mail that 'Mr. Slinger… [looks] like a cross between Bill Gates and the BBC reporter Nicholas Witchell, yet he strides and swaggers like the sexiest dude in town.' Although writing about his performance in Dennis Kelly's new play *The Gods Weep* for the RSC at the Hampstead Theatre in 2010, this by-line touches on something at the heart of Jonathan Slinger's acting. It identifies a playful and unabashed eclecticism: an ability to inhabit two seemingly diametrically opposed ideas simultaneously and revel in the uncomfortable distance between the two. It references a sensuality, a sexual ambiguity, a carnality even, that he brings to the most unlikely characters, at the most unlikely moments. It hints at an actor who is comfortable in his own skin, who likes who he is, but craves an exploration of the 'other', his 'flip-side', his own and his character's. On the outside it's a young Bill Gates on the inside it's Ziggy Stardust. 'Why do you have to be young and good looking to fall in love?' he questioned in one of our interview sessions. It's deliciously Shakespearean.

This article is an account of a four-year period of Slinger's work with the Royal Shakespeare Company (RSC), from his 2005 debut as Puck in Gregory Doran's *A Midsummer Night's Dream*, through his Syracusian Dromio in Nancy Meckler's *The Comedy of Errors*, to his Richard III and Richard II (among other parts) in Michael Boyd's complete *Histories* cycle of 2006 to 2009. The article aims to explore Slinger's processes as a Shakespearean actor, the unique influences that were brought to bear on him through participation in the *Histories*, and how he developed over those four years. I was assistant director to Meckler and Doran for the 2005/06 season and saw at first hand the creation of Puck and Dromio. I was an enthusiastic regular at the *Histories* at Stratford throughout their run and have interviewed Michael Boyd for his thoughts on Slinger's work.

It's worth noting the context in which this work took place. In autumn 2010 the new Royal Shakespeare Theatre will open. The large 1300 seat proscenium arch theatre was demolished in 2007 to be replaced by a new large thrust auditorium, in which no audience member will be more than five metres from the action. The Courtyard, an exact replica of the new theatre, was erected on the site of the old Other Place and was to be a test drive for the new permanent home for the company. Boyd chose the *Histories* as his first production in the new space as artistic director.

The work that is referenced in this article took place in an atmosphere of risk. The change in the playing space was central to Boyd's artistic vision for the RSC and particularly its actors. He would talk regularly of the need for actor and audience to 'be in the same room', the need, as he saw it, for mainstream theatre to engage with its audience with 'honesty and directness'. One of the things that attracted Boyd to Slinger was his 'appalling directness as an actor', a quality that was deemed essential for the new space. Boyd was also drawn to Slinger's 'dreadfully anarchic' work, which had a 'farcical franticness and a mad over inventiveness', work which was 'very gloomy, madly, sort of grotesquely serious'.

As well as opening the new theatre building there was a parallel risk of engaging an acting company for three years, a long period even in RSC terms (it was double the length of the *Comedies* contracts). Contemporary British actors have a myriad of opportunities in theatre, film and television. Three years in Stratford-upon-Avon playing assorted roles represented a big risk for some, quite apart from what could happen when over forty actors work cheek-by-jowl every day for three years. Boyd certainly felt that risk keenly. 'Had it not worked,' he said, 'I wasn't entirely sure what I'd do next.' Underpinning Slinger's work during this period was a sense of a lot being staked by the company, but with a sense of artistic freedom and a quiet iconoclasm – a spirit that played to the strengths of the two collaborators.

When we started working together in January 2005, I was struck by someone for whom theatre and in particular Shakespeare was something exciting and dangerous. The first day of rehearsals for *A Midsummer Night's Dream* was a microcosm of his approach to Shakespeare for good and ill. This heavy-set, ginger fellow with a Manchester accent had decided (in consultation with Gregory Doran) that his Puck 'would not run'. He had asked for a pair of Heelys: sport shoes with wheels in the heels, popular with twelve-year-old boys. Boyd would later talk about Slinger's routines in *The Comedies* season as evidence of 'Jonathan's unhealthy love affair with properties' but this was the first example I saw of how he began preparing for a role. It was a strong choice that made a clear line with a character vividly manifest.

The choice was rooted in Slinger's fascination with exploring the exact opposite of what the text appears to be suggesting. In this case, a slow trudging Puck. Slinger refers to this technique as 'flipping the script', exploring the opposite instincts to see where it leads the interpretation of the role. Many actors undertake this sort of work as an interesting academic exercise and use elements in performance, but I was struck by how central this technique is to Slinger's work. The exploration of the opposite was a well from which he drew most of his inspiration and was a source of great creative energy. By 'flipping' the script he was able consistently to shed interesting light on the psychology of his characters as well as finding much comic inspiration. His exploration of all of his characters started from a locus that was avowedly off-centre. I'm not sure that even he realised the extent to which it coloured his work throughout this period.

Like most people, Slinger had seen many more 'received' renderings of the role of Puck. He'd seen many slight young actors 'running everywhere as a human desperately trying to be a fairy'. Slinger's instinct and his own athletic abilities suggested that this was something he didn't want to do. He had never been drawn to the part and had never understood what the sexless sprite had brought to this play about love. During the audition he and Doran (neither of whom had strong feelings about the role hitherto) hit upon a kernel of an idea that became central to the production. It was rooted in Slinger's desire to explore the psychological motivations of the character. Slinger recalled:

> Puck's position as Oberon's right-hand man has been usurped by the little changeling boy, who at the opening of the play has Oberon's full affection and attention. Puck has been sidelined. He begins the play in emotional turmoil about this and spends the rest of the play trying to win Oberon back.

Doran's production foregrounded the changeling boy. Steve Tiplady of the Little Angel Theatre Company (with whom Doran had an unlikely hit with a puppet show version of *Venus and Adonis*) made an exquisite Japanese *bunraku* doll to play the role of the boy. The eighteen-inch high puppet was brought in by Titania's train and was a literal point of focus for the dissention between the fairy King and Queen. It's exotic appearance and grace of movement was a stark contrast to Slinger's stolid, pale-skinned, grungy, rather shopworn Puck. There was a sense of the new toy contrasting with the old toy. Slinger's Puck watched on damp-eyed, the rejected child in the man's body.

This idea made the precise nature of the royal argument clear. The boy was the reason why 'the nine-man's-morris is fill'd up with mud' and the cause for the high stakes civil war that had led to the apocalyptic ruination of the seasons. The elemental emotions of parenthood had been unleashed. Oberon and Titania were indeed the 'parents and original' of this bleak new reality in the fairy world. All of Oberon's meddling was clearly in order to win back his 'Lovely boy'.

In this new world Slinger's Puck felt like yesterday's man. He was discovered, vagrant-like, sweeping the streets of Athens (using the same broom that he uses in act five to 'sweep the dust behind the door' of the royal palace). The split role of First Fairy approached him with a degree of awe and bewilderment as if they were teenage autograph hunters. Puck was a washed up pop singer fallen on hard times. The line 'Thou speakest aright; I am that merry wanderer of the night' was played with shamed reluctance and a resonant bass, rather than the conventional piping tenor. After the First Fairies had finished their first speech in the quick anapestic dimeter, Slinger deliberately played against the tempo by taking the speech very slowly and deliberately on the pulse of the line. This had a comically unsettling effect rather like the *Tortoise* movement from Saint Saens' *Carnival of the Animals*, where Saint Saens has the orchestra play the can-can at a maddeningly slow tempo. The slower tempo and the sarcastic ironising of the first half of the speech prepared the ground for what was to come.

'A lovely boy', 'so sweet a changeling' and 'the loved boy' were almost spat at the First Fairy; and 'Knight of his train, to trace the forests wild' was played with a self-lacerating, wounded melancholy. Slinger had the make-up department apply the scars of the self-harmer to his wrists. The teenage dirt-bag, sk8ter-boi Puck in the body of the thirty something Slinger, was at once darkly ironic, heartfelt and daft. Having consciously thrown out the rulebook with his treatment of Puck's text, there was an opportunity for much delicious, comic subversion. Slinger trudged truculently, slowly off stage left, tired at trying to win Oberon's attention by acidly declaring 'I go, I go look how I go, swifter than arrow from the tartare's bow.' There was a sizable pause as we heard his sneakers squeak slowly to the wings, a moment that consistently brought the house down. What allowed him to treat the text in this way without appearing cloyingly self-conscious was the fact that the emotional world of the character was sincerely explored and deeply felt.

The Kurt Cobain quality of the character was not just expressed in melancholy introversion and adolescent sarcasm. Slinger also released a primal, diabolical rage and lust for chaos, as he disrupted the mechanicals rehearsal in the wood in act three. With the help of wires he literally flew above the scene releasing hellish jets of fire as he climbed ecstatically through 'A hog, a headless bear, sometime a fire, / And neigh, and bark, and grunt, and roar, and burn, / Like horse, hound, hog, bear, fire at every turn.' Here there was the sense of personal release too, through every savoured verb, as this Puck was palpably on his way back to the top of his profession.

At Slinger's instigation Puck's appearance reflected his increasing sense of self worth as the production progressed. His dull ginger hair morphed scene-by-scene in to a glittery flame red and his lugubrious *mien* transformed in to something more vital accompanied by a sweet smile behind which lurked Slinger's prominent incisors. His journey back to Oberon's affections was complete. There was a sense of touching *rapprochement* when Oberon called him 'gentle Puck' at the top of act four, his first kind words towards him the play. After Oberon and Titania's reunion dance there was a renewed sense of complicity between friends as, almost holding back tears, in a soft tenor voice he said 'Fairy King attend and mark; / I do hear the morning lark.' There was a very strong sense of nature returning to harmony. Puck or Robin Goodfellow, the personification of land spirits in English folklore, after the war, was now well.

This Puck provided a genuine streak of offbeat irreverence in a production that was self-consciously aware of its place in the production history of the play. It used the opening chords of the Mendelssohn suite at the top of act one and visually quoted Peter Brook's 'white box' in Theseus' court among other references. But this production managed to consistently subvert its audience's expectations. Slinger gave a long pause before his final couplet, making the lines 'Give me your hands, if we be friends…' a direct challenge to the house lulled in to reverie by Oberon's candle-lit benediction of the Athenian palace. This was indicative of a production that kept the audience from ever thinking that they knew what was coming next. The game of setting up expectations then subverting them was played with great skill by Doran and his company for the theatre-literate Stratford audiences. Of course there was an added poignancy in referencing some of the great RSC *Dreams* as this was the final production of the play to take place on the old RST stage. The blessing of the 'house' in act five, the celebration of regeneration and new life was therefore given added significance.

This Puck was part grown-up, part adolescent, part angel, part devil, part benign, part malignant. The performance was in places a highly wrought construction and in places naked. But crucially Slinger was comfortable with not 'solving' the part, in a play whose fairy characters are often heavily 'interpreted'. He was constantly surprising and evolving, but always true to the text. This is typical of Slinger's approach to acting. First ideas arrive fully formed and vivid, but in rehearsals they change and morph to suit the tenor of the production. He's good at throwing out his favourite ideas too when they become too cumbersome (the *Heelys* only lasted a fortnight before they were returned to the props store).

As a starting point for the role Slinger decided to actively look for the opposites throughout the text, with a role he had trouble engaging with initially. He said:

> I like flipping the script as an exercise, but this time it worked throughout: it was more than just a rehearsal game, it gave us an interesting idea which we pursued. It worked from a comedic standpoint if nothing else.

His exercise of 'flipping' the text, gave Nancy Meckler's 2005 production of *The Comedy of Errors* one of its defining moments. Rather than a teary reunion between the Syracusian and Ephesian Dromios in act five, Slinger (Syracuse) and Forbes Masson (Ephesus) were left alone on stage to regard one another suspiciously. It added an edge to Ephesian Dromio's line 'Methinks you are my glass and not my brother' and their exchange was flinty and testy, neither sure that they were happy to no longer be unique in their respective worlds. Masson's borderline sarcastic playing of the final couplet 'We came in to the world like brother and brother / And now let's go hand in hand, not one before the other' was followed by a subtle jostling for position, the offer of a hand of friendship, then, just when their hands met, they gave each other the bird. They exited in the knowledge that they were happy to keep a distance from one another.

The craggy twelve and fourteen beat final lines of the play contrast with the harmonious iambic at the reuinion of the Antipholi. By embracing the awkward rhythm, the audience was given an unsettling minor-key ending to an early comedy (perhaps a sketch of the emotionally complex and ambiguous finale to comedies like *Twelfth Night* and *Much Ado*). Masson and Slinger ensured that this *Comedy* was concluded without sentiment. This gave a depth to the Dromios and an irreverent comic 'button' to the end of the production. 'The least interesting thing that [the reunion] could be,' Slinger said, 'is a joyful, tearful reunion while we trace each others faces and do "mirror acting".'

Dromio's text too, was subject to the same rigorous psychological analysis. Slinger remarked that,

> Dromio is interesting as you have no father or mother to work with, so it becomes all about his relationship with Antipholus. The Syracusian Antipholus is the only one who is aware that he has a brother and is searching for him, the Ephesian Antipholus doesn't. The Syracusian Antipholus has a relationship with his father, the Ephesian Antipholus doesn't. The Ephesian twins thus seem to be less secure within themselves, they hit each other, they have a much more fractious relationship. It was important for me that the Syracusian relationship was solid and secure, so when Antipholus started hitting and punching me there was a real sense of betrayal, it was more deeply upsetting.

It was also much funnier and laced with pathos as a result.

Slinger's process for this part was therefore, like Puck, driven by a desire to win his friend back (interestingly the same actor, Joe Dixon, played both Oberon and Antipholus of Syracuse). With this warm relationship well established and cruelly broken by Antipholus, the famous duologue about the fat maid in act three scene two was played for high emotional stakes. It worked beautifully as a comic routine, but it was also shot through with relief and a touchingly childish joy that his friend was laughing at him again. It was both comic and poignant. Slinger's Dromio visibly grew in confidence and enjoyment throughout the scene. By the end, he too was laughing and giggling at his own quips as the scene descends in to bum jokes and casual racism:

S. ANTIPHOLUS: In what part of her body stands Ireland?
S. DROMIO: Marry sir in her buttocks, I found it out by the bogs.

Each new exchange gave Dromio a new security in the central relationship in his life. Slinger relished the naughtiness of this most famous comic scene and using his full vocal range relished inventing every disgusting image and lingered over every word. Without an indicative gesture, using only the text, Slinger managed to elicit waves of laughter and expressions of revulsion from the audience. With a pronounced Manchester accent he slid up and down the 'Rs' and the vowels of 'O sir upon her nose, all o'er embellish'd with rubies, carbuncles, sapphires, declining their rich aspect to the hot breath of Spain.' This sensuality also provided an intriguing note of sublimated eroticism.

When discussing his approach to comedy Slinger said:

> I don't approach these plays as either comedies or tragedies. I approach them as stories to be told with truth. If you play Malvolio as a man who is deeply concerned with his own personal advancement, it will be funny, dark and sad. If you only approach it as a buffoon, you may end up getting a few laughs, but you won't even be scratching the surface. I'd love to play Macbeth and find where the laughs are. *Macbeth* is full of accidents and that's very funny.

He also referenced a piece of direction he was once given by Deborah Warner, which seems to be a guiding principal to his work:

> Deborah used to talk about how interesting discomfort is. If you accurately depict discomfort, that is riveting. That is the truth of every person. No matter how polished an image people may have, nobody goes through life without that slipping. It's actually really important when you're putting characters together that you include those moments. Shakespeare has huge discomfort in his writing.

The year 2005 was a good time for an actor who understood and actively sought the comedy of discomfort and awkwardness. While it has as always been something of a staple of the best comedy, shows like *The Royle Family* and *The Office* in the UK, and *Curb Your Enthusiasm* and *Arrested Development* in the United States of America made a high art form of discomfort and were enjoying huge mainstream popularity. Their performance style is avowedly underplayed, laughs are not solicited from the audience, and punch lines are eschewed in favour of gimlet-eyed observation and truthfulness to the situation, allowing for real emotional investment in the protagonists and depth of characterisation. Audiences (particularly young DVD box set buying audiences) were perhaps more ready than ever to go on profound and complicated emotional journeys with Shakespeare's comic characters, while still laughing heartily. They were ready for a more multi-faceted approach to comedy and perhaps a little more distrustful of actors and directors that served up laughs, that told them when it was funny. Through performances like Slinger's audiences are able to experience Shakespeare as a master comedian, able to write lots of subtly shaded types of laughs. Here was a contrast to the bald, one-dimensional, gesture heavy treatment of Shakespearean comedy that seems to offer an apology for the archaic language: the sort of thinking that leads to little finger gestures accompanying a dick joke and a playing style borne out of the broader British comic traditions of music hall and pantomime. There are a generation of actors who make the case that Shakespeare's comedies might have more in common with *The Office* than with *Dick Whittington*. To come at a character form the perspective of a David Brent or a Tobias Funke rather than Widow Twankey or Aladdin is a marked and revelatory shift in perspective, which offers up the possibility of fascinating re-appraisals of Shakespeare's comedic roles.

Puck and Dromio were fecund territory for an actor with Slinger's hostility to received Shakespearean wisdom. I asked him whether this 'punk' approach to his work was something self conscious and he replied: 'I was more "acid house" myself, but I do think I feel the need to stick two fingers up as an artist and say "fuck you".'

This love of acid house is not an irrelevant part of Slinger's process as an actor within a company. There is a home-made quality and an inclusiveness about the acid house scene; it doesn't require you to dress or dance in a certain way, just to be there and move to its trancy, repetitive rhythms. Part of the attraction is to subjugate oneself to the rhythm of the whole. The drug of choice is ecstasy; you go to enjoy yourself and throw off inhibitions. This is how Slinger approaches his acting. He claims 'not to be particularly musical', but his feel for rhythm, in terms of the text, story telling and the broader framework of the production is notable. Acid house eschews melody in favour of rhythm and uses spoken lines rather than sung lyrics. His Duke of Gloucester picked up on the percussive, martial, musical score of Boyd's *Henry VIs* and found an excited, perpetual rocking movement which propelled him through the final battle scenes and gave him an elemental connection with the heart of the productions.

Making the journey from Puck to Richard Duke of Gloucester was something that had been undertaken by Aiden McArdle in the late nineties, in Boyd's first celebrated RSC productions of the first tetralogy. For many it was an obvious next step for Slinger, an actor growing in authority and temperamentally suited to working within a large ensemble. But few would have anticipated his casting as Richard II. When reflecting on this time, while he would have 'regretted' turning down Richard III – due to events in his private life he very nearly did just that – but the added carrot of Richard II encouraged him to make the three year leap in to the unknown. Michael Boyd felt that Slinger 'needed to be scared to commit'.

Despite McArdle's journey, the casting of Slinger had taken Boyd by surprise too. When he saw Slinger as Puck he was going along to see an early preview of a performance that Gregory Doran wanted a second opinion on; he was not looking for a Richard III. But Boyd was struck by

> Jonathan's ability to just hoover up an entire auditorium in to his space, to suck in a house, hold it in his lungs and blow it all out again. There have been times when I've thought 'a little less hoovering' Jonathan. But if you can do it, my God, it's special.

I think the 'hoovering' that Boyd refers to is Slinger's ability to hold a moment, to stop the play in its tracks to allow the audience to see the play through the idiosyncratic prism of his character for a brief moment and then pass on the baton. This quality is difficult to define; in Slinger's case I'd put it down to total clarity of thought and execution in the moment, synthesised with an instinctive understanding of the play's rhythms, combined with an infectious enjoyment of being centre stage. A good example of this was at the end of *Henry VI Pt. Three*. After Edward's final lines 'Sound drums and trumpets! / Farewell sour annoy! / For here I hope begins our lasting joy' as the drums built, with a half smile indicating the fomenting mutiny in his mind, Slinger was able to bring the whole attention of the house to him as he watched the royal court depart leaving him alone on stage. Many of the audience began to smile too, absolutely on Richard's wavelength as Slinger held the pause and eyeballed members of the audience before delivering the heart stopping first word of *Richard III* 'Now' before a snap blackout. I have never seen a theatrical cliff-hanger better executed.

Yet at the time of casting it remained to be seen whether Slinger's restless iconoclasm could move from being a rogue element in a production dominated by other actors to the galvanising performance of a larger ensemble in *Richard II* and *Richard III*. But the close trusting relationship between the two and their shared sensibility ensured that Boyd was able to coax the best of Slinger's talent by giving him a larger canvas on which to work. When recalling rehearsals Boyd said, 'Jonathan adored it. It was like he'd found a room big enough to play in. And he just instinctively loved the democracy of it.' But it was also important that Slinger totally trusted Boyd to edit his work when it became too much. In the foothills of this daunting undertaking, that feeling of safety was terribly important to him. He commented that, 'When Michael said it wasn't working I knew it wasn't working.'

But the canvas was vast. Slinger started and ended the eight-play history cycle. As an actor he not only had to think in terms of the plays he was in, but through a line of other parts in the cycle (such as the antagonists Fluellen in *Henry V* and the Bastard of Orleans in *Henry VI Pt. One*) and the resonances they all had with one another. An early idea that was rejected by the two was that at the end of *Richard III* there would be a quick change to transform Slinger in to Richard II, thus having the tail of the cycle bite the head. This sort of thinking was right at the centre of the life of the octology. Another example was that the actress playing Joan of Arc in

Henry VI Pt. One, on Joan's death, was immediately reincarnated as something more dangerous in the form of Margaret. The presence of ghosts and a palpable spirit realm gave a rich dimension to all eight plays and one that had to be considered by the actors. By creating this palpable sense of afterlife, in the form of thematically driven doubling, Boyd had found a driving force for the octology and found a literal form for the cycle of dynastic revenge. It also enabled the audience to think, in cosmological terms, like Elizabethans. So preparing the two roles simultaneously (the only actor in the history of the RSC to do so) provided some fascinating perspectives on both.

Once more, in order for Slinger to freely experiment in the rehearsal room he had to have a strong line through both roles at the start of rehearsals. He was looking for 'truthful resonances' through eight plays and even more roles, forward and back through history and into heaven, hell and purgatory. But as always his preparation was text first and psychological motivation second, coupled with a good deal of gut instinct. On beginning his preparation of the full octology Slinger said:

> In this extraordinary web of interwoven stories and brilliant double casting much of the work was done for you. Many relationships and resonances were already found. But Shakespeare is endlessly three dimensional, web-like and mathematical. It's like pure maths or Jazz, where everything free-forms brilliantly around a core that never alters. This brilliant virtuosic free-forming is there in the writing and you can find strands as with maths that take you on extraordinary tangents, but which ultimately take you back to the same place. So we were constantly finding things, which fitted perfectly with what we were doing already. Other brilliant bits of doubling would just shoot out of that structure without any of us having thought about it. So in amongst the chaos, in order for those extraordinary co-incidences that were not co-incidences to occur, you had to be true to it somewhere. Shakespeare's writing is incredibly malleable, but you can only bend it so far, you have to stay within the parameters of what he was writing, which is always the truth.

In preparation for *Richard II* and *Richard III* Slinger saw inherent similarities between the two characters as well as their vast differences, quite early on in his process:

> I thought that for Richard III, Richard II was like a physical ideal. At one stage I even thought that Richard III should keep a portrait of Richard II hanging in his study. Physically I wanted to make them as antithetical as I could. But then I began to consider that they were actually very similar in terms of their psychology.

When talking about Richard III Slinger felt that his deformity was the least damaging factor in the formation of his psychology. He became fascinated by the absence of his mother in the three plays in which he exists:

> Until she appears half-way through *Richard III* and utterly goes for him [the long duologue in act four scene four]. The lines in *Henry VI Pt. Three* about his birth that are the last thing that Henry VI says before he is killed by

> Richard have an impact too ['Thy mother felt more than a mother's pain / And, yet brought forth less than a mother's hope / To wit an indigested and deformed lump...Teeth hadst thou in thy head when thou wast born']. I started to get the image of a mother for whom the deformity is repulsive; that the way in which he thought about his deformity was created by the way she thought about it. She rejects and abandons him. It's a well worn path, what that sort of thing does to somebody. How much love and attention you get in those early years creates your self-esteem. If you are made to feel repulsive and you put that in the mix with the fact of the deformity and add to it a strong, ambitious, martial father who he adores and looks up to, you have the volatile psychological mix of Richard III.

The respective King's relationships with their fathers was the root of their similarities in Slinger's mind:

> Richard II is the son of the Black Prince, who pre-Henry V is the ultimate kingly role model. Richard isn't like that, he's a more sensitive aesthete, not some 'Mr. Big Dick' alpha male. He likes painting, he likes music, he's an actor. I can see what the effect would be of being found out to be a complete and utter nancy-boy and rejected by a father who is the most complete manifestation of maleness ever. For him this would be horrific.

With this in mind Slinger began to construct some clear lines through the two parts. In the first instance, working with the drums through Boyd's *Henry VIs*, he had decided that Richard III was all about drums and martial rhythms. From this came the repetitive rhythmic movements mentioned earlier, which manifested itself in him heightening the martial rhythms in the text, particularly in the section before he becomes King. The combination of pulsing rhythmic text and movement became darkly mesmeric in the duologue with Lady Anne and gave his Gloucester a manifest sense of momentum, almost like some grotesque metronome. There was a heightened sense of attack on the iambic pulse using the lower register of his voice.

If Richard III was about rhythm, in the first instance Richard II was about melody. Slinger chose to experiment with a higher more melodious tone in his voice, using his tenor register.

> It was quite interesting, but after a while it stopped me being able to control or connect with his power. So keeping the idea of melody in my mind I dropped it down to my more natural, lower register, so that authority was more accessible.

In the only moment during our interviews in which Slinger referred to extra-textual research, he talked about the image of Richard II going to the head of the mob and quelling the peasants revolt at the age of fourteen: a striking image of natural authority. He felt he had to embrace that tension between the fey, aesthetically interested, musical and very creative man and the forceful and engaging public figure. A clear, strong line was emerging and the result was an extraordinary confection.

Slinger's Richard was a Quentin Crisp-esque figure, both strongly male and strongly female. It was Richard II as Elizabeth I. Tom Piper's design had him sporting auburn ringlets, an earring, white face make up, lipstick, a ruff, with extraordinarily delicate pearl trimmed ivory breeches and cape. It was a vision of glorious Elizabethan England (it was also another prompt for the *Histories* audience to think like Elizabethans). This image was in contrast to Slinger's resonant, manly voice and his very manly frame. From the moment he entered through the auditorium, there was a strong sense of the emotional and political territory that we were in. The link to Elizabeth I was enlightening. This monarch was simultaneously male and female, a troubling mix of vulnerable and predatory, innocent and wise, beautiful and ugly, attractive and repulsive. The look was part artistic creation, part trap. It was clear how, by retreating in to every sort of ambiguity, this Richard controlled his court, and how the court of the Black Prince was threatened by their new monarch. The tension was palpable in act one scene one: he watched the squabbles of Norfolk and Bolingbroke from behind his gilded mask with an inscrutable half-smile. At the beginning of the octology strong elemental conflicts had been released and these conflicts, political, personal, psychical and sexual, were embodied by Slinger's Richard. Indeed it set the tone for the multi-dimensional exploration of power in all eight plays.

Michael Boyd remarked, when talking about Richard III, that 'Jonathan revels in the way that he repulses people and sells it as part of his charm'. The same could be said of his Richard II. It was fascinating to watch Richard II grow from the soil of Richard III. Boyd recalled that,

> Richard II emerged after Richard III's terrible dream at the battle of Bosworth, where he realised that he didn't love himself, he was sort of reborn as the image that he would never allow anyone to see himself desiring, which is elegant, beautiful, fragile, safe in the company of men. There was something very queenly, very refined, very intelligent, very high strategy. This was taken from him by Bolingbroke, a very craggy, heterosexual testosterone fuelled man coming once more to condemn him.

By having his gilded persona literally and metaphorically stripped away from him in this production, Slinger didn't move in to monstrous self-obsession, but in to a sort of ascetic, monastic enlightenment. Boyd commented that,

> There was a genuine sense of grace within him. It was a good achievement to see this fantastically inventive actor, who I would criticise for being too in love with props, to be so happy with nothing as an actor. I think he just instinctively knew that he should be alone in letting his thoughts in.

For *Richard III*, there was a sense that both collaborators were going to let their imaginations run wild. This was a role that was expected to play to Slinger's strength as an actor and as a creative force within the company. For Boyd this was an opportunity to do the *Richard III* he had been unable to do in the 1990s in his original productions of the first tetralogy. Due to personal reasons Boyd felt that he couldn't do the production that leapt out of the broadly period aesthetic of the *Henry VIs* to have a more contemporary feel for *Richard III*. But this time Boyd and Piper had decided to go for it.

Slinger playing Richard III in the new thrust space with the audience surrounding him on three sides was something that excited Boyd. He felt that there was a directness that had to be embraced in that configuration 'and Jonathan is appallingly direct'. Certainly there was a sense that in this new theatre there was nowhere to hide. Theatricality had to be embraced because of the shared nature of the space. It is a space naturally more hostile to sets and conventional theatrical spectacle, but more friendly to fearless actors.

In Boyd's modern dress *Richard III*, Slinger gave a simpler, more touching, Richard than many expected. There were moments of mad comic invention on the way. Until late on in rehearsals the opening scene of *Richard III* was to be set at a children's party and Slinger had decided to inhale some helium for parts of the opening soliloquy. Boyd cut this in favour of a starker, simpler opening. This Richard, perhaps reflecting his Richard II, was a journey towards heartbreaking self-knowledge. Boyd felt that Slinger,

> put the devil on stage and set about telling you very directly that he's right, which is very alarming and challenging. He has the ability to play an appalling egotism, which is free to be charming and to defend his position utterly. But as Richard he conquered the other side of the role, which appears after the dream, where he is skinless and naked. So that ability to suck us in becomes very important. He can draw us to him, even though we are appalled and repelled.

The dream sequence in *Richard III* encapsulated so much of Slinger's processes and tastes as an actor. He stripped down to his slightly soiled y-fronts by the end of the sequence showing plenty of cleavage to the audience sat all around him. He once more eyeballed the audience, sat a metre away from his feet. This time the connection with the audience was not one of dark, playful complicity, but one that seemed to simply say 'help me'. This moment was at once amusing, vulnerable, sad, disgusting and strangely sensual. But most importantly he allowed the text to sit beautifully and simply on top of this maelstrom of contradiction.

KING RICHARD: What do I fear? Myself? There's none else by:
Richard loves Richard; that is I am I
And if I die, no soul shall pity me
Nay wherefore should they, – since that I myself
Find in myself no pity in myself.

Slinger remarked that he didn't know how his ideas for the part would impact on the production, 'but when we had done the dream scene it all made sense: it became a complete unravelling of how he felt about the deformity and everything'.

The psychoses of Richard II and Richard III came from the place of the divided self and made manifest the idea of how the self becomes warped in pursuit of power. This profound understanding of the corrosive impact of the political on the personal seemed to be at the centre of Boyd's productions. Slinger's troubled monarchs, both monsters in their own right, tackled the idea of the public performance of monarchy but also let the audience in to a very private place.

So it's interesting to note one of Slinger's more general thoughts about acting that underpin his approach to Shakespeare. The following was laced through with some self-aware laughter as has repeated the words 'me' and 'myself':

> I think it's about exploring me, actually. Not about being somebody else, or being more comfortable in another character. It's a liberating experience, exploring things about myself through another character. I love exploring things about myself that I never get to explore whilst being me. Acting's about using as much of me as I can and using my own experience and my own imagination to make it real for me. Making it real to an audience is about making it real for me, the moment there's a truthful resonance within me, then I know it's working for me and by extension it's working for everybody else. That's what acting's about for me, it's a very self-obsessed, very selfish thing, purely about my enjoyment. If I'm enjoying myself, which is about connecting with something truthful within myself, then they [the audience] are.

In my experience it's rare to hear an actor talk about 'enjoying' himself. But it's at the centre of Slinger's appeal on stage. As is his ability to take himself just seriously enough, but never too seriously. To bring just enough of himself to proceedings, but not too much. To be totally absorbed in his character, but like many fine comedians always preserving enough of himself to be able to look the audience in the eye as if to say 'Isn't this ridiculous?'

In his brilliant 'Note on Shakespeare', Harold Pinter says that the plays are 'a wound that Shakespeare does not attempt to sew up or re-shape, whose pain he does not attempt to deaden'. For Slinger there is a conscious attempt to keep the wound open, not to cauterise it, to revel in ambiguity, to never fully be known. The metaphor of theatre is central to Shakespeare's exploration of the human condition; the sad truth that we are often poorly cast for the roles that life demands of us. By seeking not to bridge that gap but to celebrate and enjoy it in his acting, at his best Slinger taps in to an elemental energy in Shakespeare. At times his acting is not always comfortable for either performer or audience, and his experiments are not always successful, but they are rooted in a knack to be unfailingly real and vividly, messily human.

Chronology

JANUARY 2005	*A Midsummer Night's Dream* rehearsals commence in London.
APRIL 2005	*A Midsummer Night's Dream* opens at The Royal Shakespeare Theatre, Stratford-upon-Avon. *The Comedy of Errors* rehearses in Stratford-upon-Avon.
JULY 2005	*The Comedy of Errors* opens at the Royal Shakespeare Theatre, Stratford-upon-Avon.

FEBRUARY 2006	*Henry VIs* start rehearsing in London.
JULY / AUGUST 2006	*Henry VIs* open at Courtyard Theatre, Stratford-upon-Avon.
SEPTEMBER 2006	*Richard III* rehearses in London.
DECEMBER 2006	*Richard III* opens at Courtyard Theatre, Stratford-upon-Avon.
JANUARY 2007	First tetralogy plays in its entirety, Courtyard Theatre, Stratford-upon-Avon.
FEBRUARY 2007	Second tetralogy starts rehearsing in London.
JULY / AUGUST 2007	Second tetralogy opens at Courtyard Theatre Stratford-upon-Avon.
SEPTEMBER 2007	Re-rehearse *Henry VIs* in London.
NOVEMBER 2007	*Henry VIs* go back in to the Repertoire in Stratford.
JANUARY 2008	Re-rehearse all eight plays in London.
MARCH 2008	All eight plays play in repertoire at the Courtyard, Stratford-upon-Avon.
APRIL 2008	The full eight play cycle opens at the Roundhouse Theatre, London.
JUNE 2008	The final 'Glorious Moment' in which all eight histories play in historical sequence from *Richard II* finishing with the final performance of *Richard III*.

About the author

Phillip Breen is a freelance writer and director who studied at Cambridge University and trained under Terry Hands at Clwyd Theatr Cymru, where he was director of new writing from 2006–8. Selected directing credits include *Party* by Tom Basden (West End, Sydney Festival and Edinburgh Festival – Winner 2009 Fringe First), The *Stefan Golaszewski* plays (Traverse Edinburgh, Bush Theatre – Winner 2008 Fringe First), *The Caretaker*, *The Shadow of a Gunman* and his own adaptation of *The Resistible Rise of Arturo Ui* (Glasgow Citizen's), Dumb Show (New Vic Theatre, Newcastle-under-Lyme), *Measure for Measure*, *The Birthday Party*, *Two Princes* by Meredydd Barker and *Suddenly Last Summer* (Clwyd Theatr Cymru), *Far Too Happy* (Edinburgh, national tour, West End – 2001 Perrier Award nominee). For further information please visit www.phillipbreen.co.uk.

19
Kate Valk
David Pellegrini

Kate Valk is widely recognized as one of the premier actresses in American alternative theatre. She began her decades-long association with The Wooster Group shortly after graduating from New York University's performance program, where she studied under venerated Stanislavski-interpreter Stella Adler, and in the Experimental Theater Wing with Wooster founding members Elizabeth LeCompte, Spalding Gray, and Ron Vawter. As an intern to LeCompte, Valk was seamstress and stage manager for *Point Judith* (1979), and made her performance debut in *Route 1 & 9* (1981). She has been a member of the company ever since, co-creating and performing theatre, video, and radio pieces that have compelled the reexamination of the form and function of texts and their presentation. She received an OBIE (Off-Broadway Theatre) Award for Sustained Excellence of Performance (1998), and a BESSIE (New York Dance and Performance) Award for Best Performer (2002). Her interpretation of Brutus Jones in the 2006 revival of the company's 1993 production of Eugene O'Neill's *The Emperor Jones* (1920) was compared to Sarah Bernhardt in *La Dame aux Camélias*, Laurette Taylor in *The Glass Menagerie*, and Maria Callas in *Tosca* (*New York Times*, March 14, 2006), thus bringing her recognition by the mainstream theatre establishment and galvanizing hers as one of the most celebrated performances in the history of "downtown" theatre. She has co-directed the company's Summer Institute for New York City public high school students since 1998, and has participated in the Rolex Mentor and Protégé Arts Initiative program.

As both Gertrude and Ophelia in The Wooster Group's *Hamlet* (2007), Valk's performance was lauded as one in a long line in which she displayed her versatility. As evidenced by extensive scholarly interest, the production has entered the pantheon of radical, performance-centered interrogations of the play's poetics, which includes Heiner Müller's *Hamlet-Machine* (1979), Robert Wilson's one-man show (1995), and Robert Lepage's *Elsinore* (1996). Developed over a two-year process that included workshops, rehearsals at The Performing Garage (the company's base and performance venue in Soho), and previews in Europe and Brooklyn, *Hamlet* premiered at the Public Theatre/New York Shakespeare Festival in October 2007. Although it marked the first time The Wooster Group engaged a Shakespearean text, the production coalesced the company's ongoing explorations of the dramatic canon and of the performer as mediator between individual and social consciousness. To appreciate the significance of Valk's performance in *Hamlet*, therefore, is to consider her work in context of the company's collectivist ethos, eclectic development process, and pioneering use of technology. It also means situating the production within a distinctively American tradition of Shakespearean performance.

Valk has developed what many consider to be a peerless ability to simultaneously embody and critique a range of performance styles alongside the company's "appropriation and deconstruction" of works by American playwrights such as Gertrude Stein, Thornton Wilder, and Arthur Miller, and the ongoing experimentation with "spatial relationships both onstage and between the audience and the stage" (Aronson 2000: 153). In building a repertory of controversial and much-examined works, The Wooster Group aesthetic has become synonymous with

> emphasis on process over product; resistance to a univocal narrative through the creation of a nonlinear structure; employment of diverse styles of performing; the overlapping of intricate aural and visual elements, often mediated by sophisticated technology; and the recycling of scenery, props, and costumes from earlier pieces.
>
> (Arratia 2002: 332)

Valk has met the challenges associated with such departures from naturalistic acting through stage personae that often register as collages of meaning-packed and innuendo-laden gestures, expressions, and vocal stylizations. She considers it her primary responsibility to inhabit the structural frames director LeCompte adopts for each project by finding correlative "masks" to build her characters. In *House/Lights* (1997/2005), which commingled Gertrude Stein's avant-gardist libretto for *Dr. Faustus Lights the Lights* (1938) with Joseph Mawra's pulp film, *Olga's House of Shame* (1964), Valk delivered Stein's text over a pitch-changing microphone and replicated performances from Mawra's film which was projected onto video monitors. As the Narrator in *Brace Up!* (1991), Valk grounded multiple realities captured in the company's interpretation of Chekhov's *Three Sisters* in the televisual reality of talk-shows through gesture and speech acts. Though *Hamlet* varied from these kinds of intertextual constructions, it did follow a trajectory of works in which the stylistic differences associated with live and mediated performance was explored, such that Valk categorizes her performance as "channeling" more than "acting."

Valk's encounter with Shakespeare should also be considered in light of the company's absorption with the "idea of theatrical production and reproduction," and the tendency to offer "both the performance and its documentation within the same event" (Marranca 2003: 6). Her interpretation of Brutus Jones astonished not only for transgressing gender and racial bounds, but also because she refracted performance traditions drawn from minstrelsy, ancient Japanese theatre, and the production history of the play itself. If the company succeeded in producing a work long-considered unplayable due to O'Neill's conflation of "primitivism" and a well-intentioned (though highly problematic) representation of race, it did so largely on account of Valk's presentation of a "historicized and mediated" body that challenged notions of the "fixity of race," while implicating "theatre practice itself in the construction of hierarchies of race and power" (Monks 2005: 550). Significantly, Valk and LeCompte had the opportunity to revisit and expand upon their previous use of blackface in *Route 1 & 9* and *L.S.D. (…Just the High Points…)* (1984). With *Hamlet*, as in earlier works which recycled the material and specular remains of past performances and performers (including absent and deceased ones), the company sustained a "consciously self-referential and reflexive" practice that Arnold Aronson considers "virtually unknown in theatre history": the creation of an "ongoing body of work that flowed from one production into the next" (Aronson 2000: 152). *Hamlet* would extend this frame of reference to the play's performance history, emphasizing how the interplay among different representational mediums might illuminate the major themes of the play. This would be accomplished by replicating an archival recording of a noteworthy instance in theatre history, specifically the "Burton *Hamlet*," directed by John Gielgud and starring Richard Burton, which was produced on Broadway in 1964.

Any tendency towards reflexivity in The Wooster Group's productions is, according to Valk, a collateral benefit of the problem-solving inherent to theatre-making given budgetary constraints, the demands of extensive touring, and maintaining a repertory as new works are developed (Interview 2010: August 10). Her observation that each new creation is "always an extension of the reality of how to keep the group together, how to keep going" is equally revealing about the company's collectivist processes (quoted in Sellar 2007: 5). Any staging of *Hamlet* renders contemplation of the theory and practice of acting obligatory (given its thematic and structural importance), thus providing ample justification for the company to employ acting "process" as a framing mechanism. The troupe of actors in the play's *dramatis personae* also provided the means to further explore the dynamics of *ensemble*, and once again don "the mask of a theatre troupe on the road" as an allegory of their own performance identity (Siegmund 2004: 172). In earlier works, Valk developed composite characters drawn from source texts, and fictional or actual troupes of performers, ranging from Ingmar Bergman's *The Magician* (1958) for *Frank Dell's The Temptation of St. Antony* (1987), to a member of Jerzy Grotowski's Polish Laboratory Theatre in *Poor Theater* (2005). In her uncredited role as the Lead Player in *Hamlet*, Valk trafficked with the traveling players at the center of the play's action and, in bridging the spatial and temporal divide between The Wooster Group actors and those in Gielgud's production, symbolized all actors attempting Shakespeare's masterwork. As Gertrude and Ophelia, however, her primary task would be to render, as precisely as possible, "copies" of the performances from the "Burton *Hamlet*," specifically Eileen Herlie's Gertrude and Linda Marsh's Ophelia.

The multiple texts and performance frames comprising many of the company's works result in a postmodern equivalent of Richard Wagner's concept of *gesamstkunstwerke* (or total work of art); Valk has developed the capacity to embody this principle so fully as a "total" performer as to justify Elizabeth LeCompte's equation that

> Theatre is Katie in *The Emperor Jones*…the way she holds her body, the way she moves in diagonals. She inhabits something so strong that, when she speaks, the words and that "something" are equal.
>
> (Quoted in Kramer 2007)

Still, Valk maintains that her performance in *Hamlet* must be considered subordinate to the collaborative process and to the vision of the production as shaped by LeCompte (Interview 2010: August 10).

Although elements of the process might vary with each production, LeCompte's directorial pursuits rest on her "ability to allow for the space for individual expression and input while all the time setting up particular structural frameworks and scenic landscapes that situate this activity within a coherent and often challenging aesthetic" (Quick 2007: 11). She has expanded on this approach since *Sakonnet Point* (1975)—her first collaboration with Spalding Gray—in which the performers, "creatively choreographed" by LeCompte, "altered, transformed, and remolded" Gray's memories to produce "group autobiographies" that were "non-narrative, emotively free-wheeling, and very physical" (Demastes 2008: 33–34). Although the company would draw from canonical dramatic texts for primary source material thereafter (and just as Valk was beginning her involvement), improvisation continues to figure prominently, both as a "game structure set up to spur rehearsal time and develop the shared vocabulary," and within sections of productions that allow for improvisation in each performance (Valk, quoted in Salle and French 2007). Beginning her company involvement under LeCompte's tutelage, Valk has over time assumed an intermediary function between the director and the actors, and feels that she does not so much serve a hierarchical production concept as respond to fundamental questions LeCompte asks of every actor: "How far can you go, what's available to you, as a performer?" (Interview 2010: August 10). Often, such questions lead to the creation of new works so that a production idea might be generated by the performers rather than administrative fiat or directorial prerogative, as is often the case in American theatre companies.

Because the company has permanent residency at The Performing Garage, it can develop projects over extended periods of time—also an anomaly in American theatre. Valk recalls that the origins of The Wooster Group's *Hamlet* can be traced to company member Scott Shepherd's interest in the play. As part of The Wooster Group's research, they watched film versions and listened to recordings of famous performances until happening upon the Electronovision recording of the "Burton *Hamlet*." Three months after it opened (and long after Gielgud departed company), two live performances of the Broadway production were recorded and subsequently released for a two-day engagement at cinemas across the United States. LeCompte, who had seen the original, remembered it for being "experimental" for Broadway in 1964 (*The Gothamist*, March 6, 2007). Gielgud's production concept proved especially intriguing, which he explained to the company at the first read-through in Toronto on January 30, 1964:

> So often it has been my experience...that we have been through the whole play for the last time (in rehearsal) without interruptions; then all of a sudden, the scenery and the lighting come, and everybody is thrown to pieces. And even after we have seen the sets, however beautiful they are, they sort of cramp the imagination and the poetry—and they are also apt to destroy the pace. So we are going to act the play as if it were the final run-through before the technical rehearsals begin, and play it in full clothes, stripped of all extraneous trappings.
>
> (Quoted in Sterne 1967: 12–13)

Interestingly, this is a verbatim transcription by Richard L. Sterne, an actor in Gielgud's company who secretly taped the four-week rehearsal period. Valk acknowledged both Gielgud's correspondences and Sterne's transcriptions as two valuable sourcebooks throughout the company's much lengthier research and development phase.

In addition to being drawn to Gielgud's emphasis on the actor's process—at least as it appeared on the surface—the company was concurrently performing *Poor Theater* (2005), in which the actors replicated an encounter with members of Grotowski's Polish Laboratory Theatre on a research tour that they also secretly taped, as well as a BBC recording of Grotowski's legendary production of *Akropolis*. While the reconstruction of archival performances constituted a major strand of inquiry over several company works, the remains of the "Burton *Hamlet*" proved especially intriguing for a number of reasons.

Electronovision was publicized as a technique that might revolutionize theatre, as Burton indicated in a promotional interview upon the film's release:

> The film was shot in the Lunt-Fontanne Theatre, with an actual live audience and with the actors performing and either being adept or inadequate, or good or fluffing, or being articulate, just as they would be if you went to see a production tonight...we don't tone it down in order to seem like film actors or play it up because the cameras are perhaps a little further away than they would be in a movie studio...You get the immediacy of a live production of *Hamlet* on Broadway in the nervousness of the actors, knowing that they can't go back on it, that this is for all time, unlike in films, where you can, if you make a mistake, go back and do it again.
>
> (DVD: *Richard Burton's Hamlet* 1995: liner notes)

Far from revolutionizing theatre or film, however, the archive consists of grainy, black and white shots captured by seventeen cameras positioned around the theatre, which even in 1964 was reminiscent of the televised anthology shows of the 1950s, thus an "anomalous and nostalgic throwback to the already superseded days of live television recording" (Cartelli 2008: 148). Given the possibilities of exploring the interplay of performance surfaces, and the paradoxical task of copying live but mediated performances, LeCompte decided to use the Electronovision *Hamlet* as a developmental frame and to be projected behind The Wooster Group actors in performance. While the audience viewed the "Burton *Hamlet*" and the onstage copy simultaneously, the performers took their cues from television monitors situated above the audience onto which the film was transmitted with the image reversed. While the main objective would be to copy the film performances, LeCompte added another equally challenging task for the actors: matching the film's ever-changing shots and angles within the frontal perspective of the stage frame. This required that they constantly shift their positions (as well as those of rolling set pieces) so that the stage pictures mirrored the perspectives captured by the cameras at any given moment. A third task would involve further technological mediations of the live performances, as well as the company's digital manipulation of the archive itself.

Valk finds inspiration in the transformative power of the "double negative" principle in Noh theatre, in which "when you put on a mask, you're denying, you're negating yourself" (quoted in Sellar 2007: 9). In *Hamlet*, she employed multiple masks, including the performances of Herlie and Marsh, the film's montage of shots, other technological mediations of her voice and body, and Shakespeare's language. She typically begins the process of characterization by finding the costumes, which she wears and modifies throughout rehearsals; in fact, Valk has supervised the costuming for many productions since her first company assignment. Because the costumes for *Hamlet* were variations on the "rehearsal" dresses and accessories worn by Herlie and Marsh (befitting Gielgud's concept), she found the wigs to be especially helpful: flaming red for Gertrude and a shoulder-length bob for Ophelia. Valk recalls that building the characterization for Ophelia came more easily than Gertrude, but also that she overcame her skepticism about LeCompte's suggestion that she play the younger character by imagining it as a "drag role" in the tradition of Shakespeare's era (Interview 2010: August 10). Among the more playful moments in the production occurred when she was required to make rapid costume and wig changes in order to play different characters, or when the drape and flow of her dresses exactly mirrored those worn by the actresses on the screen behind her.

Although Valk watched Herlie's earlier interpretation of Gertrude in Laurence Olivier's 1948 film version "out of curiosity," her myopic focus on Herlie's and Marsh's performances did not require researching interviews or critical assessments of their work; rather, she concentrated on technical details such as: "How is she breathing? How is she sitting?" and "What is she doing with her body?" (Interview 2010: August 10). Valk attributes her preference for an external approach, in part, to her training with Stella Adler:

> She said everything was in your physical circumstances, everything was outside you, and if you had a playable action, you could make a score for yourself in your physical being, in your physical circumstances, and that's pretty much how I work.
>
> (Quoted in Sellar 2007: 27)

To this should be added LeCompte's emphasis on the style or artifice of character, and her belief in the "power of surfaces to deepen and disturb" reality (Kramer 2007: n.p.).

In her rehearsal journal for *Brace Up!*, Marianne Weems noted that LeCompte often incorporates naturalistic elements as a "formal decorative device" within a "mélange of many styles which comment on themselves through juxtaposition," adding that this often leads to a mis-identification of the "bearer of the narrative" with the characters in the "story" (Quick 2007: 69). However, it is often difficult to disassociate the personae of the performers from their characters, especially when this elision seems to be a primary objective; in *Poor Theater*, for example, Valk is listed as playing both "Kate" and "various roles." Weems's observation does indicate, however, that the commitment required of task-based performance and the juxtapositions of style and tone might engender a kind of emotional investment typically associated with naturalistic acting. Valk's total investment in performative circumstances, no matter how seemingly illogical, is a value that she also absorbed from Adler, particularly her dictum that the sort of engagement required of every actor performing any role is akin to a child's relation to play (Sellar 2007: 28). Significantly, if Valk's hyper-vigilance to the details of her predecessors' performances seemed to foreground their interpretations over her own, this does not mean that she had no emotional currency with either Shakespeare's characters or her onstage scene partners; rather, she felt fortunate to "have those performances outside of myself to get me up to speed with the language and then fill in everything else underneath." What made playing Gertrude more challenging than Ophelia, in her estimation, was that she had no personal frame of reference in regard to a mother–son relationship, and, therefore, relied more heavily on Herlie's interpretation, and also the interpersonal dynamics of her working relationship with Shepherd. She also notes that in "copying and keeping up with the screen performances," she had "no choice but to let that change me from the outside," adding that "the things I know or like to imagine that actors do, to get to an emotional place to play those scenes" can function as a "kind of emotional recall," albeit one markedly different from method acting (Interview 2010: August 10).

To some observers, the Wooster performers exemplify a "semiotic" approach to acting, in which characterization is accomplished through the accumulation of signs rather than emerging from psychological or emotional vantages. In fact, Valk recalls that she was initially drawn to the company because of the emphasis placed on "performing" over "acting," and the "formal experimentation with stage objects and signs, so that a stage prop can have equivalent significance with an actor's moment" (Interview 2010: August 10). These approaches, however, do not negate psychological or emotional engagement; for example, even though it may have appeared at times that The Wooster Group actors were satirizing or performing a camp send-up of outdated acting styles in the "Burton *Hamlet*," Valk maintains that her primary impulse was to "honor the artifact" in a kind of "worship" of her predecessors. Also, as several critics observed, in rendering the gestural and emotive nuances of Herlie's and Marsh's performances, Valk exuded a kind of empathy between the actress-characters across media, time, and place, thus shifting the correspondence between actor and character—a chief paradigm in traditional notions of characterization. These levels of commitment, engagement, and emotional investment certainly qualify any imitative aspect of Valk's performance, and render her interpretations of the characters entirely original and unique.

As with all company projects, the design and technological components of *Hamlet* were developed in concert with the performers throughout rehearsals, and not superimposed during a technical-rehearsal phase. Valk emphasized the importance of this approach thusly:

> I think what really marks our company is that we do all the work together, meaning the costumes, the video, the sound—it's all in development together. There's lots of great organic activity, lots of fantastic accidents. We get to create a lot that doesn't end up in the final show but that might inform the whole world of what we're doing.
>
> (Quoted in Salle and French 2007)

The task of matching the cinematic framing of the screen performers, therefore, would become another mask through which Valk would build and modulate her characters. For example, when the film closed-up on Marsh-as-Ophelia leaning on a chair while delivering the line "O, what a noble mind is here o'erthrown," Valk rolled a chair downstage to create a "dizzying" effect, as if the "performance was zooming out toward the audience" (Werner 2008: 325). Also, the delay between the onscreen performers' gestures and the onstage copies served to open up a critical gap between the performances; in the closet scene, for instance, Valk's meticulous replication of Herlie as she "wept, swooned, and wrung her hands," re-focused the scene's confrontation between Gertrude and Hamlet to a kind of cross-media engagement between the two actresses (Smalec 2008: 278).

Given the many physical and technical demands, it might be surprising that Valk found Shakespeare's language to be the greater challenge. It has been noted that The Wooster Group actors often function more like "figures of speech" rather than psychologically rounded characters, due, in part, to delivering the stylistically divergent texts comprising any given work. Valk has proven her vocal prowess time and again, most notably in re-imagining the dialect and syntactical contortions of O'Neill's expressionistic portrait of Brutus Jones's psychological disintegration. Sound-engineering of her voice has also figured prominently in many of her stage portraits. As Mildred Douglas in *The Hairy Ape*, the frequencies of her voice were electronically sped up and raised in pitch to make her sound like "a slightly hysterical Mickey Mouse or a teenage peroxided bombshell," thus marking her as prototypically "white" in contrast to the vocal masking of African-American and immigrant cultures for Willem Dafoe's Yank-the-stoker (Siegmund 2004: 174–75). Occasionally, such alterations produce a dislocation between the actor's image and the sounds emanating from their mouths. While *Hamlet* employed comparatively minimal vocal masking by such standards, an important element of the sound design entailed the live mixing of The Wooster Group actors' voices with those of the actors on the film's soundtrack, so that the audience heard, alternately, Valk's voice, or Herlie's or Marsh's voice as Valk mouthed the words, or some combination of the two.

Modulation of pitch, tone, and phrasing, along with the technical manipulations, all contribute to what Valk refers to as the vocal score of her performance. With *Hamlet*, Valk admits that because she did not possess "a command of Shakespearean language by any means," it took her "quite some time to even be able to hear it" (quoted in Salle and French: 2007). Though she had portrayed a character from the classical repertory as Phèdre in *To You, the Birdie!*, the company employed a translation by Paul Schmidt that dispensed with the Alexandrine verse from which Racine's play derives its baroque intensity. Both the pre-production workshops and extensive research of Shakespeare's words and imagery were essential to Valk's mastery of the language; equally important, however, was that the line readings of the actors in the "Burton *Hamlet*" were transmitted to the actors through in-ear devices in performance. The company had previously experimented with ear devices for a number of reasons; in *Poor Theater*, for example, they proved compulsory to reconstruct Grotowski's *Akropolis* since none of The Wooster Group actors spoke Polish. While Valk found the line deliveries of Herlie and Marsh helpful, she maintains that the ear devices served other equally important functions:

> A lot of how we work, with the in-ear tracks and the cues off the televisions, keeps us responding in the moment, shortening the time between impulse and action, so what we do is cued from this outside stimulus. And that can keep changing, so there is the potential for the unpredictable.
>
> (Quoted in Salle and French 2007)

Still another variation of vocal and physical masking resulted from the company's digital alteration of the film. Critics attending an early performance in Barcelona noted that as Hamlet, Shepherd seemed to be in "constant awareness of the means of reproduction" as "the one manipulating the film" (Abrams and Parker-Starbuck 2007: 96) In fact, just as Shepherd's directions to start, stop, or rewind the film reinforced the notion that the performance was emanating from his consciousness, Shepherd himself re-edited the film "so that the lines of verse, which were spoken freely in the 1964 production, are delivered according to the original poetic meter" (*Playbill*, November 2007: n.p.). Shepherd described the consequences of using Final Cut software to effect a digital re-scansion of the iambic pentameter:

> If there was a pause where I didn't like it I would just cut it out with the video attached and move it somewhere where I thought there needed to be a pause. So now we use that video which has all these jumps in it which gives us a physicality which is a little bit strange and removed. The same thing happens with the vocal performances because the tendency is to pause in order to make some sort of emotional leap from one state to another so that when you take that pause out you get a jump that is sort of startling. And inserting a pause where there wasn't one also creates interesting effects.
>
> (Interview in *The Gothamist* March 6, 2007)

On one level, this meant that The Wooster Group actors would "correct" the "Burton *Hamlet*;" Gielgud, who was initially pleased with the production, was, in fact, "appalled" by the film and the performances:

> Richard assing about and giving the most mannered and vulgar performance, shouting, grimacing, all sorts of tricks, everything I did for him destroyed. Hume [Cronyn] overacts his head off. Only Eileen [Herlie] and one or two of the others—including [Alfred] Drake [as Claudius], to my great surprise—are human. But it lasts three hours and I almost died of boredom watching it.
>
> (Gielgud 2004: 313–14)

On another level, and perhaps more relevant to the performance conditions, in copying the altered film the actors would be required to also inhabit the resulting jumps and skips so that the stage pictures matched each shot of the film. Keeping up with these technical disruptions through physical and vocal tics engendered a distinctive visceral kinetics that shaped the performances considerably.

The performance of such disruptions is actually a variation of the "safety valve" that LeCompte typically builds into a performance in order to allow for "oscillation between acting and quoting the script" (Arratia 2002: 339). This technique is related to Brecht's alienation effect—another performance modality associated with the company—only here deployed through technological means to disrupt the flow of the "performance text" as well as the text of the play. Apart from allowing a critical distance between the stage and screen performances (and the actors and their characters), this also provided LeCompte with opportunities to direct to the singular talents of her performers. As Claudius, for example, Ari Fliakos seemed to encode the cinematic jumps in the fiber of his nervous system, while Valk's constant readjustments of her stage position in space doubled the urgency and anxieties of her characters' circumstances and amplified the interpretations of the film actresses.

Another integral component of the media design was the presence of three onstage television monitors onto which images of The Wooster Group actors were transmitted, mirroring the triptych of representational systems on view: the cinematic, the theatrical, and the televisual. In many company works, video-feeds—either live or pre-recorded—are transmitted to monitors, screens, and scrims with which the performers sometimes interact. Often, the audience will see the live and mediated images simultaneously, while at other times an actor's image might appear even if not physically present onstage. These shots may be further manipulated as close-ups of gestures, facial expressions, and even discrete body parts. In *To You, the Birdie!*, the media design was composed almost entirely of shots isolating the feet, torsos, and limbs of the performers, and served as a metaphor both for Racine's play and LeCompte's conception of theatre as an "apparatus of desiring gazes which reifies bodies" (Siegmund 2004: 176). While such effects were used more sparingly in *Hamlet*, the monitors displayed live-video feeds of the action, and "portraits" of the actors' faces. In some instances, these images served a choric function, such as when a close-up on Valk-as-Gertrude appeared on the monitors during Hamlet's line "Frailty thy name is woman!"—even though neither she nor Herlie were present on stage or screen. These reaction shots transformed instances of the live performance into screen and televisual moments, reversing, paradoxically, the production's internal logic of transferring cinematic montage into live theatre. Still other moments fused the tragic dimensions of the play and any satiric intents of the production, such as when the "Burton *Hamlet*" was switched to the Kenneth Branagh film version (1996) during "the Hecuba speech" which was delivered by Charlton Heston as the Lead Actor and enacted in a flashback by Judy Dench. Valk's hilarious imitation of Dench's pantomime and the melodramatic literalism of this moment in Branagh's film culminated in a chilling expression of horror captured on Valk's face in close-up on the monitors; meanwhile, the "ghosts" of past performances circulated among the three representational modes on display. Gielgud's presence, too, was felt in The Wooster Group production, not only as the director of the archived performance, but because he also provided the voice of the Ghost, even while the specter of his own record-breaking performance in the title role shadowed Burton's interpretation.

Especially in those moments when the actors' encounters with their onscreen counterparts yielded every imaginable variation of comedy, this *Hamlet* was consistent with Marranca's categorization of the company's works as "satyr plays, to be set alongside the classics of the dramatic repertoire" (Marranca 2003: 13). But these instances, consistently dispersed throughout the performance as they may have been, gave way to equally resonant moments of high tragedy, often resulting from the interplay among the formal components of the representational mediums as well as LeCompte's interpretation of "process" derived from Gielgud's template. For example, Shepherd-as-Hamlet's directives to rewind or fast-forward the film both served as a technological abridgement and literalized the "the rehearsal mode's principle of interruptability" (Callens 2009: 544). Foregrounding process also added nuances to the performances, so that an actor-like self-consciousness tempered how moments of characterization registered. In the scene leading up to the "mousetrap," for example, Valk first played Gertrude and then Ophelia (after a hasty costume change while the film was re-wound), thus exploiting the farcical aspects of playing two roles. By contrast, when the film was fast-forwarded for Ophelia's mad scene so that Valk could take the scene someplace more demented and sadder than Marsh, LeCompte provided Valk with the opportunity to play the role unfettered by the screen performance. Furthermore, the full or partial digital erasure of the actors from the film reinforced the ephemerality of theatre and the ghosting of past performances, while re-focusing the audience's gaze more squarely on the Wooster performers at key moments. Without visual cues as a reference point to copy, moreover, the actors were given free rein to improvise. Ultimately, however, these elements projected important leitmotifs in the play—particularly the specter of the past on the present, and the famous "to be or not to be" trope—within and among the existential limits (and possibilities) of the various representational systems, while enfranchising their presumed (and actual) audiences.

Valk has described the relationship between the Wooster performers and the audience as "symbiotic," adding that the reason why the company presents open rehearsals and works-in-process is because "You don't know what a piece is going to be until it's been seen…The work totally morphs into something else. And it's something you could never imagine" (quoted in Salle and French 2007). Just as the spectral remains of the "Burton *Hamlet*" and the ghosts of past performers seemed to haunt The Wooster Group production, so, too, did past audiences, whose applause and laughter were fragmented from the film's soundtrack. This device also echoed previous company works in which "absent, dead, or forgotten" voices were added to the theatrical event through technological mediums (Siegmund 2004: 178). Considering the element of her work in which she herself was called upon to become another medium, it is no wonder, then, that Valk categorizes her performance in *Hamlet* as "channeling."

With *Hamlet*, the company expanded its exploration of the dramatic canon to consider the interpretive possibilities of performing Shakespeare in a digital and media age. It is also significant that the production would land across lower Manhattan at the Public Theatre/New York Shakespeare Festival at the invitation of Artistic Director Oskar Eustis. Though initially skeptical about presenting *Hamlet* at the Public Theatre rather than The Performing Garage, Valk ultimately came to revel in the opportunity to contribute to Joseph Papp's legacy and become associated with the current company and distinguished history of NYSF's alternative and distinctively American approach to Shakespeare (Interview 2010: August 10).

The ironic and often touching homage to *esprit de corps* discovered in the "ruins" of past productions at the heart of The Wooster Group *Hamlet* was, perhaps, best captured during a moment in Valk's performance, neither as Gertrude nor Ophelia, but as the cross-dressed boy/actor, who, in response to Hamlet's complaint about actors he had seen who "imitated humanity so abominably" replies: "I hope we have reformed that indifferently with us, sir" (III.ii. 32–41). This sentiment, equally relevant to the aims of the traveling actors in the play, the Gielgud company, and The Wooster Group's own intentions, are apropos to any troupe brave enough to mount Shakespeare's masterwork. It also provided Valk with her most giddily light-hearted moment—her obvious pleasure resulting from adopting the mask of a boy with little stake in the play's action (and, thus, temporary respite from portraying not one, but two gravely tragic characters), and also the *joie de vivre* of representing not one, but three acting companies to which she simultaneously belonged.

Chronology

1979	Kate Valk interns for Elizabeth LeCompte, building costumes and props, and stage managing The Wooster Group's *Point Judith (an epilog)*; The Performing Garage, NYC.
1981	Performance debut with TWG as Willie and various other roles in *Route 1 & 9*; TPG.
1983	Ensign Word-Processor Ann Pusey in *North Atlantic* by James Strahs; TPG. (Revived in 1999 and 2010.)
1984	Tituba from fragments of Arthur Miller's *The Crucible*, and various other roles in *L.S.D.(…Just the High Points)*; TPG.
1987	Onna in *Frank Dell's The Temptation of St. Antony*; TPG. (Revived in 1993.)
1991	Narrator in *Brace* Up!, from Chekhov's *Three Sisters*; TPG. (Also plays Masha in 2003 revival.)
1993	Brutus Jones in *The Emperor Jones* by Eugene O'Neill; TPG. (Revived in 2006, St. Ann's Warehouse, Brooklyn, NY); Asako the maid in *Fish Story*; TPG.
1995	Mildred Douglas in *The Hairy Ape* by Eugene O'Neill; TPG. (Revived in 2001.)
1997	Faustus/Elaine in *House/Lights*; TPG. (Revived in 2005 at St. Ann's Warehouse.)
1998	Receives OBIE award for Sustained Excellence of Performance.
2002	Phèdre in *To You, the Birdie!*, text by Paul Schmidt from Racine's *Phèdre*; TPG. BESSIE Award for Best Performer.
2003	Valk awarded Foundation for Contemporary Artists grant.
2005	"Kate" and various other roles in *Poor Theater*; TPG. Research & development begins for *Hamlet*.
2007	Gertrude, Ophelia & Lead Player (uncredited) in *Hamlet*; Newman Theatre, The Public Theatre/New York Shakespeare Festival (October); preview performances in Barcelona, Spain (June 2006) and St. Ann's Warehouse (February 2007).

2009 Shadow of Dido, Old Man, Guard & Sanya in *La Didone*; St. Ann's Warehouse.

2011 Jane Sparks in *Vieux Carré* by Tennessee Williams, Baryshnikov Arts Center, NY.

Note: All productions directed by Elizabeth LeCompte.

Bibliography

Abrams, Joshua, and Jennifer Parker-Starbuck (2007) 'Politics and the Classics', *PAJ: A Journal of Performance and Art* 29 (1): 88–100.

Aronson, Arnold (2000) *American Avant-Garde Theatre: A History*, London & New York: Routledge.

Arratia, Euridice (2002) 'Island Hopping: Rehearsing The Wooster Group's *Brace Up*', in Rebecca Schneider and Gabrielle Cody (eds.), *Re:Direction*, London & New York: Routledge, pp. 332–46.

Callens, Johan (2009) 'The Wooster Group's *Hamlet*, According to the True, Original Copies', *Theatre Journal* 61 (4): 539–61.

Cartelli, Thomas (2008) 'Channeling the Ghosts: The Wooster Group's Remediation of the 1964 Electronovision *Hamlet*', *Shakespeare Survey* 61: 147–60.

Demastes, William M. (2008) *Spalding Gray's America* (with a foreword by Richard Schechner), Milwaukee, WI: Limelight.

Gielgud, John (2004) *Sir John Gielgud: A Life in Letters* (edited and introduced by Richard Mangan), New York: Arcade Publishing.

Marranca, Bonnie (2003) 'The Wooster Group: A Dictionary of Ideas', *PAJ: A Journal of Performance and Art* 25 (2): 1–18.

Monks, Aoife (2005) '"Genuine Negroes and Real Bloodhounds": Cross-Dressing, Eugene O'Neill, The Wooster Group, and *The Emperor Jones*', *Modern Drama* 48 (3): 540–64.

Quick, Andrew (2007) *The Wooster Group Work Book*, New York and London: Routledge.

Siegmund, Gerald (2004) 'Voice Masks: Subjectivity, America, and the Voice in the Theatre of The Wooster Group' in Johan Callens (ed.), *The Wooster Group and Its Traditions*, Brussels: Peter Lang, pp. 167–78.

Smalec, Theresa (2008) '*Hamlet*', Performance Review, *Theatre Journal* 60 (2): 277–78.

Sterne, Richard L. (1967) *John Gielgud Directs Richard Burton in Hamlet: A Journal of Rehearsals*, New York: Random House.

Werner, Sarah (2008) 'Shakespeare Performed: Two *Hamlets*; Wooster Group and Synetic Theatre', *Shakespeare Quarterly* 59 (3): 323–29.

Interview conducted by the author

Kate Valk, August 10, 2010.

Internet sources

Kramer, Jane (2007) 'Experimental Journey: Elizabeth LeCompte takes on Shakespeare', *The New Yorker Online* October 7: n.p. http://www.newyorker.com/reporting/2007/10/08/071008fa_fact_kramer

Salle, David and Sarah French (2007) 'Interview with Kate Valk', *Bomb* 100 Summer: n.p. http://bombsite.com/issues/100/articles/2920

Sellar, Tom (2007) 'Interview with Kate Valk', *Publication and Research: The Pew Center for Arts & Heritage*, (September 7): pp. 1–28. http://www.pcah.us/m/theatre/Kate_Valk_Interview.pdf

DVD sources

Richard Burton's Hamlet (1995) DVD; produced for the screen by William Sargent & Alfred W. Crown, from the production of the play directed by Sir John Gielgud, Chatsworth, CA: Image Entertainment.

The Wooster Group *Hamlet*. August 5, 2009, Gdańsk, Poland; archival recording held at The Performing Garage, New York City.

About the author

David Pellegrini is Associate Professor of Theatre, and Chair of the Performing Arts Department at Eastern Connecticut State University. He serves as Book Review Editor of the *New England Theatre Journal*, and has contributed essays to the anthologies *Theatre and Nationalism* (2005) and *Voicings: Ten Plays from the Documentary Theatre* (1995), and articles and reviews for *Text and Presentation*, *Theatre Journal*, and *Theatre Survey*. As a member of the Unseam'd Shakespeare Company, he directed John Ford's *The Broken Heart* and *'Tis Pity She's a Whore* (cited as "Best Production 1995" by *In Pittsburgh*), Strindberg's *After the Fire*, and Shakespeare's *King Lear*, *Henry IV parts 1 & 2*, and *Antony and Cleopatra*. His production of *Our Lady of 121st Street* at Eastern was selected to be re-staged at the 2007 Kennedy Center-American College Theatre Festival (Region I), and his production of *The Women* received a Citation for "Best Ensemble 2008."

20
Harriet Walter
Paul Edmondson

Her hands are spotted and splashed with blood. She looks at them and says 'O, God', and breaks off. Clasping her hands to her breast and breathing in deeply, she stoops to wash them, quickly, furtively. It is as if they will never be clean again. She rubs them with a handkerchief and looks quickly around. Her mouth is open in disgust, but her expression changes to relief with a different, practical focus. This almost wordless sequence lasts thirty-six seconds.

This is not Lady Macbeth. Not yet. It is a moment from a B.B.C. dramatisation of Dorothy L. Sayers's *Have His Carcase* directed by Christopher Hodson in 1986. Harriet Vane discovers the body lying abandoned on a rock. For Harriet Walter, who portrayed her namesake over three series, Lady Macbeth would follow thirteen years later, but her reputation as a Shakespeare actor was already established. In this short sequence her own Shakespearian preferences and reputation are mapped on to classic crime drama.

Here readers will find a synoptic view of a highly intelligent and self-conscious performer. How does she turn Shakespeare's words into a live event? How does she speak and move? How does she prepare for a Shakespearian role and what does she seek to bring to it? What is it like watching her act moment by moment in Shakespeare? I was able to work with her on a speech of Rosalind's in *As You Like It*, a role she has not played, and I quote freely from private interviews, giving references only to published quotations. Descriptions of performance are based on my own memories (except *All's Well That Ends Well*) and the Royal Shakespeare Company archive videos available for consultation in The Shakespeare Centre Library in Stratford-upon-Avon. Shakespeare is cited from *The Oxford Shakespeare: The Complete Works* (1986; 2nd edn 2005).

She finished her training at The London Academy of Music and Dramatic Art in 1973. Her Shakespearian roles began on the professional stage in 1980 with Ophelia for Richard Eyre at The Royal Court. That was also the year she joined The Royal Shakespeare Company as Madeleine Bray and, as she recalls, 'every fifth bonnet' in David Edgar's adaptation of *Nicholas Nickleby*. The following year, she was cast as Helena in Ron Daniels's R.S.C. production of *A Midsummer Night's Dream*. This was a personally significant breakthrough, not least because it was her first experience of having to project her voice in a large auditorium. She was grateful to come under the influence of voice expert Cicely Berry who helped with her vocal pitch, projection, and control: 'she taught me not to listen to my voice but to feel it' (*Other People's Shoes*, p.156). But she admits to being disappointed by the reviews. Although a breakthrough, Helena meant engaging with knockabout farce, 'not my forte. I was better at playing fragile, broken people.'

That same season (1981–83) saw her playing Lady Percy in *Henry IV Parts One* and *Two* and another Shakespearian Helena for Trevor Nunn in *All's Well That Ends Well*. Peggy Ashcroft was playing the Countess, and the production transferred to Broadway.

Film, television and other stage work (including Aphra Behn, Anton Chekhov, and Harold Pinter) took up the next four years and she returned to the Shakespearian stage as Portia in *The Merchant of Venice* at The Royal Exchange, Manchester, directed by Braham Murray (1987). Another R.S.C. season followed (1987–89) as Viola in *Twelfth Night* (for which she won the Olivier Award) and Imogen in *Cymbeline*, followed by the Duchess of Malfi (1989–90), all directed by Bill Alexander. Theatre, television drama, and film took up most of the next decade (including a memorable portrayal of the caustic Fanny in Jane Austen's *Sense and Sensibility*, directed by Ang Lee in 1995), until she made her return to the R.S.C. as Lady Macbeth in 1999, directed by Gregory Doran (filmed in 2000 for Channel 4). There followed Beatrice in *Much Ado About Nothing* (R.S.C., 2002) and Cleopatra (R.S.C., 2006), both directed by Doran. In 2005 her performance as Elizabeth I in Schiller's *Mary Stuart* (directed by Phyllida Lloyd for the Donmar Warehouse) won her the Evening Standard Award for Best Actress and Olivier and Tony Award nominations. The production was revived for Broadway in 2009. Audio recordings of Shakespeare include Tamora in *Titus Andronicus* and Lady Macbeth (with a Scottish accent) for The Arkangel Shakespeare and Goneril in *King Lear* (opposite Paul Scofield as Lear) for The Cambridge Shakespeare, under the Naxos label. She has published several accounts of her work. There is an essay on her performance as Imogen for *Players of Shakespeare 3* (1993), and she produced a longer essay on playing Lady Macbeth for Faber and Faber's 'Actors on Shakespeare' series in 2002. Her book, *Other People's Shoes: Thoughts on Acting* first appeared in 1999 and has been reissued several times.

She is an intellectually and politically engaged performer who is able compellingly to articulate her process and preparations for a role, and the reasons for her interpretative choices. Gregory Doran stands out as one of her favourite directors of Shakespeare with whom she has worked on three R.S.C. productions because 'he puts Shakespeare first, rather than his own directorial angle, and wants to release the plays from the page through the actors' equipment and imagination'.

Walter was one of Carol Rutter's *Clamorous Voices* in 1988, 'a generation of classical actresses newly empowered by the women's movement to question the structures and systems they worked under, and the role of the female both on and off the stage' (*New Theatre Quarterly*, p. 112). Twenty-six years on from *Clamorous Voices*, Walter still feels that too often female actors are not given the same kind of attention or treatment in the rehearsal room as men. She thinks that some male directors are at their least less successful when directing women.

She encountered feminism in the same year as she started drama school. Her own political ideology makes her determined to find the humanity in a role that will speak to herself and others from her own position as a modern woman. She describes her fundamental approach to performance like this:

> Acting is what I do with who I am. That 'who I am' is in constant dynamic relationship with the world and people around me, the plays I do, and the parts I play, so it is not only a question of bringing what I know to a character, but also of opening myself to learn *from* the character via the insight of the writer.
>
> (*New Theatre Quarterly*, p. 111)

Female roles written from a male perspective usually betray elements of stereotyping: pure, virginal, desirous, nagging or monstrous women who conform to patriarchal expectations. For her, Shakespeare brings depths of psychological depiction which help to 'kick against' the stereotypes.

Although Shakespeare's women say less than his men, the roles are no less demanding or complex, except from a physical point of view ('I'm quite jealous of men sweating at the curtain call', *New Theatre Quarterly*, p. 112). When she moved from agitprop-style political theatre at the start of her career to the classical repertoire she felt liberated by the ambiguity of Shakespeare's writing. She found that she did not have to explain everything about a character by connecting scenes and episodes together, but could rather trust the language to make each moment real. Shakespeare easily accommodates her own experience and knowledge as a modern woman which she seeks to bring to the roles. But she needs other actors in rehearsal to help her understand who her character is: 'your developing theories may thwart someone else in theirs and vice versa' (White, p. 91). She asks: 'when does a part begin to look like me? Possibly not until I stand up in rehearsals without book in hand and look into the eyes of a fellow actor who is looking at me [as the character]' (White, p. 89).

What might that other actor and the audience see in her physical person? She stands tall in life and on stage. Her face is open and defined by her strong jaw-line and chin. Her mouth is wide, easily filling her expression with different moods. Her eyes sometimes close as her character relishes a word or emotion. The occasional furrowed brow brings an easy look of concern and emphasis. She has long arms and large but not over-demonstrative hands. She is powerful when standing with her hands on both hips, and can take control of a moment easily by, for example, casually leaning against a chair. But she is self-questioning about her ability to portray power, partly because of her voice. When reading a speech of Volumnia's (*Coriolanus*, 5. 3. 132–83), she explained that she herself does not have the ability to roar, unlike, for example, Irene Worth and Janet Suzman. Instead, she concentrates on different speeds within a speech, paying attention to its variety of rhythms, and cutting across other characters to gain command.

Although naturally powerful in her physical appearance she seeks to bring Shakespeare's characters to life in part by showing their imperfection or vulnerability. Women are no more virtuous or transgressive than men, and a strong-looking woman is neither more nor less likely to be either. Any easy assumptions are swept away as she seeks the real human being in the role. Imogen's virtue might be only apparent:

> When I began to delve, I could discover the flaws in Imogen. She could be underhanded, self-dramatizing, impulsive, arrogant, and so on – then, by suffering many near tragedies and near deaths, Imogen grows from a spoilt princess to a mature and generous woman.
>
> (*New Theatre Quarterly*, p. 114)

She really does delve when preparing a Shakespearian role. She is an acutely analytical reader whose 'preparatory task is to read and read the text and nothing but the text' (*Players of Shakespeare 3*, p. 202). Her way through her initial reading of Volumnia was to 'find the words to show what she is arguing, like solving a crossword puzzle'. Apart from her intellect, 'one understands with the instinct, the imagination and the emotional memory, and in this way one comes closer to the essence of the play than ever one can by intellect alone' (White, p. 91). For Imogen, she wanted to show how any apparent virtue is born from experience and knowledge. From her feminist perspective this is a reminder that any notion of a pure and perfect woman is no more than a patriarchal invention. And so her Imogen returned Giacomo's kiss while he was watching her sleep in act two, scene two (she may or may not have been dreaming of Posthumus).

A defining moment in her career was Helena in *All's Well That End's Well* (R.S.C. 1981) where her natural preferences as a performer were allowed properly to shine. She felt every bit of the responsibility that came with it and recalls walking around Mary Arden's House thinking about performing a large Shakespearian role opposite Peggy Ashcroft (who played the Countess): 'I was contemplating doing a bunk.' The production emphasised her talent for playing lachrymose fragility. Helena's great soliloquy, in which she admits to having forgotten her late father and confesses that her tears are for Bertram's leaving home, was in part underscored by a soulful sounding piano:

> What was he like?
> I have forgot him. My imagination
> Carries no favour in't but Bertram's.
> I am undone.
>
> (*All's Well That End's Well*, 1. 1. 80–83)

After speaking these lines, she fell into an armchair with her hands to her head and suddenly burst into tears. It was a moment of high emotion which, after she had briefly composed herself, brought a feeling of painful restraint to the rest of her soliloquy, moving into wistfulness for her dialogue with Paroles a few lines later (her Helena's way of coping with Paroles's vulgarity). Her tears flowed apparently effortlessly again for her sudden outburst of respect and deep affection for the Countess on 'Mine honourable mistress' (1. 3. 134) and, later, 'O my dear mother, do I see you living?' (5. 3. 321).

Her Helena was richly layered with matter-of-fact fortitude and determination, as well as a schoolgirl-like innocence, tenderness, longing, and fear. In the main it was declared a success. But in spite of her showing the vulnerability of Helena, some critics continued to judge the character according to their own interpretations.

Helena's behaviour remained for them too threatening to the patriarchal norm: she chases a man whom she traps into marriage. She was affected by the reviews which prevented her from completely enjoying the success of the production. Ten years later she shared the following critical perspective:

> I'm inclined to think that those reviews told me more about the reviewer than the play, and that the prejudice and misogyny of a few male critics is their problem, not mine.
>
> (*New Theatre Quarterly*, p. 116)

Now she can rely on her own strength of purpose and courage to help when reviews wound. Speaking in 2010 she reflects further: 'I was subversive but not brave, and seeking approval held me back. I have felt quite meek until now. Only since Cleopatra have I been brave enough to break moulds. I used to plot carefully my approach to a part, but I now see that it's about being happy in your own skin on stage.'

She recalls learning a lot from Ashcroft during *All's Well That Ends Well*. Watching great actors – she cites Judi Dench as another example – is about 'noting certain mysteries', rather than learning from what you see them do. Walter recalls her own nervous state in the wings, and her need for the emotional charge she required for Helena. She would notice how Ashcroft walked effortlessly on to the stage as though no work was being done. Ashcroft never seemed to be raising her voice, and yet she could always be heard easily. There were technical tips, too. When Ashcroft occasionally dried Walter recalls:

> I watched her while she sort of froze and then after a beat or two she would calmly carry on. She explained to me later that during that frozen pause she was waiting while an inward ear remembered the music of the line. I have often tried that and it works a lot better than panicking. The audience barely notice the hitch that to you seems like an endless pause and you get back on track and sail onward.
>
> (The George Pragnell Prize acceptance speech)

Reflecting on her early perceptions of Ashcroft's 'mystery', she recognises how she has now come to be familiar with her own inner resources, and how she can now 'access them by short-cut'. She has come to learn that volume alone is not what makes you audible. Rather, being heard and understood on stage relies on a combination of clarity, diction, modulation, intention and musicality.

She is not hide-bound by any particular way of speaking Shakespeare and knows that although there is more to a play than its language, it is the language alone which provides the key to the play's heart:

> When you've done quite a lot of Shakespeare you do seem able to highlight a word, lift it, serve up the end of a line without whacking it on the head. You can observe different twists of rhythm and, when you have a long list of things, give weight to all of them without hammering them. [...] Lines are also usually more understandable if you take them at a lick.
>
> (The George Pragnell Prize acceptance speech)

She invites us to experience Shakespeare's words as momentarily heightened, but her invitation is for us to share a critical as well as emotional perspective. She understands actors first and foremost as communicators rather than creative artists (like painters). For her, acting is a dialogue of give and take, and Shakespeare is a language like French, Italian, German or Spanish, through which to express oneself. 'A very good acting note is that, though on the page there may be twenty-six lines, you must always start as if you've only got one, and this one leads to another' ('Interview' in Davies, p. 229).

Twenty-two years after Helena came Beatrice. She found that there was 'less to hang on to in Shakespeare's prose because it does not provide the same sense of structure as his verse'. She decided to portray a Beatrice who hides pain behind her own humour. The breaking-point came in act three, scene one when Beatrice overhears Hero and Ursula talking in the garden about Benedick's love for her. In her hiding place, Beatrice was soaked with a hose-pipe as the other two women watered the 'pleachèd bower' (3. 1. 7). On their exit she came forward, soaked and shocked. It was a moment of real change and revelation. She took full opportunity of Shakespeare's emotional and intellectual structure. The effect of the hose-pipe gave the moment a keen and disarming edge. The last ripples of slapstick-induced laughter died down as she came forward and started suddenly to talk about fire. The verse provided a moment of sudden openness. There was nowhere for Beatrice to hide and her heart momentarily ruled her head. She seemed totally to surrender herself to the language in the moment. The lines 'And Benedick, love on. I will requite thee' and 'I believe it' were spoken with an uplifting and joyful abandonment, her body language intuitively reflecting Beatrice's thoughts and feelings:

> (*hands on heart*) What fire is in mine ears? (*hands on side of face*) Can this be true?
> (*hands by her side*) Stand I condemned for pride and scorn so much?
> (*hands pushing old self away*) Contempt, farewell; and maiden pride, adieu.
> (*right hand on head, left hand on heart*) No glory lives behind the back of such.
> And, Benedick, (*hands by side*) love on. I will requite thee,
> (*both hands clasped to heart*) Taming my wild heart to thy loving hand.
> If thou dost love, (*both hands clasped together in front of her*) my kindness shall incite thee
> To bind our loves up in a holy band.
> For others say thou dost deserve, (*arms open wide*) and I
> Believe it better than reportingly.
>
> (*Much Ado About Nothing*, 3. 1. 107–16)

The overhearing scene generated a great sense of release for Beatrice. Her speech is cast into the form of a truncated sonnet and constitutes Beatrice's only sustained piece of verse, as well as her only soliloquy. Seven years later, she reflected that:

> This was a moment to reveal her deepest feelings and romantic aspirations – things she wouldn't dream of revealing to anyone 'inside' the play. As actors

> we are always asked to note where the language changes from verse to prose or to rhyming. There are no hard-and-fast rules as to what Shakespeare means by these changes, but if an actor observes them, a kind of reason is revealed inside us via the different rhythms and notes that are sounded in our subconscious.
>
> ('Harriet Walter on Playing Beatrice', p. 161)

The Beatrice example illustrates, too, her careful placing of hand gestures, which she believes must be kept carefully under control in performance. Her hands moved the language and moment along, suiting 'the action to the word, the word to the action' (*Hamlet*, 3. 2. 17–18). When only reading the part of Volumnia her hands and arms were always on the move, indicative, she explained, of wanting to serve the language up as best she could without being able to perform it. 'Sawing the air too much with your hands thus is usually a sign that an actor is not trusting verbal communication enough, rather like being abroad and wanting to make yourself understood', especially the case during audio recordings of Shakespeare, when the actor is not using their whole body.

When occasion serves, she is adept at not stumbling or pausing if she should suddenly forget a line and instead keeps the iambic rhythm moving. She has taken Ashcroft's example and made the practice her own. So long as the flow continues, Walter has found (hopes) that the audience tends not to notice the occasional slippage. Very occasionally, this can lead to her speaking perfect iambic nonsense, with hilarious results for her fellow actors. In *Twelfth Night* she recalls that Viola's line to Orsino about the nature of women, 'In faith they are as true of heart as we', once came out as, '"In truth" (wrong...I've got to say "true" in a sec.; swap the "f" ["faith"] word for the "t" word ["truth"] "they are as far of fart as we."' And, instead of Cleopatra:

> shouting at the messenger 'thou shalt be whipped with wire and stewed in brine, smarting in lingering pickle...' my quarter century of experience came up with [...] 'Thou shalt be whipped with wine and spewed in Brian, smarting in gingering kipper.'
>
> (The George Pragnell Prize acceptance speech)

These anecdotes illustrate a serious point: her acting is primarily underscored by the communication she finds in Shakespeare's music and rhythm. It is interesting that for so analytical a performer, it is the score, rather than the libretto, the form rather than the content, that dominates in occasional moments of pressure.

These qualities are borne out in the sharp-edged precision she brings to Shakespeare's language, an appealing, detached quality. Her emotions never overwhelm Shakespeare's poetry. It is a question of balancing 'something between singing and ordinary speech'. To listen to her speak Shakespeare is to experience a tightly balanced and sensitive negotiation between thought, the sound of the word, and the feelings it stirs. She is able to combine a character's thought with her own intellectual sensibility as a performer. To watch her act is, in part, to watch the character she is playing think. Thought is always visually and orally present in her acting. This quality restrains emotional indulgence and has a considerable effect on how an audience receives Shakespeare's language.

She is ready to explain that her voice is a problem for her. It can sound thin and brittle, but she has turned it to her best advantage. It is an instrument for conveying fragility, wistfulness, brokenness, defensiveness, sternness and political severity. Her voice can bring a sense of restrained pain to comedy, a wryness to tragedy, and can push words around the air like chess-pieces. Occasionally, she uses a deeper register ('a chest rather than head voice'), the better to convey interiority and, especially, stillness, almost as if the language has been well digested within her and she is holding the words back.

Walter plays the flute. Music is deeply embedded into her and the way she responds to the world. This informs her poetic intuition and vice versa. When she plays Henry Purcell's 'Music for a while', for example, she knows how to phrase her playing because she can hear the words being sung in her head. When she experiences being totally present in the moment, she describes the sensation as Shakespeare playing her, rather than the other way around. 'On the whole I think I am an interpreter; I'm in no sense original. What I respond to is the music in Shakespeare.' During the great act two, scene four in *Twelfth Night* (R.S.C., 1987) when Viola and Orsino are talking about music and Viola goes on half to reveal herself to the Duke (2. 4. 107–21), she recalls once feeling as though she were 'a humming instrument in the present tense. It was not acting. It was like an epiphany.' Later, in the wings, she discovered that Donald Sumpter (Orsino) had felt something similar, too: 'We had both witnessed it, both shared it.' The moment between Viola and Orsino is intensely lyrical and she spoke her lines slowly and precisely. The words throbbed with sadness, the Shakespearian verse equivalent of sobbing. Twenty years later, she experienced Cleopatra musically as well (R.S.C., 2006). Again, the lyricism is in part intrinsic to the role and requires great sensitivity. The music was part of the psychological, emotional, physical and creative aspect of the character. Here again there were moments when she describes Shakespeare (the instrument) playing the performer, most memorably for her when Cleopatra is remembering the dead Antony:

> His legs bestrid the ocean; his reared arm
> Crested the world. His voice was propertied
> As all the tunèd spheres, and that to friends;
> But when he meant to quail and shake the orb,
> He was as rattling thunder.
>
> (5. 2. 81–85)

The moment itself alludes to music and her deep connection to it is revealing of her commitment to learning from the character as well as taking her fullest possible emotional and intellectual and imaginative response to a role.

Cleopatra was a revelation of new ground for her. Here, an actress who had consistently and carefully crept into the skin of Shakespearian roles and portrayed their contradictions and vulnerability met with the most capricious and quixotic of all of them. With Cleopatra, she found new ways of taking risks in the moment, of being less reverential, less obedient, less 'the good girl in the class'. It is a role to which audiences and critics bring their own preconceived ideas. Walter brought a suppleness of movement to the role. Creativity moved from the rehearsal room on to the stage and she delighted in keeping her Antony (Patrick Stewart) fresh and surprised. She moved quickly to the floor of the stage at key moments: crouching there with her gentlewomen for 'play one scene / Of excellent dissembling, and let it look / Like perfect honour' (1. 3. 78–80), falling at Antony's feet when he was about to leave (1. 3. 96–102). There were many moments of sheer abandonment to the part, for example:

> That time – O times!–
> I laughed him out of patience, and that night
> I laughed him into patience, and next morn,
> Ere the ninth hour, I drunk him to his bed,
> Then put my tires and mantles in him whilst
> I wore his sword Philippan.
>
> (2. 5. 18–23)

This speech was punctuated with laughter as she revelled in the pleasure of Antony and the memory of him – half gasping as she re-lived the moment – half confession, half rejoicing in the language and the emotions it makes available. And then in response to the hapless messenger a few lines later she became highly strung. 'Melt Egypt into Nile, and kindly creatures / Turn all to serpents' (2. 5. 78–79) was shouted as a sudden scream, a great moment of intuitive acting as she and the fateful country she embodies melted to the floor and found themselves among the serpents she was describing. There was a similar desperate abandonment to the language for 'Where art thou death? / Come hither, come. Come, come, and take a queen / Worth many babes and beggars' (5. 2. 45–47). Later, there was a stately flow to her grieving images of Antony as she sat on the floor and made us see effortlessly all the things she talked about which flowed from her in a rush of meditation: 'I dreamt there was an Emperor Antony [...] Realms and islands were / As plates dropped from his pockets' (5. 2. 75–90).

Viola and Cleopatra show how keen and able she is to bring a musical intention to the language. Her voice is more reedy than flutey, like the oboe at the beginning of Tchaikovsky's *Swan Lake* rather than the flute at the beginning of Mozart's concerto for flute and harp. But the sound of a voice is not the same as the tones and moods it can achieve. Walter's tonal range shows her to be peculiarly suited to Shakespeare's language, which relies on the co-mingling of comedy and tragedy. Her voice easily adopts a crisp, satirical edge and she has the ability to turn the serious into the non-serious within a hair's breadth. It is a voice that can relish words and this in itself is a quality that can encourage humour. She brought vocally to life the whole of *Venus and Adonis* when she narrated The Little Angel Theatre's exquisite puppet version of the play as part of the R.S.C.'s Complete Works season in 2006–7. Here she was nimble, compassionate, and persuasive, as well as lightly (and satirically) erotic, humorous, tender, and moving.

When reading and discussing an extract from Rosalind from 'Yes, one; and in this manner' to 'there shall not be one spot of love in't' (*As You Like It*, 3. 2. 392–408), she found the comedy and the flirtation in the language, as well as bringing them to the part. Shakespeare's language here generates an inward smile, which might become externalised and lead to laughter, but it is not about trying to induce amusement. Rosalind became a 'lesson in how to think' for her. She explained that Rosalind needs to know that she can be understood by thinking quickly, like an extrovert at a party. She recalled that this is how Nunn succeeded in trimming *All's Well That Ends Well* by twenty minutes for its Broadway transfer 'by thinking more quickly, it all naturally speeded up'. Rosalind needs to know she is being listened to, otherwise she would run out of motivation. Her list describing what she as Ganymede would do (a thirteen-line sentence) has to resonate each particular without slowing down, but must serve up the thinking lightly, playfully. Characteristic, too, is her skill at allowing the hard consonants at the ends of words to hover and buzz ever so lightly: 's', 'v', 't', 'l', 'k', and 'ple' are all letters which by emphasis can help her bring resonance to individual words or, as she says, 'a way of keeping things in flight'. She brought both music and comedy to the phrasing of 'to forswear the full stream of the world and to live in a nook merely monastic' (3. 2. 403–5). She explained that a hard 'c' or 'k' sound is known as the comic consonant: 'It's funnier to live in a nook, than in a cell.' This is a good example of Shakespeare's music combining with the imagined mood.

Rosalind's playfulness of thought was coloured by the feelings she sought to unlock. She often looks for the fear in a role and asks: what is a character trying to avoid as well as what is she trying to achieve? Rosalind disguised as Ganymede is 'playing with fire' in avoiding discovery, but needs to get back to being a woman. From her own feminist perspective, Rosalind is playful and free from having to fulfil any patriarchal ideals. She found a natural affinity with Rosalind because she could more easily access the girl than the powerful matriarch (not something Walter has been allowed to do very often).

For power, one must turn to her Lady Macbeth. There are three: her performance in Gregory Doran's 1999 R.S.C. production, its subsequent film version (2000), and an audio recording for the Arkangel Shakespeare series (1999). The R.S.C. production took place in The Swan Theatre but was filmed in The Roundhouse. In moving from stage to screen, she had to move from her more resonant 'chest voice' to her 'head voice' in order to create a much lighter, less demonstrative effect. The film version represents a clever re-invention of the performance, rather than a record of it. For the Arkangel Shakespeare audio recording she adopted a Scottish accent, which she found liberating (and which led to a quicker delivery of some of the lines). She used her theatre voice for the R.S.C. performance, which resonated in the darkened auditorium. The dangerous words made the hairs on the back of her neck stand on end. She recalls the whole theatre seeming like a haunted house, an effect impossible to convey through film or audio recording. The trajectory of this role moved from being highly motored and motivated in her first appearance to being completely unravelled by her last. 'Passion', she explains, 'is a wonderful fuel for an actor, like a fire burning inside you.' She needs to connect the images she is reaching for with something inside herself, a parallel idea or experience to conjure the same kind of force and internal fire. If this can happen, then, she believes, the audience will be caught up in it. So, in preparing for the role, she researched post-traumatic stress disorder and recalls reading about 'a young rape victim who "could not sleep without a light" ' (Walter, *Macbeth*, p. 56). On one occasion, in the rehearsal rooms in Clapham, she and Antony Sher used real knives and blood. She remembers feeling she wanted to wash her hands for the rest of that same evening. For the sleepwalking scene, she recalls wanting 'the audience to feel they were eavesdropping on Lady Macbeth cocooned in her private Hell' (Walter, *Macbeth*, p. 57). The following two moments of close description mark the beginning and end of Lady Macbeth and Walter's journey through the role.

Macbeth 1. 5. 1–53

She is immersed in her husband's words when she appears reading his letter (1. 5). Her Lady Macbeth has not read it before, and we see a woman transported in the moment as her husband's words unfold before her, one illustration of the closeness of the Macbeths' marriage, a strong interpretative arc for this production. When she arrives at 'and referred me to the coming on of time with "Hail, King that shalt be!"' (1. 5. 9), she pauses after 'Hail', and 'King' sounds as though it has stuck in her throat with a sudden gasp of excitement. Her voice reaches a deeper register at the end of the letter: 'Lay it to thy heart, and farewell' (1. 5. 13). She tucks the paper into the right breast of her dress. She conveys strength through stillness with both hands behind her neck. Her sparest of movements register clearly and she moves her hands in front of her for a matter-of-fact but imploring 'Thus thou must do' (line 22). She suppresses an excited laugh as she says 'Hie thee thither' (line 24) and revolves round with a sense of joy. Then she is still again and lightly touches her head when she mentions 'the golden round', making it momentarily palpable (line 27). Her hands return to the back of her neck until the servant interrupts, changing the dramatic temperature, briefly pulling her into dialogue. The news she receives means she returns to her inner musings and invokes the evil spirits in lines that she makes alive with lyrical texture. We are left in no doubt that she is in full possession of the situation. She stands powerfully, stock still towards the back of the stage and emphasises 'the fatal entrance of Duncan / Under *my* battlements' (lines 38–39). She kneels to begin the invocation 'Come, you spirits / That tend on mortal thoughts, unsex me here' (lines 39–40). She then places her hands on her stomach and these move slowly upwards towards her neck during 'And fill me from the crown to the toe top-full / Of direst cruelty' (lines 39–41). She continues 'Come to my woman's breasts' (line 45) with a nervous, breathy quality but then adopts a slight tremolo, as though she is being pulled forward by the enjambment against her will 'And fill me from the crown to the toe top-full / Of direst cruelty' (lines 41–42). Her voice and body are so finely in tune with the words and the feelings they inspire that she conveys a keen sense of a power overtaking and leading her where she would not ordinarily wish to follow. She conveys the sense that her frame is just able to withstand it. She stretches the monosyllabic 'g-a-a-a-ll' (line 47) as though her imagined woman's milk really were poisonous, an image echoed three lines later by her pronunciation of 'p-a-a-a-ll' (line 50). By the end of the speech, just before the entrance of Macbeth, her voice impresses something climactic upon us, part terror, part excitement, as 'Hold, hold!' (line 53) hits us with a desperate upward inflection.

Macbeth 5. 1. 30–65

She is sleep-walking and at first her delivery is underplayed. This, coupled with the light she is carrying, means she is initially still, which succeeds in drawing us in. Her first few words are frenetic, 'the jump-cut rhythms of her speech, which have the effect of an incoherent dream' (Walter, *Macbeth*, p. 58). There is a child-like gasp before she raises her voice and slows down to realise that 'Hell is murky' (line 34); a suppressed, child-like sob follows immediately afterwards. And then the frenetic pace returns, a quicksilver rush of interiorised language, perfectly enunciated. She says quickly 'who would have thought the old man to have had so much blood in him?' and then kneels (lines 36–38), visually echoing her first scene. She identifies herself with Lady Macduff for the line 'the Thane of Fife had a wife. Where is she now?' (lines 40–41). Fear that the same might happen to her raises her voice to a higher pitch. She puts down the light and then does not stop running and wiping her hands over her arms, her face, her neck, and her upper body. She flashes with anger for 'what, will these hands', and then switches to despair for 'ne'er be clean?' (line 41). Her hands continue in their urgent, frightened fidgeting and catch her nose in passing, prompting an additional exclamation 'Agh!' followed by 'here's the smell of the blood still' (line 48). Her voice rises in pitch for 'this little hand' (line 49), a moment of climax which culminates in a short sigh, 'O', and then she wails three longs sobs which also sound like screams 'O, O, O' (lines 49–50). Her body is rocking, and her right arm is in front of her at first. She then clasps her hands together with her head leaning to the right against them and she stares with fear and regret. It is a brief moment of aria before she stands and speaks her final lines with some of her earlier poise ('she forces herself out of it with her wonted practicality', Walter, *Macbeth*, p. 59), except that we now know she really is totally broken. She reaches to feel for the Doctor's hand on 'come, come, come, come, give me your hand' (line 63).

*

This essay begins and ends with Harriet Walter rubbing her hands but in very different contexts, a touchstone for her profile as a Shakespearian performer. Lying behind this 'accustomed action' (*Macbeth*, 5. 1. 27) are her analytical and interpretative processes, as well as her emotional and musical instincts. Although she may not like the sound of her voice, she has made the sound of Shakespeare her own.

Chronology

1970–73	Trained at the London Academy of Music and Dramatic Art.
1973–79	Roles in early rep. included Elizabeth Proctor in *The Crucible* by Arthur Miller and roles in *Fear and Miseries of the Third Reich* by Bertolt Brecht. Also political theatre: 7:84 and Joint Stock.
1980	Ophelia, *Hamlet*, dir. Richard Eyre, The Royal Court.
1981–83	(R.S.C) Helena, *A Midsummer Night's Dream*, dir. Ron Daniels. Helena, *All's Well That Ends Well*, dir. Trevor Nunn. Lady Percy, *Henry IV Parts One and Two*, dir. Nunn. Winnefrede, *The Witch of Edmonton*, by Thomas Dekker, John Ford and William Rowley, dir. John Caird.

	Constance, *The Twin Rivals*, by George Farquhar, dir. John Caird.
1983–85	Roles included Julia in *The Lucky Chance* by Aphra Behn and two films *Turtle Diary* (screenplay by Harold Pinter) and *The Good Father* (screenplay by Christopher Hampton).
1986	Harriet Vane in *Lord Peter Wimsey* (The Dorothy L. Sayers Mysteries), B.B.C.
1987	Portia, *The Merchant of Venice*, dir. Braham Murray The Royal Exchange, Manchester. Made Associate Artist of the R.S.C.
1987–89	(R.S.C.) Imogen, *Cymbeline*, dir. Bill Alexander. Viola, *Twelfth Night*, dir. Bill Alexander. *Three Sisters* by Anton Chekhov, dir. John Barton.
1989–90	(R.S.C.) Duchess, *The Duchess of Malfi*, by John Webster dir. Bill Alexander.
1991–99	Various roles on stage, film, and television, including: Lady Croom in *Arcadia* by Tom Stoppard, Karen in *The Children's Hour* by Lillian Hellman, Anna Petrovna in *Ivanov* by Anton Chekhov, and the films *Sense and Sensibility*, and *Onegin*.
1999–2000	Lady Macbeth in *Macbeth*, dir. Gregory Doran, R.S.C. Film of *Macbeth*, dir. by Doran for Channel Four. Arkangel Shakespeare audio recordings of Lady Macbeth and Tamora in *Titus Andronicus*. Awarded the C.B.E.
2001	Awarded Honorary Doctorate from University of Birmingham. Goneril in Naxos audio recording of *King Lear*. Beatrice in *Much Ado About Nothing*, dir. by Doran, R.S.C.
2002–5	Elizabeth I in *Mary Stuart* by Friedrich Schiller, dir. Phyllida Lloyd; Hester in *The Deep Blue Sea* by Terence Rattigan, the film *Bright Young Things*, and television work (including George Eliot, Virginia Woolf, and Mary Wollstonecraft for the B.B.C.).
2006	Cleopatra in *Antony and Cleopatra*, dir. Doran, R.S.C. Awarded The George Pragnell Prize for a career which has enhanced people's enjoyment and understanding of Shakespeare at the Shakespeare Birthday Celebrations.
2007–9	Films: *The Young Victoria* and *Antonement*.
2009	*Mary Stuart* revived on Broadway.
2010	Livia in *Women Beware Women* by Thomas Middleton dir. by Marianne Elliott (National Theatre).
2010	Curated the photography exhibition *Infinite Variety*, a celebration of the beauty of the aging female face (National Theatre).
2011	Appointed Dame Commander of the Order of the British Empire (DBE).

Bibliography

Rutter, Carol (1988) *Clamorous Voices: Shakespeare's Women Today*. London: Women's Press.

Shakespeare, William (2005) The Oxford Shakespeare: *The Complete Works*, 2nd edition, ed. by Stanley Wells, Gary Taylor, John Jowett and William Montgomery. Oxford: Clarendon Press.

Walter, Harriet (1993a) 'The Heroine, the Harpy, and the Human Being', *New Theatre Quarterly* IX (34), May (110–20).
——(1993b) 'Imogen in *Cymbeline*', in *Players of Shakespeare 3*, ed. by Russell Jackson and Robert Smallwood. Cambridge: Cambridge University Press, 201–19.
——(1998) 'Case study: Harriet Walter on Playing The Duchess of Malfi', in *Renaissance Drama in Action: An Introduction to Aspects of Theatre Practice and Performance* by Martin White. London: Routledge, 88–100.
——(1999, repr. 2006) *Other People's Shoes: Thoughts on Acting*. London: Nick Hern Books.
——(2002) *Macbeth*, Actors on Shakespeare series. London: Faber and Faber.
——(n.d.) 'Playing Hard to Get', unpublished talk given to the Dorothy L. Sayers Society.
——(2006) The George Pragnell Prize acceptance speech, The Shakespeare Birthday Lunch.

Interviews with Harriet Walter

'Interview', in *Performing Shakespeare* by Oliver Ford Davies. London: Nick Hern Books, 2007; repr. 2008, 225–30.
Interview, in 'Harriet Walter on Playing Beatrice' in *Much Ado About Nothing*, ed. by Jonathan Bate and Eric Rasmussen. Houndmills: Macmillan, 2009, 156–63.

About the author

Paul Edmondson M.A., Ph.D. is Head of Learning and Research and Director of the Stratford-upon-Avon Poetry Festival for The Shakespeare Birthplace Trust. He is a trustee of The Rose Theatre Trust, co-series editor for Palgrave Macmillan's *Shakespeare Handbooks*, and co-supervisory editor of the Penguin Shakespeare (for which he has contributed to several introductions). He is Chair of The Hosking Houses Trust. His publications include: *Twelfth Night: A Guide to the Text and Its Theatrical Life*, and (co-authored with Stanley Wells), *Shakespeare's Sonnets* and *Coffee with Shakespeare*. He has published on Shakespeare's influence on the Brontës (*Brontë Studies* and *Shakespeare Survey*). He contributed an essay on the poetry of Marlowe and Shakespeare for *The Cambridge History of English Poetry* (May, 2010). He wrote the script for The Shakespeare Centre's 'Life, Love, and Legacy' exhibition and co-curated 'Shakespeare Found: A Life Portrait'. He took another B.A. in Applied Theological Studies (University of Birmingham), 2007–2010 and was ordained deacon in The Church of England on 4 July 2010.

Index of Plays

General Index